INVISIBLE MASTER: The Puppeteers Hidden Power

1st edition

Copyright © 2019 by Leo Lyon Zagami
Published by the Consortium of Collective Consciousness Publishing™

As is common in a historic and reference book such as this, much of the information included on these pages has been collected from diverse sources. When possible, the information has been checked and double-checked. Almost every topic has at least three data points, that is, three different sources that report the same information. Even with special effort to be accurate and thorough, the author and publisher cannot vouch for each and every reference. The author and publisher assume no responsibility or liability for any outcome, loss, arrest, or injury that occurs as a result of information or advice contained in this book. As with the purchase of goods or services, *caveat emptor* is the prevailing responsibility of the purchaser, and the same is true for those who study esoteric subjects.

Library of Congress Cataloging-in-Publication Data:

Zagami, Leo Lyon
    INVISIBLE MASTER: THE PUPPETEERS HIDDEN POWER / Leo Lyon
Zagami
        p. cm.
        print ISBN 13: 978-1888729702 (Pbk.)

    ePub ISBN 13: 978-1888729726 (ePub)

    MobiPocket ISBN 13: 978-1888729733 (kindle)

    PDF ISBN 13: 978-1888729719 (PDF)

1. SOCIAL SCIENCE / Conspiracy Theories. 2. RELIGION / Christianity /
Catholic. I. Title
    Library of Congress Catalog Card Number: 2015930352

Printed in the United States of America.

10 9 8 7 6 5 4 3 2 1

LEO LYON ZAGAMI

INVISIBLE MASTER

THE PUPPETEERS HIDDEN POWER

Consortium of Collective Consciousness Publishing

LeoZagami.com ‡ CCCPublishing.com

Table of Contents

CHAPTER IV
REPTILIANS, VRIL, AND THE BLOOD LINES SERVING
THE MULTI-DIMENSIONAL WORLD

CHAPTER V
SEX WITH ALIENS

CHAPTER VI
ESOTERISM AND ALIEN ENTITIES IN
THE END TIMES SCENARIO

PREFACE

by *Cav. Luciano Fortunato Sciandra*

IIllustrious Knight of the Vatican and historian, Luciano Fortunato Sciandra, is a Member of the Equestrian Order of the Holy Sepulchre of Jerusalem and the Pontifical Equestrian Order of St. Sylvester Pope, as well as Grand Master of the Ordo Nova Militia Templi (Militia Spiritus Sancti, Rosae+ Crucis et Graal), and President of C.R.E.S.T. (Centro Ricerche E Studi della Tradizione).

*V*eritas vos liberabit ("the truth shall set you free") were the words left by the Sage of Sages, the Prophet of Prophets, the Master of Masters, the Son of God ... Jesus Christ ... that reach us in a time where we find all sorts of alleged exposure and research for the truth, even made by the average Joe, seeking to discover, modify, rectify, and even rewrite history at times, raising continous doubts about what has been transmitted to us from the past, often creating uncertainties with the erroneous interpretation of facts described by those who lived such truths in a profane way, perhaps "from the outside" and now shout out their interpretation in the name of exasperated and exasperating liberalism, tending to exalt and highlight heresies by presenting them as truths.

Mysteries that have been hidden from their persecutors, using symbols and rites of a seemingly incomprehensible nature, that after initiation and an allegoric or esoteric path, become ready for interpretation. The so-called Secret Societies that have transmitted these "truths," and still lead the study and research of them through their ancient rituals with the help of objects, perfumes, music of various kinds, including songs, accompany the neophyte in the strange field of wisdom and esoteric understanding. Constitutions, statutes, rules, and rituals, are, in fact, mysteriously or accidentally found in the most remote corners of the planet in a variety of traditions. The paternity of such documents, books, chalices, stones or "sacred" objects is, however, attributed to important figures of the past, so to suggest an alternative version of history from the known one, which thanks to these mystery schools, reach us to this day, as a kind of *fil rouge* or "underground stream."

In the past history of mankind, one finds with some perseverance, the contradiction in the two adversarial fields of Faith and Science, Spirit and Reason. It looks like there is an underground thread that from time immemorial, challenges, and often attacks the superstar of Ancient Wisdom aka the Holy Roman Catholic Church, which seeks to eliminate all ideas contrary to the supposed "True Faith." Leo Lyon Zagami has analyzed, studied and verified these Secret Societies, and in particular, he speaks in this book about the S.R.I.A (*Societas Rosacruciana In Anglia*), Cagliostro's Egyptian Rite legacy, and the O.T.O. (*Ordo Templi Orientis*), among other Illuminati sects.

Remember, The Sacred Society of Rosicrucians exists in a visible and invisible way from the dawn of time, and as Jean d'Heliopolis once wrote, *"En Agartha ... douze Rose+Croix, chargès de controller l'evolution spirituelle des hommes."* Meaning they control the evolution of humanity from Agartha ... nevertheless in *The Secret History of the Rose Cross*, Sedir writes that: *"The Rosicrucians of 1614 will take as an example and propose to their neophytes as an infallible guide,"* the text *"The Imitation of Christ"* (Latin: *De Imitatione Christi*), by Thomas à Kempis, reaffirming their Christian nature.

The author has analyzed founding documents, statutes, initiations, ceremonial regulations and the rituals of many secret societies, studying and investigating the behavior of the various characters who characterized the history of Secret Societies and the various Brotherhoods. He has sought in many parts of the world traces of the real Illuminati, by getting in touch with them and their organizations for an in- depth and first-hand investigation. St. Thomas Aquinas, the author of the *Summa Theologiae* reminds us that: *"In all ages there have always been people inspired by supernatural illumination, not to reveal a new doctrine of Faith, but rather to help the direction of human conduct and behavior."*

In his new work, Leo Lyon Zagami has not avoided a wide study and discussion on the so-called "paranormal" phenomena of our era, that reach us from the yellow pages of the past, to the glossy and colorful chronicles of the current age, and are often connected by some Ufologists and authors, to the so-called UFO/alien phenomenon. Other writers and researchers, approach the subject in a different way, talking about good and bad spirits (i.e. *Angels and Demons*), and interdimensional entities that are evoked into our reality by the use of various rituals, Zagami mentions also the sects, and secret societies of men, who operate following such ancients practices as Theurgy or Goetia, and also, in some cases, like CERN, with the apparent use of highly sophisticated modern technology. Some characters have approached such "paranormal" techniques to aspire to become the World's Masters, having allies in other dimensions or even other planets and galaxies.

Zagami, who writes for both the "initiates" and the "profane," makes it clear that the Roman Catholic Church, to discover and punish heretics deemed as a threat, made extensive use of their Holy Inquisition, which used obvious and covert operations to silence them if judged dangerous, such as Count Cagliostro, who was their last victim. He also explains how the occult elite is presently trying to overthrow governments, wishing to become the sole masters of this world, annulling the sovereign nations, by the establishment of a New World Order, using for this purpose, Masonic institutions and in some cases Para-Masonic Lodges, almost invisible, for the implementation of their "Plan."

The author, having also been part of some of these organizations, makes the readers aware of their progress, their development, and their goals that have been set in secretive and otherwise inaccessible environments. He speaks of Invisible Masters and Secret Chiefs, both spiritual and material, and of so-called "contactists" who allegedly know the access to multi-dimensional doors where they can psychically or physically enter, "What is above and what is below."

To conclude, Leo Lyon Zagami, a conspiracy expert like no other, whose books seem to be more like manuals, shows he is capable of the mission that Fate (for the Pagans), or Divine Providence (for the Catholics), has entrusted him, so to make visible what is in the fog ... *"Surge Naebula Vidi Sion"* ... **Rome, November 25, 2014 (Saint Mercurius Martyr) Luciano Fortunato SCIANDRA (Equites Christi)**

INTRODUCTION

by the Author

For a moment imagine yourself as an initiate in an old Rosicrucian Fraternal Order. Place yourself at the beginning of the Aspirant to the Zelator degree, where the ritual is done in the following way: Two Heralds enter and stand one on each side of the entrance of the Preparation Room. The Conductor of Novices, who is robed in black, with a cowl on his head, takes the left arm of the Aspirant, and approaches the door leading from the Porch to the Sacred Hall. He does five circuits of the Sacred Hall with the Aspirant, according to the path of the Sun, where all the *Fratres* and Officers are addressed, during which the following ode is sung:

> *Before God began the Universe, all matter lay in a rough clot devastated by wild disorder, nor knew the light a radiant ray*
>
> *As darkness reigned uncontrollably over all confusion*
>
> *Then God rose, threw his thunder, and commanded the elements to rise in the air suspended the leaning World, and spread the blue skies over it;*
>
> *He made the stars circulate, and in the middle was the sun.*
>
> *Then he created Man from dust and formed it with a Living Soul*
>
> *He entrusted all things to him, and he did so to the Lord*
>
> *Yet he showed himself ungrateful to Heaven and was driven out of Eden.*
>
> *From here all our misfortunes came, nor did humanity share a consolation As long as the Rosicrucians were not born and formed another Eden here:*
>
> *Where true pleasure reigns eternally and retrieves native innocence.*
>
> *Crystal fountains flow here, nothing that is defective can enter*
>
> *Here the Tree of Knowledge really grows, whose fruits we taste, but free from sin While sweet friendship really abounds, and Guardian Angels roam around.*

I have chosen the *Guardian Angels* ritual of an English Rosicrucian Order, and the words sung by the officers, to help deepen your studies on the rituals of the Illuminati of the various traditions in relation to the alien world. These mysterious figures are sometimes referred to as the **Secret Chiefs, Invisible Masters,** or **Unknown Superiors**, who have had an influence on the history of humanity, whether this theory is accepted, or not.

I am a former Rosicrucian Commander of the Fraternitas Rosicruciana Antiqua (FRA), a Rosicrucian Order originally established by German Illuminati **Dr. Arnold Krumm-Heller,** and the present Grand Master of the **Rite of Strict**

Observance and the *Ordo Illuminatorum Universalis,* and in the past, a Freemason of various Rites and Orders. The history of this invisible reality has influenced society since the days of Atlantis. A millennial tradition we find in all mystery schools, as well as in the history and practices of the various religions, that link us to mysterious and invisible beings through particular places around the world, where magic is said to naturally gather in large amounts, and where we have access to multi-dimensional realities driven by occult knowledge and secret rituals that throughout history, few have had the courage to divulge.

In chapter IX of the book, *Magick Without Tears,* by celebrated black magician Aleister Crowley (his real name was Edward Alexander Crowley 1875-1947) entitled, "Chiefs of Secrets," we find a letter addressed to a *Soror,* meaning *Sister,* in the Illuminati of A∴A∴ *(Astrum Argentum),* a magical co-fraternity founded by Crowley in 1907, where he clearly and unequivocally spoke of the matter, pointing out his wish to be more strict in regards to the curiosity of his own disciples on the theme of the Secret Chiefs:

Cara Soror,

Do what thou wilt shall be the whole of the Law.

Very glad I am, since at one time I was obliged to be starkly stern about impertinent curiosity, to note that you wish to be informed about the Secret Chiefs of the ∴A∴ is justified; it is most certainly of the first importance that you and I should be quite clear in our minds about Those under whose jurisdiction and tutelage we both work.

Crowley explains the role of the Secret Chiefs, in relation to the Secret Societies he is part of, emphasizing that: ***"For one thing, the 'Chief' is so far above me that I can rely on him to take the necessary steps, whenever contact would be useful; for another, there is one path always open which is perfectly sufficient for all possible contingencies."***

So what is this "path always open" that Mr. Crowley mentions to his disciples? In the following pages, I will explain what unites the mysterious alien beings or Invisible Masters, to the complex hierarchy of the Illuminati network, and the creation of humanity, and the links of the Invisible Masters with the greatest prophets and wizards in history. I consider this the fourth volume of my *Confessions of an Illuminati* trilogy, as I felt the need for further study on these complex and intricate subjects.

The alien in front of you could be an angel, but it is most likely the usual demonic trickster. In this book, I hope to help you better understand the difference between the two, so that you can distinguish their actions in the invisible realm. Saint Thomas Aquinas, who was an Italian Dominican friar, a Catholic priest, and doctor of the Church revered by the Jesuits, and more generally by the exorcists of the Church of Rome, explains that angels are organized in a hierarchy of nine ranks. In order from the closest to God to the furthest from God, whose ranks are divided into three categories, as follows:

The highest three ranks are nearest to God:

| Seraphim | Cherubim | Thrones |

The next three ranks are named for their governing function:

| Dominations | Virtues | Powers |

The final three ranks are named for the work they do:

Principalities   **Archangels**   **Angels**

Thomas Aquinas states that demons are also organized in a hierarchy, but does not tell us the names or functions of their ranks:

> *The fallen angels are engaged in battle against man's salvation and in torturing lost souls in hell. The fallen angels that beset man on earth, carry with them their own dark and punishing atmosphere, and wherever they are they endure the pains of hell.* [Note: For further discussion of angels, see Qq. 106-114.] – from **Summa Theologica**.

In short, it would appear that demons are an almost necessary evil in the Kingdom of God. Aquinas specifies: *"The fallen angels did not lose their natural knowledge by their sin; nor did they lose their angelic intellect, their actions are subordinate to those of their superiors, the demons are not equal to each other; Between them, there is natural subordination."*

So, there is a natural hierarchy of evil. It would appear that a superior demon can illuminate a lower one, but of course, true enlightenment can only come from God. The atheist, of course, may not believe any of this, but as Carl Gustav Jung wisely said, *"All that I have learned has led me step by step to an unshakable conviction of the existence of God."* If you have ever wondered if good angels have authority over the bad ones, unfortunately, the answer is no, for as Aquinas explains:

> *It would seem that men are not guarded by the angels. For guardians are deputed to some because they either know not how, or are not able, to guard themselves, as children and the sick. But man is able to guard himself against his free-will,*

FIG. 1 *Oil on canvas By Paul Gauguin Museum of Fine Arts, Boston entitled* **Where Do We Come From? What Are We? Where Are We Going?**

and knows how by his natural knowledge of natural law. Therefore, man is not guarded by an angel.

If we carefully consider the structure and faculties of man, we can perceive that our existence on Earth is only a test condition and nothing more. When life ends according to our earthly choices, reward or punishment follows, a reality that exists beyond eons. This is, in essence, what is taught by the Rosicrucians. The initials of the four secret words of the Order, form the word *FIAT,* which is the keyword of the **Western Initiatic System,** that, combined with the word Lux, gives life to the famous Latin phrase, *Fiat lux,* which translates literally to: *"Let there be light,"* found in Genesis 1:3 of the Torah, the first part of the Hebrew Bible.

So let's shed light on the UFO phenomenon, by asking the questions: *Where Do We Come From? What Are We? Where Are We Going*? Just as the French artist, Paul Gauguinin did in his famous artwork from 1897.

~ Leo Lyon Zagami

Acknowledgements:

Italian version first printed in April, 2015

Artwork concept by Christy Zagami

Translations by Leo Zagami, Jennifer Fahey

Adaptation by Christy Zagami

Edited by Christy Zagami, Brad Olsen

Cover and Book Design by Mark J. Maxam

WHO ARE THE INVISIBLE MASTERS?

The supposed alien ancestors of Jesus

 aurence Gardner (1943-2010) was a well-known Masonic author in the 1990s, for some of his books that reached an international level, such as Bloodline of The Holy Grail: The Hidden Lineage of Jesus Revealed (1996). [1] Until his death, he worked hard to trace the true lineage of Jesus, and despite the fact that traditional historians call him a pseudo-historian, his actual influence on contemporary culture is remarkable. As the English newspaper, The Independent wrote after his death: "His work inspired the now famous Da Vinci Code of 2003, offering a bit of inspiration for Dan Brown's novel development." [2]

Gardner even came to determine a supposed alien origin for Jesus through the line of blood that came from his anointed, King David. In his book *Genesis of the Grail Kings* from 1999, [3] Gardner determined that the real bloodline of Jesus ultimately descended from the biblical Cain of alien origins, whose sons and his following bloodline were, therefore, of extraterrestrial origin.

Gardner discussed this further during a conference, where he stated that they, the sons of Cain, were the true children of the Gods, the Annunaki from the Stars, who were briefly bred to be the leaders of the human race. Annunaki is the Sumerian denomination of the tyrannical Jewish **Nephilim,** descendants of the Giants, the two hundred Ben Elohim, or fallen angels that **Yahweh** (one of the **Elohim** creators of humanity) kicked out of Heaven, a notion disclosed initially by **Zecharia Sitchin** (1920-2010), the famous unconventional scholar, often criticized for his translations from ancient Sumerian texts. In addition, Sitchin

1   *See* Laurence Gardner, *Bloodline of The Holy Grail: The Hidden Lineage of Jesus Revealed* (Boston, US:Element Books,1996).

2   http://www.independent.co.uk/news/obituaries/laurence-gardner-alternative-historian-whose-work-helped-inspire-dan-brown-2056096.html ‡ Archived 28th November 2017.

3   *See* Laurence Gardner, *Genesis of the Grail Kings*, (Ealing, London, UK: Bantam Press,1999).

FIG. 2 Laurence Gardner (1943-2010)

had direct contact with the Vatican through Monsignor Corrado Balducci (1923-2008), as described in Volume III, of my *Confessions*.

The significance of Gardner's strange claims and those made by Sitchin and others will become apparent after understanding why their position is so different from that of traditional historians, and the importance of their thesis. Gardner developed his work with an almost encyclopedic approach to his already mentioned *Genesis of the Grail Kings,* and focused on the period of the Old Testament, in particular, on the biblical parts of *Genesis* and *Exodus.* He begins with a description of the origins of the Jewish faith as a mixture created by Egyptian worshippers of the sun, assimilating to some notions of the tradition of the Sumerians and their belief system, to which they would be strongly influenced. Gardner followed those who did not revert to the official version of the history of humanity because they were influenced by the mystery schools that traditionally guide both the good and bad Illuminati.

One such person, well before Gardner, was Gerald Massey (1828-1907), an unconventional archeologist linked to the Theosophical Society, who wrote, *A Book of the Beginnings,* issued in 1881, that later influenced Kenneth Grant, who was linked to Crowley. Massey's work is still used today as a reference for the Theosophical Society, a religious-philosophical movement founded by **Helena Petrovna Blavatsky (1831-1891)**. Massey was a poet, who was passionate about Egyptian civilization, but never a true Egyptologist in the traditional sense, but rather someone who taught himself the art of deciphering hieroglyphs, using his very good intuition. Massey was also the Grand Master of an Order of Druids (A.O.D.) that was highly influential in the Illuminati network. He is still well-known in the New Age movement today, for his seemingly bizarre theory that establishes a parallel between the life of Horus and that of Jesus, a theory that he said was based on a mysterious ancient relic found in Luxor, that Massey examines and interprets in the work, *The Historical Jesus and the Mythical Christ* (1886).

There are no other sources of reference to assert his thesis, aside from his own. In reality, Massey was just proposing an old theory, made popular by Christian Ernst Wünsch, in Adam Weishaupt's Illuminati Order, one hundred years earlier.

In fact, Ernst Wünsch wrote in, **Horus or the Astro-Gnostic final judgment on the Revelation of John** published in 1783: *"Horus of the Egyptians was the messiah of the Jews, as we have often shown. Horus was the bread and wine. The Messiah was thus also, in the opinion of some in the Jewish sect, to present. He put forth namely life's bread and life's wine, that is, he was the soul's food and the soul's drink, heavenly food and heavenly drink. Jesus had to do all of this. He had further said, that he was going to come in a different relation to situations with his disciples, that he would now like to succeed in his designs on the temple. For this reason, he metaphorically gave them bread and wine, instead of eating his body and blood, as a memorial to his custom until this time community and to drink a toast with them, and since then the communion has been used."*

However, in 2007, a popular documentary loved by globalists, entitled *Zeit-geist* [4] will resume this Illuminati theory, to brainwash the masses, proposing it as Massey's own, and exponentially amplifying it to the whole world in the era of the internet. The statements about the fact that Jesus would be a sort of copycat product of ancient religious figures like Horus or others, have, in fact, been widespread. Anti-Christian atheist websites have been used against Christians in religious debate, even unjustly. This theory originated in the Illuminati, according to traditional historians, and has no basis in reality. However, I still think the truth is found somewhere in between, and is not simply a mythical vision, as seen in Masonry or in other sects where myth often reigns over reality. For Mystic Masonry, the religions and myths of the past are an obvious trace left to us by extradimensional beings able to travel the cosmos since ancient times, to join the human race in secret rituals orchestrated by the Illuminati and the Illuminist, for both evil and good deeds, to be operated on mankind, in order to establish religions and civilizations, at times even requiring human sacrifice. Something that is still happening in the most secret lodges of Occult Masonry, and other more nefarious sects of the Illuminati.

There has been talk of "Contact" between Freemasonry and Aliens, recently relaunched by advocates of the theory of the ancient astronauts known as "paleo-astronautics," originally introduced in the 1960s, by a mathematician of the Soviet establishment named **Matest M. Agrest**, later popularized by a Swiss writer named Erich von Däniken (b. 1935), in his book, *Chariots of the Gods* (1969), that became an international bestseller translated into many languages. Paleo-astronautics has been promoted a lot in recent years by the TV channels of the New World Order controlled by the usual Illuminati groups, and was originally created in the 1960s, but these notions were present for a long time in the

4   http://en.wikipedia.org/wiki/ Zeitgeist: _the_Movie ‡ Archived 28th November 2017.

FIG. 3 Gerald Massey (1828-1907) photo by John and Charles Watkins ("circa 1856")

lodges of fringe Masonic rites and certain Illuminati sects like the *Ordo Templi Orientis*, or the Temple of Set Society. In general, the media has become an involuntary instrument of control exercised by the Illuminati, who for some reason now seem to want to publicly indoctrinate the population with their alternative vision of man's history and origins.

What has so far been considered as a dark secret theory hidden behind the walls of Masonic lodges or other mystery schools, has now become, for motives related to current plans of the occult elite, an alternative version of the history of humanity. The word occult comes from the Latin word *occultus* meaning hidden. Since the Illuminati is an occult secret society, they **hide** things in plain sight, and now they seem to also reveal them without anyone questioning why they are doing so.

Perhaps we should be wondering why such information, which was once considered top secret, and could often get you jailed or killed, back in the days of the Inquisition, as with the famous Italian Dominican friar and philosopher, Giordano Bruno (1548-1600), is today at the disposal to millions of people, from many TV networks worldwide. Are they preparing something for humanity? Obviously, the answer is yes, but what? In 1584, Bruno wrote in *The Infinite Universe*: "*Innumerable suns exist; innumerable earths revolve around these suns... Living beings inhabit these worlds.*"

The basic theme of Bruno's *Spaccio*, also written in the year 1584:

"The glorification of the magical religion of the Egyptians."

Bruno believed this worship was really the worship of "God in things." Bruno wrote in *Spaccio*: "*for diverse living things represent divine spirits and powers, which, beyond the absolute being which they have, obtain a being communicated to all things according to their capacity and measure. Whence God as a whole is in all things.*"

No wonder Bruno is considered today by many, not only a ufologist, but recent studies have linked him to the origins of Rosicrucianism, a cultural movement which arose in Europe in the early 17th century, that we know is an emanation of a much older mystery school of the Illuminati network.

FIRST ACCESS TO A MULTI-DIMENSIONAL "STARGATE"

*I*n *Genesis of the Grail Kings,* Gardner speaks in detail of the Great Pyramid of Cheops and considers of great importance the fact that the Kings Chamber, placed inside of it, could be used as a superconductor capable of carrying the pharaoh into another space-time dimension for a very unusual initiation. And it was in the Kings Chamber that the pharaoh's ritual of passing was handled according to the tradition of *The Book of the Dead* of ancient Egypt. This strange room, used by the pharaoh during the rituals in question, apparently, led him to the Gods of Antiquity, entities duly described by Gardner as transdimensional, rather than just extraterrestrial. The Kings Chamber hypothesis as a dimensional portal was reaffirmed in the summer of 2014, during an important conference in Italy, by author and internationally renowned researcher Robert Bauval, who has, among other things, a background in engineering. Bauval said that after thirty years of research, it is now safe to say that the Kings Chamber is an interdimensional portal.

Napoleon also had a profound experience in the House of Kings, as my friend Adrian Gilbert writes in *Mysteries of the Stone of Destiny*: *"In 1798, his army had just won a great victory on the Mamelukes that had ruled Egypt for centuries. After the battle, Napoleon entered the pyramid, insisting that he was left alone in the House of Kings. When he left, about an hour later, he was pale but refused any question as to what had happened in that place; He kept that secret with him to the grave."* [5] In this place, there was an extra-dimensional "Stargate" used by the pharaoh. Édouard Schuré (1841-1929) in *The Great Initiates: A Study of the Secret History of Religions*, a mysterious book of tremendous importance for the Illuminati mystery schools, gives the following explanation of the famous stories of Herodotus in Old Egypt:

> *For a long time archeologists have seen in the sarcophagus of the Great Pyramid of Gizeh the tomb of King Sesostus, on the testimony of Herodotus, who was not an initiate, and to whom the Egyptian priests hardly confided anything except trifles and folk tales. The kings of Egypt, however, had their tombs elsewhere. The strange inner structure of the Pyramid proves that it was to be used for initiation ceremonies and secret practices of the priests of Osiris. The Well of Truth which we described, the ascending staircase and the room of the arcana are found there.*

> *The room called the Kings Chamber, which contains the sarcophagus, was the one where the adept was led on the eve of his great initiation. These same arrangements were reproduced in the great temples of central and upper Egypt.* [6]

Schuré continues, *"'No man,' said the hierophant, 'escapes death, and every living soul is destined to resurrection. The adept goes through the tomb alive, that afterward, he may enter into the light of Osiris. Lie down, therefore, in this coffin and wait for the light! Tonight you will go through the door of Fear you will reach the threshold of Mastery.' The initiate lay down in the open sarcophagus. The hierophant extended his hand over him in blessing and the procession of initiates left the cave in silence."* [7]

Schuré was another very interesting character connected to the Illuminati, and the Hermetic school of French initiate Antoine-Joseph Pernety, known as Dom Pernety (1716-1801), a former Benedictine, and librarian of Frederic the Great of Prussia, who was considered a key figure in the origins of the Ancient and Accepted Scottish Rite. Dom Pernety was also influenced by the Christian mysticism of Swedenborg and he founded in 1760 the secret society of *Rite Hermétique* or Illuminati of Avignon, very much in vogue in the first Enlightenment period, as a more mystical and esoteric alternative to the Illuminati Order of Adam Weishaupt.

Schuré, who was an initiate, was influenced by Rudolf Steiner (1861-1925), bound in turn, by the already mentioned Helena Petrovna Blavatsky, founder in 1875 of the Theosophical Society, originally created in New York. Thus, we find a certain affinity between the perceptions we have mentioned so far, whose glue always seems to be the Theosophical Society, that has, more than anyone else,

5   See Adrian Gilbert, *Secrets of the Stone of Destiny: Legend, History, and Prophecy*, (Italian Edition-Arezzo, IT: Harmakis Ed., 2014), p. 16.

6   Édouard cé, *The Great Initiates: A Study of the Secret History of Religions*, (Italian Edition-Bari, IT, Gius. LATERZA E FIGLI, 1929, 2nd reprint of the 5th edition), p. 114.

7   *Ibid.*

promulgated in the modern era, the idea of the Invisible Masters and the Secret Chiefs of a New and Imminent Age.

As all theosophists and Illuminati, he was obsessed with ancient Egypt and its characters, including Moses, described by Schuré in this way:

Moses, the Egyptian initiate, and priest of Osiris, was indisputably the organizer of monotheism. Through him, this principle, until then hidden beneath the threefold veil of the Mysteries, came out of the depths of the temple and entered the course of history. Moses had the courage to establish the highest principle of initiation as the sole dogma of a national religion, and the prudence to reveal its consequences to only a small number of initiates while imposing it upon the masses through fear. In so doing, the prophet of Sinai evidently had before him distant vistas which extended far beyond the destinies of his people. The establishment of the universal religion of mankind is the true mission of Israel, which few Jews other than its greatest prophets have understood. In order for this mission to be fulfilled, the swallowing up of the people who championed it was implied. The Jewish nation was dispersed and annihilated. The idea of Moses and the Prophets have lived and increased. Enlarged and transfigured by Christianity, taken up by Islam, although on a lower plane, upon the barbaric West, and was to influence Asia once again. Henceforth it would be useless for mankind to rebel and struggle against itself in convulsive efforts; mankind was to revolve around this major idea like the nebula around the sun which organizes it. This was the tremendous work of Moses. [8]

Moses was a great interdimensional magician, who in fact, thanks to his privileged contact with God, and extra-dimensional aliens/angels, managed to lead the Jews out of Egypt, according to the Bible. Moses was the one who began the path that would lead them to the "Promised Land," that the Jews are still craving and suffering for, to this day. That is why Schuré devotes a whole chapter in his book *The Great Initiates*, called *"MOSES: The Mission of Israel."* A century later, the late Laurence Gardner, a typical representative of contemporary Masonic / Illuminist thought, will also focus on this subject inspired by the work of Alexandre Saint-Yves, Marquess of Alveydre (26 March 1842 – 5 February 1909), who was a French occultist that adapted the works of **Fabre d'Olivet (1767-1825)**, and wrote the book *Mission des Juifs*, or "Mission of the Jews."

Let's return to the role of Moses, who is bound, if you think about it, to a special interdimensional location and *Stargate*, constructed to initiate the pharaohs to the highest mysteries, and project them into parallel dimensions and distant worlds.

We are for the first time in front of unusual open Stargates, where the interconnecting extra-dimensional doors could be found in a cave, behind a bush, or on top of a mountain, which Schuré calls the *Sacred Mountain*. It is, therefore, worthwhile to look even closer at the important and enigmatic figure of Moses, tied to the constant support of a Superior guide that I would call an "alien," in his mission to guide the chosen people here on earth. A race, that apparently, has a specific task, a divine mission, which puts them above the rest of humanity, while for others critical of the Jewish belief system, is the result of a diabolical compromise. It is a controversial subject for sure, which would require a separate book for its complex nature.

8   *Ibid.*, p. 128.

MOSES THE HIGH PRIEST OF OSIRIS
AND HIS ALIEN GUIDE

*M*oses is undoubtedly one of the most enigmatic characters in the Bible. I would like to expand on this figure beyond the "Hollywood" image that we can see recently, thanks to *Exodus: Gods and Kings* by Sir Ridley Scott (b. November 30, 1937), a film director who also gave us *Prometheus*, another 2012 success story based on paleo-astronautics, and the alleged alien origins of humanity inspired by the Illuminati. Moses was born in Egypt, around the year 1600 BC. This date is following the indications of historians Titus Flavius Josephus, who was born Yosef ben Matityahu (37 – c. 100), and was a first-century Romano-Jewish scholar, historian and hagiographer; and the Greek historian Herodotus (c. 484 – c. 425 BC), who was the first to identify the Hyksos with the Jews. Indeed, both advocate the theory that links the Exodus of the Jews, with the expulsion of the Hyksos from Egypt (about 1550-1525 BC). Instead, according to Jewish tradition, Moses' birth date, 7 Adar 2368, corresponds to the years between 1391-1386 BC, a period which would make him a contemporary of **Pharaoh Akhetaton** (who lived in the 14th century BC).

Ahmed Osman conducted a very elaborate study published later in the book entitled *Moses and Akhenaten—The Secret History of Egypt at the Time of the Exodus,* (originally published by Bear & Company in 1990). Today, however, many scholars and historians believe that the events of the Exodus are only literary fiction inspired by some priests at the time of deportation, to emphasize their religious characteristics. Moses is said to have died at the venerable age of 120 years on mount Nebo and was buried in the Moab Valley in a mysterious place. Moses wrote the first five books of the Bible, the so-called *Pentateuch*, although there are, of course, scholars of biblical exegesis who in some historical periods have attempted to assert the opposite. He then wrote *Genesis, Exodus, Leviticus, Numbers*, and *Deuteronomy*.

But as far as *Genesis* is concerned, according to the aforementioned Gardner, Moses derived it from the Phoenician history of **Sanchoniathon** and other ancient tales, while for Édouard Schuré on *Genesis* he states: *"Considering Moses' education, there is no doubt that he wrote* Genesis *in Egyptian hieroglyphs with three meanings. He entrusted the keys and oral explanation to his successors. When, in Solomon's time,* Genesis *was transliterated into Phoenician characters, when, after the Babylonian Captivity, Esdras edited it in Chaldaic-Aramaic characters, the Jewish priesthood could make but imperfect use of these keys. At last, when the Greek translators of the Bible appeared, they had no more than a vague idea of the esoteric meaning of the texts."*

Massey, in *The Book of the Beginnings,* writes more pragmatically, that *Genesis* would simply symbolize an allegory present in Egypt in the famous *Book of the Dead*, and again in Africa from time immemorial. Massey writes: *"The first words of the Hebrew* Book of Genesis*, 'In the beginning, God created the heavens and the earth,' have simply no meaning; no initial point in time, or place in space; no element of commencement whatever, no means of laying hold, to begin with. Whereas the beginnings in mythology were phenomenal, palpable, and verifiable; they were the primary facts observed and registered by the earliest thinkers. The Egyptians did not begin with anywhere, in particular, to arrive at nothing definite in the end. The Hebrew beginning* *does not enable us to begin, it is a fragment from a primitive system of thought and expression which cannot be understood directly or according to the modern mode. When the ancient matter has been divested of all that constituted its character as real myth, it only becomes a false myth and is of no value whatever until restored to its proper place in the mythical system. This can only be done by recovering the phenomenal origin and mold that shaped the matter of mythology. The primitive genesis was no carving of chaos into the shape of worlds, according to the absurd modern notion of a creation. The mapping out of the heavens and measuring of time and period were the registered result of human observation, utterly remote from the ordinary notion of divine revelation; it was a work of necessity accomplished for the most immediate use. The creation belongs to the mythological astronomy, and has no relation at all to the supposed manufacture of matter—about which the early thinkers knew nothing and did not pretend to know— the formation of worlds, or the origin of man, but simply meant the first formulation of time and period observed in the heavens, the recurring courses of the stars and moon and sun, and the recording of their motions by aid of the fixed stars. It was the earliest means of telling time on the face of the celestial horologe which had been already figured for the use of the primitive observers of its 'hands.' In a description of this creation or beginning of time and formation, found on one of the monuments restored in the time of Shabaka, it is said of the Maker, 'A blessing was pronounced upon all things, in the day when he bid them exist, and before he had yet caused gods to be made for Ptah.' So in the Hebrew version, when the two heavens were finished and the starry circle of night and day was limned, the Elohim saw that everything was created good. But we require knowing who was the maker and what were the Elohim here postulated as the creators. The three first words of the Hebrew Genesis and professed account of creation by means of the Elohim are b'rashith elohim bara, translated, 'In the beginning God created.' ... Those who have rendered this ancient language and sent forth their versions in hundreds of other tongues were altogether ignorant of the one original which could have explained and corrected the derivative Hebrew, held to be the primeval speech; God's own personal utterance. With their one book in hand and that uninterpreted according to the gnosis, unillustrated by the comparative method, they have assumed the preposterous proportions and pretensions of teachers of the world, and yet the very first words of revelation reveal nothing of phenomenal origin. For that, we must seek elsewhere."*

So Massey's work seems to indicate that the Jews are an Egyptian tribe, which in part share the same vision of Schuré. Moses was the adopted son of Pharaoh Ramses II, and received from his priests, all the teachings usually received by the sons of Pharaohs, including the most important scientific and historical notions, and above all the knowledge of the Royal Arts, which included alchemy and magic. After escaping from Egypt to avoid punishment for the murder of a guard, Moses went beyond the Red Sea and the Sinai Peninsula, to the land of Madian, where there was a temple that was not under the control of the Egyptian priesthood. There he met **Jethro,** the high priest of Madian or the Raguel (the watchman of God). He was a man of black skin, who belonged to the purest type of the ancient Ethiopian race, which had ruled Egypt four or five thousand years before Rameses. Jethro was neither an inspired man, nor a man of action, but was a great sage. Moses will marry **Sephora**, one of the seven daughters of Jethro. Later (Numbers 3:1) after the Exodus, Aaron, and Miriam, Moses' brother and sister, according to the Bible, reproached him for having married an Ethiopian. Schuré explains that:

*When a priest of Osiris had committed a murder, even involuntarily they were severely judged by the priestly college. Already the Pharaoh suspected an usurper in his sister's son. The life of the scribe hung by only a thread. So he preferred voluntary exile, and to submit himself to the expiations the law of the initiates imposed upon murderers. When a priest of Osiris had committed even an unpremeditated murder, he was supposed to lose the benefit of his anticipated resurrection **in the light of Osiris**, a privilege he had obtained through the tests of initiation, and which placed him far above the masses. In order to expiate his crime and to find his inner light once again, he had to submit himself to further cruel tests and once more to expose himself to death. After a long fast and with the aid of certain potions the atoning one was plunged into a deep sleep; then he was placed in a cave beneath the temple. He remained there for days, sometimes for weeks.* [9]

So this was a cruel journey for Moses, typical of the practices and teachings of ancient Illuminati mystery schools, exposing him once again to death, and extra-dimensional dangers, with no assurance of surviving this terrible ordeal. Schuré continues:

During this time he was to undertake a journey into the other world, into Erebus or the region of Amentis, where float the souls of the dead who are not yet detached from the terrestrial atmosphere. There he had to search for his victim, to undergo the latter's anguish, obtain his pardon and help him to find his way to the light. Only then was he considered to have expiated the murder; only then was his astral body washed of the black stains which the poisoned breath and the curses of his victim had soiled. But from this real or imaginary journey, the guilty one very well might not return, and often when the priests went to awaken the expiator from his sleep, they found nothing but a corpse. [10]

However, it was in the underworld that Moses eventually regained a privileged contact with the invisible dimension after his murder, and after his astral cortex had been totally cleansed from sin, he was reawakened, and it is at that time that Moses took his name which means "the Saved;" In fact, before then he was known in Egypt as Hosarsiph, not Moses. Moses then married Sephora, the daughter of Jethro, and lived for many years in the village of Madian. Then one day he went without fear to the cavern of Serval, described by Schuré as *"a place dedicated from time immemorial to supernatural visions, to Elohim, or to luminous spirits. No priest, no hunter would have consented to lead a pilgrim there."* [11] A sacred place dedicated to contact with what we now commonly call UFOs.

Fearlessly, Moses climbed past the ravine of Horeb. Courageously he crossed the valley of death with its chaos of rocks. *"Like every human effort, initiation has its phases of humility and pride,"* writes Schuré. In climbing the mountain, Moses had reached the summit of pride, for he was approaching the summit of human power. Already he felt himself at one with the Supreme Being. The burning red sun hung low over the volcanic massive form of Sinai and purple shadows were lying in the valleys below when Moses found himself before a cavern where a few terebinths protected the entrance. He prepared to enter, but suddenly he

---

9   *Ibid.,* p. 142.
10   *Ibid.,* p. 138.
11   *Ibid.,* p. 153.

was blinded by a light that enveloped him, similar to a flame.

An angel with a drawn sword blocked his way. He was thunderstruck and Moses fell prone upon the ground. All his pride had been broken in that moment by this alien interdimensional force, his *Invisible Master*.

The angel's alien gaze had pierced him with its light. And then, with that deep sense of things that are awakened in the visionary state of the real Illuminati, he finally understood that this alien being was about to impose a serious task upon him. He would have liked to escape his new mission and creep into the earth like a miserable worm but it was too late, he was chosen by the very powerful interdimensional entity. A voice said.

"Moses! Moses!"

And he answered: *"Here am I."*

"Come no closer; take off your shoes. For the place where you are standing is holy ground!"

Moses hid his face in his hands. He was afraid to look at the angel again, to face his gaze. And the angel said to him, *"You who seek Elohim, why do you tremble before me?"*

Moses replied, *"Who are you?"*

"A ray of Elohim, a solar angel, a messenger of the One Who is and Who will be."
"What do you command, Who am I," asked Moses, *"that I should lead the Children of Israel out of Egypt?"*

"Go," **said the angel,** *"for I shall be with you. I shall put the fire of Elohim in your heart, and His word upon your lips. For forty years you have been calling upon Him. Your voice has reached Him. Here I seize you in his name! Son of Elohim, you belong to me forever!"*

And Moses cried out boldly: *"Show me Elohim, that I may see His living fire!"*

He raised his head. But the sea of flames had vanished.

Today, the New Age cult known as the *Raëlian Movement* teaches that life on Earth was scientifically created by a species of extraterrestrials, which they call the Elohim. Not all scholars accept the plural nature of the Elohim as Biblical Hebrew. However, the Biblical term Elohim was considered plural a long time before the birth of the *Raëlian Movement*. The King James Version of the Bible makes it plainly obvious that the word God (Elohim) was being used in the Bible in the plural form.

"I am, that I am!" said Moses after receiving his ultimate mission from his alien overlord. He thought for a moment that his weak human body had been consumed by the fire of ether, but his spirit was stronger than any vision transmitted by the alien messengers of God, after training in the Egyptian priesthood. When he went down to Jethro's temple again, he was now ready for his new task as leader of the Jewish people. However, beware of New Agers that say there is no God and Moses was simply led by aliens. Moses understood the real nature of the angel of the Lord, the interdimensional alien, which appeared to him in flames of fire from within a bush. The popular tradition writes Schuré, *"still has* *it that sometimes in the flashing fire, the God of Sinai appears in the form of a Medusa head with eagle's wings. Woe to those who see His face! To see Him is to die!"*

The nomads spoke of strange alien events while sitting in their tents during the evening when the women and camels were asleep and they felt free to discuss these matters. In reality, only the boldest of Jethro's initiates ever climbed to the cavern of Serval and spent several days in fasting and prayer as the task was very demanding. A question remains after analyzing why the Lord doesn't want to be seen. To give Moses credibility in his mission, the Lord gives him a magic stick that will allow him to do things that must impress people and induce them to follow him. In short, this was a sort of magic wand, not forgetting that the first magic wand in history was that of Circe in the *Odyssey*, who used it to transform his men into wild beasts. Italian *fairy tales* put them into the hands of the powerful fairies, and by the late Middle Ages and in *Wicca* and Ceremonial magic, practitioners use several magical tools including wands. [12]

In ceremonial magic in general, the magic wand is considered an essential energy conductor to carry out a magical operation. It makes you wonder why Moses was not able to visualize the magic flame? Could he possibly have known more about the illusion projected by the alien Matrix that surrounds and dominates from the invisible world? Was he too respectful of that sacred flame from the etheric plane? The term aether (also written as "ether") was adopted from ancient Greek philosophy and science into Victorian physics (see Luminiferous aether) and utilized by Madame Blavatsky to correspond to akasha, the fifth element (quintessence) of Hindu metaphysics. The etheric plane is the highest plane in the dimension of Matter; a plane that is as concrete and real as the physical plane (and even more so) but is experienced through the senses of the soul in a dimension, and a consciousness beyond physical awareness. For the Illuminati, it is the world of ascended masters and their retreats. Certainly, there are also deceptive illusions in this realm, often due to demons and etheric parasites, but other times, as in this case, the subsequent result of a presumably divine message of a higher entity such as Yahweh (**Jahve**), confirm the genuineness of the original message. So, in the case of Moses, given his subsequent influence on the Jewish people, the phenomenon is believed to not be influenced by etheric parasites, that are negative thought forms, which are temporary beings generated in the etheric plane.

Remember, the etheric plane is a non-physical substructure underlying our material reality. Etheric energies and constructs are invisible "metadata" that can influence physical events at the quantum level. The lack of certainty for us, and common morals, which certainly are not operating at the level of Moses, Jesus or Mohammed, is mostly due to the fact that the majority of people ignore that there is a vast range of different entities in the various planes of existence. In the *astral plane*, there exist many different levels or realms, each realm has a slightly different vibration, ranging from the simplest expressions of lower telluric forms, sometimes called "elemental" or demonic, that in occultism are also called tulpas, vampiric egregores, or larvae, often used by the Illuminati, up to the supreme angelic intelligence and manifestations of the *divine plane,* charged with governing more worlds. Not always what we perceive coincides with what appears in front of us.

---

12   *See* https://en.wikipedia.org/wiki/Wand ‡ Archived 28th November 2017.

With Moses, as well as high magic, it could be said that we are in front of *God's technology*, which for us humans is obviously an "alien" technology, that allows us to do extraordinary things. According to some occult teachings, all souls are born on the divine plane and then descend down through the lower planes; however, souls will work their way back to the divine plane as Maffeo Charles Poinsot reminds us in, *The Book of Fate and Fortune, An Encyclopaedia of the Occult Sciences.* On the divine plane, souls can be opened to conscious communication with the sphere of the divine known as the *Absolute*, and receive knowledge about the nature of reality.

Initiates have come to realize, that in esoteric cosmology, a plane other than the physical plane is conceived as a subtle state of consciousness that transcends the known physical universe. A world of forces invisible to us and unknown to most people, but visible and well-known to the magician and true Illuminati like Moses. **Jorg Sabellicus** writes in the fourth volume of *Practical Magic* (*Magia Pratica*), that the conviction of the existence of different planes of reality are an important corollary to the concept of the existence of more "bodies" capable of acting on any of the planes in question. Along with the physical body (although being the most strident and farthest from God, but, however, the most important, because it is the starting point for climbing to higher worlds), there are a number of other "immaterial bodies," The number of which varies or depends on the planes of being identified by the various mystery schools. So according to the most widespread tradition of modern occultism, beside the body of flesh and blood, we have a so called "etheric" body, acting on the same plane, representing the intricacy of impalpable forces that assign the form to the biological structures (for the spiritists this body would be the "ghost" which in some cases remain in the places where physical death occurred). [13]

Moses was aware of these different fields of energy (present in the so-called etheric body), that are in continuous vibration, connected to energy vortexes called *chakra* (which in Sanskrit mean "wheel," as well as "circle" and "cycle"), that are in turn, placed in the etheric body. These seven doors, connect us to the upper, as well as the inferior planes, by emitting specific frequencies which are perceived by a developed eye, and attentive to color; That is why Jesus, the prophets the saints, and so on, are represented in the old paintings surrounded by a yellow aura, for example. Each chakra also emits a sound, an energetic expression that extends to our outside knowledge, a call for interdimensional entities that can be vampiric and naughty, or angelic and benevolent.They are positive if we emit a clean and pleasant sound, while they are malicious and parasitic if our sound is distorted because of our internal conflicts and misconduct.

The *Ordo Templi Orientis*, as well as other sects of the Crowleyan milieu (see the A.·.A.·. or the *Ordo Templi Astartes* (O.T.A.), related to the Thelemic Law, which is the name of a spiritual philosophy whose prophet was **Aleister Crowley**, influence their members through initiation rituals written by the English magician, for the various degrees of his Order (O.T.O.), that gradually and consciously distort the chakra energy, thus polluting them so badly and sometimes irreversibly, to facilitate demonic control of their minions. Unfortunately, they think they are elevating themselves to new levels of consciousness, but they are

---

13   *See* Jorg Sabellicus, *Magia Pratica vol. 4*, (Rome, IT: Ed. Mediterranee, 2001), pp. 12-13.

actually doing the exact opposite, falling most of the time into the abyss that Crowley described as the last impediment before illumination, but also the most dangerous. The risk of being overwhelmed in the abyss is high, even for a high-level Initiate, as Crowley pointed out. Hence the famous admonition of Crowley, "*Babe of the Abyss,*" which appeared in his famous work called The *Book of Lies,* published in 1913, which I will investigate later in my book, of being literally vampirized by interdimensional alien entities, something that happens to the majority of practicing occultists.

This was obviously not the case of Moses, a true Prophet and adept of the mysteries, a "Great Initiate" who worked on what the occultists call the "mental body," the only possible way to access the angelic plane, and the "spiritual body," which constitutes the divine glint enclosed in the complex psycho-physical structure of man—which, if released through a true illumination and proper knowledge, goes spontaneously toward the highest of worlds.

After many miracles, the Bible tells us that Moses left Egypt with his people, the Jews, wandering into the desert using magic Illuminati knowledge gathered in the priesthood of Osiris. Schuré, speaks about this in a specific chapter of his book on *The Great Initiates* entitled, *Exodus – The Desert – Magic and Theurgy:*

The Exodus was coordinated and preparations made well in advance by the prophet, the chief Israelite leaders, and Jethro. To put his plan into effect, Moses took advantage of a moment when Menephtah, his former study-companion, now Pharaoh, had to repel the mighty invasion of Mermaiu, king of the Lybians. The entire Egyptian army was occupied on the western borders of the country and could not stop the Hebrews. Thus the mass emigration occurred peacefully. Now we see the Beni-Israel on the march. The long file of caravans, with tents carried on camels' backs and followed by great herds, prepares to go around the Red Sea. They still number only a few thousand men. Later the emigration will grow larger "with all kinds of men," as the Bible says. They will include Canaanites, Edomites, Arabs, Semites of all kinds, attracted and fascinated by the desert prophet, who calls them from all directions and shapes them to his liking. The nucleus of his people is formed of the Beni-Israel, straightforward men, but rough, obstinate and rebellious. Their hags or their leaders have taught them the cult of the One God. This religion constitutes a high patriarchal tradition among them. But in those primitive and violent natures, monotheism is still only a better and intermittent consciousness. As soon as their evil passions reawaken, the instinct toward polytheism, so natural for man, takes the upper hand. Then they fall back into the superstitions, witchcraft and idolatrous practices of the neighboring peoples of Egypt and Phoenicia. Moses will fight this with Draconian laws.

Around the prophet who leads these people is a group of priests presided over by Aaron, Moses' initiate brother, and by the prophetess Miriam, who already represents feminine initiation in Israel. This group constitutes the priesthood. With them, seventy elected leaders or lay initiates press around the prophet of Ieve. Moses will entrust to them his secret doctrine and his oral tradition, will transmit to them a part of his powers and sometimes will make them sharers in his inspirations and visions. In the midst of this group is carried the golden Ark. Moses borrowed this idea from the Egyptian temples where it served as the secret place for the theurgic books, but he refashioned it in line with his personal plans. The Ark of

Israel is surrounded by four cherubim in gold, similar to sphinxes and resembling the four symbolic animals of Ezekiel's vision. One cherub has the head of a lion, another, of a bull, the third, of an eagle and the fourth, of a man. These personify the four elements of the universe: earth, water, air, and fire, as well as the four worlds represented by the letters of the sacred Tetragrammaton. With their wings, the cherubim cover the mercy seat, the throne of God.

This Ark will be the means of producing electrifying and splendid phenomena. The latter will be brought about by the magic of the priest of Osiris. These phenomena, exaggerated by legend, will produce the Biblical accounts. In addition, the golden Ark enclosed the Sepher Bereshith, or Book of Cosmogony, written by Moses in Egyptian hieroglyphics, and the magic wand of the prophet, called the rod by the Bible. Later it will also contain the Book of the Covenant or the law of Sinai. Moses will call the Ark the throne of Elohim, for in it rests sacred tradition—the mission of Israel, the idea of leve.

The Jews were led by an immense "cloud column" flying during the day. The Islamic tradition also alludes to similar manifestations by Jinn, supernatural alien creatures we also find in the **One Thousand and One Nights** fairy tales, on which I will also dwell later, no wonder by night the Israelites were conducted by a huge "column of fire" as the Jinn are called "fire spirits." Remember like human beings, the jinn can be good, evil, or neutrally benevolent and hence have free will like humans. These were definitely unusual events, which were visible to all the multitude of Israelites, who followed Moses their leader and never stopped trusting his relation with the god who guided him. For many paleo-astronautics researchers, the cloud column and the column of fire could represent the classic bizarre cigar-shaped UFO, but their hypothesis is only partially justified. A more in-depth and less materialistic vision must make us understand the true nature of these interdimensional beings and their unique method of traveling to the cosmos, using these "Stargates" or inter-dimensional doors, as a highway to move around the universe, but also to move from one dimension to another, which does not only mean a change in the vibrational state of these multi-dimensional beings at the entrance of our dimension, but often also a vibrational change in those who observe them.

That is why, outside of the unusual mass UFO sightings, these visions are often granted only to a few selected people that vibrate and resonate in a particular way and have a specific energy field around them. The human energy field is composed of seven levels. Many people have the erroneous idea that this field is like the layers of an onion but is not. Each level penetrates through the body and extends outward from the skin. Each successive level is of a "higher frequency" or a "higher octave." The production of various forms of electric phenomena at the will of powerful initiates is not only attributed to Moses by antiquity. Chaldean tradition attributed it to the Magi, Greek, and Latin traditions, to certain priests of Jupiter and Apollo. In similar cases, the phenomena are indeed of an electric nature. But the electricity of the earthly atmosphere would be put in motion by a more subtle and **universal force active everywhere, and which the great initiates agreed to attract, to concentrate and to project. This force is called akasha by the Brahmans, the fire element by the Magi of Chaldea, the great magic agent by the Kabbalists of the Middle Ages.** From the point of view of modern science, it can be called **etheric force.** One can either attract it directly or invoke it through the intermediary of invisible agents, conscious or semi-conscious, of which the earthly *atmosphere is full, and which the will of the Magi knows how to control. This theory is in no way contrary to a rational concept of the universe, and it is even indispensable in explaining a large body of phenomenon which would remain incomprehensible without it. It is necessary only to add that these phenomena are governed by changeless laws which are always proportioned to the intellectual, moral and magnetic strength of the initiate.* [14]

Energy is also a theme that permeates many areas of complementary health care, including Reiki, but for the characters who played a specific role and had a privileged and direct bond with their gods or certain entities, it is something much more profound. Interestingly, when the Jews needed food in the desert, the Lord informed Moses that he would rain food from the sky, and the next morning the Israelites would find the food they needed, a strange food, because of the high energy content they called *manna*. So God, with his army of angels, according to the Bible, does exactly what is normally done with an army to help people in difficulty, that is, distributes food rations from the sky. And of course, it is not a matter of common foods, but of highly energetic artificial foods, created in this case in a parallel world, another dimension, where Jinn and other entities live, angelic if spiritually superior, or demonic, if spiritually inferior, and in both cases able to astonish us with their creations or deceive us with their illusions. Finally, Kabbalists, who are said to be inspired by the work of Moses, arranged and reduced in a single vision, a series of concepts expressed by Gnostics, Neo-Platonists, and Pythagoreans, who, in turn, according to occultist historiography, have an ancestral tradition known as "**hyperborean**" where they divide reality into four worlds:

1. Atziluth or Atzilut, the Divine World, archetypal home, corresponding in some way to the world of Platonic ideas.

2. Briah, the Creative World, the Spheres of the Archangels, and other spiritual entities, who realize divine will by transforming it into acts in the lower worlds.

3. Jesirah, the World of Formation, lying immediately above the plane of matter and composed of a super thin substance (the quintessential of alchemists), which imposes form and quality on material bodies and can be molded with thought and guided by disciplined will.

4. Assiah, the World of Matter, the one in which our common virtue is overcome. [15]

THE IMMORTALITY DOCTRINE OF THE ILLUMINATI

The *Fraternitas Rosicruciana Antiqua* teaches in their mystery school that Moses believed in the doctrine of the fate of the elected announced by the Shaï-en-sinsin, an ancient Egyptian text translated into Latin, and originally published in Berlin in 1851, under the title, *Sai an Sinsin sive Aber Metempsychosis veterum Aegyptiorum* by Egyptologist **Heinrich Ferdinand Karl Brugsch**, also known as **Heinrich Brugsch** (1827-1894), not to be confused with his brother, junior by fifteen years who was **Émile Charles Albert Brugsch** (1842-1930), another important Egyptologist known as the assistant curator of

14   Eduard Schuré, *THE GREAT INITIATED, Ibid.*, p. 163.
15   Jorg Sabelicus, *MAGIC PRACTICE VOL. 4, Ibid.*, p. 11.

the Bulaq Museum—the core element of what is today's Egyptian Museum. Émile was also the one who helped Aleister Crowley in 1904, in the translation of a funeral artifact of great importance for the future Thelemic religion, which Crowley calls *The Stele of Revealing* or *Stele 718*, also known as the *Stele of Ankh-ef-en-Khonsu*. This is a painted, wooden offering stele, originally located in the former Bulaq Museum under inventory number 666, that was moved around 1902 to the newly opened Egyptian Museum of Cairo (inventory number A 9422; Temporary Register Number 25/12/24/11), where it remains to this day.

I would like to focus on the content of the *Shaï-en-sinsin* considered of some importance in Illuminati circles, especially in the *Fraternitas Rosicruciana Antiqua* (F.R.A.), a Rosicrucian Order originally established by German occultist and Illuminati Dr. Arnold Krumm-Heller, also connected to Crowley. The first scholars that study this ancient text were impressed by its high moral tone, and strong resemblance to the Bible, for some historians it bears the imprint of an essentially religious feeling and contains moral maxims whose striking agreement with the precepts of the Jewish Lawgiver as with those of Christ. It can be summarized as follows, reminding us that in Ancient Egypt this kind of secret occult teaching was also transmitted before actual death, with a symbolic initiation, a bit like what happens in the third degree of the F.R.A.:

The candidate dies purified in physics and in the soul and is tested in front of Osiris for his qualities and good deeds. The deceased reconnects to the Sun and descends with him through the gates of the eastern horizon, in the lower sky, the Egyptian Ade. Ptah forms a new cover of flesh and bones, similar to what he possessed on earth; Amon enlivens him with the breath of life; His heart, the principle of material life, *is now returned to him through the medium of breath. Ptah (Pteh, Peteh) was one of the triad of Memphis along with Sekhmet (or Bast) and Nefertum.*

When Memphis became the capital of Egypt, Ptah became the ultimate creator who made everything, including the gods of the Ogdoad of Hermopolis, and the Ennead of Heliopolis and was given the epithet, *He who set all the gods in their places and gave all things the breath of life.*

When I was initiated to the third degree of the *Fraternitas Rosicruciana Antiqua*, many years ago, the key element of this initiation was without any doubt the breathing of Ptha, the final moment in which the initiate symbolically deceased, resumes all the functions of his body organs, and he can finally see, understand, speak, walk, drink, sleep, and wake. From that point onwards, he will not fear his enemies and will enjoy perpetual health. He will retain his individuality, and the instructions in the ancient text say he will also possess the privilege to take on any forms he wants, and he will instantly be able to move from one place to another or even be able to visit the earth every day, establishing a new bodily existence. These preparatory lessons, what is defined as a "second life" are supplemented also by other texts.

The posthumous world is represented in the image of the earth. Spiritual life is, so to speak, a trick of human life, the occupations of the elect being the same as man. It is not a contemplative existence for all eternity, passive happiness, but an active and labor-intensive life, and, using the expression of French Egyptologist François Joseph Chabas (1817-1882), endowed with an infinite and longer life. This is the Egyptian concept of the Divine life of the righteous people, of which I have decided to expose the theory without trying to explain it. It is well-known that most of the scrolls that the ancient Egyptians buried with the mummies contain more or less complete copies of some sacred texts, considered as talismans, with property to operate or facilitate the entrance of the deceased to a new existence and to protect it in the overriding regimes. The subject of these texts is almost invariably about the fate of man after death. Among such compositions, *The Book of the Dead* and *The Books of Breathing* have long been known. Then there are still others, namely *The Book of Passing through the Eternities*, the *Amduat*, and the *Book of Gates*, in which we recognize most of the ideas and even phrases of the Shaï-en-sinsin Papyrus. The soul lives eternally but separated from the Manes. In ancient Roman religion, the Manes are chthonic deities sometimes thought to represent souls of deceased loved ones. *The Books of Breathing* and the *Shaï-en-sinsin*, date back to the Bas-Empire, but it is generally believed that it has been drawn up with the help of much older documents: the numerous specimens that have been found are all in hieratic writing.

If you judge according to the titles of the dead to whom they were devoted, the **Shaï-en-sinsin was specifically reserved for the priests and assistants of Amon-Ra.**

It is therefore, legitimate to think that Moses had studied, and knew his mysteries. *The Emerald Tablet*, also known as the *Smaragdine Table*, or *Tabula Smaragdina*, attributed to Hermes Trismegistus ("Hermes the Thrice-Greatest") highlight the most important bodily functions: *breathing*, and the secrets of breathing, that are transmitted in this text. According to the esoteric teachings, good breathing does not only have the function of oxygenating the lungs but also brings in that essential element for the initiated, that helps to penetrate and store in its organism the vital fluid, the **Prana or universal strength.**

Text of the Book of Breathings

I. [They drag Osiris in] to the Pool of Khonsu, (2) and likewise, [Osiris, Hôr, justified] born of Taikhebyt, justified, (3) after he has grasped his heart. They bury (4) the Book of Breathings which <Isis> made, which (5) is written on both its inside and outside, (wrapped) in royal linen, and it is placed <under> the (6) left arm near his heart. The bearer makes (7) his coffin on the outside of it. This document is made for him so that (8) he might breathe like the souls of the gods forever and (9) ever.

II. Beginning [of the Book of Breathings] which [Isis] made [for her brother, Osiris to cause his soul to live, to cause his body to live, to rejuvenate all his limbs] (2) again, [so that he might join] the horizon with his father, Re, [and to cause his soul to appear in heaven as the disk of the moon, so that his body might shine like Orion in the womb of Nut, to] (3) cause [the same] thing to happen to Osiris, Hôr, justified, [born of Taikhebyt, justified. Keep it secret!] (4) Do not let anyone read it. It is useful for one in the necropolis. He will live again successfully millions of times.

(5) O [Osiris,] Hôr, justified, born of Ta[ikhebyt, justified. You have been purified. Your heart has been purified. Your front is in] a state of purity, your back (6) is in a state of cleanliness. Your midsection is <cleansed> with soda [and natron. No part of you is involved in wrongdoing. The Osiris, Hôr,] justified, born of [Taikhebyt, justified, begotten of] Remny-qa, is purified in

that pool of [the Field of Offerings to the north of the Field of the Grasshopper.] Wadjet (8) and Nekhbet have purified you in the fourth hour of the night and the [fourth] hour [of the day.]

[Come, Osiris, Hôr, justified, born of Taikhebyt], justified. May you enter the Hall (9) of the Two Goddesses of Truth. You have been purified from every sin [and misdeed. Stone of Truth is your name.]

[O] Osiris, Hôr, justified, may you enter (10) into the afterlife [in] a state of great purity. [The Two Goddesses of Truth] have cleansed you [in the Great Hall. A purification has been performed for you in the Hall of Geb. Your body has been purified in the Hall] (11) of Shu. You see Re when [he] sets [and Atum in the evening. Amon is with you, giving breath to you. Ptah (12) is fashioning] your limbs. May you enter into the horizon together with Re. [Your soul has been received into the Neshmet ship with Osiris. Your soul is made divine in the House of Geb. You are justified forever and ever.]

III. [Osiris,] Hôr, justified, born of Tai[khebyt, justified. May your name endure. May your body last. Then your mummy will endure. [1] You shall not be turned back from heaven or earth. May you be made happy in the presence of Re.] (2) May your soul live in the presence of Amon. May your body be renewed in the presence of Osiris. May you breathe forever [and ever.]

[May your soul make invocation offerings for you of bread, beer, beef and fowl, libations and] (3) incense during the course [of every day. Your flesh is on] ‹your› bones, made like your form on earth. May you drink with [your throat. [2] May you eat with your mouth. May your receive] (4) offerings with [the souls of the gods. May] Anubis [protect] you and may he guard you. You shall not be turned back from the gates [of the afterlife.] May the twice [great] and mighty [Thoth,] Lord of Hermopolis, come to you and write for you the Book of Breathings with his own fingers. May your soul breathe (6) forever. May you assume again your form on earth among the living. You are divine with the souls of the gods. Your heart is the heart of Re. Your limbs (7) [are the limbs of the Great God.]

[O Osiris,] Hôr, justified. Amon is with you every day ... in the House of Re. May you live again. May Wepwawet open for you the [beautiful] path. (8) [May you see with your eyes and hear with your] ears, speak with your mouth and walk with your legs. Your soul is divine in the afterlife so that it can assume any form it desires. May you cause the rustlings(?) [3] of the noble *Ished*-tree in Heliopolis. May you awake every day and see the rays (10) of the sun. May Amon come to you bearing the breath of life. May he cause you to breathe [in] your coffin. May you go forth to the earth every day. May you be given the Book (11) [of Breathings of Thoth for] your protection. May you breathe by means of it like Re.

May your eye see the rays of the (sun's) disk. May truth be spoken to you (12) [in the presence of Osiris. May "justified" be written upon your body. Horus, the Avenger of His Father, Horus of Edfu, may he enfold your body in protection, [4] and may he cause your soul to be divine like all the gods do. The soul of Re is animating [your soul]. (13) The soul of Shu unites with your [nos]trils. O Osiris, Hôr, justified, born of Taikebyt, justified. May your soul breathe [anyplace you want.]

IV. [You are in the seat of Osiris. Foremost of the Westerners is your name. May the Great Inundation come to you from Elephantine, and may he fill your offering table with provisions.] (2) Osiris, Hôr, [justified, born of Taikhebyt, justified. May the gods of Upper and Lower Egypt come to you and guide you to the *Alcha'a* [5] together with your soul. May] you [accompany] (3) Osiris and may you breathe within the necropolis [together with the Great God. May your body live] (4) in Busiris and the Thinite Nome. May your soul live in heaven every day.

[Osiris, Hôr, justified, born of Taikhebyt, justified. May Sekhmet have power over those who conspire against you. Horus,] (5) Great of Heart, is protecting you. Horus of Edfu [does what you want. Horus the Beloved guards your body. May you endure in] (6) life, prosperity, and health. You have been established upon your seat in the Sacred Land.

[Come now Osiris, Hôr, justified, born of Taikhebyt, justified. You] have arisen in your likeness, the likeness of your royal regalia. May you be established in life. [May you spend your time in health. May you walk and breathe] (8) anywhere. May Re shine upon in cave [6] like (he did upon) Osiris. May [you] breathe [and live on his rays. May Amon animate] (9) your *ka*, may it live, prosper, and be healthy. [7] May he cause you to flourish by the Book of Breathings. May you accompany Osiris [and Horus, Lord of the Henu-boat. You are the Great God,] (10) foremost among the gods. May your face live and your form be beautiful. Your name is established every day. May you enter into the god's [great hall (or council)] (11) in Busiris, and may you see the Foremost of the Westerners at the Wag-festival. [8] May your odor be as pleasant as a young man. [May your name be as great as] (12) an august [noble].

O Osiris, Hôr, justified. May your soul live by means of the Book of Breathings. [May you join with] (13) <your> soul. May you enter into the afterlife without your enemy. You are a divine soul [in Busiris.]

(The remainder of the papyrus is missing. Louvre Papyrus 3284, III, 21 to V, 11 can be used for the missing text.) III. (21) You have your heart. It is not far from you. [9] (22) You have your eyes, which are open every day.

IV. Words spoken by the gods who are in attendance on Re. Osiris NN (3) May you accompany (4) Osiris. May your soul live forever and ever.

Words spoken by the gods who are in the afterlife (5) to Osiris. Foremost of the Westerners, and to Osiris NN (6) in order to open for him the doors of the afterlife.

May you be received (7) in the necropolis. Come, let your soul live forever. May it build a portal in the necropolis. (8) May your *ka* praise its god, for it has received the Book of Breathings. Come, let it cause breathing.

(9) A boon which the king gives to Osiris, Foremost of the Westerners, the Great God, Lord of Abydos. May he give an invocation offering (10) of bread, beer, beef, fowl, wine, milk, offerings, provisions, and every (11) good thing to the *ka* of Osiris NN (12) May you be healthy. May your corpse live, enduring at the command of Re himself, and like Re neither perishing (13) nor being sick forever and ever.

(14) O Far Strider [10] who has come forth from Heliopolis. Osiris NN has not done (15) any wrong. [11]

(16) O Great of Strength, who comes forth from Hery-aha. [12] Osiris NN has not committed (17) any robbery.

(18) O One with the Nose, [13] who comes forth from Hermopolis. Osiris NN has not (19) shown favoritism (?). [14]

(20) O Eye Swallower, who comes forth from the Double Caverns. [15] Osiris NN has not made (21) any seizure of property by theft.

V. O Terrible of Visage, [16] who comes forth from the necropolis, Osiris NN has not engaged in any disputes. (2) O Ruty, who comes forth from heaven. Osiris NN has not caused a false reading of the balance [17] (3) O Ho Whose Eye is on Fire, [18] who comes forth from Letopolis. Osiris NN has not committed any deception.

(4) O Gods who are in the hereafter, hear the voice of Osiris NN. He has come before you (5) without any evil committed by him, without any wrong-doing held against him, and without any witness who rises up against him. He lives by righteousness. He consumes righteousness. The hearts of the gods are content with all that he has done. (6) He has given bread to the hungry, water to the thirsty, clothing to the naked. He has given offerings to the gods and invocation offerings to the blessed dead. There is no accusation against him before any of the gods. Let him enter into the afterlife without being turned away. Let him accompany Osiris together with the gods (8) of the cavern, for he has life, prosperity, and health among the living, and he is divine among the justified dead. Let him live, and let his soul live. Let (9) his soul be admitted to any place he desires. Accept his Book of Breathings. Let him breathe together with that soul of his in (10) the afterlife with any form his heart desires together with the Westerners. Let his soul go wherever it wants. Let him live upon the earth forever and ever. [16]

MOUNT SINAI, COUNT CAGLIOSTRO, AND THE FORTY-DAY EXPERIENCE

*M*oses arrived at Mount Sinai three months after leaving Egypt with the Israelites. The Lord met Moses several times on his favorite mountain, surrounded by a dense cloud, warning that no one could climb up for any reason during the sacred meeting. Exodus 19:12 is very clear on this point: *"Put limits for the people around the mountain and tell them, Be careful that you do not approach the mountain or touch the foot of it. Whoever touches the mountain is to be put to death."* (New International Version)

This suggests that an interdimensional door was created for Moses on this mountain, where an alien angelic entity appeared to him earlier in the Serbal cave and was handling the whole affair on behalf of God, who was creating a sort of transcendental operative base for him. Subsequently, many luminescent clouds covered the top of the mountain, as other alien entities were possibly ar-

---

16   Translation of *The Book of Breathings* by Michael D. Rhodes , Department of Ancient Scripture Brigham Young University.

riving on top of Mount Sinai to meet up with Moses. Most extraterrestrial beings visiting our planet are actually extra-dimensional in nature but limited to travel within and across specific dimensional portals like Mount Sinai in this case. Moses entered the clouds and disappeared for several days or weeks, just like some alleged alien abductees. Here, in an extra-dimensional reality, the space-time continuum is certainly different from ours. Moses was taught many things, and given various orders to build different objects. Even Schuré wrote that this was typical of the Egyptian priestly tradition to which Moses belonged. However, the alien forces leading Moses seem to have instructed him on the construction of objects much more powerful than the ones used by the Egyptian enemy. In this context, Moses received from the Lord and his angels, the design for a weird arc-shaped instrument later called **The Ark of the Covenant** also referred to as **The Ark of Elohim**, a gold-covered wooden chest with a lid, described in the *Book of Exodus* as containing the two stone tablets of the Ten Commandments. For some researchers, this device is supposed to be a communication device or a very powerful weapon, and for others a device that allowed to travel between dimensions/alternate universes/planes of existence/etc.

It was called The Ark of the Covenant because it represented the covenant between God and the Jewish people. It is said to be composed of pure gold, a noble metal considered of great importance by some alien species like the Annunaki, and it is suggested by Zecharia Sitchin that the Anunnaki were brethren of the Elohim. The Bible, in Exodus 25: 10-22, describes it in great detail: *"it was a kind of acacia wood, covered inside and out with pure gold, measuring 2.5 cubits long and 1.5 cubits long. Width and height (about 1.25 meters long by 0.75 meters wide and 0.75 meters high). A golden cornice or garland surrounded its upper part, and on the outside was fixed with four rings of gold on both sides, through which were inserted two long poles, also made of acacia wood covered with gold, to be able to carry it. Its top cap, called 'propitiatory,' was solid gold and had on top the image of two gold cherubim, one facing the other and with the wings unfolded, that looked towards the center of the box. Between the cherubim and the mercy seat, there was an open space, a kind of sacred triangle-which was called the oracle, and was the most sacred part of the Ark."*

Back in 2004, while I was in Egypt, a member of the highly influential Boutros-Ghali family told me that gold and diamonds are the only minerals used for the construction of spaceships by these alien species, and they were the same ones revered and worshipped by the Illuminati. So the mysterious Ark of the Covenant could be many things, but it is definitely an alien artifact of some kind.

Lon Milo DuQuette, occultist, author, and Freemason of the Ancient and Accepted Scottish Rite, describes it as a sort of electric battery in use in ancient Egypt in his book *Chicken Qabalah of Rabbi Lamed Ben Clifford*. This hypothesis is supported by the studies of some fringe archaeologists on a bas-relief found in Hathor Temple, located about 2.5 km south-east of the town of Dendera, where we find what is now known as the Dendera light, a supposed ancient Egyptian electrical lighting technology depicted on three stone reliefs (one single and a double representation). Mainstream Egyptologists take the view that it is a typical set of symbolic images from Egyptian mythology, but shortly after the discovery of the Temple of Dendera (made in 1857), the English scientist Sir William Crookes, who was later initiated into the Hermetic Order of the Golden Dawn in 1890, built what is known as the Crookes tube or the Crookes–Hittorf tub. This is an early experimental electrical discharge tube with partial vacuum used in 1895 by Wilhelm Röntgen, to discover X-rays. Röntgen stumbled on X-rays while experimenting with Lenard and Crookes tubes and began studying them. This object has so many visible similarities to the battery that appears in the bas-relief found in the temple of **Hathor** at **Dendera** that one wonders why they are still covering up this important discovery. Lon Milo writes: *"I hear you laughing, dear students, but I must remind you that viable batteries have been found in Egyptian tombs of this period and before."* [17]

In reality, a real antique artifact, known as the *Baghdad Battery*, with the features of a modern battery that would confirm the interpretation of the bas-relief of Dendera, was made public in 1938, but as the name suggests it was found in Persia, and not in Egypt. DuQuette also reminds us that the Ark was considered: *"A lethal weapon and the Israelites treated it as one. They kept it wrapped in cloth and leather, and the men carrying it had to wear special clothes and special shoes."* [18] In addition to the Ark of the Covenant, Moses had to build *the tent of meeting* described in *Exodus* 33:7 in the following manner:

> *7 Now Moses used to take a tent and pitch it outside the camp some distance away, calling it the "tent of meeting." Anyone inquiring of the Lord would go to the tent of meeting outside the camp. 8 And whenever Moses went out to the tent, all the people rose and stood at the entrances to their tents, watching Moses until he entered the tent. 9 As Moses went into the tent, the pillar of cloud would come down and stay at the entrance, while the Lord spoke with Moses. 10 Whenever the people saw the pillar of cloud standing at the entrance to the tent, they all stood and worshipped, each at the entrance to their tent. 11 The Lord would speak to Moses face to face, as one speaks to a friend. Then Moses would return to the camp, but his young aide Joshua son of Nun did not leave the tent.* [19]

This tent was clearly built so that outside you could not see what was happening inside, and the God of the Jews gave Moses precise instructions on how to build all these objects back on Mount Sinai. So Moses received some kind of technological preparation from his "alien" godly sources during his long stay on Mount Sinai, as did other characters who have changed the history of humanity with their inspired inventions more or less of a divine nature. All this is further confirmation of the fact that Moses had to deal with extra-dimensional entities with a well-defined hierarchy that he knew and respected, because tied to the one who should be our "Creator," is obviously an alien God, as he dominates a multiverse reality, where nothing is as it seems. After a while, the alien Lord invited Moses again to Mount Sinai. Here the *Lord* came into the cloud and abducted him for forty days. The same forty days that we also find mentioned for Jesus in *Acts* 1:3: *"3 After his suffering, he presented himself to them and gave many convincing proofs that he was alive.* ***He appeared to them over a period of forty days and spoke about the kingdom of God.***" (New International Version)

The number 40 is frequently used in major Biblical stories. Here's a quick list:

40 days and nights of rain during the flood of Noah

---

17   Lon Milo Duquette, *THE CHICKEN QABALAH OF RABBI LAMED BEN CLIFFORD*, (York Beach, ME: Weiser Books, 2001), p. 77.

18   *Ibid.*, p. 76.

19   From the New International Version.

40 days after flood Noah opened the door to the ark

40 years the children of Israel wandered in the desert

Moses was in Egypt (ego, flesh) 40 years, Midian 40 years, and then in the desert 40 years.

Moses was on the mountain for 40 days and 40 nights

Solomon reigned 40 years

Jonah said it would be 40 days until Nineveh would be destroyed

There are literally hundreds more verses that involve the number 40, but this short list from **The Old Testament** should suffice to show you how important it is. So what does the number 40 really represent? Mentioned 146 times in Scripture, the number 40 generally symbolizes a period of testing, trial or probation. During Moses' life, he lived forty years in Egypt and forty years in the desert before God selected him to lead his people out of slavery. He also sent spies, for forty days, to investigate the land God promised the Israelites as an inheritance (*Numbers* 13:25, 14:34). Forty, in the end, represents the testing and trial of our physical life as a whole, and the number forty can also represent the regeneration and transformation of man. The same kind of transformation that illuminated Jesus, and was mentioned in *The Gospel of John: "14 Just as Moses lifted up the snake in the wilderness, so the Son of Man must be lifted up, [a] 15 that everyone who believes may have eternal life in him."* [20]

"Must be lifted up"? Well in an unusual interpretation, this looks like a classic abduction scenario. The Travis Walton UFO incident, for example, an alleged abduction of an American logger by a UFO on November 5, 1975, saw Mr. Walton lifted in the sky by a beam of light, that reappeared only after a five-day search. Of course, he was not given any particular instructions or groundbreaking revelations for mankind, but this phenomenon is more common than most people think.

Within the tradition of the Illuminati linked to "alien" contact, the **forty days topic** is also present in the Great Work of the famous **Count of Cagliostro**, the controversial figure who had in Moses and Solomon, two important points of reference for his Masonic doctrine, along with the prophets **Enoch and Elijah**, considered by Cagliostro to be his Secret Chiefs and Invisible Masters, chosen intermediaries to the **"Architect of all worlds."** These teachings are also found in his Egyptian Rite of Freemasonry, the Masonic ritual created by the Grand Copt, Count Alessandro of Cagliostro, which was the alias used by the occultist Giuseppe Balsamo. At the very moment the Worshipful Master of the Egyptian Rite elevates a Fellow Craft (second-degree) to the Sublime degree of Master Mason, blowing three times on his face, following this way the ancient tradition of **Ptah**, the demiurge of Memphis, god of craftsmen and architects and at the same time wrapping him with a red cord, doing simbolically what Ptah does in the Shaï-en-sin, when he wraps the deceased in a new body, after showing him the new apron and gloves, Cagliostro's new Master Mason will also be blessed and consecrated by the angels, as well as by **Enoch, Elijah, and Moses.** In addition, in the Catechism of the Egyptian Rite we find, as I mentioned earlier, the instruction for the forty days period, in which through a series of spiritual

20   From the New International Version.

exercises, one enters another dimension, regenerating both spirit and body, as Cagliostro used to say.

Here is a brief extract from the 2nd degree of Cagliostro's Egyptian Rite:

Q. Did you find much happiness in your forty days of meditation and prayer?

A. No, but I know of the reason for it and its purpose.

Q. What are they?

A. Every man who wishes to travel with profit in natural and supernatural philosophy, must build in his heart a temple to the Eternal and search to regenerate himself not only physically but also morally. It is necessary that he employs all his efforts to discover the apostle and the celebrant of the grandeur and the Omnipotence of God; he is obliged in the highest degree to hide and render his individuality impenetrable to all profanes. The Eternal, in creating the primary matter, has endowed it with such perfection, that it alone can serve and prolong the years of mortals, that which it accomplishes through the redemption and the conduct of the forty days with a love for the natural and spiritual being. For the spiritual or natural operation, forty days is the time both determined and necessary to perfect our morality and bring us to the desired age. This spiritual regeneration consummated and perfected, we have no further need for protection or security from any mortal and one will be principal and master, and with the continuance of the grace of the Eternal one can conserve that power, so long as one conforms scrupulously to that which I will show you.

In the Islamic tradition, as well as in the Jewish one, admired by Cagliostro, who took inspiration from both for his Masonic rite and his own teachings, the collaboration between entities, spirits and men, for those who do not have the necessary prequisites and access codes to these realities, is only narrated, but strictly forbidden. Later I will talk about these entities, using the term **UFOnauts**—someone or something that travels in a UFO. After all this occult work, Cagliostro however, as some of you may already know, did not enjoy a happy ending to his otherwise adventurous and epic life around the courts of Europe. He was instead condemned by the Vatican to a barbaric ending, with a brutal imprisonment and a forced isolation in a cell of the Castle of San Leo, until his supposed death in 1795. The relationship with certain entities for the Vatican was, and still is to some extent even today, a sort of exclusivity that should not have been violated by the Illuminati Grand Master, Count Cagliostro, who became the last victim of the infamous Inquisition.

The mysterious Count had learned a lot, perhaps too much, in his famous Middle Eastern travels, that he often used to brag about, and where he seems to have acquired the teachings of a secret book of the **Sheikh Abu'l Muwai jid of Gudscherat**, entitled *Dschawahiru'l Chamsa (The Five Precious Stones)* quoted only in relatively recent times by Rudolf von Sebottendorf (also known as Rudolf Glauer), an important figure in the activities of the Thule Society, a post-World War I German occultist organization that influenced many members of the future Nazi Party. Von Sebottendorf does this in his celebrated essay *Orientalische Magie,* that appeared on numbers 4, 5 and 6 of *Theosophie* published in Leipzig between 1924 and 1925, which reconnects not only to the forty-day theme, so dear to the Illuminati and the Prophets, but also shows us the hidden secrets of esoteric Islam, and the *Jinn*, supernatural or supersensible beings, who along with humans and angels are an essential alien component of the cosmos, that have apparently helped a lot the early practitioners of what became that monstrosity called esoteric Nazism.

The only aim of black magic is to lead people astray, and to make their souls wretched, and that's what Nazism eventually did when they put the whole country of Germany under a spell. This is always the key goal of evil magicians who deal with devilish Jinn. Actually, among the alien Jinn, there are believers and disbelievers, the believing Jinn are called Jinn, while the disbelieving Jinn are called Shaytan (the devil). Thus, when Muslims talk about Shayatin (devils), they mean the second kind of Jinn.

Sheikh Abu'l Muwai jid of Gudscherat explains that this science serves to:

1. Create friendship or enmity between two people;

2. Provide someone with healing, illness or death;

3. Make sure you reach your own desires, temporal or eternal;

4. Get to a win or defeat situation on the battlefield.

Let's remember, however, that these occult practices are obviously contrary to the basic tenets of traditional Islam, that considers magic to be an act of blasphemy, even if you are using it to simply get in touch with the spirit world, in the usual **forty-day marathon.** To have clearer idea of why we shouldn't use magic in our day to day life, it might be worth reading the following words from the actual ***Quran***: *"Suleiman (Solomon) did not disbelieve, but the devils disbelieved teaching men magic."* [Quran 2:102]

During the preparation to this magical ordeal envisioned in the *Dschawahiru'l Chamsa,* to get in contact, and eventually win the collaboration of certain alien entities, the courageous or blasphemous aspirant depending on the point of view, must be scrupulously clean, he doesn't have to miss any of the laundry list of restrictions by the Islamic religion, no dogs, cats or strangers must enter his home, that must be suffused with natural incense and fragrances. It is very important to fast during the forty-days of what is defined by Sheikh Abu'l Muwai jid of Gudscherat as the *Chilla,* a spiritual practice of penance and solitude well-known in Sufism. You must rest on a mat laid on the floor, and you must sleep as little as possible during the forty days, and not be involved in any conversation during this time. Those who want to practice this retreat for forty days must do it in solitude. The diet to be observed must be oriented according to the divine names you are reciting during your prayers. Islam knows two types of divine names. The ones regarded as friendly or beautiful, and the terrifying ones. If you are reciting the beautiful names, you should not swallow butter, curdled milk, vinegar or salt. If you are using the terrifying ones, avoid flesh, fish, eggs, and honey. If you are using both categories, you should not eat onions and garlic. In any case, alcohol and pork are prohibited as the Islamic tradition prescribes. During the forty days of fasting, the practitioner must recite ten phrases from the Quran ten times.

These are all reminders that the Islamic world and belief system if analyzed in- depth, have accommodated traditional, pagan and pre-Islamic practices of the highest level in their magical teachings. The Islamic faith is shaded with the supernatural and occult, especially at the popular level, but they always tend to hide this element I am now investigating further, because of its connections to the alien reality. You can find visible manifestations of the occult in Islam everywhere— even on streets and in names. Protection from the evil eye is usually sought after. On the back of trucks in Islamic countries, one can see at times the picture of an eye with an arrow drawn through it. This means that anyone envious of the truck will not be able to cause an accident to happen to it; the eye of greed will be rendered powerless. Even small children often carry protection with them against the evil eye in the form of small blue pearls. Women wear gems to divert the evil eye so that its glance can do no harm, a bit like Crystals are used to offer protection against negative energies by New Agers. These items also serve in the Islamic tradition to frustrate the eyes of lust, distracting them. The Middle East is full of such elements, terms, and fetishes. If you suggest them to get rid of these practices, they will find it nearly impossible even if considered sinful by their own religion. They depend upon these beliefs and are not willing to abandon them.

Many believe in the power of the evil eye and its effects on men here in Italy, especially in Southern regions like Sicily, that have a strong Islamic influence. If you look at someone from behind or beside, he may sense it quickly and turn to you abruptly, staring into your eyes and even beat you up. Another form of the occult in Islam is the *mandil* or reading of the cloth. This is one of many ways in which secrets are revealed in the Muslim world. Once in a school in the Middle East, a watch was stolen and all the girls of that class had to go home. The headmaster said that she would not allow the teachers to teach until the watch was found. This went on for two days. On the third day, the parents came and said that they would not agree to this punishment because it put their daughters under suspicion of having stolen the watch. They resented this because they insisted that their daughters were innocent. An easy solution to the problem was suggested through a visit by a soothsayer (one with knowledge of the extrasensory world) who lived in the neighboring village. She would be able to reveal the whereabouts of the watch, for she had recently disclosed the exact location of two stolen cows which had been hidden fifteen kilometers away from the owner's farm. The headmaster of the school did not accept this method, but fortune telling in the Middle East is part of daily life.

In Egypt once, I was forced to accept a reading made in a coffee cup from a known psychic advisor, they interpret the residual coffee grounds in the cup and on the saucer and tell your future. I remember on that same occasion, the famous Egyptian psychic also told me the story of a girl who vanished, and when the psychic was consulted by the police, she apparently gave all the details of the kidnapping thanks to the Jinn, including the name of the abductor and the country to which the girl had been taken. The most famous fortune tellers accept military generals, government officials and business people as customers, as well as ordinary citizens in Egypt. They all line-up in front of their doors and have to wait their turn, I saw this with my own eyes.

There is another form of fortune telling and soothe-saying; namely, predictions, as to whether one should marry a particular person and whether the union will be a happy one. Many are involved in these practices and are bound by them all their lives. **In Islamic countries, Qur'anic texts, prayers or curses are sometimes** written on small papers, not only for protecting a person but also to actively influence certain people in special situations. A sheikh once said that he was writing verses from the Qur'an that would help a businessman have a successful business trip. Also, a young man wanted to influence a girl to love him, so he asked someone to hide pieces of written texts under her mattress. Merchants who want the businesses and projects of their competitors to fail, also practice similar customs. An old leading figure in the world of the Islamic Illuminati called **Ahmad ibn Ali al-Buni**, who was a 12th-century author and esoteric student, investigated the occult properties of the 99 names of God, and advised the faithful on how they could harness their supernatural power through amulets and talismans in his book *Luma'at al-nuraniyya* (**Brilliant Lights**). We find the same approach also in the *Dschawahiru'l Chamsa* quoted by Rudolf von Sebottendorff, who indicates the following praying formula that is also an important spell: *"Be praised, there is no God outside of You, Lord of all things, Provider, Donor, Consoler."* This spell for example, originally consists of 45 letters, for a total numeric value of 2613.

Von Sebottendorf conducts a detailed analysis of a series of snapshots of Arabic numerals and godly names related to the compulsory practice in the Islam Faith which is called the *Zakat*, which means "purity" or "purify," and represents the charity that all Muslims, who are sufficiently well-off, must do in order to spiritually purify their wealth. So Rudolf von Sebottendorf, based his work on this mysterious, almost unknown text, left by a certain Sheikh Abu'l Muwai jid of Gudscherat, explaining that certain formulas must be recited during the forty days, about 70,000 times, which amounts to 1710 recitals a day, an effort requiring the total involvement of the practitioner that will absorb all of his intellectual abilities. As I told you earlier, for most traditional Muslims seeking the presence of a Jinn is not permissible regardless of the method by which it is done.

Jinn are dangerous and can cause chaos if interfered with, but generally, they keep to themselves. They live in our world and take their place where it suits them, usually remote or sacred areas. Evil Jinn, however, tend to stay in impure places like toilets, etc. Sebottendorf warns us that when we are involved in this kind of practice, ghost and demons are always watching us, both when we are awake and while we are sleeping, attempting to confide secrets of all sorts, often fueled with dangerous lies and perversions. It is clear that this kind of exercise, as Sebottendorf points out, requires tremendous effort for the human psyche, and very few people will attempt this kind of occult practice. These exercises are, therefore, considered very dangerous. The powers gained, however, are used by the practitioner according to what is indicated with great care.

In the rest of his essay, Von Sebottendorf, who tells us that in traditional texts you find a series of tables showing the original Arabic alphabet in relation to the numeric value of the letters, but Von Sebottendorf decided instead to propose these tables in a simplified version for the Western reader, reproducing the names using the Latin alphabet, also in use in the modern English and German alphabet. The letters present in the tables in the text are also correlated with the twelve signs of the Zodiac, with the four elements, and the seven planets. Once an Islamic expert using this occult method was asked if a man and a woman called **Akram and Rahima** were compatible with each other. It turns out that both names belong to the same manifestation of God, and that their quality also coincides with friendship. The corresponding planets present are not enemies, indeed according to the charts of planetary trends they show a mixture of friendship and enmity; so they are indifferent. The Zodiac signs involved indicate however the possibility of change from friendship to enmity between the two sides. According to the tables, the elements are conflicting and presumptuous. If, for example, the expert wants to help a certain individual called Bahran, by consulting the tables, he will find out that the five letters of the name (b.a.h.r.m.) Correspond to certain Jinn called **Danusch, Husch, Rahusch, Qajapusch,** and **Madschbusch,** and by calculating the corresponding names of God in the tables of the text, you will determine how many times you have to repeat a certain prayer. So in order to have the help of the genies in question, the expert must, therefore, recite no less than 24,000 times the following formula:

O Danusch, in the name of the Durable,

O Husch, in the name of the Chief,

O Rahusch, In the name of the Lord,

O Qajapusch, in the name of Allah,

Or Madschbusch, in the name of the King.

As the practitioner of Islamic magic is reciting this, he has to direct his face towards the home of the one he wants to put under his or her influence, and at the same time, as indicated in the tables of the book in question, he must also burn five times particular herbs to suffuse the ambience. In short, it is not an easy game to evoke or work with these genies, but for certain Illuminati, it's a necessary requirement in their long trial for obtaining illumination, or their ultimate quest for occult power. In the Islamic texts, it is stated that the Jinn are able to materialize or disappear at will. This would imply one of three things:

1) They have control over the matter that we consider to be "everyday reality;"

2) They have control over certain aspects of our own psyche, and can create in us the subjective experience of matter;

3) They can create illusions of an external and very realistic nature in the same way that we create holograms. It is possible that this last suggestion includes the first.

Various researchers on the cutting edge of nuclear physics (i.e. Paul Davies) and also in the border-line medical field (i.e. Harry Oldfield) have speculated that there exists a kind of blueprint for physical beings and physical materials— this may be an electromagnetic lattice or hologram which tells each atom or molecule what to do and where to go. The reason for this kind of speculation is that our present knowledge of natural control systems is unable to explain the degree of specialization that many atoms/molecules/cells exhibit. [21]

However, away from the battlefield and the materialist world of fundamentalist Islam, this religion and the supernatural frequently meet to this day, and the use of sacred words and phrases to cure the unwell, offer us a powerful reminder of the value traditionally attributed by Islam to sustained supplication and remembrance of God but also to his invisible Hierarchy.

21   Article by Chris Line on *Flying Saucer Review* Vol. 34 No. 4 December Quarter, 1989.

Jinn, demons, humans, and angels make up the known sapient creations of God. Like human beings, *Jinn* can be good, evil, or neutrally benevolent and hence have free-will like humans. Since the Jinn, like humankind, face the judgment of God, they are on no account to be confused with God, who is alone to be worshipped. Yes, King Solomon appears to have had Jinn working for him, but only with God's special permission.

Let's not underestimate the power of these creatures and their connection to the Illuminati network. If we want to truly understand the alien phenomena, but also the present manipulation of mankind made possible now more than ever by modern technology, we need to understand the Invisible Masters and Secret Chiefs that rule us from their interdimensional reality.

MOSES' RADIANT GLOW

*W*hen Moses, after completing his forty-day marathon, returned to his people, he returned looking different, his skin was *radiant* to the point that the Jews began to fear him. A fear that obliged Moses to put a veil in front of his face, as reported in *Exodus* 34:29:

29 *When Moses came down from Mount Sinai with the two tablets of the covenant law in his hands, he was not aware that his face was radiant because he had spoken with the Lord.* (New International Version)

Obviously, Moses was subjected to some kind energetic treatment that empowered his magnetic flux or **animal magnetism,** a name given by Illuminati member Franz Anton **Mesmer** (1734-1815), to a science already practiced since ancient times. Mesmer was one of the two major protagonists of the esoteric scene of the eighteenth century, the other being Count Cagliostro.

Moses was a much more than an ordinary magnetizer. Many researchers, among them Protestants, spiritists, and other writers, claim that even Jesus was the greatest of all magnetizers and that the source of his miracles was animal magnetism. Meanwhile, the Lord on board his glory cloud decided when the Jewish people were to depart or to move toward the next stage of this liberating mission led by Moses. When the cloud moved, the people of Israel left for the next stage of their trip towards the Promised Land. Strangely enough, during the previous century, some churches began to report the appearance of various "glory clouds" around the globe.

They believed this to be a physical manifestation of God's presence in the form of a glittery cloud that lingered over worship services. Such clouds have been reported in services all over the world, from one-room house churches in Brazil to mega-churches in California, and in places where UFO sightings have been usually reported. Those who have witnessed this phenomenon describe it as a glittering swarm of gold-like particles that settle on skin and hair and then vanish upward. Some describe hands and faces covered in oil or a glittery residue that returns even after wiping it off. There are also reports of feathers or "jewels" falling from these clouds. Some pastors, usually in the Charismatic or Pentecostal movement, claim that the cloud has so enveloped them before preaching that they could hardly see the congregation. They attribute it to the tangible presence of God anointing them for preaching, and they obviously use it as a reference for their biblical foundation, the Old Testament and passages from *Exodus,* as the actual term "glory cloud" is not found anywhere in Scripture, and many rightly wonder whether such a thing is biblical. It is significant that the "proof texts" for the so-called "glory cloud" come entirely from the Old Testament, and the experiences mainly made by Moses and the Israelites. Those who encountered the cloud of God's glory in the Old Testament were often unable to approach it (see: *Exodus 40:34–35; 2 Chronicles 7:2;* and *1 Kings 8:11*).

By contrast, those experiencing the modern version of a "glory cloud" greet it with singing, dancing, shouting, and basking in the glitter that engulfs them. This response is inconsistent with biblical accounts but is consistent with some UFO reports. When the glory of God was present in a cloud, the power of His presence was so overwhelming that mortal man could not enter it because at the time the alien forces at work for God didn't want any contact with the majority of mankind, only with a few chosen ones that became their Prophets.

Ezekiel was also one of the privileged few that experienced this kind of alien encounter with God. He writes:

"Like the appearance of a rainbow in the clouds on a rainy day, so was the radiance around him. This was the appearance of the likeness of the glory of the LORD. When I saw it, I fell facedown, and I heard the voice of one speaking" (Ezekiel 1:28; cf. 44:4).

When the Lord gave Isaiah a vision of His glory, Isaiah's response was to cry, *"Woe to me! I am ruined! For I am a man of unclean lips, and I live among a people of unclean lips, and my eyes have seen the King, the Lord Almighty" (Isaiah 6:5).* **Abject humility akin to horror always followed Old Testament displays of the glory of God** (2 Chronicles 5:14; 7:3; Isaiah 6:5).

The response of Ezekiel and Isaiah, to the glory of the Lord, were similar to the responses of those in modern Charismatic churches, but the same can be said of the way most ordinary people today when they encounter UFOs, do not connect this kind of event to a religious one. In descriptions, it has never been written that the "glory cloud" could be demonic, with close affinity to Jinn, whose dark and malicious nature are often prone to fool mankind with illusions. The Jinn or Jinni or Genies or Djinn are part of what the Ancient people of this Earth used to call "Elemental Spirits."

What are Elemental Spirits?

Elemental Spirits are what some call the Nature Spirits or Devas or the Faeries, these type of Spirits have only one element to their nature, usually **Air, Fire, Water** and **Earth,** so Djinn are part of the Fire Spirits, but in Arabic the other groups are also known as **JINN,** since no human eye can see them. This is what most Arabic scholars call (Jaan al Bahar, Jaan al Hawa, Jaan al Ar'd, and Jaan al Nai'r) in English you can translate it to (Water Spirit, Air Spirit, Earth Spirit and Fire Spirit).

Do they have any names besides their Natural Elements?

Yes. Spirits of the Four Elements are divided into four categories, earth, air, fire, and water. Let us look at each of them, in turn.

1. **EARTH:** *(Jaan al A'rd) Earth spirits, that is the beings, which relate to rocks, stones, minerals, precious gems, hills, and mountains are traditionally called in English (Gnomes). All aspects of the solid physical structure of the planet come under their domain.*

Although they can be found within rocks, they also have a freedom to move around but generally stay close to the ground. They are a) Gnomes b) Kobolds c) giants d) mountain spirits also in Arabic they are called the (Ghul or Qu'laz) they are short about 1 to 2 feet tall and they look old with full beard those are the Gnomes or the Ghulz, the other type are bigger and bit taller, most of them live underground, under the trees or on hilltops.

2. **WATER:** *(Jaan al Bah'ar) Water spirits are connected to all liquids, but their presence can be felt in a much more powerful way by streams, rivers, lakes and, of course, the sea. They are traditionally known as Undines or Al'Aunabiy'in although stories of mermaids or A'rusatual Bah'r and mermen are accounts of these beings. They are a) Nymphs b) undines c) nixies and d) na'iads. They have males and females, but females shine as if wet. The females are nude and without wings, the exquisite limbs gleam through the white auric flow, the arms are particularly long and beautiful, and she waves them gracefully in her flight. She is about four feet in height and her general coloring is silvery white, with gold stars around the head. (Al-si'ah)*

3. **AIR:** *(Jaan al Ha'wa) The spirits of the air are connected to all gaseous substances, but like water beings, are best sensed in winds and breezes. Because air moves so quickly they can be difficult to pin down. They are known as Sylphs in tradition although the perception of a "fairy" with tiny wings that can fly is a close approximation to how they appear to children. This type of spirit is what most scholars call "Al'arwah al Khaf'i" (the simple spirits) and they are very strong. They are: a) Sylphs b) storm spirits c) fairies. They live in the element of air and are like light in the atmosphere. Sensitive to the movement of the atmosphere, they have a sleepy consciousness. Their task is to transfer light to the plants. The stream of air caused by a flying bird creates a sound they can hear. They are like birds flying through the air. Sylphs are connected to movement in space, like modeling and directing the wind. Elves (or fairies) are more connected to the expansion of life in their area this is what some Scholars call the Al'irfid.*

4. **FIRE:** *(Jaan al Na'r these are what most people call the JINN) Fire spirits can be found in volcanoes in nature, but also in any fire, from candle to inferno. They are known as Salamanders or Vulcanii and are the most difficult of all of the elementals to connect with, that being said, they are to only associate with philosophers and adepts of the magical arts.* [22]

The scholars Gordon Creighton and Chris Line, back in the 1980s, wrote two important articles published by the prestigious magazine **Flying Saucer Review**, stating that the UFOs were actually Jinn, and the famous scientist of ancient Persia Zakariyya al-Qazwini, states that "*the Jinn are aerial animals with transparent bodies, which can assume various forms.*"

This is a category of Jinn that lives in the atmosphere, the just mentioned **Jaan al Ha'wa,** that reminds us of the volatile plasma creatures of Trevor Constable,

----

22   *See* https://somalisufisam.wordpress.com/2011/06/06/the-realm-of-jinn-the-elemental-spirits/ ‡ Archived 28th November 2017.

and even Kenneth Arnold, who, as I will show you later, practically started the modern phenomenon of Ufology, and believed that what we now call UFOs, are actually living beings. Obviously, to be visible from afar, Jinn must utilize plenty of **electromagnetic** energy to look enormous and luminous. This alien presence would be able to appear to the human eye, like the cigar-shaped alien space-ships that are often spotted all over the planet, and this would seem like one of the vehicles favored by some of the extra-dimensional beings that through dimensional passages can span the cosmos from one side to the other, showing themselves in various ways. Muslims believe that the Jinn can fly and adopt to whatever form. On the FBI website **The Vault,** accessible on the Internet since 2011, [23] aliens are described in one of the declassified documents of the FBI *Memorandum,* as beings of a multi-dimensional nature coming from extraterrestrial planets. However, according to this document generated within the mysterious Illuminati group known with the acronym **B.S.R.A**, namely the *Borderland Science Research Association* (later B.S.R.F. still in existence), these "ultraterrestrial" beings would sometimes operate in transdimensional flying disks with a crew on board; other times they would only be able to fly empty spaceships with a remote control. Both cases would, however, fall into what we call the *UFO phenomenon,* also in line with what I said about the Jinn phenomenon.

In 1996, Robert Dean (b.1929) a well-known American Ufologist who retired from the U.S. Army as a Command Sergeant Major after a 28-year career, was guested in Rome for an important World UFO Conference. He spoke of encounters with extraterrestrial entities and spaceships while serving in the U.S. Army and working at SHAPE, in the NATO headquarters of NATO Allied Forces. He said there were confirmed hypothesis by U.S. Navy scientists and pilots, that UFOs, were actually **bioships**, meaning alien ships that worked like *living organisms.* A shocking statement, for sure!

Matter, space-time, physical laws, and the human mind work flawlessly, along with the physical laws of space-time, in a logical and understandable way, what we all define as rationality. Logic, action and reaction, cause and effect, these are the rules to follow in order to fit into this material world from which we are surrounded (at least in appearance), otherwise we are considered crazy or New Age, especially when we are trying to lift the so-called veil of Isis on the UFO phenomenon, in its most hidden essence. They are linked not only to flashing lights in the sky but also to the occult, and the secret beliefs and practices of the Illuminati network made up of Secret Societies and religions that control our society.

CERN researchers were baffled when they made a new discovery in 2017, on how matter thrived in the early universe when it should actually have been destroyed by antimatter, a discovery that in itself evokes a theory that the universe is controlled by a mysterious realm lying outside space and time. This is, basically, evidence that boasts a 2009 theory of the existence of a Hypercosmic God, a discovery clearly in contrast with the rubbish promoted every day by globalists and leftist freaks, who push atheism and materialism every day. In the meantime, they deny the existence of aliens, and make statements like: *"It will be too difficult for these aliens to ever reach us,"* or, *"they are light years away, so it is physically impossible as journeys in space can last hundreds of years,"* and, *"how could they ever cover these vast distances?"*

---

23   *See* http://vault.fbi.gov/. ‡ Archived 28th November 2017.

FIG. 4 *Professor Giuseppe Vatinno and Jack Sarfatti in Rome in May 2014, while Sarfatti signs the book entitled* How the Hippies Saved Physics *by David Kaiser*

These pseudo-scientific statements are given with an embarrassing limit of understanding of the reality of space-time law, a reality that works only on a material level, that for interdimensional entities has absolutely no value. What we have today, thanks to the scientific community, is fundamentally a religion based on matter, or a religion of matter, which is from all points of view ruling planet Earth today. Especially because of the constant disinformation dictated by the pragmatist system imposed by the New World Order, an evil conspiracy that imposes a mathematic model from the past. This is a bit like what happened to Galileo, who ended with the infamous *Galileo affair*.

Even today's Ufology has heavy limitations, obsessed with materialistic phenomena like lights in the sky, and nothing more. I have often found myself in so-called Ufology centers, where a long-lasting light in the sky was taken more seriously than a video of a presumed alien, or of a human being possessed by entities clearly not of this world, the latter considered garbage not worth further investigation. In short, they devote most of their time to research light effects, often and willingly generated by other humans or joker entities. There are the so-called tricksters and demonic entities, who live in the spaces between the spaces, the practical jokers who manipulate our reality. This is a short story about the figure of the joker, also known as the trickster. Its affairs are almost never motivated by a noble cause, so it is better not to trust their special effects. Most Ufologists are naïve or deliberately misguided or censored. When Gordon Creighton published his first controversial article on the *True Nature of UFO Entities* on November 18,

1990, he wrote something significant in the introduction, words that should make us understand more about the conspiracy of silence behind Ufology:

> *This article, which appeared originally in FSR 29/1 (October, 1983) is reprinted now at the request of a number of readers, and to remind all our readers of what lies ahead for Mankind. Ever since its publication, the article has been treated throughout the world with total silence, and there is a general agreement among all Ufologists on both sides of the Atlantic never to give it a mention.*

> *FSR Consultant Dr. Richard F. Haines expected me to print his comprehensive REVIEW OF EXPLANATORY HYPOTHESIS FOR UNIDENTIFIED AERIAL PHENOMENA, and I promptly did so (FSR 32/2–1987).*

> *But it might be noted that he did not deem it necessary to include the slightest reference to my work in his survey, even as a minimal gesture of courtesy. Four of the leading experts in Ufology in the world have written me privately to say that they think I am on the right track. Only one of them—Ann Druffel—has had the guts to say so publicly.*

So what does contemporary Ufology do apart from silencing the truth on the true nature of UFO entities? What is its purpose nowadays?

The extra-dimensional reality and the paraphysical hypothesis on the different planes of existence that these beings can use at will, annulling in most cases any known physical law that we are aware of, needs to be taken seriously. The infamous *Greys*, which, according to authors like Nigel Kerner or Raymond E. Fowler, could even be a kind of *biological robot* created by an alien race ready to exploit us, a truth that seems farfetched and distant from what myself, and other researchers, who usually connect the Greys to Islamic *Jinn* or elemental entities, without discussing their possible bioelectric nature. But perhaps the truth lies somewhere in the middle, as this kind of hypothesis is not so blunt, after listening to the experience of contemporary physicist **Jack Sarfatti.**

Between 1953 and 1954, a group of American scientists, including the well-known Sarfatti claim to have been in contact with *"extraterrestrials, or those who seemed extraterrestrial"* as Sarfatti himself says: *"That's why I am so forward as a physicist. And there are others contactees among us, we are a good group."* Sarfatti made these statements in a shocking interview given to Italian journalist and Ufologist Maurizio Baiata in Rome in 2006, where he states:

> *I heard a metallic voice that I think belonged to an EBE, a Grey. Perhaps they were Androids because they said they were a computable computer. ... One of my other interests in physics, in addition to propulsion, is conscience, but from a physical and non-spiritual point of view. I do not speak of spiritual or religious things, but of pure psychotronic engineering, or how to create a car that is as conscious as we are, because we are machines, in a way. At the level of a billionth of a meter, we are nanomachines. This is also one of the books of Sir Roger Penrose, such as **"The Emperor's New Mind," "Shadows of the Mind,"** or **"The Road to Reality,"** and Stuart Hameroff's work on microtubules, a kind of nano-switch that would make us a sort of incredible chemical-quantum computer. The fact is that if you look at the nervous system, neurons with a sub-neural microscope and show a photo to an engineer who creates Intel chips, he'll think it's a chip. The structure of neural cells on a nanoscale resembles a large computer chip. Likewise, looking at images of the Universe with dark energy patterns in evidence,*

FIG. 5 Giuseppe Balsamo, "Conte di Cagliostro," by Jean-Antoine Houdon, 1786, marble—
National Gallery of Art, Washington, DC, USA.

it will seem to look at a great, immense cosmic brain. [24]

24   https://mauriziobaiata.net/2015/07/20/jack-sarfatti-entanglement-ufo-e-paranor-
          male-il-fisico-quantistico-rivela-tutto-in-unintervista-straordinaria// ‡ Archived
          28th November 2017.

A different, but an interesting view is that of Sarfatti, which is built on the mystery school teachings. In both cases, whether you are interested in learning about the most technological and physical nature of these beings, or the most magical or mysterious, these aliens are interested in our soul, and our vital force. It is their motivation for possessing us, and possession, as we all know, is liberated only through a good exorcist. Be careful, then, in contacting this type of entity if you are not really prepared, for the result could ruin your life at best, and in the worst case scenario, it might kill you.

A WANDERING ENTITY COULD INVADE YOUR LIFF

*I*n 1964, art student Alexandar Paunovitch discovered two strange depictions in a 16th-century fresco of the crucifixion of Christ, located above the altar of the Visoki Dečani Monastery in Kosovo. In this fresco entitled *The Crucifixion*, that was painted in 1350, we find objects similar to UFOs. They represent two comets that look like spaceships, with two men inside of them, and are often quoted by Ufologists. More recently on the walls of the Svetitskhoveli Cathedral in Georgia, there is another image of Christ that has sent conspiracy theorists into a frenzy. These frescos might not necessarily be linked to the UFO phenomenon, but they are definitely linked to our perception of Jesus being no ordinary man. Throughout history, Jesus Christ and Christianity have been linked to what is clearly alien activity. At this point the questions we need to ask are:

Why was Jesus Christ considered the Savior of humanity?

Why was Moses a key figure and prophet in all the Abrahamic religions?

And finally, why was the Grand Master of the Illuminati Giuseppe Balsamo known as Count Cagliostro, inspired by both of them?

How were these three important figures connected to non-worldly beings, called angels or demons by some, and Jinn by others? And in more recent times addressed as extraterrestrials, or even extra-dimensional beings? There is a link that most people ignore. **Steven Greer**, who is a well-known American physician who founded the Center for the Study of Extraterrestrial Intelligence (CSETI), and later the Disclosure Project, which seeks the disclosure of allegedly suppressed UFO information from governments, media and corporations, states that these entities are in fact, non-human, but at the same time they are not extraterrestrial. So what are they? Greer states that in evaluating the data and reports of alleged human-alien contacts, less than 10 percent of those cases are what they really seem, the remaining 90 percent is a combination of the following factors at work: incorrect identification of other paranormal experiences (mistakenly labeled as such) related to lucid dreams, out-of-body experiences, pre-death cases, astral encounters with other non-human (but not extraterrestrial) entities, and similar related phenomena. [25]

I wonder what source gave Greer so much certainty on the true nature of alien beings, maybe his friends in the Democratic Party? Dr. Greer, a former emergency room doctor, was also involved in the unsuccessful Rockefeller initiative in the mid-1990s that involved both Bill and Hillary Clinton, with the late tycoon

25   *See* Roberto Pinottti, *UFO: oltre il contatto Prospettive e scenari di un incontro epocale*, (Milan, IT: Mondadori, 2013), p. 233.

Laurance Rockefeller (1910-2004) who tried to get the Government to release all classified files about UFOs and aliens.

Dr. Greer thinks that **Hillary Clinton** would likely have revealed aliens exist if she made it to the White House in 2016: *"There's no question in my mind that Hillary Clinton is aware of the issue. Her campaign chairperson John Podesta came out in favor of disclosure and said that the government should come forward with this information."*

Greer's message is that technology will save the Earth. That the aliens are good, and that current classified projects threaten the constitution, so they must be declassified. His message is: *"We must not attack the ETs."* The Stargate Conspiracy by Lynn Picknett and Clive Prince has proven like other books, that the CIA pushes this disinfo message over and over again. Also Nick Redfern's books have proven the same promotion of techno-spirituality that is also linked to the New Age Movement. And why would non-human entities be considered by Greer terrestrial, and not extraterrestrial, when they clearly operate from another dimension? Obviously, in addition to the usual interpretations typical of people who accept without asking, it seems to me that Dr. Greer would rather distance himself from some researchers, than classify many unconventional experiences with UFOs or supposed aliens, as abductions, and define the people involved as abductees. Greer seems to think there is, in fact, the external involvement of shadowy groups that manipulate and use the abduction syndrome to spread disinformation that can discredit the UFO-ET phenomenon. [26]

In this case, I agree with Dr. Greer on the disinformation factor at work in Ufology. I believe there is also a clear link with fragile subjects and victims of psychological problems, often manipulated by Illuminati sects, operating on behalf of Intelligence agencies, and although there is a great deal of casualties linked to mental illness, others fall into the reality of possession. Many people shudder when they hear the word possession, as it conjures up thoughts of frightening movies they have seen, stories they have read, reports they have heard from the media, or things they have been told within their family or friendship circles.

In other words, possession for a lot of people is strongly connected to the negative, the demonic, and to death, and not linked at all with the abduction phenomenon. Certainly traditional Ufologists tend to ignore the many similarities with other phenomena, but in his classic study *Passport to Magonia* (1969), French scientist **Jacques Vallee** (b.1939) presented many examples of similarities between fairy and UFO sightings for example, and Jean Bastide, in *La memoire des OVNI* (1978) went further and said: *"modern contacts established with extraterrestrials precisely the same rules as contacts in the past with beings more or less human in form."* Similarities between UFO encounters and demonic encounters have also been outlined by various researchers. So, what exactly is happening here? The answer to that depends upon the time that you live in. Most people today would readily acknowledge this as a typical alien abduction story, but what if you asked someone who lived one or two or even ten centuries ago. How would they define all this? [27]

---

26   *Ibid.*

27   http://www.danielrjennings.org/SimilaritiesBetweenUFOActivityAndDemonicActivity.html ‡ Archived 28th November 2017.

I ask you now to open your minds to discover through my research, the real nature of the alien reality, made up of the Invisible Masters, but also of invisible attackers and vampiric alien entities, always ready to drain your energy, and participate at times in poltergeist activity. Some suggest a minority of poltergeist events are occurrences of playful aliens having a bit of sport at our expense. However, raised scratch marks often appear on the bodies of some poltergeist victims, and on one occasion an investigating police officer saw cuts spontaneously appearing on the legs and chest of a screaming poltergeist victim. Here is an example containing elements of sex, poltergeist, stigmata, and possible alien vampirism from a UFO abduction case reported by the late expert Dr. Karla Turner:

> He woke up in his bed with a strange female alien being beside him. "She was trying to get me worked up," he said. "She got on top of me and tried to make me respond, you know, sexually. But I kept refusing, I pushed her away and begged her to leave me alone ... she was naked, though, and she felt really cold when she touched me." ... "I found these marks this morning," he pointed ... three large puncture marks on the skin on the back of his calf arranged in an equilateral triangle.

Dr. Karla Turner died of fast-moving cancer on January 10, 1996, after being threatened for her work. She was just 48. Shortly after her suspicious and untimely death (murder?), her publishing company was intimidated into halting the printing of Karla Turner's haunting conclusions about the agenda of the evil Greys, and how it factors into the human power elite occultist's agenda for a New World Order. Since then, several other people involved in UFO investigation have also experienced threats followed by highly unusual cancers.

Several of her case studies are also dead. Dr. Turner was widely respected in the UFO community for her research on alien abduction. A scholar and professional educator, she earned a Ph.D. in Old English studies and taught at university level in Texas for more than ten years. But in 1988, she and her husband and son endured a shocking series of experiences and recollections that forced them to recognize that they were all abductees. Dr. Turner was actually working on another book when she became ill in early 1995, this is an interesting extract from her courageous book *Into the Fringe*, published in 1992:

> He was staying alone in a friend's apartment, collapsing in bed after hours of walking the streets alone, and when he awoke he was covered with bruises and scratches all over his back ... "I was sitting on the couch, and it was late at night. And all of a sudden, the couch started hopping up and down, and then this footstool started hopping, I mean, really hopping. It was shaking me! ... I felt the whole bed started to shake, and when I tried to move, I found I was paralyzed. I couldn't even speak, but somehow I finally managed to whisper a prayer, asking the god of truth and love to make this frightening force go away. I repeated the prayer again and again, until the paralysis broke, but the bed shook even more violently as my strength increased ... I tried to rouse Casey and tell him what had happened, but he rolled over sleepily without responding. At that point, three women came in and approached me. They held me comfortingly and told me, 'You did the right thing. You passed the test.'"[28]

28 See Karla Turner, *Into the Fringe*, (New York City, US: Berkley Books, 1992), pp. 64, 73, 77.

In all these accounts there are certainly striking parallels. The first thing we notice in studying this phenomenon is that some encounters with entities seem to be accidental, and others seem to be clearly directed at the specific person for reasons I will try to make clear in this book. We wonder whether the seemingly accidental encounters are as accidental as they appear, but don't be fooled. Does the manifestation occur in response to some hidden need, a psychological state that calls for outside intervention of some kind? In this regard, French ufologist Jean-Francois Boeded, in his book *Fantastiques rencontres au bout du monde* (1982) suggested that we should conceive of sightings as starting long before the actual experience. He points to many cases in which witnesses had premonitions that something was about to happen, or for some reason, they went home by a different route, or took an unaccustomed walk. Somehow, it would seem, the witnesses were being prepared for the experience they were about to undergo.

For the sake of comparison, let's look at a condensed version:

A light appeared outside the window. The rest of her family appeared to go into a state of suspended animation. Four small creatures entered the room passing straight through a door. One of them communicated with her telepathically and led her outside where an oval craft was waiting. On board, she was subjected to a painful physical examination. A probe was pushed up her nose. Another probe was inserted into her navel and she was told she was being measured for procreation. She was made to sit in a glass chair where she was enclosed by a transparent cover and immersed in fluid; she could breathe through tubes attached to her nose and mouth. A sweet liquid oozed into her mouth. When she was released from the chair she found that she had traveled to the alien's planet. Two of the creatures took her along a tunnel and through a series of chambers. The first was full of small reptile-like creatures; the second was a large green-colored space where they floated over pyramids to a city of mysterious crystalline forms. She was taken into one of the crystal shapes where she was confronted by a giant bird that burst into light and then collapsed into a pile of embers. A voice told her that she had been chosen for a special mission which would be revealed to her. When Betty stated she believed in God, the voice told her that that was why she had been chosen ... the leader, Quazgaa, told her that secrets had been locked in her mind. She was then escorted back to her home where she saw the rest of her family still in a state of suspended animation.

In his book *The Invisible College* (E.P. Dutton, 1975), Jacques Vallee posits the idea of a control system, UFOs, and related phenomena are the means through which man's concepts are being rearranged. **Their ultimate source may be unknowable, at least at this stage of human development:**

When I speak of a control system for planet earth, he says, I do not want my words to be misunderstood: I do not mean that some higher order of beings has locked us inside the constraints of a space-bound jail, closely monitored by psychic entities we might call angels or demons. I do not propose to redefine God. What I do mean is that mythology rules at a level of our social reality over which normal political and intellectual action has no power. [29]

I AM THAT I AM

Count Cagliostro said:

---

29   *See* Jerome Clark, *FATE Magazine*, 1978.

I AM NOT OF ANY TIME or of any place; beyond time and space, my spiritual being lives an eternal existence. I turn my thoughts back over the ages and I project my spirit towards an existence far beyond which you perceive, I become what I choose to be. Participating consciously in the Absolute Being, I arrange my actions according to what is at hand. My name defines my actions because I am free. My country is wherever my feet stand at the moment. Put yesterday behind you if you dare, like the forgotten ancestors who came before you, give no thought to the morrow and the illusionary hope of greatness will never be yours, I am that I am. I have only one Father; different circumstances of my life have made me come to this great and moving truth, but the mysteries of this origin and the relationships that unite me to this unknown Father are and remain my secrets. Those who will be called to become, to understand more like me, know me and approve me. As for the hour and time at which my material body at the age of forty will leave this land, as far as the family I choose, not to increase the already heavy responsibilities of those who have met me—because it is written: You will not let the sky fall—I can tell you that I was not born of the flesh, nor the will of man, I was born of the spirit. My name, which is mine, and the one I chose to appear amongst you, here is what I claim. Those I have been given to on my birth or during my youth, those for which I was known, are of other times and places; I have left, as I have left yesterdays fashionable and now useless clothes. But behold, I am noble and adventurous, I speak, and your caring souls will recognize the ancient words. A voice that is in you and who for a long time was silent answered my call; I act and peace finds your hearts, health arrives in your bodies, hope, and courage in your souls. All men are my brothers, all the countries are dear to me, I traveled everywhere so that the Spirit can descend on us from a road and come to us. I do not ask the Kings, of whom I respect the power, that the hospitality on their lands, and when it is granted to me, I take the best possible benefit around me: but I can not pass it. I'm a noble traveler. Like the south wind, like the shining light of the noon that characterizes the full consciousness of things and active communion with God, so I go to the north, to the fog and the cold, leaving somewhere to my passage some of me Myself, spending myself, dropping me at every stop, but leaving a bit of light, a bit of heat, until I finally arrived and settled at the end of my career; then the rose will bloom on the Cross. I'm Cagliostro. Why do you need more questions? If you were children of God, if your soul was not so in vain and so curious, you would have understood it already. Instead, you need details, signs, and parables, so listen. You go back to the past as you like it.

All light comes from the East, all beginning from Egypt; I've been three years old like you, then seven years, then I became mature and from that age on I have not counted. Three cycles of seven years make twenty-one years and realize the fullness of human development. In my early infancy, under the law of rigor and justice, I lived in exile, like Israel among foreign nations. Just as Israel had in itself the presence of God, who as a Metatron leading them in their footsteps, I have a mighty Angel that watched over me and directed always my actions, cleansed my soul, developing the latent forces in me. He was my Master and My Guide. My reason was formed and clarified; I was interrogating, studying, and taking consciousness of all my surroundings; I traveled, many trips, all around the room of my reflections in the temples and in the four parts of the world; But when I wanted to penetrate the origin of my being and ascend to God in the thrust of my soul then my helpless reason silenced and left behind my conjecture.

A love that attracted all the creatures impulsively, an irresistible ambition, a profound feeling of my rights to all the things of the earth and of the sky possessed me, and they led me toward the life and the progressive experience of my strength, pf their play and their limit, it was the struggle I had to stand against the powers of the world, I was abandoned and tempted in the desert, I struggled with the angel like Jacob, with men and with demons, and these, once overcome, taught me the secrets of the domination of darkness, so that I never lose myself in one of those ways from which there is no return. One day—after so many years and journeys— Heaven met my efforts: he remembered his servant who, clothed in bridal dresses, had the grace to be admitted as Moses in the presence of the Lord. Since then, it has been like receiving a new name, a unique mission. Free and master of life I did not think that to use this force for the work of God. I knew that he confirmed my acts and my words, as I confirmed His name and His dominion on earth. There are beings who no longer have Guardian angels, I was of those. Here is my childhood and my youth, so that your restless and generous spirit asks them; But did they last for more or less years, that they have stopped in the countries of your fathers and in other cities, which matter to you? Am I not a free man? You judge my habits, as if to say my actions, say if they are good, tell me if you have seen them more powerful and then perhaps you will no longer care for my nationality, my rank, and my religion. If, following your happy journeys, one day you approached that land of the East that saw me born and reminded of me, you will pronounce my name, then you will see my father's servants opening you the doors of the holy city. Then, when he comes back, he will tell his brothers if I have abused you with a false prestige, if I have taken something that was not mine in your dwellings. [30]

Cagliostro's speech revolves around four very important points to reflect on:

1. *"But the mysteries of this origin and the relationships that unite me to this unknown Father are and remain my secrets;"*

2. *"Just as Israel had in itself the presence of God, who as a Metatron leading them in their footsteps, I have a mighty Angel that watched over me and directed always my actions, cleansed my soul, developing the latent forces in me;"*

3. *"I was abandoned and tempted in the desert, I struggled with the angel like Jacob, with men and with demons, and these, once overcomed, taught me the secrets of the domination of darkness;"*

4. *"Heaven met my efforts: he remembered his servant who, clothed in bridal dresses, had the grace to be admitted as Moses in the presence of the Lord."*

The ways in which Cagliostro managed his "alien contacts" were only revealed to the initiators of Occult Freemasonry in the *Arcana Arcanorum,* the infamous system called **The Naples Arrangement,** cited several times by Aleister Crowley, and still present today in the latest degrees of the Misraïm Rite of Freemasonry, part of the so-called Egyptian Rites of Freemasonry (The Rites of Memphis and Misraïm or the Rites of Misraïm and Memphis depending on the Masonic lineage). This secret reveals a transcendental message of angelic communication that demonstrates how one clearly meets a superior reality, and therefore, extra-terrestrial within Occult Freemasonry, which also in its more traditional style is

---

30   From *"Memory for Count of Cagliostro, accused against the Attorney-General"* — Paris 1786.

based on its allegories and its mysteries on the Temple of Solomon, in turn, built by extra-dimensional entities.

Among other things, *The Conjuration of the Four Elements*, by Eliphas Levi or the conjuration of the seven angelic entities of the *Arcana Arcanorum*, drawn from the Rites of Misraïm and Memphis of **Count Gastone Ventura** (1906-1981), known by the initiac name of *Aldebaran*, that some view as the closest to the originals of Count Cagliostro, are exactly like those reported by Eliphas Lévi, in *Sanctum Regnum*, used in the consecration ritual to the degree of the Unknown Superior (S::I::/*Supèrieur Inconnu*) of the Martinist Order, which is considered to be the depositary of the knowledge of the true Illuminati.

As **Allen H. Greenfield** wrote in *Secret Rituals of the Men In Black*:

The Conjuration of the Four is a Ritual used by the Hermetic Brotherhood of Luxor, in its Initiation ceremonies. It, too, is a development of an earlier cycle of rituals, employed by its predecessors in the Fratres Lucis, and before that, the Asiatic Brethren. These, in their turn, go back to the Gold Rosicrucians and the authentic Kabbalah, embodied in the teachings and practices of Jacob Frank, Sabbatai Zevi, and so forth, ultimately taking us to the dawn of Kabbalah in the Languedoc, when Isaac the Blind of Posquičres and his circle achieved communication with Elijah on the Day of Atonement early in the 12th Century of the Common Era.

Masonic Grand Hierophant General and Grand Initiator of Italian Martinism, Count Gastone Ventura, was definitely a class A Illuminati, and he used for his occult operations so-called Olympian spirits (or Olympic spirits, Olympick spirits), a term that refers to seven or sometimes fourteen spirits, mentioned in several Renaissance and post-Renaissance books of ritual magic and ceremonial magic, such as the *Book of Magic Science*, or the *Arbatel de magia veterum*, and *The Secret Grimoire of Turiel*.

The mythological pantheon may change at times, or another language is spoken for convenience or respect of the forces in the field, this happens for example, in the case of Latin or ancient Greek, but the essence, remember, remains the same, that is, the attempt by initiates in the occult arts to contact an alien guide, in this case of a presumed angelic nature. When the conjuration of the seven elements is recited, to any conspired entity, the framing of the Masonic *Arcana Arcanorum* requires the burning of the Olympic seal, or the corresponding Archangel, written on a piece of paper, where they draw the pentacles of the same planetary color of the seals themselves (corresponding color of that plane). At this point, after the conjuration of the entities, the Wizard Mason draws with his magic wand the **Seal of Solomon** in the air and then on the ground, the six-pointed star placed **as above so below**. Magic wands are also used in Mystic Masonry, but the operator identifies himself during the conjuring ritual of the *Arcana Arcanorum* with King Solomon, and he must find himself during this final phase constantly within the seal of Solomon he has drawn on the ground. It would appear that this ritual is considered similar to that in which King Solomon would have access to the alien angelic reality, at least according to the practitioners of the Masonic *Arcana Arcanorum*. And if the Old Testament focuses on the **"fall" of King Solomon** due to the "perversion of the heart" caused by the strange influence of foreign wives, which led him to worship other gods (*Astarte, Milcolm, and Camos*) in the Apocryphal tradition as well as in the Quran, they fully describe in detail

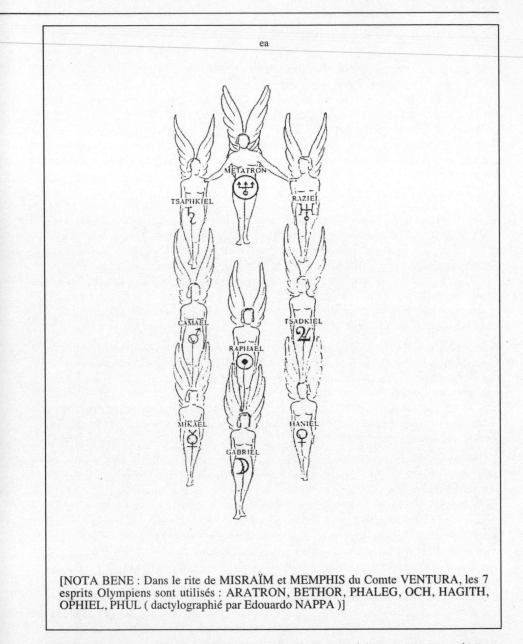

[NOTA BENE : Dans le rite de MISRAÏM et MEMPHIS du Comte VENTURA, les 7 esprits Olympiens sont utilisés : ARATRON, BETHOR, PHALEG, OCH, HAGITH, OPHIEL, PHUL (dactylographié par Edouardo NAPPA)]

FIG. 6 Image extracted from the Masonic Arcana Arcanorum of the Egyptian Rites of Misraïm and Memphis by Count Gastone Ventura shows Freemasonry dealing with supposed angelic forces.

the King's magic abilities on these entities that the Quran calls Jinn.

The Testament of Solomon is a text originally written in Hebrew, in a Judaic setting in the first century AD, subsequently redrafted in Greek in a Christian environment in the 3rd century AD. The text, attributed to the same King Solomon, describes his repentance on his deathbed, when he confesses that he was able to build the legendary Temple bearing his name by using demons commanded by a magical ring entrusted to him by the Archangel Michael. (The classic alien gift?) From here came the legend that Solomon would have sealed in a bronze vase with magic symbols, the seventy-two demons he evoked to help him build the Temple, thus reciting the topos of the genie enclosed in the bottle.

During the late Middle Ages, *The Solomon Key* or *Clavis Salomonis* appeared, as a text of medieval magic originally attributed (by mistake) to King Solomon. Many of these grimoires attributed to him at that time were and are nevertheless, considered to be of paramount importance to the Illuminati network, because they were influenced by much older books by Jewish Kabbalists and Arab alchemists, who, in turn, often referred to the Greek-Roman mystery schools of the late ancient world. For this reason, *The Key of Solomon* was translated from Hebrew to English in 1889, by the supposed founder of the **Hermetic Order of the Golden Dawn**, Samuel Liddell MacGregor Mathers, mentor, and later enemy, of Aleister Crowley. However, during the period of their intense collaboration, Mathers gave Crowley the key rituals to help him access the invisible world of the Secret Chiefs, known only to the Illuminati of the upper levels, who are those who want to come into contact with their Invisible Masters and nourish their power.

YAHWEH AND THE ALIEN ORIGINS OF ISRAEL

*A*lbert Pike was a Masonic thinker and a reformer of the Ancient and Accepted Scottish Rite. Pike is known not only for his work, but also as a target of several anti-Masonic attacks made posthumously. Due to the gravity of these attacks, some Masonic authors have openly acknowledged his controversies and extravagance, and sought to distance themselves from him. For most Masons, Pike remains a legendary and enigmatic figure with an aura of mysticism and scandal. Few people read his books, which may be considered too complex for today's readers. Nevertheless, within the Scottish Rite of Freemasonry, Southern Jurisdiction, U.S.A. he is still highly esteemed almost to the degree of veneration. [31] *Morals and Dogma* by Albert Pike published in 1871, is Pikes' 861-page volume of lectures on the esoteric roots of Freemasonry.

Until 1964, this book was given to every Mason completing the 14th degree in the Southern jurisdiction of the U.S. Scottish Rite Freemasons. Masonic lectures are standard oral presentations given during initiation to a new degree. Lectures provide background material for initiates and the discuss duties of the degree in general terms. They do not present details of the rituals, gestures, regalia, etc., for which one must consult other books on Masonry. Pike states right off that half of the text is copied from other works. Unfortunately, none of these quotes are properly cited, and in most cases it is only a shift in style that allows us to identify a quote. There are also lapses of fact and logic. So it would be a mistake to use this work as an authoritative source without additional research and critical thinking. That said, *Morals and Dogma* is a huge, rambling treasure-house of esoteric data, particularly on the Kabbalah and ancient mystery religions.

31   *See* https://albertpike.wordpress.com/albert-pike-and-his-vision-of-masonry/ ‡ Archived 28th November 2017.

Whether you just browse these pages or study it from beginning to end, this is a must-read book for anyone looking for long-lost knowledge. [32] *Morals and Dogma* has been described as a collection of thirty-two essays dedicated to each degree of the Ancient and Accepted Scottish Rite, which attempts to provide a philosophical rationale for the degrees in question.

Basically, Pike's teachings are a backdrop for each of the degrees by supplying in-depth lessons in comparative religion, history and philosophy. An upgraded official reprint was released in 2011, with the benefit of annotations by the famous Arturo de Hoyos, a figure I talked about in my trilogy, who is the Scottish Rite's Grand Archivist and Grand Historian.

My main reason for mentioning Pike, is that he talks extensively of the Elohim in his *Morals and Dogma*, mentioning the fact that we descend from them because of an act of self-sacrifice:

*"**Man descended from the elemental Forces or Titans [Elohim]**, who fed on the body of the Pantheistic Deity creating the Universe by self-sacrifice, commemorates in sacramental observance this mysterious passion, and while partaking of the raw flesh of the victim, seems to be invigorated by a fresh draught from the fountain of universal life, to receive a new pledge of regenerated existence. Death is the inseparable antecedent of life; the seed dies in order to produce the plant, and the earth itself is rent asunder and dies at the birth of Dionusos. Hence the significance of the phallus, or of its inoffensive substitute, the obelisk, rising as an emblem of resurrection by the tomb of buried Deity at Lerna or at Sais." (**Pike's teachings for the 24th Degree**: Prince of The Tabernacle, p. 393—**emphasis added**)*

Richard L. Thompson, writes in *Alien Identities,* that the geologist Christian O'Brien argued that these [ancient Hebrew and Sumerian] texts describe a race of beings called Shining Ones—his translation of the Hebrew word Elohim. These beings created modern humans from earlier human forms by genetic manipulation. Some of these beings, called Watchers, mated with humans, but this was considered a crime by the Shining Ones. One of the Watchers was named Shemjaza, and **Yahweh was one of the Shining Ones**. However Pike, has yet more illuminating words on this subject that bring us once again back to *Genesis* and to Mount Sinai, where the Israelites apparently became emancipated from their alien Lord (or at least tried too):

In the Hebrew writings, the term "Heavenly Hosts" includes not only the counsellors and emissaries of Jehovah, but also the celestial luminaries, and the stars, imagined in the East to be animated intelligence, presiding over human weal and woe, are identified with the more distinctly impersonated messengers or angels, who execute the Divine decrees, and whose predominance in Heaven is in mysterious correspondence and relation with the powers and dominions of the earth. In Job, the Morning Stars and the Sons of God are identified; they join in the same chorus of praise to the Almighty; they are both susceptible of joy; they walk in brightness, and are liable to impurity and imperfection in the sight of God.

The Elohim originally included not only foreign superstitious forms, but also all that host of Heaven which was revealed in poetry to the shepherds of the

---

32   *See* http://www.sacred-texts.com/mas/md/index.htm ‡ Archived 28th November 2017.

desert, now as an encampment of warriors, now as careering in chariots of fire, and now as winged messengers, ascending and descending the vault of Heaven, to communicate the will of God to mankind.

*"The Eternal," says the Bereshith Rabba to Genesis, **"Called forth Abraham and his posterity out of the dominion of the stars; by nature, the Israelite was a servant to the stars, and born under their influence, as are the heathen; but by virtue of the law given on Mount Sinai, he became liberated from this degrading servitude."** The Arabs had a similar legend. The Prophet Amos explicitly asserts that the Israelites, in the desert, worshipped, not Jehovah, but Moloch, or a Star-God, equivalent to Saturn. The Gods El or Jehovah were not merely planetary or solar. Their symbolism, like that of every other Deity, was coextensive with nature, and with the mind of man. Yet the astrological character is assigned even to Jehovah. He is described as seated on the pinnacle of the Universe, leading forth the Hosts of Heaven, and telling them unerringly by name and number. His stars are His sons and His eyes, which run through the whole world, keeping watch over men's deeds. The stars and planets were properly the angels. In Pharisaic tradition, as in the phraseology of the New Testament, the Heavenly Host appears as an Angelic Army, divided into regiments and brigades, under the command of imaginary chiefs, such as Massaloth, Legion, Kartor Gistra, etc.—each Gistra being captain of 365,000 myriads of stars. The Seven Spirits which stand before the throne, spoken of by several Jewish writers, and generally presumed to have been immediately derived from the Persian Amshaspands, were ultimately the seven planetary intelligence, the original model of the seven-branched golden candlestick exhibited to Moses on God's mountain. The stars were imagined to have fought in their courses against Sisera. The heavens were spoken of as holding a predominance over the earth, as governing it by signs and ordinances, and as containing the elements of that astrological wisdom, more especially cultivated by the Babylonians and Egyptians. (Pike's teachings for the 25th degree, Knight of the Brazen Serpent—**emphasis added**, pp. 509-510)*

Let's analyze the Elohim through another key figure in the Illuminati network. Eliphas Levi is the author of the similarly entitled occult masterpiece, *Dogme et Rituel de la Haute Magie.* The late Charles Lobinger, once official historian of the Scottish Rite of the Southern Jurisdiction, said about Pike's book: *"swarmed with citations from Eliphas Levi,"* and that *Morals and Dogma:* *"is shown to be literal and verbatim extractions from those of the French Magus."* Well, Eliphas Levi, in *Transcendental Magic,* makes a clear statement in the chapter entitled, *The Nuctameron of the Hebrews* declaring *"the Elohim made all things."* Earlier in the same book, on page 267, Levi also states: *"it is the luminous and living manifestation of Ruach-Elohim which, according to Moses, brooded and worked upon the bosom of the waters at the birth of the world."*

Therefore, there is no question of a privileged alien contact for the Jews. It is also important to remember that the two key figures of Jewish Kabbalah, a practice that goes far beyond ordinary demonology, where practitioners live the most esoteric side of Mystical Judaism, are in fact, Moses and King Solomon. The Jews believe, among other things, that the latter was the first great Kabbalist and ritualist in history, but Moses, however, was given the task of the first voluntary agreement with the *"Lord" Yahweh,* one of the Shining Ones. The Shining Ones true identity is considered by most people to be one of the greatest secrets ever kept from mankind by the Illuminati and their mystery schools. The Church tried to erase this almost forgotten race from history, but the legacy of the Shining Ones lives on, in each one of us. When the Lord called Moses into the famous *Tent of Meeting,* and dictated a statute that was to regulate the life of the Jews and the rest of the landlords who interacted with superior entities, their mission was to dictate new rules to people judged possibly as inferior and barbaric at the time by the Elohim. This statute consisted of a series of often very controversial, and violent rules, which suggests that the alien Lord Yahweh regarded Jews as very primitive people, unless these statutes were invented by the Jews themselves, and then attributed to the Lord to give some kind of credibility and respect.

I must also say, that the Lord in question, seemed very violent and unforgiving to believers of the Jewish faith, since it not only threatened with death and destruction those Jews who had not obeyed certain rituals, but went as far as burning alive two poor people who made an offer with the Lord, without following the ritual to perfection, and even put to death a little boy, who during a fight had blasphemed his name. In short, with the alien Lord Yahweh, no joking or light behavior is ever possible for the Israelites.

The alien Lord suddenly makes a long list of horrible threats for the transgression of the laws he imposes. In fact, Yahweh tells his people that if they do not put all his laws into practice, he will send terror, illnesses, and enemies who will decimate them. If, after all this, the Lord's people will still not put all his commands into practice, then the Lord will make the land of his people infertile, mutilate the cattle, and even have their children kidnapped by wild beasts. And if his people insist on not putting his commands into practice, he will then devastate the cities of his people personally, place in them their enemies, and ultimately persecute all the remaining people. These threats are something that would be more logical to hear from Adolf Hitler, the man most responsible for the devastation of the Second World War and the disturbing horrors of the Holocaust, than God himself, or his alien overlord Yahweh.

It is, however, incredible for us, simple men from Earth, to believe that the supposed "Lord" used so much cruelty on his people, and that's why some scholars prefer to think that some of these threats have been added later by Jewish scholars, to impose Israelite law. Nevertheless, we need to understand that we have been placed on this planet to serve the divinity that created us, that can use us in whatever way feasible.

Alien conspiracy theorists have been saying for years that extraterrestrials have already visited Earth, and world leaders all know this as proven fact, as well as Secret Societies, working together to keep us under an alleged truth embargo, amid fears over the impact the truth would have on religion and the rule of law. This is partly true from my own experience, but are we really ready to deal with the truth of what seems to be a kind of alien dictatorship? An alien dictator does its job on behalf of a very strict hierarchical structure at a universal level, where every entity in the organization including angels and demons, except the one we commonly refer to as God, are subordinate to a single other entity.

Indeed, the growing Luciferian nature of our society today will probably end with hell on earth if we were ever to deal directly with Yahweh, as in the days of the Old Testament, without a very long preparation. Do you understand now why we don't encounter the shining aliens so easily as their demonic counterparts?

Worth citing in this case is *Lucifer and Prometheus*, a classic work of psychological literary criticism published in 1952, written by an important figure of the occult elite named **R.J. Zwi Werblowsky**, (1924-2015), an Israeli scholar of religion specializing in comparative religion and interfaith dialogue, who served as Dean of the Faculty of Humanities at the Hebrew University of Jerusalem between 1965-1969.

Werblowsky argues that the Satan of John Milton's *Paradise Lost*, became a disproportionately appealing character in modern society, because of attributes he shares with the Greek Titan Prometheus, who is as we know, very important for the occult elite. For Werblowsky's purposes, however, the names "Satan" and "Lucifer" are used more or less interchangeably in his work, and in the book in question, Werblowsky also points out the essential ambiguity of Prometheus and his dual Christ-like/Satanic nature as developed in the Christian tradition. Werblowsky sets out to explore the heroic at its limits, and not only makes explicit the motivating factor of World War II and its horrors in undertaking his study, but he also points out on the growing influence of the devil:

> *The apocalyptic beast let loose has become a reality to our generation, and nobody knows what is still ahead of us. It is understandable therefore, that books on the devil have been on the increase lately... If the attempts of this school have not yet borne much fruit, it is because we fear the devil's sight more than his activity, and because of a very understandable reticence to force open our whited sepulchres."*

Going back to the at-times difficult relationship between God and his chosen people, a term that originally referred to Israelites, let's remember that the phenomenon of the so-called chosen people throughout history has involved not only Christian denominations, who traditionally believe the church has replaced Israel as the People of God, but also groups of people who are not linked to the Abrahamic tradition, and consider themselves to be chosen by a deity or an alien deity for a purpose, such as to act as the deity's agent on earth for a specific mission.

Anthropologists call it ethnocentrism, but often this type of attitude hides a true godly mission handed down by God's hierarchy and given to the recipient by an Invisible Master. Let's remember the Jews refer to this mission as a burden imposed on them to spread the message of One God, and I repeat, not a pleasure but a burden. [33]

So after a long series of massacres operated by the "Lord" against his people to subjugate them, the Israelites finally arrive to the Promised Land, and the first thing Yahweh orders is to kill those who live there, and to destroy and pillage their cities, something that, unfortunately, continues to some extent even today. He then adds that if they do not obey, he will do to his people what they should do to the pre-existing local populations. The Jews are therefore, from Moses onwards, under some kind of constant alien blackmail, which is also why they are now in bed with the Vatican at the top of the **New World Order**, rewarded for their loyalty and in the past punished for their disloyalty. The ruthless Lord of the Old Testament directed the Jews to exterminate certain populations, where whole cities

---

33   *See* https://en.wikipedia.org/wiki/Jews_as_the_chosen_people ‡ Archived 28th November 2017.

with men, women, and children, were raided and killed, while cattle and the ruins of the Cities were literally taken away or destroyed by the Lord's command. It is possibly like what we see these days with supposed aliens stealing cattle, or cattle mutilations, and of course, with human abductions, only on a much bigger scale.

Most of us have heard of cattle mutilations, especially in the 70s, perhaps we have even seen disturbing pictures of such incidents. While most can put these incidents out of their minds as simply something strange that happens. This terrifying mixture of terror and mystery might have facilitated Moses and his alien overlord, in their mission to impose the choice of monotheism upon the Jewish people, at a time when polytheism, from Phoenicia to Babylon, was indeed prevalent. Different was the policy and the way of thinking of those who later supported the Messiah Jesus Christ, called "The Redeemer," who promoted a belief system originally based on tolerance and peace. However this peace never came to fruition, and we are still waiting for the hopefully imminent establishment of the Kingdom of God, a complex operation given the inability of the majority of people to dominate their demonic side and the corruption of institutions like the Church, in promoting true Christianity. This means Jesus is basically part of an unfinished plan, but unlike Moses, he did not carry the sword of punishment but that of sacrifice and victory. The figure of Jesus is, of course, a revolutionary one within the Jewish world, but it must also be understood as part of a much wider and more unusual plan established by Secret Chiefs and Invisible Masters, which remains difficult to fully comprehend.

Returning to Moses, just before the Jews occupied the Promised Land, he named his successor Joshua, who received instructions directly from the Lord in the *Tent of Meeting*. Moses' life ends, and the alien objects donated to him by his Lord Yahweh and his angelic entities, begin an obscure and secret legacy with certain power groups and secret societies, that will eventually attempt to dominate the world using such objects. All of them are obviously obsessed with **The Ark of the Covenant.**This object with others given to Moses, was entrusted to the Levites, who placed it in an underground cell of the Temple of Jerusalem in 587 BC. The Ark should still be there, located on the Temple Mount in the Old City of Jerusalem, the current site of the Dome of the Rock and Al-Aqsa Mosque, although Orthodox Christians in Ethiopia say they own the only true "Ark of the Covenant" in The Church of Our Lady Mary of Zion, the most important church in Ethiopia, that claims to contain the Ark of the Covenant, where there existed a population who embraced Judaism.

His Holiness Abuna Paulos, patriarch of the Ethiopian Orthodox Church for the Smithsonian said: *"Queen Sheba visited King Solomon in Jerusalem three thousand years ago, and the son she bore him, Menelik, at age 20 visited Jerusalem, from where he brought the Ark of the Covenant back to Aksum. It's been in Ethiopia ever since."* There is another equally interesting hypothesis that says that the Ark of the Covenant eventually wound up in the hands of the Knights Templar. This story was confirmed by a document that French author **Guy Tarade**, a well-known and prolific French writer devoted to paranormal themes, passed on a few years ago to his friend, the American writer George C. Andrews, who will later speak about it and publish, *Extra-Terrestrial Friends and Foes.* This is an alleged document about the Templars and their involvement with The Ark of the Covenant.

Unfortunately, it is impossible to verify the validity of the information contained in the text, as the original documents that surfaced in France have apparently disappeared. We can only go back with certainty to 1937, when a Catholic priest, Abbot Corriol, submitted to a publisher named M. Reynaud, based in Forcalquier, a commune in the Alpes-de-Haute-Provence department in southeastern France, the manuscript was entitled *Recueil des Actes du Clergé Regulier et Seculier de la Haute Provence* (Collection of Acts of the Recognized and Secular Clergy of Upper Provence).

The publisher never published the manuscript but, in 1972, showed it to some friends who had expressed a certain interest in it. The part of the manuscript that we are interested in is the transcription of notes written by one of the Inquisitors during the persecution and arrest of the Knights Templar, in which are quoted phrases of a Templar under torture for the fourth time, transcribed on February 13, 1310. The Templar, referred to as *Brother Arnold* said: *"In the document, after finishing his testimony to the inquisitor whose name is not provided, gave a detailed list of the objects present in his castle were we find, in addition to ordinary furnishings, a few ceremonial objects and some ancient clay tablets plus the mention of a mysterious box."*

The Inquisitor asks the Templar about the box: *"How was this box made? Where did it come from?"* And the Templars reply is rather shocking:

"It was built of a metal unknown to me. Brother Blacas told me that it was the Ark of the Covenant, brought back to Jerusalem in 1127 and then deposited at the Abbey of Senanque, at the request of St. Bernard und St. Malachi."

Unfortunately, at this point in the text Father Corriol suddenly stopped transcribing the original notes, explaining that the Templar in question must have been out of his mind because of great pain. In the end, remember, this was a Catholic priest living in France in the Thirties, so he certainly did not want to give rise to any dangerous speculation on his faith by writing about certain things. Father Corriol reports that in the rest of the Templar testimony he spoke of weird things like; traveling through time in the sky on chariots that spat fire, the Kindom of the Swan, a deep well of darkness lost in the sky through which one can obtain immortality and the possibility of reaching unknown stars and empires, that George C. Andrews thinks could be a Black Hole. The Templar also spoke of the Apocalypse, and celestial warfare between the powers of light and darkness. [34]

The hypothesis that the Ark of the Covenant passed in the hands of the Templars, though with a very different version of the events, was reiterated recently by Graham Phillips in his book *The Templars and the Ark of the Covenant: The Discovery of the Treasure of Solomon.* [35] For Graham Phillips: *"According to legend, the Ark of the Covenant was an ornate golden chest that was both a means of communicating with God and a terrible weapon used against the enemies of the ancient Israelites. In order to use it the high priest had to wear a breastplate containing twelve sacred gemstones called the Stones of Fire. These objects were kept in the Great Temple of Jerusalem until they vanished following the Babylonian invasion in 597 BCE."*

---

34   *See* George C Andrews, *Extra-Terrestrial Friends and Foes,* (Lilburn, GA Illuminet Press, 1993), pp. 101-102.

35   *See* Graham Phillips, *The Templars and the Ark of the Covenant: The Discovery of the Treasure of Solomon,* (Rochester, UK: Bear & Company, 2004).

At the ancient ruins of Petra in southern Jordan, Graham Phillips uncovered evidence that the 13th-century Templars found the Ark and the Stones of Fire, and that they brought these treasures back to central England when they fled the persecution of French king Philip the Fair a century later. The author followed ciphered messages left by the Templars in church paintings, inscriptions, and stained glass windows to what may well be three of the Stones of Fire. When examined by Oxford University scientists, these stones were found to possess odd physical properties that interfered with electronic equipment and produced a sphere of floating light similar to ball lightning. The Bible asserts that the Ark had the power to destroy armies and bring down the walls of cities. Now Graham Phillips provides scientific evidence that these claims may be true and offers compelling documentation that the Ark may be located in the English countryside, not far from the birthplace of William Shakespeare at Stratford-upon-Avon. [36]

And what happened to the other sacred objects involved in Moses' history? As for the bronze serpent donated by the Lord to Moses, it was destroyed in 725-697 BC by King Hezekiah, because it was worshipped as a sort of God. Of Moses' magical wand, there is not a trace, but it seems it was also used by King Solomon to cut the stones of the famous temple that was built according to the Quran, with the help of alien entities, the Jinn, as I mentioned earlier. Concluding this whole affair, we can say that Moses is one of the most important and controversial characters that have ever existed.

A human being who was chosen from beings not of this world, to become the leader and the prophet of his "Chosen People," who would have contributed in spreading the monotheistic belief, as both Christianity and Islam descend from the practices of the ancient Israelites and the worship of the God of Abraham, a new religious layout that will help the birth of a New World Order, thanks to an Invisible Master called Yahweh. The Gnostics concluded that the Demiurge Yahweh demanded faith (*pistis*) from his creation and because of this he was the bad God; contrasted by the good God, who can only be reached by "gnosis."

Plato refers to the Demiurge frequently in the *Timaeus* as the entity who *fashioned and shaped* the material world. And Plato was the one who used for the first time the term *gnostikos* meaning; having knowledge, in the *Politicus* 258e-267a, referring to *gnostike techne, the art of knowing*, or perhaps the art of managing things known, in order to argue *that the ideal politician is defined as the master of the gnostic art.* However, the original Gnostics refrained from assuming any role in politics because their intention was not to change, or control our society through social engineering, and mind control but to produce a balanced and well-skilled enlightened individual, who would eventually be able to create a truly enlightened society, good enough to not be run by external alien management.

However, in certain Gnostic creeds that later became prevalent and belong to the dark side of the Illuminati, this *good God* is compared to the Ancient Greek god Prometheus, the Titan who stole fire from Olympus and gave it to mankind, who is also identified as Lucifer, the spirit of evil and adversary of God in the Christian and Islamic religions. According to author and teacher **John Lash** (b. 1945), a comparative mythologist who has been called the true successor of Mir-

36   http://www.simonandschuster.co.uk/books/The-Templars-and-the-Ark-of-the-Covenant/Graham-Phillips/9781591430391 ‡ Archived 28th November 2017.

cea Eliade and the rightful heir of Joseph Campbell, the Gnostics were: *"Skilled in theology and dialectical argument, they were able to refute fanatical beliefs, but unable to protect themselves against the violence driven by those beliefs. And they had no recourse to the establishment powers either. Not only were gnostics like Hypatia apolitical, they deliberately refrained from involvement in politics in order to dissociate themselves from the other type of initiates, the Illuminati who had been enmeshed in patriarchal and theocratic power games from their outset."* [37]

As a well-known artist author and publisher Uri Dowbenko once wrote:

The controversy began when certain initiates of the Mystery Schools began to abuse their mystical knowledge and redirect it into behavioral manipulation, psychological programming and mind control technology. In essence, the Illuminati gave up their role as teachers to become social engineers and advisors to the Ruling Class. This coincided with the rise of the patriarchal Abrahamic religions of Judaism, Islam and Christianity, which also required techniques of mind control to keep their followers ("believers") in line. [38]

Sometimes the relationship with the invisible world, both in the angelic or the demonic realm, is very complex, as in the case of the Gnostics, who consider even the *Son of God* concept to be a delusional idea insinuated into the human mind by an alien species of aberrant, nonhuman entities or mental parasites, called the Archons. Archons and Jinn are said to be the same thing, so you have malevolent and benign Archons, and for some they have the role of the angels and demons of the Old Testament, but we also need to keep in mind that in the Gnostic view there is no absolute opposition of *Good versus Evil.* In fact, Gnostics did not characterize the problem posed by the Archons in terms of evil, but in terms of a godly error, and say that good and evil do not come from the same source, for this reason the relations with the Invisible Masters might have been simplified for mainstream humans, but not for the Gnostics.

If you were to ask me if the material universe is all evil, while the non-material world is good, as various Gnostic systems within the Illuminati claim, and if God can only be perceived as a Slave God, like the Yahweh of the Jews, or an extraterrestrial entity, as some authors depict Him these days with absolutely no evidence, I will say to you that the Supreme creator God certainly isn't limited to the classic Jewish perception of Yahweh, or to an extraterrestrial figure. We need to consider Him well beyond such material concepts, and His presence is always felt everywhere in our Universe, and beyond our comprehension. The Anunnaki are not our creators, as the Illuminati would like you to believe.

They have indeed participated in our material evolution as human species by means of genetic manipulation in very ancient times, but they only help to create our physical bodies, not our souls. They are in no way the source of our spiritual side, created out of the pure energy by God. Zecharia Sitchin, in an interesting discussion attempts to answer a question that would have become unavoidable: *"So, who was Yahweh? Was He one of them? Was He an extraterrestrial?"*

37   John Lamb Lash, *Not in His Image: Gnostic Vision, Sacred Ecology, and the Future of Belief*, (White River Junction, VT: Chelsea Green Publishing, 2006) p. 276.

38   https://www.newdawnmagazine.com/articles/the-illuminati-renegades-of-the-mystery-schools ‡ Archived 11th December, 2017.

FIG. 7 Image with an alien twist based on The Creation of Adam the famous fresco painting by Michelangelo, which forms part of the Sistine Chapel's ceiling, painted c. 1508–1512.

Well, in one sense he is, of course, an extraterrestrial, since he seemingly comes from beyond the Earth. But is—or was—he an Anunnaki? Or, more generally speaking, an inhabitant of Nîbiru? Sitchin establishes a series of comparisons with gods named on ancient clay plates. Even though there are various similarities with each of these gods in the biblical descriptions of Yahweh, the comparison doesn't work out with any one of them, since there are often contradictions. However, for Sitchin the question, with its implied answer, is not so outrageous:

> Unless we deem Yahweh—"God" to all whose religious beliefs are founded on the Bible—to have been one of us Earthlings, then He could only be not of this Earth—which "extraterrestrial" ("outside of, not from Terra") means. And the story of Man's Divine Encounters, the subject of this book, is so filled with parallels between the biblical experiences and those of encounters with the Anunnaki by other ancient peoples, that the possibility that Yahweh was one of "them" must be seriously considered. [39]

KOOT HOOMI, THE INVISIBLE MASTER OF BLAVATSKY

I have often quoted Schuré's classic, *THE GREAT INITIATES A Study of the Secret History of Religions,* a book of great importance for the Illuminati, that I studied with great attention since my adolescence, thanks to my father, the late Dr. Elio Zagami, a well-known Jungian psychologist, who passed away in 2010. In this book, Schuré talks not only of Moses, but of all the great initiates, from Rama to Krishna, Pythagoras, to Plato, and of course, Jesus

39   See Zecharia Sitchin: *Divine Encounters: A Guide to Visions, Angels and Other Emissaries,* (New York: Avon, 1995), p. 347-380.

and others, showing them in a very different light from which we are tradition-ally accustomed.

Of course, traditional Christians might not agree with all the content of this book, but Freemason and Illuminati member Rudolf Steiner, wrote these very interesting words in the introduction to the German translation of this book by Marie von Sivers, published by the firm of Max Altmann in Leipzig in 1909:

> Schuré is convinced that there is a future for spiritual culture ... His artistic cre-ativity rests upon this faith, and this book has grown out of it. It speaks about the "Great Illuminated," the Great Initiates, who have looked deeply into the back-ground of things, and from this background has given great impulses for the spiri-tual development of mankind. It traces the great spiritual deeds of Rama, Krishna, Hermes, Pythagoras, and Plato, in order to show the unification of all these impuls-es in Christ ... The light streaming from Schuré's book enlightens those who wish to be firmly rooted in the spiritual sources from which strength and certainty for modern life can be drawn. One who understands the religious needs of our time will be able to recognize the benefits Schuré's book can provide in this area particularly. It offers historic proof that the essence of religion is not to be separated from the concept of "initiation" or "illumination." The need for religion is universally human. A soul that assumes it can live without religion is caught in a deep self-deception. But these needs can be satisfied only by the messengers of the spiritual world, who have attained the highest level of development. Religion ultimately can reveal the greatest verities to the simplest hearts. Thus its starting-point lies where fantasy lays aside the cloak of illusion and becomes imagination so that the highest reality is disclosed to the soul, and where the search for truth becomes inspiration, at which stage not the reflected light of thoughts, but the primordial light of ideas, speaks.

> Inasmuch as Schuré describes the great founders of religion as the highest initi-ates, he presents the religious development of mankind from its deepest roots. One will understand the essence of "initiation" of the future when one gains an insight into this through the great religious phenomena of the past.

> Today there is much talk about the limits of human knowledge. It is said that this or that must be hidden from man because with his understanding he cannot penetrate beyond a certain point. In the future, one will recognize that a person's limits of understanding will widen to the extent that he develops himself. Things that seemed unknowable enter into the realm of knowledge when man unfolds his capacities for knowledge which slumber within him. Once one has gained confidence in such a widening of the human capacities for knowledge, he has already entered upon the path, at the end of which stand the Great Initiates. Schuré's book is one of the best guides for finding this path in our day. It speaks about the deeds of the Illu-minated. These deeds can be recognized in the spiritual history of mankind, and this book traces the path from these deeds to the souls of the Illuminated themselves ...

> When people can become convinced that the spiritual impulses of the past, which continue to live on in their souls, have originated from the faculty of spiri-tual insight, then they will be able to work their way to the recognition that this faculty can also be attained today. "One who can trace the spiritual life of the pres-ent, not merely on the surface, but in its depths, will be able to observe how after the ebbing away of materialistic streams, sources of the spiritual life open up from many directions. Whoever observes this clearly will not question the transitory

necessity of materialism. He will know that this materialism had to develop in these last centuries because the fruits of external culture were possible only under its one-sided influence. But such a person will also see the dawning of a new age of spirituality. In Schuré's Great Initiates we believe we have one of the best symptoms of this approaching spiritual age. We include the author of this book among those who boldly step forward into the dawn of this age. The strength which flows from searching into the souls of the Great Initiates has given him the daring and the freedom necessary to write such a courageous book as the one before us."

I came to understand, with the help of this book, the role of the Great Initiates, who represent the perennial wisdom of the real Illuminati, to be found in the lives and accomplishments of figures of truly extraordinary stature, that after their alien contact went on shaping what became the most influential religions. In the course of his investigations, Schuré covers such topics as the mysterious dawn of pre-historic Europe • the Bhagavad Gita: India's dream of eternity • death and resurrection in ancient Egypt • the light of Osiris • esoteric wisdom of Moses • Orpheus and his lyre: a divine cosmogony • Pythagorean initiation, secrets of numbers, the divine Psyche • Plato: initiate and idealist • the Greek mysteries of Eleusis • the Essenes and their spiritual training • and the significance of Christ in human evolution.

The aliveness, the freshness, the excitement of discovery that breathes through *The Great Initiates* explains its continuing popularity to this day in certain knowledgeable circles. Born out of Schuré's deep experience and observation, *The Great Initiates* encompasses long centuries of life on earth and reflects the greatest search of all, being the quest for the spirit made by those true Illuminati, who had not sold their soul to the dark side. "The world has never known greater men of action," Schuré declared about the protagonist of *The Great Initiates,* [40] a statement that my father, who encouraged me to study this book, seemed to like very much.

Schuré traces the story of the founders of the various religions that influenced so much of our society and traditions, by linking their teachings together in a fascinating manner, so as to reveal a single great divine plan. A *universal* religion crafted by the Invisible Masters in the course of millennia and known in its entirety only to the true initiates. Schuré knew both the Theosophical Society and Rudolf Steiner's Anthroposophical Society, with whom he collaborated for several years. Speaking of Invisible Masters and Secret Chiefs, I always wonder how much spiritual influence and magical power was given by certain alien forces to **Helena Petrovna Blavatsky,** the creator of Theosophy and a key figure in the advent of the One World Religion? She hypnotized the masses with her more or less fantastic stories about these mysterious beings that became the foundation of the future New Age movement, and she had an indifferent following, including illustrious figures, such as **Thomas Edison,** the inventor of the light bulb, also interested in Spiritism and the paranormal.

Amongst Blavatsky's fans, were Scientists and Inventors like Alfred Russel Wallace or Abner Doubleday, historically credited with inventing baseball, although for some this is untrue. Even the wife of the Archbishop of Canterbury followed Madame Blavatsky's work. When she died in 1891, the Theosophical movement

40   E.Schuré, *I GRANDI INIZIATI, Ibid.,* p. 18.

she founded only a few years earlier, was said to have 10,0000 adepts. And now after a supposed Jesuit take over of the organization that took place after her death, Theosophy is at the heart of the pseudo-spirituality of the New World Order.

Even today, those who embrace this community are numerous, especially in English speaking countries, and among Freemasons. Let us now analyze the character of Blavatsky. Apparently, she did not have the magnetism or beauty to entrance thousands of people, let's face it, frankly, she was rather ugly. So how did she do it? To fascinate all these people, she made public her alleged correspondence with the Invisible Masters, including Koot Hoomi Lan Singh, whose wisdom had been accumulated thanks to numerous reincarnations, according to Blavatsky. The messages from the Invisible Master Koot Hoomi could materialize everywhere, under pillows, in Blavatsky's luggage, and sometimes even in the morning mail. In many pictures, Koot Hoomi seems to be depicted as a sort of Jesus figure. In our collective imagination he certainly fits the image of a spiritual master.

Certainly, it is hard to believe that these Invisible Masters could be involved not only with the benevolent side of humanity but also with the wicked, as in the case of Nazism and Himmler, who also admired the figure of Blavatsky and her studies. When German race theorists incorporated Blavatsky's narrative, it was within a larger program of asserting German superiority, but there was also in it the hidden hand of the Invisible Masters. In 1888, Blavatsky published her *magnum opus*, the two-volume set *The Secret Doctrine*. In this work, she outlines a new vision of humanity's evolution, one that places the Aryans at the top of a racial hierarchy. She claimed these revelations came from occult sources, meaning her Secret Chiefs, and she went on informing of various German occult organizations of the Illuminati network which, in turn, would later lay the foundation for the racial theories of Nazism.

The creation of a temple for communication by the SS elite, with the Secret Chiefs, considered the true Invisible Masters of esoteric Nazism, shows the ambivalence of the values of these entities from a typical human perspective. Often we have a limited understanding of their intervention in human affairs because we view it from their immortal perspective, not tied to our space-time reality. If we want to think like a Secret Chief or an Invisible Master, we have to have, first of all, a good idea of infinity... and then proceed as Jesus did, but also Gautama Buddha, the historical Buddha. That is why Esoteric Nazism had a very strong bond with Tibetan Buddhism, and with a few Buddhist sects who work in this direction in the hope of overcoming the impositions of our present understanding of the space-time continuum, so that we may have an otherwise *inaccessible* vision for common mortals.

Oxford physicist and mathematician Roger Penrose says that space and time are secondary constructs that emerge out of a deeper level of reality. Both quantum physics, where the future is unknown, and recent experiments verifying quantum entanglement, where particles instantaneously communicate over infinite distances, challenge our basic ideas about space-time. Alternate theories where space and time are minor players in our physical reality are still tentative, and so mathematically dense that physicists can barely follow what is going on. [41] However, the *Great Initiates,* as well as the Invisible Masters that secretly

---

41   http://www.ws5.com/spacetime/ ‡ Archived 11th December, 2017.

FIG. 8 Koot-Hoomi, the Invisible Master of Madame Blavatsky in a portrait by Hermann Schmiechen in 1884, with an absolute resemblance to the classic image of Jesus.

work with adepts on humanity's evolution, often behind the closed doors of certain occult lodges of the Illuminati, know very well what is going on.

THE POLAIRE BROTHERHOOD, OTTO RAHN, AND THE GRAIL

O tto Rahn, who enjoyed for a time a great prestige among Nazi leaders, is defined by the English newspaper *The Telegraph,* as the original Indiana Jones: *"Like Jones, Rahn was an archaeologist, like him he fell foul of the Nazis, and like him he was obsessed with finding the Holy Grail—the cup reputedly used to catch Christ's blood when he was crucified. But whereas Jones rode the Grail-train to box-office glory, Rahn's obsession ended up costing him his life."* [42]

Rahn was born on the 18th of February 1904, in Michelstadt, Southern Hesse, near Marburg in Germany. It was his father Karl who introduced him to the great German legends of Parzival, Lohengrin, and the Nibelungenlied, for this reason in secondary school he developed a fascination with the history of the medieval Cathars, their faith, and revolt against king and pope. Otto soon became passionate about the cultural aspect of the Languedoc region of southern France. He went on trying various faculties in the University of Heidelberg, Giessen, and Freiburg, but he was eventually inspired by his professor, Baron von Gall, to study the Albigensian (Catharism) movement and the terrible massacre that occurred at Montségur. It is uncertain if he graduated or not. I found disturbing evidence that Rahn intended to write a dissertation on Guyot, the Provencal Troubadour on whose lost Grail poem Wolfram von Eschenbach claimed to have based his *Parzival.* The medieval German romance of Parzival revived in the 1800s by **Wilhelm Richard Wagner,** inspired both Hitler since the tender age of 12, and Otto Rahn's modern quest for the Holy Grail. Wagner was fascinated with Medieval legends, especially those concerned with the Knights Templar, which after their suppression evolved for some fringe historians like the late Laurence Gardner, into Speculative Freemasonry.

Consider also the following; around 1865 Wagner allegedly visited the area around Montségur while supposedly researching Grail material for his *Parsifal,* and strangely enough the composer, artist, music producer and inventor, **Adrian Wagner (b. 1952),** who is the great-great grandson of the famous nineteenth-century Grail opera composer, is described on the Internet as a colleague of the late Laurence Gardner, a scholar who examined the secret ties linking the Masons and the Knights Templar, to the supposed descendants of Jesus and Mary Magdalene, who fell under the protection of these groups. [43]

Otto Rahn soon pieced together a series of clues obtained from a detailed study ranging from the history of the Cathars to the poem of Wolfram von Eschenbach, and his deep interest in the Cathars and Grail legends, eventually pushed him to travel extensively from 1928 to 1932, in France, Spain, Italy and Switzerland, and in the summer of 1929, Otto Rahn finally made his first appearance in the Languedoc region of southern France. He quickly settled in the village of Lavelanet and over the next three months systematically explored the ruined Cathar temple-

---

42   http://www.telegraph.co.uk/culture/film/starsandstories/3673575/The-original-Indiana-Jones-Otto-Rahn-and-the-temple-of-doom.html ‡ Archived 11th December, 2017.

43   *See* http://littlemurphydog-sacrifice.blogspot.it/2013/05/esoterica-wagneriana.html ‡ Archived 11th December, 2017.

fortress on Montségur as well as the surrounding mountain grottoes. Rahn believed that the secret teachings of Gnostic Manichaeism practiced by Cathars, preserved in some way by the late Troubadours, the traveling poets and singers of the medieval courts of France, contained the answer to the Grail mystery, and the secrets of the ancient Druids, the elite of the Western Illuminati. Rahn thought to be the key to this incredible secret was found in the caverns somewhere beneath the mountain peak, where the ruins of the fortress of Montségur are still located. It was the last Cathar fortress to fall during the Albigensian Crusade, the first ideological genocide in Christianity that gave rise to the infamous Inquisition.

The adherents to what is commonly known as Catharism were also sometimes known as Albigensians after the city Albi, in southern France, where the movement first took hold. In the days prior to the fall of the fortress on Montségur, after a terrible nine-month siege, several Cathars allegedly slipped through the besieger's lines, carrying away a mysterious "treasure" with them that they apparently hid in these grottoes visited by Otto Rahn. However, most of the ruins of the present fortress at Montségur are not from the Cathar era—the original castle was completely pulled down by the French royal forces working for the Vatican against the heretical Cathars.

The castle is, nevertheless, still seen and considered by many as the last Cathar stronghold. The current ruin occupying the site is referred to by French archaeologists as "Montségur III," slowly rebuilt after the destruction of what is considered "Montségur II" in 1244, precedently rebuilt by Raymond de Péreille in 1204, one of the two lords of Montségur, who decided to rebuild this castle that had already been in ruins for 40 years or more, considered "Montségur I." So it was de Péreille who refortified the castle originally built on an ancient settlement that dated back to the stone age, later used by the Romans, and made it the most influential center of Cathar activities until the persecution and the final destruction of 1244. Otto Rahn's knowledge of *sacred geography*, Nigel Pennick suggests, can be traced back to the Druids and Templars. The Cathars were also said to be familiar with this tradition. In many meetings with the local people (he is said to have spoken the local Provencal language fluently), Otto Rahn gathered everything concerning the Cathars and the Grail. These formed the basis of Rahn's thrilling accounts of his exploration of the caverns of Sabarthes south of Montségur and especially the Lombrives caverns called "the Cathedral" by the local people. He described this magnificent cavern as follows: "*In time out of mind, in an epoch whose remoteness has been barely touched by modern historical science, it was used as a temple consecrated to the Iberian God Illhomber, God of the Sun. Between two monoliths one which had crumbled, the steep path leads into the giant vestibule of the cathedral of Lombrives. Between the stalagmites of white limestone, between walls of a deep brown color and the brilliant rock crystal, the path leads down into the bowels of the mountain. A hall 260 feet in height served as a cathedral for the heretics.*" Rahn tells how: "*Deeply stirred I walked through the crystal halls and marble crypts, put aside the bones of fallen pure ones and knights.*"

An old Languedoc shepherd's tale recorded by Otto Rahn and incorporated into his first book, also displays profound mystical symbolism:

During the time when the walls of Montségur were still standing, the Cathars kept the Holy Grail there. Montségur was in danger. The armies of Lucifer had besieged it. They wanted the Grail, to restore it to their Prince's diadem from which it had fallen during the fall of his angels. Then, at the most critical moment, there came down from heaven a white dove, which, with its beak, split Tabor [Montségur] in two. Esclarmonde, who was the keeper of the Grail, threw the sacred jewel into the depths of the mountain. The mountain closed up again, and in this manner was the Grail saved. When the devils entered the fortress, they were too late. Enraged, they put to death by fire all of the Pures, not far from the rock on which the castle stands in the Field of the Stake. All of the Pures perished on the pyre except Esclarmonde de Foix. When she knew the Grail to be safe, she climbed to the summit of Mount Tabor, changed into a white dove and flew off toward the mountains of Asia. [44]

There was endless speculation whether Rahn went initially to France as part of a Nazi plot—or spy—or whether it was only after the publication of his first book that he was enrolled as a valuable Nazi propaganda asset. The evidence suggests the latter scenario was more likely, if only because Rahn is known to have had serious financial problems, often having to borrow money to make his trips—and often unable to pay people back. If the Nazi's wanted him in the south of France, it is likely they would have guaranteed his presence, simply by paying him to get there—and be able to stay there.

But a quick survey of his travels makes it immediately apparent Rahn was never "their man" on the ground, but rather an agent of the Secret Chiefs. Evidence of this appeared in March 1932, after a controversy broke out in a local French newspaper still in existence called *La Depeche*, which published articles about the activities of a group known as *Polaires* that were excavating in Montségur. Otto Rahn was mentioned—though his name was twice misspelled, once as Rams, once as Rahu. It was clearly said that he was the leader of this mysterious group, [45] described in *Le Bulletin des Polaires* from June 9, 1930 in the following way:

The Polaires take this name because from all time the Sacred Mountain, that is the symbolic location of the Initiatic Centers, has always been qualified by different traditions as "Polar." And it may very well be that this Mountain was once really Polar, in the geographical sense of the word, since it is stated everywhere that the Boreal Tradition (or Primordial Tradition, a source of all traditions) originally had its seat in the Hyperborean regions.

The foundation for what would later become *La Fraternité des Polaires* was laid in 1920 by the Italian Illuminati and Intelligence operatives **Mario Fille** and **Cesare Accomani**, with the help of **Fernand Divoire** (1883-1940), a French journalist and author. According to limited sources, the history of this secretive Illuminati Order begins in Italy back in 1908, when a young Mario Fille meets a mysterious hermit during a holiday in Bagnaia, a small and charmingly historical town in Northern Lazio, in the Province of Viterbo on the slopes of Monte Cimino, an area renowned for its hot springs, Renaissance villas and Etruscan ruins. Here Fille met the local hermit, a certain Father Julian, during one of his long walks. The locals of the village were fearful of the hermit, or so the story goes. Mario Fille befriended **Father Julian (Padre Giuliano)** and visited him frequently during his stay in Bagnaia. Father Julian enjoyed so much the long and deep conversations

44   https://otto-rahn.com/it/node/7 ‡ Archived 11th December, 2017.

45   *See* http://philipcoppens.com/rahn.html ‡ Archived 11th December, 2017.

with the young Franco-Italian that when Fille left Bagnaia, Father Julian gave him a special gift consisting of some old and withered parchments later referred to as *L'Oracle de Force Astrale*. This was an unusual gift from a supposed monk, that would, in turn, trigger 12 years later, the birth of the Polaire Brotherhood, and became a direct link of its members with the Unknown Masters and the alien world.

Father Julian stated the following when giving Mario Fille this important gift: *"What you have here are some pages taken from the Book of Science of Life and Death: these pages contain a successful Method of Divination on an arithmetical basis. If you,"* Father Julian spoke to the astonished young man, *"want the answer to a really important question or issue, then write the question down, add your first and last name as well as your Mother's name to it. Then you have to convert the letters into numbers and carry out certain lengthy arithmetic operations. But do not let this put you off because when you finally convert the results back into letters, you will have the answer to the question. But please beware, you are the only one who has the key, you are commanded not to pass on this knowledge without the authorization of the Unknown Superiors."* [46]

Father Julian expressively warned young Mario not to reveal this knowledge because of the severe consequences which would follow; insanity or even death would be the price one had to pay. Consultation of this method, this Oracle, called for processes that were allegedly "painstaking and lengthy."

As a matter of fact, because of this warning from Father Julian, Fille did not bother to apply the learned skills and knowledge for the following twelve years. It was in, or around 1920, that, during a time of personal crisis, Mario Fille began working with Father Julian's Oracle. According to some sources, this was what Father Julian also had advised him to do; only to use the magic oracle in times of trouble or desperation. He followed the old man's instructions as it was laid out by him back in 1908, and after several hours work, a final series of numbers emerged which, when retranslated into letters, gave a cogent and grammatically correct answer to his question. Mario Fille was truly left amazed. Although the question had to be phrased in Italian, its answers were sometimes in English or German. Nevertheless, the Oracle apparently never *"failed to behave with perfect reliability."* [47]

In 1920, Fille allegedly visited Egypt, where he met his fellow countryman Cesare Accomani. Fille told Accomani about his experiences with Father Julian in the hills north of Rome. Both Accomani and Fille began working together with the Oracle and it was notably Accomani who *"became very enthusiastic"* about the Divination method of Father Julian. But it was Fille and Fille alone who possessed the key to the Oracle's manipulation. Mario Fille decided to pay a second visit to Father Julian, but what he apparently feared came true; Father Julian no longer lived in the small hut in the mountains just outside of Bagnaia. He finally had the idea to apply the divination method to find out the whereabouts of the old Italian hermit. But first, he became acquainted with the magic oracle.

During one of the first divinatory sessions, the Oracle revealed its name,

46   From the article *Die Brüderschaft der "Polarier" Ein Kapitel zur Geschichte der geheimen Orden* by Ing. Lambert Binder published in *Mensch und Schicksal*, Jg. 4, Nr. 24, Villach 1951.

47   *See* Joscelyn Godwin, *Arktos: The Polar Myth in Science, Symbolism and Nazi Survival* (London, UK:Thames & Hudson Ltd , 1993).

L'Oracle de Force Astrale (The Oracle of the Astral Force). Fille also learned that it was not a mere method of divination, but an actual channel of communication, a channel between the user and the Invisible Masters operating from the *Rosicrucian Initiatic Center of Mysterious Asia*. This center was supposedly situated in the Himalayas and was directed by the so-called *Three Supreme Sages* or the *Little Lights of the Orient*. These Sages supposedly lived in Agartha, a place where the spiritual activities of our Earth were/are directed by the Secret Chiefs. Fille soon learned that Father Julian was one of them, and according to some sources, Fille received this answer in 1918. This simple and modest hermit turned out to be one of the highest initiates on earth, directing the fate of humanity in secret from a hidden monastery in the Himalayas.

The *Three Supreme Sages* were directed by the Superior head, who was allegedly from Europe. The claim of a Rosicrucian center in the Himalayas has been around since at least the seventeenth-century in Illuminated circles. In 1618, a certain Henrichus Neuhusius published a manifesto, *Pia et Utilissima Admonitio de Fratribus Rosae Crucis* (the title translates something like: *A practical and explicit warning/reminder from the Brethren of the Rose and Cross)*, which states that the Rosicrucians left for the East due to the outbreak of the Thirty Years War (1618-1848) and the instability in Europe. A similar claim was later made in 1710 by Samuel Richter, and in more recent times, by René Guénon (1886-1951). Both presented the idea in some of their works. After the first sessions with Father Julian's Oracle, Fille and Accomani decided to settle in Paris (at Monmartre) where they began demonstrations with the Oracle, with a group of writers and journalists. The sources claim that the Oracle sent the message that Fille and his friend should journey for Paris. It is stated that demonstrations were given in the hopes that the writers present would publicize what they saw and experienced. In other words, for some reason, both Fille and Accomani wanted to promote the Oracle to the public. According to a German source, Fille had received authorization to demonstrate the Oracle (translated from German) to a *"small group of experts."*

Although this source does not elaborate on the details of the authorization, the German text suggests that Fille needed to find suitable candidates to form an occult working group. The articles were supposed to attract these candidates. The Great Sages in Tibet prepared both the leaders of this group for the coming of the Spirit under the sign of the Rose and Cross. The group of writers and journalists who were approached by Fille consisted of Maurice Magre (writer), Jean Marquès-Rivière (writer), Fernand Divoire (journalist), Jean Dorsenne (journalist), Jeanne Canudo, René Guénon and others. The personalities mentioned above were favorably impressed and began a collaboration with both Fille and Accomani. During this period both men associated themselves with many influential personalities. [48]

L'Oracle de Force Astrale (*The Oracle of the Astral Force*) opened up many doors for both Fille and Accomani. It turns out that available sources are relatively silent about this period. Officially, the Polaire Brotherhood, *La Fraternité des Polaires*, did not exist until 1929, the year in which the group received the task to

---

48   See Victor Blanchard, *A Brief Summary of his life and work*: http://www.hermanubis.com.br/artigos/EN/ARENVictorBlanchard.htm ‡ Archived 11th December, 2017.

establish an Order, the Polaire Brotherhood. Cesare Accomani, whose initiatic name was **Zam Bhotiva,** wrote that he received a number of communications from the Oracle during the months of June and July 1929, which referred to the foundation, or better, the reconstruction of a group called *Polaires.*

The Oracle literally gave them a mission; the reconstitution of the Polaire Brotherhood whose members were dispersed in the fifteenth century through hatred of the True Light. The Oracle furthermore revealed that the establishment of the Brotherhood could no longer be postponed, because the time was near; when rods of fire will once again descend upon certain countries of this earth, and men shall have to rebuild everything once again what he has destroyed because of his thirst for gold and his egoism. For a year or two René Guénon, who is one of the more well-known luminaries of the twentieth century, and somebody I wrote about extensively in my trilogy, was captivated by the Oracle and its messages, but his interest slowly faded, and he eventually decided to disassociate himself from the newly founded Brotherhood. His attitude towards the *Polaires* changed so dramatically, that he decided to publish a very critical and negative article about them, which was published in the February, 1932 issue of *Le Voile d'Isis*, a publication that started in 1890 as the official organ of the **Groupe Indépendant d'études Esoterique.** [49]

However, the regular communications between the Polaire Brotherhood and Alien Intelligence resurrected a movement of real Illuminati, which Fille and Accomani claimed had previously been known as Cathars, Gnostics, Albigenses, Knights Templar, and the Essenes. *They claim as incarnated Brothers those who have always been men of great capacity such as Jesus, St. John, Shakespeare, Francis Bacon, Arthur Conan Doyle, etc.* [50]

As mentioned earlier, the beings they communicated with had intelligence, knowledge and spiritual power, and lived in a place called Agartha a.k.a. "the Rosicrucian Initiatic Center of Mysterious Asia," situated somewhere in the Himalayas. They were also referred to as the **Great White Brotherhood**, a phrase that came into use through the Theosophical Society of Madame Blavatsky and Annie Besant. Maurice Magre, who published *Pourquoi je suis Bouddhiste* (Why I am a Buddhist) in 1928, stated the following on the subject: *"The existence of this Brotherhood, variously known as Agartha and as the Great White Brotherhood, is what it always has been, but unproven by those 'material evidence' of which the Western mind is so fond."* As mentioned on page two, the Sages of the Himalayas, the *"Troit Petites Lumières,"* were headed by someone from Europe to whom the oracle referred to as Le Chevalier Sage, *"The Wise Knight."* It is stated that this European Sage is named *"Celui qui attend" ("He who waits")* and that he is a Rosicrucian.

Joseph George Caldwell wrote that the communications received by the group after April 8, 1930 are said to have come from a Chevalier Rose-Croix (Rose-Croix Knight), who some identified as the Master Racoczy, a favorite of the neo-Theosophists. So as far as the foundation of *La Fraternité des Polaires*, the

---

49   *See* Pierre Geyraud, *Les Sociétés Secrètes de Paris*, (Paris, FR: Editions Èmile-Paul Frères, 1939) pp. 56-66.

50   From the article *Phantoms of Reality* by Keith Shelton – The information in it comes from the English White Eagle Lodge, which was founded in 1936 with the help of the *Polaire Brotherhood* of Paris.

story goes that Accomani and Fille received all the necessary instructions via the Oracle, of the Invisible Masters, regarding the rules and regulations of the Order, its rites, as well as its goals and aims. The first meetings of the Brotherhood were organized in the office of a Parisian newspaper, whose chief editor let the Polaires use the offices based in Rue Richelieu during the evenings.

For a short period, the newspaper's address was also the correspondence address of the Polaire Brotherhood. On August 27, 1930 the Order moved into a studio on the ground floor of a major building at 38, Avenue Junot, in Paris. It contained a large room with a high ceiling with a large, massive table in its center. Oak chairs of an archaic style were placed along the walls. On the left of the entrance stood a Tibetan magical statue, a so-called **Kwal-Ynn**, placed on a small wooden platform attached to the wall. The statue became an issue of debate among the *Polaires* because apparently it was not doctrine-related. Eventually, the magical statue was removed and replaced with a map of the world. On the right, were stairs leading to a small, high-ceiled room, which was intended for initiation-ceremonies, the actual Lodge room. This Lodge was located at 36, Avenue Junot in "e XVIIIème arrondissement," which was for the Illuminati, a sign that the Lodge was under the protection of the Invisible Masters. **36 and 18 are in fact, multiples of the numbers 3 and 9. Let's remember the magic oracle is based on numbers.** So with regard to the symbolism of the Polaires, it is clear that certain numbers were frequently used and repeated within the organization.

The numbers 3, 7, and 9 (3x3) were privileged numbers and it is not a coincidence that the membership of the Polaire Brotherhood in France did not exceed a total of 63 members at any given time because the number 63 is the outcome of 7x9. This is just one of the many examples of how number symbolism was used in the Polaire Brotherhood. The "Central Group" was lead instead by nine people known as *Les Neuf* (The Nine). "The Nine" consisted of, amongst others, Cesare Accomani; **Henri Meslin du Champigny** (1896-1949); a Martinist and Gnostic Bishop known as *Tau Harmonius*, who later consecrated the famous Illuminati of Robert Ambelain in Paris on 15 June 1945, according to the pontifical of the *Eglise Gnostique Universelle*; the French author **Ernest Gengenbach,** also known as Jehan Sylvius (1903-1979), who is the co-author of *La Papesse de Diable* (1931); **Madame Fernande Guignard**; **René Odin**, an old Martinist and Kabbalist involved with Fille, in shady espionage activities on behalf of the infamous O.V.R.A., the Italian secret police founded by Mussolini.

The highest dignitary of the Brotherhood was, despite contrary belief, not **Mario Fille** but a Catholic priest, **Mgr. Lesètre**, a Papal Chamberlain, a court title given by the Pope to high-ranking clergy as well as influential lay persons prior to 1968. It had been decided that the Grand Maître de L'Ordre's secret dignitary had to be someone of a high rank or position and of course, Mgr. Lesètre in his position was the ideal choice. Lesètre headed the Order for a brief period of time.

Pierre Geyraud in his book, *Les Sociétés Secrètes de Paris – Parmi les sectes et les rites, Les Petites Eglises de Paris,* describes a scene in which Lesètre, wearing a mask, interrogates the *Three Little Lights*, considered the Invisible Masters of the Order, through conciliation of a trance medium. Undoubtedly, Geyraud describes a scene in which the *Oracle of the Astral Force* was consulted and the use of a medium mentioned by Geyraud shines new light on their method of divination. Allegedly, Mgr. Lesètre was too authoritative and was forced to step down as leader. He returned to his career in the Catholic Church and was succeeded by Henri Meslin du Champigny. The *Polaires* advocated the theory that **Christian Rosenkreuz** the legendary, possibly allegorical, founder of the Rosicrucian Order had been initiated into Catharism by Albigensian refugees in Germany.

Maurice Magre a member of the *Polaires*, in his book *Magiciens et illuminés (Magicians and Illuminati)* published in 1930, tells the story of a man named Christian Rosenkreutz who was the last descendant of a German family called Germelshausen, a family that allegedly had embraced Albigensian (Cathar) doctrines during the 13th century. They were all put to death, except for the youngest son. He was carried away by an Albigensian priest from the Languedoc, and was brought up in their monastery, and the rest is history. Magre claims that his account was derived from oral tradition. There's another theory also connected to the Polaires which claims that they believed that Christian Rosenkreutz had visited the region when he left Spain, after his decision to return home.

THE ULTRA-DIMENSIONAL PORTAL OF LUCIFER

O tto Rahn mysteriously disappeared during a snowstorm on March 13, 1939, on the Kaiser Mountains in the Austrian state of Tyrol, a few months before the beginning of World War II, which officially began on the 1st of September 1939, with the invasion of Poland by Nazi Germany. But his book was published just two years earlier entitled, *Luzifers Hofgesind, eine Reise zu den guten Geistern Europas* (in short *Lucifer's Court*), was imposed by the Reichsführer SS Heinrich Himmler to the main dignitaries of Nazism,[51] thus giving Rahn a mythological status within Esoteric Nazism.

The late Rahn had actually written and published two books linking Montségur and Cathars with the Holy Grail: *Kreuzzug gegen den Gral* (*Crusade Towards the Grail*) in 1933 and *Lucifer's Court* in 1937. After the publication of his first book, Rahn's work came to the attention of Himmler, the head of the SS, who was fascinated by the occult and had already initiated research in the south of France. Himmler, who was deeply interested in Otto Rahn's research at **Montségur,** had acquired the **Castle of Wewelsburg** in 1934, under the auspices of the SS *Brigadeführer* Karl Maria Wiligut, Himmler's Rasputin, who felt there was great spiritual strength in this castle, and knew its real nature as an interdimensional portal. It is said that Wewelsburg was going to be the Grail Castle of the Nazi regime once they had established themselves as rulers of the world.

The castle was not built by the Nazi regime, but its history started several centuries before the National Socialists came to power in 1933. The castle was built from 1603 to 1609 as a secondary residence for *Fürstbischof* Theodor von Fürstenberg, the prince-bishop of Paderborn, whose primary residence was the castle at Neuhaus. However, an older fortress existed on the site from the 9th century onwards. At the time, it withstood an invasion of the Huns, and its location was auspiciously close to what was believed to be the site where the Battle of the Teutoburg Forest occurred. This battle occurred in 9 AD, when various

---

51   *See* http://www.centrosangiorgio.com/occultismo/articoli/il_nazismo_esoterico.htm
        ‡ Archived 11th December, 2017.

FIG. 9 *Cover of the Italian edition of the book* Luzifers Hofgesind (Lucifer's Court) *by* **Otto Rahn.** *In this Antichristian work, Rahn identifies Lucifer with the true principle of good engaged in an eternal struggle against the true principle of evil, then incarnated by The Church of Rome and its corrupt hierarchy.*

Germanic tribes made an alliance and ambushed and destroyed three Roman legions. The battle was the start of a seven-year long war, whereby the Rhine became the boundary of the Roman Empire. It should, therefore, not come as a surprise that it was seen as a symbol of German unity and a demonstration that a united Germany could conquer all. It meant that the estate had the shape of a spear, underlining the unconfirmed belief that the site would become the location where the Spear of Destiny would be held.

There is a story that Hitler saw his future when he visited the Museum in Vienna where the Spear was on display, and that he became convinced that whoever possessed it would control the fate of the world. That Wewelsburg was going to be the New Jerusalem at the epicenter of Germany is in evidence from 1941 onwards, when the architects called the complex the **Center of the World**. In line with sacred mythology, the design would have the castle on a mountain, surrounded by a lake, as there were plans to flood the valley. [52] To acquire this place Heinrich Himmler signed a castle rental contract for one hundred years for the symbolic amount of one hundred marks with the district of Paderborn in Westphalia, where the castle is located. Under the main floor of the castle, we find an awesome underground meeting room referred to as the "Crypt of Himmler"—a spooky vault that was supposed to be *The Holy of Holies* for the SS, where the high priests of Nazism communicated with the hidden chiefs of the inner world, their Invisible Masters, in a secret chamber known amongst the high priesthood of the SS, as the Walhalla, or Hall of the Dead. The most sacred of places for the Nazi's that, according to some claims, was supposed to become the site where Himmler's body would reside after his death.

The swastika in the crypt's ceiling is physically linked with a sun wheel known as the *Schwarze Sonne*, embedded in the center of the marble floor of the room above known as the *Obergruppenführersaal*, within the inner sanctum of Wewelsburg castle. The vault was also made to eventually receive the Holy Grail on an altar of black marble engraved with the letters "SS" in silver, written using a Runic alphabet. A Catholic publication in the early 1970s wrote: *"Wewelsburg's guests meditated on mysticism on the morals of honor, on the spiritual myth of blood, and on other Gnostic and dualistic themes dear to the German elite. These retreats were made in the scenery, of a room of almost five hundred square meters, above the vault where was located the altar of the new religion."* [53]

The Temple used by the SS Nazi's to communicate with their Invisible Masters has been open to visitors since 2010, as today's Germans have created a somewhat controversial and *"macabre museum,"* as pointed out by the British tabloid *Daily Mail*. Now dubbed *Naziland* by critics, the space is dedicated to the history of Nazi Germany's evil SS *"in the eerie castle that was once home to its boss Heinrich Himmler."* [54]

----

52   http://www.militaryhistorytours.co.uk/tours/third-reich/himmlers-ss-wewelsburg-castle/ ‡ Archived 11th December, 2017.

53   Article extracted from the magazine *Catolicismo* n. 249, September 1971, available online at: http://catolicismo.com.br/Acervo/Num/0249/P01.html ‡ Archived 11th December, 2017.

54   *See* http://www.dailymail.co.uk/news/article-1267405/Heinrich-Himmlers-eerie-castle-plays-host-macabre-Nazi-memorabilia.html

In 2010, the so-called Crypt at Wewelsburg castle was opened during an exhibition called **"Ideology, and Terror of the SS."** One of the portraits exhibited for the occasion clearly resembles the image of a grey alien. Is this an indirect confirmation of alien forces behind the esoteric side of Nazism? The crypt, before its public opening, was repeatedly visited and used for occult workings since the early 1980s by the infamous Satanist, and founder of the Temple of Set, former Lieutenant Colonel of the US Military Intelligence, **Michael Aquino.** The well-known British journalist and reverend of the Church of Satan, Gavin Baddeley states: *"Undeniably in 1984, Aquino—like Nikolas Schrek—made a visit to the SS Castle of Wewelsburg, conducting a rite in the notorious Hall of the Dead. 'The reality of this chamber rushed in on me,' Aquino later wrote. This is no Holywood set, no ordinary room painted and decorated to titillate the senses, 1235 inmates of the Nierderyhugen concentration camp prisoners died during the construction of Wewelsburg for the SS."* [55] Aquino also indicates on the official website of the Satanic *Order of the Trapezoid* two years earlier, that he conducted occult activities in Castle of Wewelsburg:

The emblem that is used today for the Order of the Trapezoid was conceived in the Wewelsburg Castle, Westphalia, Germany during the Wewelsburg Working on Octo-ber 19, XVII / 1982 in the Hall of the Dead (Walhalla), was sketched out on a desk in the Wewelsburg caretaker's office (when I returned the Walhalla keys to him following the Working), and was drafted in precise mathematical proportions on a table in Eva Braun's tea-room in the Eagle's Nest at Obersalzberg. I could have done the drafting ear-lier but wanted the environment to be magically appropriate. There were a few tourists milling around the main room of the Eagle's Nest, but as it turned out I had the wood-paneled tea-room to myself. [56]

Aquino conducted the rituals in order to connect with the Secret Chiefs and Invisible Masters of esoteric Nazism, along with other U.S. Intelligence officers of his dangerous sect, like Col. John B. Alexander, while officially in Europe on a NATO mission. Baddeley confirms: *"He had visited Wewelsburg while on Second-ment for NATO in Europe."* [57] Secondment means the transfer of a military officer or corporate executive to another post for temporary duty. So what kind of duty is this supposed to be? Baddeley points out that Aquino was merely *"interested in techniques used by Nazi occultists, rather than racial or political issues."* [58]

Aquino managed to practice Satanic rituals internationally, at the expense of the unknowing taxpayer, but Aquino was not the only one in recent times to use Wewelsburg and its surroundings for rituals. A few years earlier, it was used by underground film director, magician and Satanist (despite that he says the contrary), **Kenneth Anger, IX° degree honorary member of the O.T.O.,** quoted several times in my publications. Anger used the Externsteine, a distinctive sandstone rock formation located in the Teutoburg Forest, near Wewelsburg Castle, for some ritualistic scenes in his film *Lucifer Rising*, because it is a particularly powerful location connected to the energies of various entities.

55   Gaving Baddeley, *Lucifer Rising: A Book of Sin, Devil Worship and Rock n' Roll*, (London, UK: Plexus, 1999), p. 153.

56   http://www.trapezoid.org/thought/evolution.html ‡ Archived 11th December, 2017.

57   Gavin Baddeley, *Ibid.*, p. 154.

58   *Ibid.*, p. 153.

FIG. 10 The Castle of Wewelsburg. In the ritual crypt of SS, an unmistakable image of an alien emerged over a period of several months in 2010, during an art exhibition.

Like Glastonbury Tor (a hill near Glastonbury in the English county of Somerset), it was the focus of pagan rituals before being co-opted by the Christian church. *Externsteine* was the *Irminsul,* which in ancient times was considered to be the sacred pillar bearing the Universe and linking Heaven to Earth, a pagan symbol from Germanic paganism identical to the *Cosmic Tree* of Norwegian mythology, the *Yggdrasil*, since both are the representation of the reality behind the apparent and ephemeral material world. *Externsteine* was profaned with the destruction of the *Irminsul* by Charlemagne in the 13th century, defeating the Saxons, forcing them to convert to Christianity.

"We must never forget what happened in Verden in 782 ... There was the massacre. Four thousand five hundred Saxon prisoners were killed by the Christian soldiers of Charlemagne," wrote Jean Mabire, an important historian and political journalist from the French far-right in an article entitled *Thule the Sun rediscovered by the Hyperboreans*. [59] For the Nazis to leave for the legendary Thule, (which many scholars believe to be Iceland), doesn't mean only navigating to this mysterious island that the ancients consecrated as the land of origins of wisdom, but also to discover, beyond the known world, the very secret of life. I spent a lot of time in Iceland during my 20s and early 30s, in search of knowledge to dominate certain occult forces in me and around me. Iceland is definitely a magical island from

59   *See* Jean Mabire, *Thule. Il sole ritrovato degli Iperborei*, (Turin, IT: L'Età dell'Acquario, 2nd edition 2016).

all points of view. The strong presence of Illuminati groups like the *Theosophical Society* and the *Ordo Templi Orientis* (**Caliphate**) remains there to this day.

There are alien entities that the Illuminati collaborate with from the beginning of time, to achieve the supreme fulfillment of the Great Work, that of achieving immortality. The Guardians of the Threshold are often called dwellers on the threshold, are supposed to manifest as soon as the student of the occult is in contact with the alien realm. Only then would it be possible to fully join the spiritual center of the world's Initiatic system, that of the Invisible Masters, who together with their Secret Chiefs would encapsulate the immortals of all the epochs and their vital energy that could render immortality. One of the few who seem to have achieved this was the famous **Count of Saint-Germain.** French author and Illuminati **Serge Hutin** wrote in his book, *Invisible Government and Secret Societies:* [60]

> *In 1784, Saint-Germain died in one of the Castles of his faithful disciple, the Prince Charles of Hesse-Kassel. Was it a real death, or rather a cover-up, to conceal a temporary disappearance, and to allow Saint-Germain to escape the embarrassing curiosity of the people? The evidence that the count was not dead is given by the testimony of his participation in the general assemblies of Freemasonry in Paris and Wilhelmsbad in 1785.*

This could only take place through contact with celestial beings, the true Invisible Masters of the Cosmos, whose technology is unlimited and can grant humans the gift of immortality. In the Zelator ritual of the S.R.I.A., the ultimate purpose of this Order of Rosicrucian Illuminati is made clear: "*The greatest secret yet lay hid, the prolongation, the rejuvenation of animal life. 'Twas death to strike the tocsin bell, save by him whose skill had solved one of four problems: First, the rejuvenation of the ever-burning lamp; Second, the transmutation to Silver; Third, the transformation into Gold, and Fourth, the Discovery of the Elixir of Life.*" [61]

60   Serge Hutin, *Governi occulti e societ segrete*, (Rome, IT: Ed. Mediterranee, 1973, **Second Edition, 1996,**) pp. 99-100.

61   *See Rituals of the Societas Rosicruciana in Anglia (Zelator).*

FIG. 11 Thomas Edison had an interest in the occult, and was tied to Madame Helena Petrovna Blavatsky and The Theosophical Society. Edison was the inventor of the light bulb and the phonograph, one of the first instruments designed to record and reproduce sound, which subsequently gave life to the most famous turntables originally created by Edison, in an attempt to communicate with the dead.

MY EXPERIENCE: FROM CAGLIOSTRO TO THE "STARGATE" OF THE ALCHEMIST

||

Cagliostro, my Secret Chief, and Invisible Master

 s a 9-year-old child, while walking in the center of Rome with my father Elio, near Piazza Navona, I discovered the figure of the Count of Cagliostro. My parents talked about the mysterious magician, and Freemason (a word I still did not understand), a character who even challenged the Vatican with magical arts and knowledge. All this intrigued me, for the first time I learned that Giuseppe Balsamo, known as Count of Cagliostro, was actually a member of my family, but when I asked for clarification about him, my father Elio replied, "He was the black sheep of the family, just like you Leo." My father had probably perceived my early interest in magic, and the fact I never wanted to conform to the system and its Matrix from the earliest age. From that moment on, more than any other, Cagliostro in some way became my Secret Chief, my invisible guide to the mysteries of the occult.

Count Alessandro di Cagliostro, alias Giuseppe Balsamo, was born on June 2nd 1743, and after a lifetime of *"riding the tiger"* as the Eastern saying goes, on December 27, 1789, Pope Pius VI ordered his arrest and initially imprisoned him in Castel Sant'Angelo. After the farce of a trial and forty-seven interrogations, on April 7th, 1791, Count Cagliostro was finally sentenced to life imprisonment. In Piazza della Minerva in Rome, they solemnly burned his Masonic insignia and regalia and the unjustly confiscated books. He was imprisoned on the 21st of April of the same year in the fortress of San Leo (near Rimini), which seemed to me almost a divine sign. In the Castle of San Leo, Cagliostro spent the rest of his life in horrible conditions, relegated to a secret cell called *Il Pozzetto*, a sort of well or sewer. He died on August 26, 1795, two and a half years before the arrival of the French troops lead by his disciple Napoleon, who could have freed him, but that was not the case, and some historians even said that French troops wanted to drink a toast with his skull upon their arrival to the infamous castle.

Cagliostro was the last victim of the Inquisition. The fact that he was a charlatan is truly a questionable matter, also because influential and uncomfortable figures operating within the intelligence community, or the Illuminati Network and Freemasonry, are often described as charlatans to the outside world, to

FIG. 12 Dom Fra' Manuel Pinto da Fonseca (1681 – 24 January 1773) was the 68th Prince and Grand Master of the Sovereign Military Order of Malta from 1741 until his deat. He was considered by Count Cagliostro as a true Illuminati.

cover-up the real importance of such figures in front of profane and mundane society. His secret teachings and the rituals of his famous Egyptian Rite, are regarded as very important by those who intend to learn the deepest secrets of the real Illuminati. That's why I founded some years ago, in London, the Cagliostro Lodge (*Aula Lucis Cagliostro*) of the *Fraternitas Rosicruciana Antiqua* (known as F.R.A.), operating between 2001 and 2003, where I was Classroom Director, the Worshipful Master of this Rosicrucian Lodge.

The Egyptian Rite of Cagliostro is considered an anomaly by so-called *regular* Freemasonry, because of the divinatory and magical practices in it. Cagliostro was admired but also hindered by the most remarkable figures of his age. His particular personality led him to outsmart the Masonic paradigms of his time, to consider Masonry with the sufficiency of the Great Initiates, among men looking most of the time for vain glory.

Giuseppe Balsamo had many aliases, such as Count of Cagliostro, Comte de Phoenix, Marquess Pellegrini, and others. In 1766, he operated alchemically with his Secret Chief called Manuel Pinto de Fonseca, Grand Master of the Order of Malta, whose initiatic name was *Althotas*. The two met in the city of Messina during a walk in the harbor, another episode my father, who was born and raised there, loved to talk about. I often found myself in Messina, a Sicilian city of great importance for Christian Knighthood Orders, because during the Crusades, it was the last port where the Knights usually stopped before continuing their journey to the Holy Land.

A few years after Cagliostro's first visit to Malta, a lodge of the Order of Illuminati founded by Adam Weishaupt would be opened, thanks to the groundwork done by Cagliostro years earlier. After numerous trips to Europe and North Africa, Cagliostro returned to Malta, where the new Grand Master of the Order of Malta, *Fra' Emmanuel Marie des Neiges de Rohan-Polduc,* would grant him a chivalrous dignity. Cagliostro had his first Masonic initiation in the *Loge de Saint Jean d'Écosse du Secret et de l'Harmonie,* based in the eastern part of Malta, but not being a recognized lodge by the Grand Lodge of England, and in desperate need of a Masonic passport valid throughout Europe, Cagliostro eventually was initiated again on April 12th, 1777 in *Loge d'Espérance No. 289* in London, where he received the three degrees of the Craft on the same day. This episode of the life of Cagliostro is very familiar to me, since I did more or less the same thing after receiving my first initiation considered "irregular" by Prince Alliata of Monreale in the early Nineties in Rome, and then repeating it in London years later with utmost regularity by the United Grand Lodge of England, inside **Kirby Lodge 2818** in Great Queen Street, simply to have a valid Masonic passport to travel around the lodges of the world.

Loge de Saint Jean d'Écosse du Secret et de l'Harmonie in Malta was later indicated as the first lodge to be in possession of the famous *Arcana Arcanorum,* linked to Cagliostro's teachings, and to the alien entities that he worked with. This lodge apparently also became involved with the Illuminati Order of Adam Weishaupt. Michel Monereau, in *The Secrets of Hermes of La Franc-Maison et les Rites de Misraïm and Memphis*, published in Paris in 1989, writes that the lodge in question received a regular charter from the Grand Lodge of England on March 30, 1789. In a letter addressed to this Masonic power a few days before February 4, 1789, the main officers of the lodge stated that their legitimate Masonic affiliation had

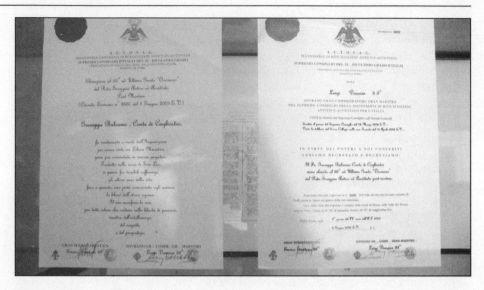

FIG. 13 Diploma attesting the post-mortem elevation of Giuseppe Balsamo Count of Cagliostro to the 33rd and last Degree of the Ancient and Accepted Scottish Rite. Sovereign Decree No. 8537 issued on the 5th of June 2003, from the Gran Loggia d'Italia degli ALAM (http://www. granloggia.it/).

been present since the beginning of the century and that in 1764 they had also been affiliated with the Scottish Mother Lodge of Marseilles.[1]

Most of the members of this Maltese Lodge were **Knights of the Order of Malta** and, according to lodge documentation, of different origin, French, Venetian, Neapolitan, and the initiation of Giuseppe Balsamo was apparently recorded and present in surviving documentation. The lodge will later cease its activity when Napoleon banned the Order of the Knights of Malta from the island, but it served a very important role in the creation of the so-called *Naples Arrangement* or *Arcana Arcanorum,* elaborated later in Naples by Cagliostro, also thanks to the logistical and financial support of members of the *Loge de Saint Jean d'Écosse du Secret et de l'Harmonie* in Malta.

This was when Cagliostro first met his mentor from the occult elite, **Francesco Maria Venanzio Aquino, Prince of Caramanico (1738-1795),** ambassador to London and Paris for the Kingdom of Naples, and later viceroy of Sicily, a character of fundamental importance for the cognitive and initiatic development of Cagliostro, cousin of the famous alchemist Raimondo di Sangro Prince of Sansevero, who would invite Cagliostro to Naples. It is this connection with Prince D'Aquino that would lead Giuseppe Balsamo to become the legendary Count Alessandro di Cagliostro, acquainting him with the secret teachings of *Arcana Arcanorum,* connected to alien communication and the Invisible Masters. The Hermetic society—continued under different denominations—known as *Neapolitan School,* which claims to be the oldest Alchemical Transmutation School in the West today.

---

1   *See* Michel Monereau, *The Secret Secrets of La Franc-Macconnerie and the Rites of Misraïm and Memphis,* (Paris, FR : Editions Axis Mundi, 1989.

It seems that the members of this Lodge in Malta, were interested in so-called inner alchemy, linked to the ancient Egyptian tradition, which was said to have allowed them to acquire immortality and create a *body of glory*. The same symbolic finalization was expressed by the Eleusinian and Orphic mysteries, along with those of Isis and Osiris.

Two centuries after his death, and after many slanders and lies about him, Giuseppe Balsamo, alias Count Cagliostro, received posthumously the 33rd Degree of the Ancient and Accepted Scottish Rite, a honorary degree in recognition of his outstanding service to the Rite, registered with **Sovereign Decree No. 8537 issued on the 5th of June 2003 by the Gran Loggia d'Italia degli ALAM** (Antichi Liberi Accettati Muratori), also known as Grand Lodge of Italy of the A.F.& A.M. (Antient Free and Accepted Masons), and popularly referred to as the *Freemasons of Piazza del Gesù,* due to their former headquarters in Piazza del Gesù, 47 in Rome, and now based in nearby Palazzo Vitelleschi, in Via San Nicola de' Cesarini, 3 in Rome. An influential Italian Obedience with over 7000 members, with mixed-gender lodges after the Second World War, founded in 1910 as a schism from the Grande Oriente d'Italia and a member of the international association of Liberal Masonic jurisdictions, called CLIPSAS. Better late than never for Count Cagliostro, however it is a shame the only Masonic Obedience that would grant him this kind of posthumous recognition, now present in the Castle Of San Leo, was actually a Masonic Obedience considered "irregular" by most regular Masonic Obediences in the USA, especially after realizing how much Count Cagliostro influenced the Founding Fathers of the Declaration of Independence, and who were involved in Freemasonry.

THE POWER OF MAGIC IN MY CHILDHOOD

*T*he Lyon family is said to descend from Jesus and King David, who, according to Gardner's theory, were of alien ancestry. Magic for me was tied to Invisible Masters who mysteriously helped me survive a strange and dangerous episode I had in the early years of my life, when I nearly died, after falling in a spring near my family home. The experience opened up direct contact with the invisible realm, and with entities that pushed me in the following years to become more and more interested in the occult and the hidden mysterious forces.

The first book I ever read was *The Magic Power of Witchcraft* by Gavin Frost (1930-2016) and Yvonne Frost [2] founders of the Church and School of Wicca in 1968. I found it by accident (or probably pushed by some invisible force), advertised in the back of a famous Italian comic book at the end of the Seventies, and after preserving the cutout of the ad for months, and thanks to the modest savings I put together, I eventually ordered it. I remember being extremely happy when the book finally arrived as if it was Christmas all over again. I noticed that the English title was very different from the Italian one, *The Power of White Magic,* clearly a much more innocent approach than *The Magic Power of Witchcraft*.

When I opened the book, and in the presentation of the authors, I discovered that they were related to the Wiccan religion, also known as The Craft, Wicca, Benevolent Witchcraft, and The Old Religion, of which the authors were high

---

2   Authors known in Italy with the pseudonymsJohn and Katy Fair, Il Potere della
        Magia Bianca/The Power of White Magic, (Rome,IT : Editions Sans Egal 1979).

FIG. 14 *The Magic Power of Witchcraft by Gavin Frost and Yvonne Frost published in 1976 by Parker Publishing Company, Inc., West Nyack, N.Y.*

priests. I began investigating and practicing the teachings of this unusual book, that included astral traveling, and other exercises, like rituals of evocation and much more. I did all this with the group of children I was playing with, and I was naturally leading at the time, almost like a sort of lodge master, sometimes drawing these magic circles in the most unlikely places and scaring more than one person in the process. However, this book, in the end, left me rather confused because what was described as White Magic, was used for the control of people, and not just for good ends, but also for acts of manipulation and what was clearly **Black Magic**.

It is repeated (especially in the first chapter) that thanks to this book a magical power can be acquired to do basically, whatever you wish, even cause harm to others. This saddened me as a kid, as I always thought that white magic meant good magic used to do good, and not some doorway to Hell. However, after this disappointment, I decided to venture into the family library in search of true magical text and ancient grimoires. I discovered red magic, whose origins relate to the propitiatory rituals of the Egyptian Ptolemaic High priests, operating in the 3rd–1st centuries BC, that took the name "red magic" from the red-colored tunics worn by the priesthood. I even drifted into the darker reality of black magic of the ancient medieval grimoires, though with many reservations and a bit of healthy fear.

I also devoted myself to music and the art of DJing with a turn-table, originally invented by Thomas Edison, a proud member of the Masonic Fraternity, a unique invention, where I began experimenting with sounds and alchemy A bond between music and magic, that will always be present in my life, and to which I have devoted ample space in my book, *The Illuminati and the Music of Hollywood*. [3]

THE OPENING OF THE GREAT BOOK OF NATURE

*D*riven by my infinite curiosity, I continued my study of alchemy, after my initial study of magic. From there I discovered in the private library of my family a book called *The Great Book of Nature*. [4] This is a very rare French Hermetic and Alchemical text published after two centuries, in an obscure Italian book from the 1920s, purchased years earlier by my father, with a preface and a top-level appendix, written by the great Sardinian Rosicrucian called Vincenzo Soro. An important figure of the Italian Illuminati, Soro claimed himself to be of an ancient Gnostic and Rosicrucian lineage, that originally operated from Sardinia, a truly magical place, full of powerful energy and dimensional portals.

In *Silentium post clamores* (1617), Michele Mayer writes that Rosicrucians are the successors of the Hindu Brahmins, the Egyptian High Priests, the Eleusinian Mysteries, the Magi of Persia and of Ethiopia, the Pythagoreans and the Arabs. In an original drawing by Vincenzo Soro, positioned in the first pages of *The Great Book of Nature,* we can see a simple circular diagram divided in a gradual and consecutive way, wherein the end we find at the center of the system **The Invisible Masters**, the "aliens" at the heart of the Western Initiatic System. The text is described as, *"A Curious work of the eighteenth century about occult philosophy, the intelligence of the hieroglyphics of the ancients secret Society of the Brothers of*

3   Available at the moment only in the Italian language: Leo Lyon Zagami, *Illuminati e la Musica di Hollywood* , (Arezzo,IT: Harmakis Editions, 2014).

4   *See* Vincenzo Soro, *Il Gran Libro della Natura*, (Todi, PG, IT: Atanor ,1921).

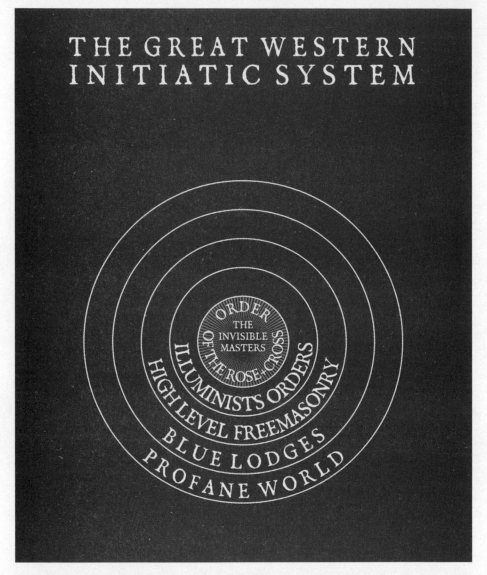

FIG. 15 Scheme translated and adapted in English by the author and Brad Kwiatek, originally created and drawn by the Sardinian Illuminati Vincenzo Soro that appeared on the Masonic essay from 1921 **The Great Book of Nature** *that shows in the center of* **The Great Western Initiatic System** *the Invisible Masters.*

The Rose Cross, of the transmutation of metals, and of the communication of man with Superior entities and intermediaries between him and The Great Architect."

This book (*The Great Book of Nature*), now unavailable and out of print, was originally published in Italy by the publishing house Atanor in 1921, after being published in France several times since the pre-revolutionary era, as a secret publication of the Order of the Philalethes, not to be confused with the more

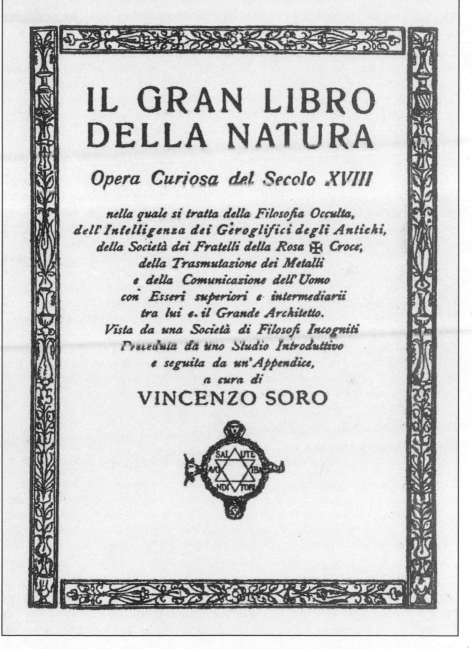

FIG. 16 The cover of the Italian edition of The Great Book of Nature states it talks about Occult Philosophy, of the intelligence of the hieroglyphs of the ancients, and of the communication of man with Superior beings, and the Great Architect (the aliens?)

modern Masonic research society based in North America called *The Philalethes Society*. This group included The French elite of the Illuminati, who worked in the period prior to the French Revolution.

This book contained all the hidden keys and all the secrets of the Illuminati, Freemasonry, and the Western Initiatic System at large, with all its various elements. In short, *The Great Book of Nature* was a book of a much higher level than that Wiccan piece of crap I bought as a young boy, and I ended up reading it over and over again, and carrying it with me for years to come around the world during all my adventures, never ceasing to appreciate it. A real goldmine of information about the Secret Societies that are responsible for the Illuminati network, which in all its emanations take orders from the aliens called *The Invisible Masters*.

It was yet another ancient text that brought me to a more direct contact with these alien entities, a grimoire entitled **The Book of the Sacred Magic of Abramelin the Mage,** today widely available in various editions. What impressed me most about the *Great Book of Nature* was a note about the word **enlightened**, which is *"Illuminati"* in Italian. What Vincenzo Soro wrote at the beginning of his commentary, revealed to me for the first time, the connection between the Illuminati and the Invisible Masters. Soro then describes the Rosicrucian Order as: *"A Universal Mystic Communion that resides, unique and indestructible, at the center of the Initiatic System formed by all the Illuminati of the East and the West, of the one and the other Hemisphere, presided on top by the Custodians of Threshold, and the invisible hierarchy of secret societies, that are defined as the true Illuminati whose leadership guided all the spiritual evolution of our Planet. From which sprung all the Light Ambassadors, the instructors and the Messiahs, the illuminators of the peoples, and the founders of all Religions, that write and shape all the mystical currents that push mankind into becoming more."*

IN SEARCH OF A "STARGATE"

This is a brief excerpt from a commentary added to the Italian version of *The Book of the Sacred Magic of Abramelin the Mage*:

The Malignant Spirits are there, around you, though invisible, and examine whether the one who evokes is courageous or timid if he has prudence and faith in God. We can take it and make them appear with little pain. But how many words wrongly spoken by an ill-intentioned person will come back against the same person who pronounced them with ignorance. And he who has such a character must not undertake this kind of operation because it means humiliating God and tempting him.

My most conscious result of contact with interdimensional entities was obtained at the age of 23, during and after the practice of the *Magic of Abramelin,* as outlined in Volume III of my *Confessions*. This is a long long ritual lasting several months, where it is necessary to isolate as much as possible from the rest of the world, in an ascetic manner. What we call "aliens" are hyperdimensional beings that have always been present in magical grimoires. They hide behind the veil of our perceptions and can project themselves into our visible reality at will, or when we evoke them using magic. They are not recent visitors to earth but have been here for hundreds of thousands of years, protected by an interdimensional reality we ignore. Some "aliens" helped genetically engineer the human race, while other factions later crippled human genetics in order to turn mankind into little more than a source of physical and etheric food. Today, those inter- acting with humanity via abductions, are not the same ones interacting with Moses, they are demonic and have a negative orientation, and intend to create a race of human-alien hybrids, capable of ruling over humanity while having total allegiance to the interdimensional demonic alien empire.

In a ceremonial magical operation conducted by a number of people, the mode is quite different, and it is crucial that individual efforts are coordinated, and so generally there is a master of a lodge or chapter, appointed for a par- ticular magical operation, whose task is to monitor the course of the student, who can eventually be promoted, when a particular stage has been reached, and when it is time to move him to the next level. This, however, does not happen when you undertake the most complex ritual ever originated in the Illuminati, which the majority of initiates still feel too dangerous to this day, *The Book of the Sacred Magic of Abramelin the Mage,* is *"knowledge and conversation with your Holy Guardian Angel,"* that is after all, Alien Contact, and not an easy task to be sure.

It contains extremely powerful tools if mastered because it links the human to the preterhuman consciousness, but when you are alone in dealing with these forces, you could risk losing yourself in the abyss of cosmic consciousness and never return. If you are not prepared, you are more likely to create a form of thought, a vampiric Egregore, which can become your own abyss and a dead end. The real wizards of the Illuminati sects before succeeding not only in participat- ing in the rituals of the occult lodges which they preside, but also while becoming a true enlightened teacher in the various mystery schools of origin, must travel on an introspective journey, and work profoundly on themselves. This kind of opera- tion can even last several years. The alchemists, and later the Freemasons, call this work **V.I.T.R.I.O.L.** *Visita Interiora Terrae Rectificando Invenies Occultum Lapi- dem (Visit the Interior of the Earth; by Rectification thou shalt find the Hidden Stone).* Even the mythical Rosenkreuz's crypt, according to the description presented in the legend, is located in the interior of the Earth, recalling the alchemical motto V.I.T.R.I.O.L. linked to the Invisible College and the Invisible Masters.

The tradition of the Unknown Superiors in Freemasonry hides in turn, that of the Secret Chiefs, sometimes called Invisible Masters, the alien link of the Illuminati. In ancient traditions, every tribe, every religion, every brotherhood, had entities that guide and protect their evolution and the tradition itself. These entities then incarnate primarily into associated bloodlines of the ruling elite, because DNA and the soul tend to correspond to a specific bloodline and lin- eage of people dear to that entity. So tracing bloodlines can show potentiality of destiny. It is said in the Illuminati mystery schools that bloodlines of a certain type rise via genetic modification by alien occult factions, or by a mutation in response to the soul frequency of ancestors who made negative soul pacts with higher dark powers to achieve material wealth and influence. These bloodlines have a physical and spiritual symbiotic relationship with their alien counter- parts, often corrupt by greed and matter, if not truly spiritual and devoted to the angelic realm. In the Sabian tradition, a religious group mentioned three times in the Quran as a People of the Book, there are entities that guide and watch over their people and humanity just like the Watchers of Mount Tabor of the Jewish tradition. In the Islamic tradition alien entities even have their own Mosque of the Jinn in Mecca, also known as the Mosque of Allegiance, built at the place where a group of jinn are said to have gathered one night to hear the recitation of a portion of the Quran by Muhammad. Muslim pilgrims circle the Kaaba inside the grand mosque in Mecca, but what is less commonly known is the presence of a holy relic, literally a cornerstone that is part of the worship shrouded in mystery, and there is much speculation over what the stone might be. Many Muslims believe the stone is in fact, a meteorite possessing supernatural powers. The Invisible Master *par excellence* of the Islamic tradition is **Khiḍr** or **al-Khiḍr**, which literally means "**The Green One.**" Yes, like a green alien who according to the 9th-century Muslim writer Tabari: *"because he sat on a white pelt, and when he got up from it, it was green."* Islamic scholar Gordon Newby, who translates this passage from Tabari, comments: *"Al-Khiḍr is usually associated with fertility and fecundity, as indicated by his color and the story that he sat on a white skin which turned green. Muslim commentators usually identify the skin as the earth and the green as plants."* Another medieval writer, Thalabi, says that Moses saw al-Khiḍr *"standing on a green carpet in the middle of the sea engaged in prayers."*[5]

In Muslim tradition, al-Khiḍr is widely known as the spiritual guide of Moses and Alexander the Great, a wali (saint), a prophet, and one of four immortals along with Enoch (Idris), Jesus, and Elijah. Qur'ānic commentators say that al-Khiḍr is one of the prophets; others refer to him simply as an angel who functions as a guide to those who seek God, just as the typical Invisible Master. Al-Khiḍr is mentioned in the Qur'an, but not by name. He's called "a servant from among our [Allah's] servants"; the Islamic exegetical tradition is left to fill in the details. His story appears in what is perhaps the strangest and most cryptic of the surahs (chapters) of the Qur'an: Surah 18, *Surat al-Kahf, the Chapter of the Cave.* As we see, Jung found a special significance in this title. Khiḍr is associated with the Water of Life and immortality, another subject dear to the Illuminati, and he is described as the one who has found the actual source of life. He's an "alien," all right—as C. G. Jung perceptively called him. If Jung's reading has even a grain of truth, he owes his existence to one of the deepest longings of the human soul: renewal and rebirth. In the East, where it is believed that human beings, after a multiplicity of births and deaths, can reach a level of spiritual evolution, there is a trace of masters of great spiritual strength who after finishing the cycle of existences chose not to associate with the absolute, as they would rightly deserve to complete their *Sadhana.* Instead, they decide to remain on the earth materially present and in secluded places to help humanity in its evolution, thus becoming themselves Invisible Masters.

MY FATHER DESCRIBES THE DIFFERENT ASPECTS OF FREEMASONRY

*M*y father Elio once told me that the spiritual and initiatic connotations of so-called Modern Speculative Masonry, created in 1717, referred to true spiritual entities that secretly guided the Order from the invisible realm, thanks to the Rosicrucians. This occult link was kept a secret to the majority of Freemasons, that these days are incapable of understanding the esoteric side of their Craft because they are too busy with some of its superficial

---

5   Quoted by Haim Schwartzbaum in *Fabula*, 1959.

materialistic aspects. This mysterious tradition is the same one we find in one of the most prominent figures of the British intelligence services, Sir Francis Bacon. Bacon's alleged connection to the Rosicrucians and the Freemasons has often been discussed by authors and scholars in many books. A number of writers, some of whom were connected with Theosophy, have claimed that Francis Bacon (1561-1626), the English philosopher, statesman, scientist, jurist, and author, was a member of secret societies. On the 22nd of January, 1621 in honor of Sir Francis Bacon's sixtieth birthday, a select group of men assembled in the large banquet hall in York House without fanfare, for what has been described as a Masonic banquet. This banquet was to pay tribute to Sir Francis Bacon. Only the Rosi cross (Rosicrucians) and Masons aware of Bacon's leadership role were invited. [6]

Sir Francis Bacon was considered one of the chief occultists in England during the Elizabethan age and was instrumental in the founding of America— the New Atlantis of the real Illuminati. Sir Francis Bacon believed that the New World was this New Atlantis. This idea was more than some fanciful intellectual dream, as it was originally transmitted to him by the Invisible Masters at the center of the Western Initiatic System. Bacon inspired an agenda to realize the idea that will finally result in the United States of America. Some of the most influential men of his day backed Bacon's agenda and eventually set in motion the machinery for what became the American democracy. Bacon's own secret society, the Rosicrucians, was established on American soil by the mid-1600s and among the colonizers of the New Atlantis were very powerful men, called the Order of the Quest, who sought to re-establish the glory of the Pagan Golden Age. America's destiny was planned out over 150 years prior to the American Revolution. Bacon believed that in the far, far ancient prehistoric past, gods dwelt with man during a golden age. These gods taught man ancient wisdom that was eventually lost in the destruction of Atlantis. These gods envisioned by Bacon were the typical Invisible Masters, who handpicked specific humans who were then anointed as priests and mediators between the gods and humanity. [7]

These special humans like Moses and Cagliostro were given keys to unlock the secrets of ancient wisdom, the keys I will unveil to you in this book, that are the secret to truly understand the alien interdimensional world we live in.

Biblically, Bacon's gods were the fallen Watchers and their offspring. The so-called keys of the ancient wisdom are none other than the biblical **Knowledge of Good and Evil**, and forbidden angelic technology that the book of Enoch speaks of. America's ancient name, *Amaruca*, was literally the Land of the Plumèd Serpent, which for the occult elite has a central role in the Last Days.

In *The Secret Teachings of All Ages*, Manly Palmer Hall (1901-1990) writes:

No other sacred book sets forth so completely as the Popol Vuh the initiatory rituals of a great school of mystical philosophy. This volume alone is sufficient to establish incontestably the philosophical excellence of the red race.

"The Red 'Children of the Sun,'" writes James Morgan Pryse, "do not worship

6   *See* https://en.wikipedia.org/wiki/Occult_theories_about_Francis_Bacon ‡ Archived 11th December, 2017.

7   *See* https://israelinprophecy.wordpress.com/america-the-new-atlantis-the-womb-of-the-antichrist/ ‡ Archived 11th December, 2017.

the One God. For them that One God is absolutely impersonal, and all the Forces emanated from that One God are personal. This is the exact reverse of the popular western conception of a personal God and impersonal working forces in nature. Decide for yourself which of these beliefs is the more philosophical. These Children of the Sun adore the Plumèd Serpent, who is the messenger of the Sun. He was the God Quetzalcoatl in Mexico, Gucumatz in Quiché, and in Peru, he was called Amaru. From the latter name comes our word America. Amaruca is, literally translated, 'Land of the Plumèd Serpent.' The priests of this God of Peace, from their chief center in the Cordilleras, once ruled both Americas. All the Red men who have remained true to the ancient religion are still under their sway. One of their strong centers was in Guatemala, and of their Order was the author of the book called Popol Vuh. In the Quiché tongue, Gucumatz is the exact equivalent of Quetzalcoatl in the Nahuatl language; Quetzal, the bird of Paradise; coat, serpent—'the Serpent veiled in plumes of the paradise-bird!'"

The Popol Vuh was discovered by Father Ximinez in the seventeenth century. It was translated into French by Brasseur de Bourbourg and published in 1861. The only complete English translation is that by Kenneth Sylvan Guthrie, which ran through the early files of The Word magazine and which is used as the basis of this article. A portion of the Popol Vuh was translated into English, with extremely valuable commentaries, by James Morgan Pryse, but unfortunately, his translation was never completed. The second book of the Popol Vuh is largely devoted to the initiatory rituals of the Quiché nation.

These ceremonials are of first importance to students of Masonic symbolism and mystical philosophy since they establish beyond doubt the existence of ancient and divinely instituted Mystery schools on the American Continent.

In 1793, the cornerstone of the Capitol building was laid by George Washington and hundreds of Freemasons. A silver Masonic trowel was made for the ceremony and hundreds of masons paraded to Washington D.C. to witness the historical event. This would be the first of many buildings and monuments to be erected by the Freemasons, and George Washington would be the first of at least fourteen known masons to take the office of President of the United States. [8]

So that's why Washington, D.C. was precisely located on the 77th Meridian West, and why the original five colonial cities—Boston, New York City, Philadelphia, Baltimore, and Washington, D.C. were built in precise alignment with each other, with Stonehenge across the Atlantic, and on a specific occult Ley Line suggested by the Invisible Masters of Freemasonry and the Rosicrucian tradition. Easter Island, the Nasca Lines of Peru and the Giza Pyramid, all line up along another Ley Line which is exactly 30 degrees to the equator. We are definitely connected to Mother Earth through the subtle electrical current that runs around the entire planet, that is involved with the activities of the Invisible Masters and their interdimensional travels. These electrical currents are known as *Ley Lines* and are almost like Mother Earth's veins. The ancient wonders and holy sites of the ancient world—temples, shrines and pyramids, are all built on these Ley Lines, also known as Great Circles, which encircle the earth in perfect alignment.

8   Manly P. Hall, *The Secret Teachings of All Ages*, (San Francisco, CA: H. S. Crocker Company Inc.,1928), p. 195.

FIG. 17 *The Temple of the Rose Cross by Teophilus Schweighardt Constantiens, 1618.*

Ley lines, also known as Energy Lines, are hypothetical alignments of a number of places of geographical interest, such as ancient monuments and megaliths. Some say that the Ley Lines are a lost ancient man-made technology when in reality it's an Alien interdimensional technology still in use. These lines may be part of the planetary energy grid theory which operates through geometrical patterns that follow a specific symmetry linked to sacred geometry interdimensional portals. Perhaps the most adventurous explanation is that they involve energy that is now explainable by the String Theory.

This relatively new mathematical concept allows for the existence of extra dimensions as well as the idea of passage from one to the other, something the various Illuminati sects and Invisible Masters from the upper or lower realms have known for thousands of years. These extra dimensions represent profoundly different realities and forms of life, where our own laws of physics are replaced by others. Ancient societies and various mystery schools and religions understood the concept of interdimensional travel, but have kept it secret. Many of the great ancient sites were set in harmony with each other, along shared ley lines of alien energy that can be still be felt if physically aware. In a recent interview with *Hotelchatter.com*, Hollywood psychic Aiden Chase said: *"There's an energy field in the land here that supports wishes and dreams. L.A.'s natural 'good vibe' energy, from the Hollywood Hills to the ocean has supported people's dreams from actor to entrepreneur for over 100 years."* Okay, that sounds interesting, but are we sure there isn't something else of a darker nature at work after viewing all the recent scandals? I will direct the interested parties to check out Volume II of my *Confessions* series of books for the definite answer.

THE INTERDIMENSIONAL NATURE OF THE INVISIBLE MASTERS

Since antiquity, the true Hidden Masters (who are certainly not the black magicians of the elite), in contact with the divine through angelic and benevolent entities, hid in an impenetrable shadow. However, in order to encourage deserving adepts in their research, certain Masters have published allegorical and hermetic treatises that were impossible to fully decipher if not initiated into the ancient mysteries. They also addressed from time to time special emissaries that went from village to village, and even wandered the cities from time to time, looking for someone who deserved their attention. Cagliostro was also known as the *Noble Traveler*, and at times one of the mysterious figures who moved from town to town, visiting isolated alchemists, exchanging knowledge and secret occult instructions received from the alien interdimensional realm, or the **Invisible College,** as the Rosicrucians called it.

The secrecy of these adepts of the occult arts was often justified by the great fear of being discovered by the Church of Rome, that viewed them not only as heretics but as a possible competition to their Occult elite represented by the Jesuits. Obviously participation of the esoteric mysteries, in search of Invisible Masters, and Elemental Spirits of Nature that could help them in the discovery of the Philosopher's Stone, said to be a substance or something which is said to render those who possessed it all-powerful, or the Universal Medicine, or *panacea*, to cure all forms of disease, are interests the Church never encouraged. Many historical facts seem to confirm the truth of such statements, and certain still-existing legal documents go on to prove that gold on certain occasions has been indeed produced by the alchemist using artificial means. The Rosicrucian's always insisted that this art was only one of the most insignificant parts of their divine science and that they possessed far more important secrets.

The Rosicrucians themselves did not contradict such stories; on the contrary, they asserted that there were many occult laws and mysterious powers; of which mankind, on the whole, knew very little, because the spiritual powers of perception are not sufficient among mankind as a whole, to enable them to perceive spiritual things. They say that if our spiritual powers of perception were fully developed, we should see this universe peopled with other beings than ourselves, and of whose existence we know nothing at present.

They say that we should then see this universe filled with things of life, whose beauty and sublimity surpass the most exalted imagination of man, and we should learn mysteries in comparison with which the art of making gold sinks into insignificance and becomes comparatively worthless.

They speak of the inhabitants of the four kingdoms of nature, of **Nymphs, Undines, Gnomes, Sylphs, Salamanders, and Fairies**, as if they were people they were intimately acquainted with, and as if they did not belong to the realm of the fable, but were living beings of an ethereal organization, too subtle to be perceived by our gross material senses; but living, conscious, and knowing, ready to serve and instruct man, and to be instructed by him. **They speak of Planetary Spirits who were formerly men, but who are now as far above human beings as the latter are above animals**, and they assert that if men knew their divine powers, which are dormant in their constitution, and were to pay attention to their development, instead of wasting all their life and energies upon the comparatively insignificant and trifling affairs of their short and transient external existence upon this earth, they might in time become like those planetary spirits or gods. [9]

However, there are often misconceptions about the true nature of *Hidden* or *Invisible* Masters, that guide from behind the scenes of the Rosicrucian reality. One of the most prevalent is that the Hidden Masters conspire to "rule our lives," when in reality the ones dealing with the angelical realm are only trying to help us in our evolution as a species. Of course, these don't include black magicians or witches like Aleister Crowley, and during the last few thousand years the vast majority of the world's population were exploited, misled and manipulated by those seeking material power. In human history there have always existed as self-seeking opportunists that will sell their soul to the darkest forces, dealing with interdimensional demons for this reason. Whether such people are known to the public, or simply pull the strings of their puppets from behind the scenes, these are our enemies, and the enemies of true Freemasonry, those who plot various political, monetary and social agendas for their own selfish ends. Hidden Masters, Secret Chiefs, and Invisible Masters are concepts popularized in the 19th century, by the occultist and teacher, H. P. Blavatsky, to describe concealed preceptors, but we never know if the nature of these preceptors is truly benign, or, like in most cases, totally evil and manipulative.

In calling them in a certain way Blavatsky wasn't simply following the age-old practice of referring to a teacher of spiritual verities as a terrestrial "Hidden Master," but she was also referring to **disincarnated entities,** who existed on higher or lower planes of existence. Invisible Masters that incarnated in certain living beings reputed of importance for their mission, and could later gather in a special spiritual or magical location, such as Shambhala for example, a place very dear to the Theosophists, or scattered through the world, working anonymously. This is a concept exposed by the Unknown Philosopher / Claude de Saint Mar-

9   Franz Hartmann, *Cosmology or Cabala Universal Science Secret Symbols of the Rosicrucians* (Boston: Occult Publishing Company. 130 Tremont Street, 1888), p .1.

FIG. 18 The Alchemical Door, also known as the Alchemy Gate or Magic Portal (Italian: Porta Alchemica or Porta Magica), is a mysterious monument built between 1678 and 1680 by Massimiliano Palombara.

tin (1743-1803). The Invisible Master is an extra-dimensional entity or a human immortal, who only imparts his esoteric teachings to his carefully chosen disciples in secret, to plant the seeds of something greater. Jesus fulfills this role in the Gospels, as did Buddha before him. The fact that the words Hidden Masters may now mean anything or nothing and has even been adopted by a group of silly contemporary musicians playing with occult lore, does not alter its original value and importance. The real **Hidden Masters** in connection to what popular culture will call the good aliens, not the ones from the dark side, have indeed no desire to rule or control your life. Such coercion goes against all universal occult laws, and most manmade ones as well. But we know how the dark side attempts to operate beyond laws, they act as present guardians of the material world, the previously mentioned Archons, who are most of the time dangerous intrapsychic mind-parasites, just like most of their Islamic counterparts, the *Jinn*, used by the occult elite and the Intelligence agencies to trick and manipulate us.

However, freedom of thought and action is an inalienable right of mankind granted to us all by our Creator, don't ever forget this. If it were not so, man would be no better than a mindless robot with no possibility of evolving to a higher state—something the occult elite is trying to stop before they lose their grip on materialistic reality. You may argue that some human beings are not free, such as those in prison, or who are enslaved in some way or another in their present human existence. But if you think about it, you will agree that at some time—in some way or other—whether in this life or a previous one, they exercised their **Free Will** to bring about their present circumstances. For the conditions in which

we find ourselves are in every case the result of our own actions in this or a former life, a topic I touched in detail in my suppressed, and now rare book, *The
Decline of the Western Initiatic System and the rise of Satanism in our Society*.

Higher dimensions are outside of our classic range of perception, so expanding our consciousness with the knowledge I am providing you is in my modest
opinion, is the best way to gradually become more aware and conscious that we
are multi-dimensional beings living in a multi-dimensional universe.

DOORWAYS TO MULTI-DIMENSIONAL WORLDS

*T*he multi-dimensional reality of our world is a topic I began studying
in my early twenties, in a period that coincided (i.e. a typical case of
synchronicity), with the release of a movie called *Stargate* directed by
Roland Emmerich. This film was Hollywood's approach that I found illuminating, because God does not exist in only one place, and neither do you. That's
why in the so-called Egyptian Freemasonry of the Ancient and Primitive Rite of
Memphis and Misraïm, God is known as the *Great Architect of the Universes,* not
as the Great Architect of the Universe, as in all the other Masonic rites. Lately,
there has been news of a radical new theory, that proposes the universe began
from a hyper-dimensional black hole and for over a decade a group of scholars
from different branches of science support theories that relate to the possible
existence of a **hyperdimensional universe**. In particular, with regard to Ufology,
well-known experts such as Harvard psychiatrist John Mack and astrophysicist
Jacques Vallée, have singled out the issue of parallel dimensions on the basis of
research in a controversial and fascinating field, that of abductions. [10]

Others still argue—not because of their personal opinion, but because of
deep knowledge of the cause—that although the extra-dimensional origin of
aliens is not certain, they are certainly capable of traveling dimensionally, that
is, certain ET races come from different levels of our reality, rather than distant
galaxies. As I mentioned earlier, interdimensional travel could be the gateway to
distant worlds. Too many, in fact, are the cases in which the supposed ET seems
to appear to the abductee, in places with closed doors and windows, or even ce-
ment walls, and then disappearing shortly after into thin air, leaving no trace.
Moreover, the machines we define as UFOs, also appear to be able to appear and
disappear to and from strange worlds, or parallel realities, using physical laws
not yet known to us. In science fiction films, the idea of a parallel dimension is
often discussed, but as one realizes in certain cases, this is not fantasy, as everything is based on concrete scientific postulates, which occur within physics.

Electromagnetic fields became known by **James Clerk Maxwell (1831-1879)**,
Scottish mathematician and physicist, dating back to the late 19th century. He
demonstrated these forces with the publication of *A Dynamical Theory of the Electromagnetic Field* in 1865, that electric and magnetic fields travel through space as
waves moving at the speed of light. Maxwell is best-known for his research in
electromagnetic radiation, which unites the science of electricity, magnetism,
and optics. Electricity flows through many metals because of the movement of
electrons among the atoms of the metal.

---

10   *See* http://www.noiegliextraterrestri.it/2014/03/i-mondi-paralleli-e-la-connessione-
con.html ‡ Archived 11th December, 2017.

Moving electrons also produce a magnetic field, the strength of which depends on the number of moving electrons. [11] These theories were later elaborated by **Karl Ernst Ludwig Marx Planck (1858-1947)** at the beginning of the twentieth century. Planck was studying black-body radiation and suggested that the energy carried by electromagnetic waves could only be released in "packets" of energy. Planck then developed the theory of *quanta,* that is, elemental particles whose presence explains the abnormal behavior of electromagnetic fields, especially in relation to the discontinuous emission of energy. From that point onwards in physics, a quantum (plural: *quanta*) is the minimum amount of any physical entity involved in such interaction. In 1905, **Albert Einstein (1879-1955)** perfected this theory in front of the general skepticism of his contemporaries, when he presented his paper, *Concerning a Heuristic Point of View about the Creation and Transformation of Light,* in Bern, Switzerland, on March 17, 1905, three days after his twenty-sixth birthday. From then on, 1905 became the year that Einstein referred to as "very revolutionary," as he had introduced the concept of *light quanta*, as an indivisible packet. It was not until 1926 that this theory was fully embraced by the academic community, with the more modern term *photon*, coined by Gilbert Lewis (1875-1946), who first wrote about it in an article in *Nature,* substituting forever Einstein's light quanta.

During more recent studies it was noticed that the extremely uneven behavior of atoms, was related to electrons which instead of performing a correct orbit around the nucleus, seemed to vanish from one point and reappear mysteriously in another. Such apparitions and disappearances of electrons were called **quantum leaps.** So a quantum leap is where the electron on rung X simply disappears and instantaneously appears on rung X+1, without ever traversing the space in between them. This is why the jump is called discontinuous, and why the quantum leap is not only considered surprising and interesting from a classical academic point of view but because of the much wider implications related to interdimensional travel or even time travel. Let's not forget Quantum Leap, the American science-fiction television series that originally aired on NBC for five seasons, from March, 1989 through May, 1993. While the followers of Niels Henrik David Bohr's theories (1885-1962) concluded that the irrational behavior of what was happening was due to the total unreliability of the used detection tools of the observer, other luminaries, including Bryce Seligman DeWitt (1923-2004) of the University of North Carolina, came to new, disconcerting conclusions.

According to them, the thing did not jump from one side to the other, but temporarily disappeared from this plane of reality and then reappeared. Today the most avant-garde scientists—including the aforementioned Jack Sarfatti and Fred Alan Wolf—have concluded that the only way to explain this bizarre behavior of what was a new scientific theory based on the wave function in quantum physics, is the theory of the **Many Worlds interpretation,** originally formulated in 1957 by physicist and mathematician Hugh Everett III (1930-1982), operating from Princeton University. In 1954, a young Princeton University doctoral candidate named Hugh Everett III came up with a radical idea: *"That there exist parallel universes, exactly like our universe. These universes are all related to ours; indeed, they branch off from ours, and our universe is branched off of others. Within*

11   *See* https://digital.nls.uk/scientists/biographies/james-clerk-maxwell/discoveries ‡
        Archived 11th December, 2017.

these parallel universes, our wars have had different outcomes than the ones we know. Species that are extinct in our universe have evolved and adapted to others. In other universes, we humans may have become extinct." [12]

This thought boggles the mind and yet, it is still comprehensible only to a privileged few who have the understanding for it. Giuseppe Vatinno, who was a member of the Italian Parliament until 2013, described at one point as being *"the world's first transhumanist politician,"* is a professor of physics residing in Rome. After a weird and unsuccessful political campaign based on his book, *Transhumanism: A new philosophy for the man of the 21st century (Il Transumanesimo. Una nuova filosofia per l'uomo del XXI secolo)*, Vatinno, who I know personally, in 2012, was involved in a strange controversy in parliament when he submitted a question about the existence of UFOs. He told me later that he did it to invite the Italian parliament to deepen their knowledge of the extraterrestrial phenomenon. However, this unusual event created a subsequent social media quarrel, that eventually led one of the two Italian transhumanist association members that previously supported him, to explicitly disassociate from his activities, and at the same time, Giuseppe Vatinno received life-threatening messages on Twitter that were followed by a police investigation. Obviously someone disliked his questioning of the UFO phenomenon in the Italian parliament, and in the end, he returned to his previous job, as University professor.

Vatinno, who is a friend of the aforementioned Jack Sarfatti, pointed out to me that the quantum interpretation of the *Many Worlds Interpretation*, is part of a more general category of *parallel universes* elaborated in the superstring theory, Brane cosmology, and it appeared in work done in two of the most important early detecting devices used to study subatomic particles, known as cloud and bubble chambers.

Michio Kaku is the famous TV personality, theoretical physicist, author, and science educator, who is the co-founder of the Field String Theory, explains the existence in the universe of eleven dimensions. Well, that's interesting, if you connect the Illuminati fixation for this number that Aleister Crowley singled out as the key to all rituals. Going back to Professor Giuseppe Vatinno, he also told me in private that the category of parallel universes is becoming in recent years particularly relevant in cosmology. Very well-known scientists, such as Hawking, Gell-Mann, Weinberg, and Feynman deployed in favor of the *Many Worlds Interpretation,* usually referred with the acronym **M.W.I.** Moreover, Vatinno specifies that there are parallel universes endowed with the same physical laws of ours, there are in fact, (and should not be confused), even parallel universes generated during the Bing Bang, as taught by Andrej Linde's, *Theory of Bubble Universes*, and others that may be generated by nothingness (Theory of Continuous Inflation); but these kinds of universes might not have the same physical laws as ours. According to the theory of the multiverse (or metauniverse), there exist a plurality of parallel universes, so that every decision that each of us takes in this world, would create new ones in another. Based on this interpretation there would be, for example, a world in which the Third Reich came out victorious from World War II, and another in which Hitler is an unknown painter. It may sound like a screenplay for a movie, yet physicists have

---

12   *See* https://science.howstuffworks.com/science-vs-myth/everyday-myths/parallel-universe.htm ‡ Archived 11th December, 2017.

been studying these scenarios for at least fifty years, and there are complicated and elegant mathematical calculations that can describe them.[13]

According to the latest research published in *Physical Review X*[14] while I was writing this book back in October 2014, a team from The University of California, Davis (also referred to as UCD, UC Davis, or Davis), and one from the Australian Griffith University, stated that not only do parallel universes exist, but they could even interact with each other. No wonder in her book, *Knocking on Heaven's Door*, from 2011, well-known Harvard University theorist **Lisa Randall** explores how physics may truly transform with the latest discoveries of our whole understanding of the fundamental nature of the world. As the Smithsonian outlines: "*She thinks an extra dimension may exist close to our familiar reality, hidden except for a bizarre sapping of the strength of gravity as we see it. She also ponders the makeup of dark matter, unseen particles that have shaped the growth of the entire cosmos. These ideas, once the sole province of fiction writers, face real tests in a new generation of experiments.*"[15]

WHAT IS VRIL, AND DOES QUANTUM PHYSICS CONFIRM THE OCCULT?

*L*ike others have pointed out, rather than discrediting the occult, recent scientific discoveries in quantum physics seem to reaffirm a place for mystical ideas. When John Whiteside "Jack" Parsons (1914-1952), the American rocket engineer and rocket propulsion researcher, chemist, and Thelemite occultist, first visited the Agape Lodge of the O.T.O., he stated that as a scientist he found that Crowley's magick teachings seemed to correlate with the work of the quantum field folks. The illogical nature of quantum physics is a subject that I gradually discovered myself, mostly while dealing with certain interdimensional beings as part of my own occult training in the Illuminati groups I joined early in my life. Orders and confraternities, where through ceremonial magic and rituals, I was involved in a reality entrenched with quantum physics, where I eventually taught what some call illumination or at least what I regard as a higher level of consciousness.

It's synchronicity, as the great Swiss psychiatrist, and psychoanalysis **Carl Gustav Jung** (1875-1961) called it. At the base of Jung's work on synchronicity is the so-called *quantum entanglement*, that also attracted the attention of Nobel Prize winner **Wolfgang Pauli** and gave rise to a close correspondence between the two, known as *The Pauli/Jung Letters 1932-58*. They were later published by Jung's successor Carl Alfred Meier (1905-1995), of who my father Elio was the leading Italian collaborator at the end of the sixties and early seventies. To Jung, synchronicity was a meaningful coincidence in time, a psychic factor which is independent of space and time, but truly relevant. This revolutionary concept

13   Article by Davide Patitucci, *Universi paralleli, "ecco la prova della loro esistenza e interazione,"* in *Il Fatto Quotidiano*, 3rd of December 2014.

14   *Physical Review X* is a peer-reviewed open access scientific journal published by the American Physical Society that covers all aspects of physics.

15   *See* https://www.smithsonianmag.com/science-nature/opening-strange-portals-in-physics-92901090/ ‡ Archived 11th December, 2017.

of synchronicity both challenges and complements the physicist's classical view of casualty that the Illuminati and the Freemasons never believed. It also forces us to a basic reconsideration of the meaning of chance, probability, coincidence and the singular events in our lives.

Returning to the film *Stargate,* dealing with the theme of interdimensional passages in a new way, though still linked to a commercial and materialistic vision typical of Hollywood films, it can be said that from that moment onwards the Alchemical Door, also known as the Alchemy Gate or Magic Portal in Piazza Vittorio, built between 1678 and 1680, now found in the heart of the Esquilino district in Rome became my favorite "Stargate."

This strange and unusual monument built by Rosicrucian Illuminati Massimiliano Palombara belongs to an original set of doors of Villa Palombara, destroyed over time. Once Rome became the capital of the new kingdom of Italy, it was completely removed, for the construction of the new Esquilino district. The only small part spared was the very doorway of the detached outbuilding, what today is known as the Magic Door of Piazza Vittorio, although probably Alchemic Door would have been a more appropriate name for it.

In this Villa, Palombara held meetings, attended by the most important Illuminati figures of his time, who shared his interests for alchemy and the Invisible Masters, people like the Swedish Queen Christina, who lived in Rome after having abdicated, the distinguished astronomer Domenico Cassini, the renowned Jesuit scholar Father Athanasius Kircher, and others linked to the mysterious Rosicrucians operating in Italy under Jesuit supervision. The Rosicrucian Illuminati was an important part of the Occult elite, that may even be seen as prefiguring the eighteenth century alchemical *Gold-und Rosencreutz Orden*, made public by Rosicrucian Magus *Sincerus Renatus* (Salomon Richter) in 1710.

Queen Christina's practice of alchemy preoccupied her for most of her adult life. Her interest in alchemy also had some intriguing Rosicrucian connections. The original Rosicrucian pamphlets of 1614 spread high expectations for a new age, and a universal reformation of the arts that circulated among radical Paracelsians in Northern Europe. The Rosicrucian elements that were to surface in Italy, however, appear to have grown out of a purely alchemical interest, where the transmutational operations promised a future restoration of the golden age. [16]

The ancient wisdom of transmutation, the secrets of the cosmos and longevity—this is what they were searching for—but (also) a link with the invisible world. Throughout the Middle Ages and the Renaissance, there were many scholars who claimed that they had received late night visits from mysterious members of a secret society that had accomplished the transmutation of metals, the means of prolonging life, the knowledge to see and to hear what was occurring in distant places, and the ability to travel across the heavens in heavier-than-air vehicles (UFOs?). Some students of the history of alchemy have stated that crumbling, yellowed records of the alchemists remain in dusty libraries—more than 100,000 ancient volumes written in a code that has never been sufficiently deciphered. Numerous occult groups and mystery schools within the

16   http://www.alchemywebsite.com/queen_christina.html ‡ Archived 11th December, 2017.

Illuminati network like the Rosicrucians, have been created around the belief that centuries ago a secret society achieved a high level of scientific knowledge that they carefully guarded from the rest of humanity.

This is almost common knowledge in the Illuminati. According to these occultists, certain men of genius in ancient Egypt and Persia were given access to the records of the advanced technologies of the antediluvian world of Atlantis. Many hundreds of years ago, these ancient masters learned to duplicate many of the feats of the Titans of the lost continent. There are persistent legends in nearly every culture that tell of an Elder Race that populated the Earth millions of years ago. The Old Ones, who may originally have been of extraterrestrial origin, were an immensely intelligent and scientifically advanced species, who eventually chose to structure their own environment under the surface of the planet's soil and seas.

The Old Ones are said to usually remain aloof from surface dwellers, but from time to time throughout history, they have been known to visit certain of Earth's more intelligent members in the guise of alchemist or mysterious scientists, in order to offer constructive criticism and, in some cases, to give valuable advice in the material sciences. The Old Ones seem to be, after a close analysis, another emanation of the Invisible Masters at the center of the Western Initiatic System. In 1871, occultist and Rosicrucian Edward Bulwer-Lytton wrote, *The Coming Race*, a novel about a small group of German mystics who discovered a race of supermen living within the Earth's interior. The super race had built a paradise based on **The Vril Force**, a form of energy so powerful that the older beings had outlawed its use as a potential weapon. The Vril was derived from the Black Sun, a large ball of *Prima Materia* that provided light and radiation to the inhabitants of inner Earth. [17]

After all, the magicians of the Illuminati, as Aleister Crowley taught, clearly expressed the importance of communion with such beings, and Crowley was also a Rosicrucian, and included their secret teachings in the 5th degree of the O.T.O., in the Sovereign Prince Rose-Croix section. Crowley himself in one of the last statements, he made in 1944, clearly said: *"My observation of the Universe convinces me that there are beings of intelligence and power of a far higher quality than anything we can conceive of as human; that they are not necessarily based on the cerebral and nervous structures that we know, and that the one and only chance for mankind to advance as a whole is for individuals to make contact with such beings."*

Crowley's erstwhile secretary Kenneth Grant (who claims to have formed a link to his alien "angel" Aossic, and calls himself Aossic, Ossik, or A'ashik) has—together with his followers—developed a more or less comprehensible outline of a new cosmos, on the basis of an occult alliance with the alien world. Interested readers are referred to Grant's books, many of which remain in print. We shall now concentrate on Grant's resulting theoretical alien expansion of Crowley's demonology. The latter never seems to have regarded angels or demons as very definite beings; for him, they ruled the material world and were used for things like obtaining money. Under Grant's influence, they were elaborated into **complex transcendental schemes of alternate dimensions outside the circles of space and time**: *"The terrestrial vehicle is an outcropping in three dimensions of the Angel: the Angel is the fountain of living waters which empowers the terrestrial vehicle."*

---

17   https://www.bibliotecapleyades.net/sociopolitica/sociopol_brotherhoodss30.htm ‡ Archived 11th December, 2017.

WHY SIRIUS MATTERS

*T*hrough contact with the **Holy Guardian Angel (HGA)**, the gate of re-membrance of our supernatural reality opens, what Grant calls *"the continuum often glyphed as the Goddess of which we are terrestrial facets."* Grant and his adherents remember the origins of Being, and have constructed a remarkably complicated collection of metaphors drawn from sources such as the Kabbalah, H.P. Lovecraft, Salvador Dalí, Michael P. Bertiaux, Austin Osman Spare, Lemuria, Atlantis, **extraterrestrial visitors from Sirius**, the promotion of at least one "New Aeon," and a whole slew of "revelations," Grant placed great emphasis on the development of an IX° degree dream-control technique, bor-rowed from Thomas Lake Harris, introduced into the Crowleyan O.T.O. by Ida Nellidorf under the name of **croto-comatose lucidity.**

Before going to sleep the sexual energies were first raised by constant sexual stimulation without orgasm and then concentrated onto a talisman bearing a requisite symbol so that in the dream-state, the aroused libido would copulate with a dream-partner. The talisman would thus become magically charged and would make a particular wish—be it for gold or Gnosis—come true. But the greatest interest has been shown in the supposed alien entity called Lam, which Crowley "beheld" in 1918.

In October 1979, Kenneth Grant (under his alias of "Aossic Aiwass 718"), de-scribed Crowley's Amalantrah Working of 1918 as an *"active reflex and extension of Lam"* and released *"An Official Statement of the O.T.O concerning the Cult of Lam, the Dikpala of the Way of Silence."* Grant drew up a ritual meditation for making con-tact with Lam. The entity was imagined as an egg, and the practitioner would enter its eyes with the aid of the mantra *Lam* so that once united Tantrically with Lam, one could "see" the world from beyond. Grant judged the sex-magic versions of this meditation to be extremely dangerous, and most emphatically rejected all homosexual variations of it (in some O.T.O. groups like the Caliph-ate, the XI° it is the homosexual degree). To gain the most objective results from all contacts with Lam, Grant stated that none of its practitioners should inform each other of their own results for several years. [18] We will talk more about Grant later, I would like to now discuss the direct link between interdimensional enti-ties, the Crowleyan O.T.O. and NASA, before going deeper into the relationship between the Illuminati and the interdimensional alien beings linked to them.

In 1997, syndicated talk show host Art Bell received a frantic call from a man claiming to have **worked in Area 51**. The entire radio station was zapped off the air as soon as the caller began to reveal detailed plans concerning extra- dimen-sional aliens, the government, and population control.

Here is a transcript of the disturbing talk:

Hello, Art? Art? Hi ... I don't have a whole lot of time ... um, I was a former em-ployee of Area 51 ... I was let go on a medical discharge about a week ago ... and ... and ... (starts to cry) I kinda been running across the country ... um ... um ... man ... I don't know WHERE to start ... they'll triangulate on this position re-

ally, really soon ... (starting to break up and get more frantic—Art tells him to give us something quick) ... OK ... um ... um ... What we're thinking of as Aliens ... they're EXTRA-DIMENSIONAL BEINGS ... that an earlier precursor of the SPACE PROGRAM MADE CONTACT WITH ... uh ... they are NOT what they claim to be ... uh ... they have INFILTRATED a lot of aspects of the MILITARY ESTABLISHMENT particularly Area 51 ... uh ... the DISASTERS that are coming ... the GOVERNMENT knows about them ... and there's a lot of SAFE AREAS in this WORLD THAT THEY COULD BEGIN MOVING THE POPULATION TO ... NOW—Art ... but they are NOT doing anything about it ... THEY WANT THE MAJOR POPULATION CENTERS—WIPED OUT SO THAT THE FEW THAT ARE LEFT WILL BE MORE EASILY CONTROLLABLE ... (breaking up more, starting to cry) ... I started getting ...

Silence—Art went off the air at that point. Well, the comment on the "precursor of the space program" is very interesting. As one of the Californian leaders of Crowley's O.T.O. in the 1940s, **John Whiteside "Jack" Parsons (1914- 1952)**, an American rocket engineer and rocket propulsion researcher, credited with an important role in the founding of Jet Propulsion Laboratory (JPL) and Aerojet, and is regarded as being among the most important figures in the history of the U.S. space program. Let's remember he was one of the principal founders of JPL currently owned by NASA. Parsons was eventually expelled from JPL and Aerojet in 1944, due to the Lodge's infamy, and allegedly illicit activities, along with his hazardous workplace conduct. In reality, he went on conducting a series of occult rituals for the Illuminati, that opened interdimensional portals, possibly helping interdimensional beings in their alien invasion.

The topic I will now unravel is the actual method of contact developed by certain Illuminati groups that have dealt for a long time with the alien overlords of the UFOs, understating their nature and their secrets. Everywhere, in the mineral, vegetable, and animal kingdom, we see innumerable gradations of existence, without any hard line of separation between them, or, if such lines are seen, it is because the "missing links" have been lost. Moreover, there are amphibious beings which are equally adapted to live in the air and in the water, in the earth and air, or in the earth and the water, and the same may be said about the Elementals, or Spirits of Nature, interdimensional beings living in a parallel reality.

As there are innumerable gradations of visible forms, likewise, there are innumerable gradations of invisible ones in the interdimensional realm, and there are amphibious existences in the realm of the Universal Soul which may exist in two different states—which may appear sometimes in visible forms, while at other times they are invisible to us. There are beings on the Astral Plane which are only seen by those who have developed their inner senses to an extent sufficient to enable them to perceive such forms from another dimension; but certain conditions may exist which may cause such ethereal forms to become more dense and material, so as to become perceptible even to the physical senses of man, (80) leading in some cases to mind blowing revelations and true "Contact," but most of the time forcing us into unpleasant experiences where we are literally vampirized by these entities.

THE UFONAUTS AND ALIEN VAMPIRISM

III

Choronzon & Crowley opened the doors to hell in 1909

 n the history of Ancient Rome, which has always been the operative center of the Illuminati, there are an enormous amount of events and manifestations that can now be attributed to the UFO phenomenon. Famous is the legend of Emperor Constantine and the crucial Battle of the Milvian Bridge, that would seal the future of the Christian Faith. From Eusebius, two accounts of the battle survive. The shorter one in Ecclesiastical history promotes the belief that God helped Constantine, but does not mention a vision. Later, in *Life of Constantine*, Eusebius writes a detailed account of the vision and stresses that he heard the story from the Emperor himself. According to this version, Constantine and his army were marching (Eusebius does not specify the actual location of the event, but it clearly is not in the camp in Rome), when he looked up to the sun and saw a cross of light above it, and with it the Greek words "Εν Τούτῳ Νίκα." The term *En toutō níka* translated into Latin is *in hoc signo vinces*, and the literal meaning of the phrase in Greek is: *"In this (sign), conquer,"* while in Latin it means *"In this sign, you shall conquer."* A more free translation would be: *"Through this sign (you shall) conquer."* At first, he was unsure of the meaning of the apparition, but the following night he had a dream in which Christ explained to him that he should use the sign against his enemies. [1]

This was a typical intervention from above, but also a clear intervention from the alien overlords to direct the future of the Empire towards Christianity, at the time still considered the faith of a minor sect. Regarding in particular, Ancient Rome, there have been a few UFO sightings reported, such as in *De Prodigiis,* by the Roman historian Julius Obsequens, who was believed to have lived in the middle of the 4th century AD. Obsequens tells of a series of extraordinary facts, wonders i.e. *prodigi* in the Latin language, which occurred in previous centuries in the territories of the Roman Empire, referring to stories narrated by Tito Livio. Three events in particular, between 216 and 90 BC, caught the attention of followers of the theory of Paleocontact, that this was a critical time in which

1   https://en.wikipedia.org/wiki/Battle_of_the_Milvian_Bridge ‡ Archived 11th December, 2017.

some of these UFO sightings occurred. George C. Andrews writes about the Council of Nicea (325 AD), that decided the future of Christianity and the New World Order, and Andrews explains that all references to extraterrestrials and reincarnation were systematically deleted from the Bible. [2]

The concept of life on other dimensions, planets, or universes, would confuse Christians, but it doesn't mean that the Christian paradigm is false. According to much of my research, the existence of interdimensional aliens from other planets or planes of existence (i.e. different dimensions) doesn't refute scripture at all. In fact, scripture seems to indicate that there is, in fact, life on other dimensions, supporting the existence of entities of various natures. The term **Angels**, Fallen Angels, **Demons**, Hosts of Heaven, Stars, Creatures, Sons of God, and the Nephilim, also known as "Rapha," or "Rephaim," all three of which refer to *giants*, must be defined. Within these terms lies the key to unlocking the mystery of what modern society calls *aliens*, and the modern Illuminati calls *Ufonauts*.

Freemasons must place their hand on *The Book of Revelation*, often called the Revelation to John, the Apocalypse of John, The Revelation, or simply Revelation or Apocalypse, which is a very revealing part of the New Testament, and possibly the only one still retaining some important references about the interdimensional alien overlords. The Book of Revelation teaches of three evil spirits, who are demons, who look like frogs. Frogs and grey aliens, both have large eyes, and similar facial features. It says these three frog-like demons will gather the kings of the world together for the battle of Armageddon, against Jesus Christ before His return. Some passages of note:

Rev 16:12-21: *The sixth angel poured out his bowl on the great river Euphrates, and its water was dried up to prepare the way for the kings from the East. Then I saw three evil spirits that looked like frogs; they came out of the mouth of the dragon, out of the mouth of the beast and out of the mouth of the false prophet. They are spirits of demons performing miraculous signs, and they go out to the kings of the whole world, to gather them for the battle on the great day of God Almighty. Jesus says, "Behold, I come like a thief! Blessed is he who stays awake and keeps his clothes with him, so that he may not go naked and be shamefully exposed." Then they gathered the kings together to the place that in Hebrew is called Armageddon. The seventh angel poured out his bowl into the air, and out of the temple came a loud voice from the throne, saying, It is done!? Then there came flashes of lightning, rumblings, peals of thunder and a severe earthquake. No earthquake like it has ever occurred since man has been on earth, so tremendous was the quake. The great city split into three parts, and the cities of the nations collapsed. God remembered Babylon the Great and gave her the cup filled with the wine of the fury of his wrath. Every island fled away and the mountains could not be found. From the sky huge hailstones of about a hundred pounds each fell upon men. And they cursed God on account of the plague of hail, because the plague was so terrible.*

(Two chapters on the details of Babylon's destruction follow, there is praise to God, and it is said that the time of the wedding of the Lamb has come, and then...)

Rev 19:11: *I saw heaven standing open and there before me was a white horse, whose rider is called Faithful and True. With justice he judges and makes war. His*

2   *See* George C. Andrews, *Extra-Terrestrial Friends and Foes, Ibid.*, p.100.

eyes are like blazing fire, and on his head are many crowns. He has a name written on him that no one knows but he himself. He is dressed in a robe dipped in blood, and his name is the Word of God. The armies of heaven were following him, riding on white horses and dressed in fine linen, white and clean. Out of his mouth comes a sharp sword with which to strike down the nations. "He will rule them with an iron scepter." He treads the winepress of the fury of the wrath of God Almighty. On his robe and on his thigh he has this name written: KING OF KINGS AND LORD OF LORDS. And I saw an angel standing in the sun, who cried in a loud voice to all the birds flying in midair, "Come, gather together for the great supper of God, so that you may eat the flesh of kings, generals, and mighty men, of horses and their riders, and the flesh of all people, free and slave, small and great." Then I saw the beast and the kings of the earth and their armies gathered together to make war against the rider on the horse and his army. But the beast was captured, and with him the false prophet who had performed the miraculous signs on his behalf. With these signs he had deluded those who had received the mark of the beast and worshiped his image. The two of them were thrown alive into the fiery lake of burning sulfur. The rest of them were killed with the sword that came out of the mouth of the rider on the horse, and all the birds gorged themselves on their flesh.

After the fall of Babylon, Jesus will come again. It is right before this time that the three frog-like demons will deceptively lead all the kings of the world to Armageddon. So who are the three evil demon spirits that look like frogs? What we can understand is that these evil spirits gather people together to war against Jesus before he returns. The people that are preparing to war against Jesus are not Christians. Also, they are preparing to war against Him before He returns. How do they know Jesus is about to return? If they are being gathered together to war, it must mean they think they will have someone to fight—yet Jesus hasn't returned yet. And do these people know it is Jesus they are preparing to war against? No matter what they think of Jesus, they are not Christians, and their view of Jesus must be negative.

Let's review some facts about evil spirits, or demons. Demons don't have bodies, and they cannot materialize physically. Bodies are something that indicate fallen angels. Yet here demons are said to look like frogs. People can't see demons, so how could a demon look like a frog? In order for a demon to be seen, it would have to be in the body of a person or animal. In this case, the animal that they describe is a frog. So let's say these three demons were inside of and controlling three frogs. How likely do you think it is, that people would follow three frogs to gather for war? Would an army of humans let themselves be led by three actual demon-possessed frogs? These frogs would be doing (deceptive) signs and wonders, under the power of Satan and his fallen angels, but it still seems unlikely that people would let themselves be led by three frogs into battle, no matter the circumstances. It sounds as convincing as a fairy tale, for the kings of the earth to be led to battle by three demon-possessed frogs that seem to be working (false) miracles and wonders.

But note that John doesn't say the three evil spirits "are three frogs." He says they *"looked like frogs."* So assuming they are not frogs, what else might these demons be aside from an actual frog? Let's say that John was shown in his *Revelation* vision an image of something he had never seen before. Let's say he saw a body that was of no known animal that he was familiar with, and obviously to him was not a man either. It makes sense that if John didn't know what this creature was, and had never seen anything like it, that he would describe it as *"looking like"* something he was familiar with. John chose a frog. But if John had never seen this creature before, that doesn't mean we never have. Closer to Jesus' return in a more linear time than John, and closer to *The Book of Revelation* being fulfilled, it stands to reason that we may have become familiar with this frog-like creature, even though John was not. Is there any creature today that is a familiar image to us, which John would have never seen before? Is there some creature that if we had to describe it as looking like a known animal, we would choose to say it looks like a frog? Is there perhaps something we call by another name, because we have been taught to for whatever reason, but if we had never seen or heard of it before, and we had to describe it, we would say it looks like a frog? I propose that the culturally common image of a "grey alien" looks much like a frog. [3]

Interestingly enough, Crowley's ritual of claiming the grade and role of Magus of the Aeon for the Illuminati of the A∴A∴ saw him symbolically consecrating a frog as Jesus Christ, then killing it. (And it didn't rise again!). He said it was his formula of killing the power of Christianity and the old aeon, but it hides much more.

THE CRUCIFIED FROG AND THE ALIEN APOCALYPSE

*C*rowley performed *Liber L X X – The Cross of a Frog* on July 17th, of 1916 during his retreat to Lake Pasquaney, (now Newfound Lake) in New Hampshire.

This is the opening of the ritual:

STAUROS BATRACHOU,

the Ceremonies proper to obtaining

a familiar spirit of a Mercurial

nature as described in the

Apocalypse of St. John the Divine

from a frog or toad

STAUROS BATRACHOU

He had crucified a toad

In thee basilisk abode,

Muttering the Runes averse

Mad with many a mocking curse.

Aleister Crowley mentions clearly what seems to be the recipe to invoke an alien spirit of a Mercurial nature, and indicates as the basis for this weird ritual the *Apocalypse of St. John the Divine.* Something truly strange and alien is going on with this ritual where: *The Chief Officer representeth a Snake, because of Mercury. (the proper food for snakes is frogs.) The Mystery of Conception is the catching of the frog in silence, and the affirmation of the Will to perform this ceremony.*

---

3   *See* http://paradoxbrown.com/aliensinthebookofrevelation.htm/ ‡ Archived 11th December, 2017.

First of all, let's keep in mind Snake worship is typical of the devotion to serpent deities, and this tradition is present in several ancient cultures. Some Jinn in Islamic mythology are described as alternating between human and serpentine forms, and the Serpent is a character from the *Genesis* creation narrative, occasionally depicted with legs, and sometimes identified with Satan. Remember, when Crowley is talking to us, he is using a coded Illuminati language, that permits him to talk freely about his interdimensional Satanic beliefs and practices. These three demons we find in *The Book of Revelation*, who look like "grey aliens" are specified to come out of the mouth of the Beast, Dragon, and False Prophet. This is symbolic of speaking these creatures into being. When God spoke in Genesis, the universe came into being, with the words that came out of the mouth of God. In a dark parallel, it seems that Satan, the Beast from the Sea, and the False Prophet, will speak them into being, or create these animal-monsters. And then the kings of the earth will follow these three "grey aliens" to battle, and be deceived.

In fact, they will be following three demon-possessed genetically engineered animal-monsters, but it seems they will believe they are "aliens," biological extraterrestrials from outer space. Among all the visible paranormal activities that are going on today, including ghosts, fairies, Bigfoot, orbs, and many others, it is the Alien phenomenon that stands out as unique. Out of all the activities of demons and fallen angels today, it is the alien phenomenon that is mentioned in The Book of Revelation, showing great Biblical prophetic significance. [4] Not surprisingly, "The Beast 666" became the pseudonym of Crowley, who earlier, in December 1909, with Victor Benjamin Neuberg (1883-1940), went to Bou Saada, a town and municipality in M'Sila Province, Algeria, situated 245 km south of Algiers, and from there in the middle of the desert proceeded to the call of the tenth *Aethyr*, called *Zax*, evoking Choronzon, also known as 333, Lord of Hallucinations, one of the most feared umbrood in existence:

> First let the scribe be seated in the center of the circle in the desert sand, and let the circle be fortified by the Holy Names of God—Tetragrammaton and Shaddai El Chai and Ararita. And let the Demon be invoked within a triangle, wherein is inscribed the name of Choronzon, and about it let him write ANAPHAXETON—ANAPHANETON—PRIMEUMATON, and in the angles MI-CA-EL4: and at each angle the Seer shall slay a pigeon, and having done this, let him retire to a secret place, where is neither sight nor hearing, and sit within his black robe, secretly invoking the Aethyr. And let the Scribe perform the Banishing Rituals of the Pentagram and Hexagram, and let him call upon the Holy Names of God, and say the Exorcism of Honorius, and let him beseech protection and help of the Most High.

This magical operation was done between 2 o'clock and 4.15 in the afternoon to open the gates of the underworld. As Crowley points out in note 11 of the commentary to his magical text, *The Vision and the Voice (Liber 418)*, in which he explains that the words in question were even used by Adam to open the gates of hell. This was the ultimate aim of Crowley's magical operation, which seems to have achieved some success in his terrible mission.

Victor Benjamin Neuberg, who attended and assisted *Frater Perdurabo* (Crowley's Initiatic Name in the A∴A∴) in his ritual, reported that Crowley put himself inside the triangle of the invocation deliberately positioning himself from any

---

4   *Ibid.*

protection. Thus defying every common sense, ready to attract the deeds of the gods on himself. Neuburg had been initiated earlier by Crowley in the A∴A∴ taking the initiatic name of *Frater Omnia Vincam,* realizing perhaps too late the true evil intentions of his diabolical Master and lover. Crowley on that occasion wanted not only to open the gates of hell for humanity but also wanted to allow his own possession of the evoked demon. This a secret and very dangerous practice defined by the Illuminati as a ***controlled possession***. Crowley did this so that he could fully become the 666 announced in the Book Revelation.

Neuburg never managed to describe with precision and lucid mentality the apocalyptic and scary visions to which his master had been subjected to that afternoon, and the experience in question left him scarred for life, later breaking his relationship with Crowley in 1914. On that day, in a crazy sequence of events, Crowley was possessed by the entity that Sir Edward Kelly, assistant to celebrity John Dee, defined as the first and the most dangerous of the powers of evil. Crowley apparently turned momentarily dark, assuming in the process various sullen forms during the ritual. At one point Crowley was transformed into a naked and voluptuous woman, while the demon swirled with fluid and obscene inhumanity from his mouth, he would vomit satanic anger and absolute hate towards poor Neuburg, pervading the atmosphere with shameful and brutal curses. After a period of time that probably appeared infinite, to poor Neuburg, Crowley returned to normal.

However, Crowley/Choronzon's behavior during the ritual did not only cover the topos of the infernal ranks to which this demon traditionally belongs, but also the Jinn of the Islamic tradition. The ability to change form to seduce and deceive man as Choronzon is one of the most visible characteristics of Jinn, and more generally of the fairy trickster, but also of some specific divinities. Fairies have often been noted for their mischief and malice. Some pranks ascribed to them, such as tangling the hair of sleepers into "Elf-locks," stealing small items, or leading a traveler astray, are generally harmless. But far more dangerous behaviors are also attributed to fairies.

Any form of sudden death might stem from a fairy kidnapping, with the apparent corpse being a wooden stand-in with the appearance of the kidnapped person.

Consumption (tuberculosis) was sometimes blamed on the fairies, forcing young men and women to dance at revels every night, causing them to waste away from lack of rest. Fairies riding domestic animals, such as cows, could cause paralysis or mysterious illnesses. Due to belief in fairies as tricksters, a considerable lore developed regarding ways to protect oneself from their mischief,[5] but they are also related to the phenomenon of the dimensional portals. Humor, laughter, and irony pervade the adventures of the extra-dimensional Trickster, even the cruelest ones have at times shown an amorous appearance, from which animals or men are mumbled, even if they cause their death. Similarly, the demon Choronzon explains to Neuburg that *he laughs as he kills.* The demon also warns those who evoke him of his destructive fury, but he can also give certain forms of knowledge to the endearing wizard as an obvious reward.

From this contractual form, *do ut des* (Latin for *I give that you may give)* often

---

5   *See* http://www.newworldencyclopedia.org/entry/Fairy ‡ Archived 11th December, 2017.

said or written in magic for sacrifices, when one *gives* and expects something back from the gods. In the case of Crowley, however, there was no deception from the trickster in question, as Crowley was sent to the desert in that distant December 1909, with a specific mission by the Secret Chiefs, after rediscovering in a drawer six months earlier, in June 1909, the sacred text of the future New Age religion, the controversial writing is known as *The Book of the Law,* which was transmitted to him in 1904 by the alien praeter-human entity named Aiwass, a messenger of Horus that occult experts identify with Lucifer, and some of Crowley's successors say was an extraterrestrial entity. Alexandra Owen, Professor of History and Gender Studies, and a social and cultural historian specializing in nineteenth and twentieth-century Britain explains that despite that Crowley rejected originally the teachings received in *The Book of the Law* in 1904, they came back dramatically years later before his trip to North Africa. Crowley stated that he found the manuscript of *The Book of the Law* lost in the attic in his home of Boleskine shortly before Victor Neuburg emerged from his Magical Retirement. Crowley was significantly struck by the sudden reappearance of his manuscript from 1904, almost like a lightning strike had suddenly hit him. Taking the ground under his feet and forcing him into two days of meditation. He emerged with a clear understanding that the Secret Chiefs wanted to impose on him this new mission. [6]

Crowley was constrained by the clauses dictated by the entity five years earlier, to take back that pseudo-sacred text, that from then on he would start promoting within the Western Initiatic System as the basis for his new religion of Thelema, the religion of the Illuminati now so popular in Hollywood. This was done originally in Germany, where part of the O.T.O. was born, but also The Order of the Illuminati of Adam Weishaupt, and earlier on the Rosicrucians. With his new religious mission, he created in the following year's strong dissensions, and schisms within the world of the Illuminati, that even brought to life a non-Thelemic version of the O.T.O. (ie non-Crowleyan), that developed with some success in Switzerland, where it eventually died out in the first decade of the new millennium, due to a lack of funding and the increasing pressure of the O.T.O. in the USA.

UFONAUTS AND THE SECRET CIPHER OF THE ILLUMINATI

*A*llen H. Greenfield (born 1946), is a high-level contemporary Illuminati and illuminist, who was elected to the mystical episcopate of the Neopythagorean Gnostic Assembly in both 1986, and 1994, and further consecrated within the *Ordo Templi Orientis* (O.T.O.) by Frater Superior William Breeze in 1987, and later again by David Scriven "Sabazius," by their mysterious Grand Master for North America. Greenfield has long parted ways with the O.T.O., in favor of what is described as a broadly-based free illuminist movement. His episcopal title "Tau" is sometimes abbreviated as "T" and prefixed to his legal name, thus he may also be referred to as **T Allen Greenfield**. A former member of the *Ordo Templi Orientis* and editor of the Eulis Lodge journal *LASHTAL*, Greenfield has more recently become a critic of the Order's upper management. In February 2006, he called for their resignation and stepped down from all man-

---

6   See Alex Owen, *The book The Place of Enchantment: British Occultism and the Culture of the Modern,* (Chicago: The University of Chicago Press, 2004), p. 213.

agerial duties in protest, issuing a strong criticism of the current Outer Head of the Order, William Breeze. [7] Allen H. Greenfield states in his official blog:

I was consecrated by Tau Silenus, William Gary Keith Breeze in Brooklyn NY on November 19, 1988. I cross consecrated with Tau Apiryon, David Forrest Scriven in Atlanta GA December 10, 1993. I was reconsecrated by Scriven, Lynn Scriven (Soror Helena) assisting at the Scriven home in Riverside, California May 25, 1997. Allen Greenfield was Elected to the Episcopate by the Holy Synod of the Neopythagorean Gnostic Church August 21, 1986, He was consecrated by Patriarch Bertiaux in Chicago IL USA December 4 1993. Please note that, as Tau Michael Bertiaux has held, since June 16, 1979, all major independent lines of the traditional apostolic succession through consecration at that time by Bishop Forest Gregory Barber, all such lines flow to me by virtue of my consecrations by Bertiaux. Bertiaux, later reconsecrated by Jorge Rodriguez, then also consecrated me. In line with MY FORMER ASSOCIATES AT "O.T.O.'s" Ecclesia Gnostica Catholica, Patriarch Tau Silenus and Primate Tau Apiryon, I hold that there is a distinction between, on the one hand, Spiritual Appointment and Consecration in the lineage of Edward Alexander Crowley (Baphomet 33 * 90* 96* XI° MA&P R MM) and, on the other, the traditional Apostolic Succession. Both have their importance and validity.

The issue is the passage of egregore and empowerment, not any particular faith or creed. In my view, and, in having held both, I believe I can render a rather well informed and detached opinion on this. I held the succession of Baphomet as a Bishop "now and forever" through Consecration by both the Absolute Grand Patriarch of the **Ordo Templi Orientis Ecclesia Gnostica Catholica** *(November 19, 1988 Brooklyn NY). While I am no longer associated with E.G.C.-O.T.O., I hold with the Augustinian doctrine "once a bishop-always a bishop" though I claim—and would have—no authority within O.T.O. as of late July, 2006. As Tau Silenus recognized me in writing unconditionally as Bishop in writing prior to my becoming an O.T.O. initiate, I maintain I hold the succession of Baphomet, such as it is. Others are free to disagree; nobody questions my Full Apostolic Succession, which is what counts magically. The "Baphomet descent" doctrine peculiar to the current O.T.O. management was, in my opinion, a reaction to questions about their own Apostolic Succession, and nothing more, a silly overreaction typical of them. I also hold the Latter Day Saints succession (Restored Apostolic Church of Jesus Christ of Immaculate Latter-day Saints) through Bishop William Conway, and the Doinel Succession through various consecrations. The Honorary Title of "Rabbi" was recently also given me by the Fellowship Assembly, which I accept in the sense of being a "teacher of spirituality" in the Reform Jewish tradition.* [8]

In Greenfield's book *Secret Cipher of the UFOnauts,* released for the first time in the mid-1990s, he revealed to the world what is possibly at the heart of the UFO mystery, with the discovery of hidden Secret Ciphers and Rituals used by UFOnauts, Contactees, Occult Adepts and Secret Chiefs, who have maintained communication with these mysterious Ultraterrestrial beings, who control forces almost totally beyond our comprehension, with human adepts, stretching from

7   *See* https://en.wikipedia.org/wiki/Allen_H._Greenfield ‡ Archived 11th December, 2017.

8   *See* https://allengreenfield.wordpress.com/2016/01/29/masonic-dignities-egregoric-successions-updated-january-29-2016-ce/ ‡ Archived 11th December, 2017.

remote antiquity to the present moment.[9] These secrets include the infamous vampirism operated by the grey aliens, and how to resist it in their physical examinations, were developed within the Illuminati organizations inspired by **Frater Achad**, also known as **Frater Parzifal**, real name **Charles Robert John Stansfeld Jones (1886-1950)**, one of the early leaders of the O.T.O in North America. Again, according to Greenfield, these revelations would be compatible with the secret teachings of the Theosophical "**Great White Brotherhood**," in the ways of communicating with these interdimensional aliens, which, unfortunately, are seldom benevolent, and more often vampire parasites. Greenfield writes:

> *These terms are consistent with the inner secret teachings of the Great White Brotherhood. The terms also provide a clue, as noted, as to how to do battle with the UFOnauts. As others have remarked, UFOnauts frequently use bizarre forms of sexuality in their physical examinations or probes on humans, in order to obtain certain secretions of a physical, emotional and even spiritual nature.[10]*

Regarding the dark forces at work, to stop you from learning the truth about the UFO phenomenon and their alien overlords, Greenfield adds:

> *Often when a person or institution allied with the historical Great White Brotherhood approaches success (variously defined) or comes into possession of certain aspects of transcendent wisdom, Something Intervenes. That "something" has been defined as the Man in Black, the Men In Black, the black lodges, or The Black Lodge. The latter term most nearly accommodates my own view. That they need to do this, and that they often fail in their efforts, is itself an indication that (A) the Black Lodge is opposed by Something Else, equally as strong, and (B) they are afraid of something we might find out—about them, about their opposition, about ourselves or all three. The story of our interaction with the UFOnauts begins with the Qabalistic Tree of Life and the Chakra system of the body. According to the primal occult and frequently secret and subversive view, the manifest universe emerges from an Ultimate NOT-Thing, a Consciousness or Beingness beyond words or expressions sometimes referred to as the Unmanifest or The Limitless Light. Limitless Light. This Unmanifest cannot be understood in the external sense but can be Known in the Gnostic sense by the initiate or perfected sentient being, the Ubermensch. It can be plugged into. For reasons equally inexpressible, this uniqueness unfolds itself in manifestation. Thus, the limitless light becomes a series of emanations or expressions or Intelligence that devolve increasingly toward our material form of existence and thus towards accessibility in the conventional sense. But the manifestations also increasingly become subject to subdivision into arbitrary concepts such as "good" and "evil" as these are commonly understood. And they also become closer and closer in form and content to our own mundane reality, though in the relativity of things, these Higher Intelligence may seem unspeakably powerful, mythic and divine. The Gnostic view has tended to be that what the external world of the conventional person understands as god, devil demon, angel or, more recently, extraterrestrial beings are, in fact, such emanations of the unspeakable ultimate.[11]*

---

9   *See* http://www.paranoiamagazine.com/2016/07/complete-secret-cipher-ufonauts/ ‡ Archived 11th December, 2017.

10   Allen H. Greenfield, *Secret Cipher of the UFOnauts* (Los Angeles, CA: IllumiNet Press, 1994), p. 55.

11   *Ibid.*, pp. 58-59.

Greenfield, explains that one of the central figures in exposing this Secret Cipher of the UFOnauts was Aleister Crowley, but it was perfected by Crowley's "magical son," Charles Stansfeld Jones, aka Frater Achad, who partially deciphered and transmitted it to his own disciples. Frater Achad was at that time one of the highest representatives of the Illuminati of the *Ordo Templi Orientis* in North America. Crowley and Frater Achad (a Jesuits agent), frequently discussed entities and the importance of the Ouija board, as it is often mentioned in their unpublished letters. Throughout 1917, Achad experimented with the board as a means of summoning mainly what he described as Angels, as opposed to Elementals. Frater Achad was a high-level occultist and exemplary ceremonial magician, known also as *Tantalus Leucocephalus*, after reaching the Tenth Degree of the O.T.O. However, he was eventually kicked out and later expelled from the O.T.O., after holding the supreme post of Grand Master of British Columbia, considered at that time the Grand Master for the whole of North America, for the relatively small O.T.O. Crowley expelled him after he became more and more involved and absorbed by another Secret Society, that is said to be run by the infamous Jesuits, the **Universal Brotherhood** (U.B.).

In 1921, Jones joined the Universal Brotherhood (U.B.), also known to its members as the Integral Fellowship, or as the Mahacakra Society (or M.), depending on the level of participation. This group was actively recruiting among Theosophists for a decade or more, in a period of time when the powerful Society of Jesus took over the Theosophical Society, and Charles Stansfeld Jones was one of a number of prominent Thelemites who eventually joined them.

The methods of the U.B. involved one-to-one correspondence, with an elaborate set of rules regarding strict secrecy of instructions, envelopes-within-envelopes, purple typewriter ribbons, and special paperclips. It is said that aspirants were provided with typescript lectures ("sutras") on metaphysical topics, using idiosyncratic terms like "integrality" and "partitivity." A system of alms provided for funds to be remitted back up the same chain from which these instructions descended. Organizational titles and pseudonyms in the U.B. were generally taken from Sanskrit. To this day, few if any of the U.B. writings have become accessible to non-members, and suggest that their doctrines *involved a baroquely intellectualized form of sentimental monotheism.*

In 1924, Charles Stansfeld Jones was superintending about 70 members of U.B., and formed a plan for subsuming Thelema into the U.B. as a Grama or Integral Body, which would perpetuate some O.T.O. and A∴A∴ materials in their pure form. He communicated this idea to **O.T.O. member Wilfred T. Smith (1885-1957) Frater Velle Omnia Velle Nihil (aka Fra. 132),** who was at that time his subordinate in both the U.B. and A∴A∴, but Smith's interest in the U.B. was slight and waning, he was more interested in launching the O.T.O. in Hollywood, as he eventually did after renting 1746 Winona Boulevard. His marketing choice was indeed the right one in light of today's O.T.O success in Hollywood. In the meantime, Annie Besant, as head of the Theosophical Society, strictly forbade cross-membership in the U.B., knowing of the Jesuit involvement, and as Crowley became aware of the involvement of his followers with this Catholic Order, he likewise denounced the U.B., calling it a "swindle" in correspondence with Charles Stansfeld Jones. Confirming the Jesuit nature of this operation is the fact that many of those who left the Theosophical Society for the U.B. under pressure from Besant, converted later to Roman Catholicism. In 1928, Jones himself, *Frater Achad,* became a staunch Roman Catholic, undergoing baptism and confirmation into the laity of the Church. At roughly the same time, he succeeded to the U.B. office of **Mahaguru**, thus becoming the Grand Master of this Illuminati Jesuit controlled organization. Jones continued to hold that office, apparently until his death. Jones was succeeded as Mahaguru by John P. Kowal (1900-1978).

The true aim of the U.B. remains obscure, but it has been accused by Wilfred T. Smith, of acting as a front for Roman Catholic infiltration of occult groups, and by former member Paul Foster Case, the founder of the B.O.T.A. (*Builders of the Adytum*) **of being inspired by the Bavarian Illuminati.** Mahaguru John P. Kowal told Martin Starr that its purpose was "*to make men think.*" [12]

But in reality, it was a Secret Society created and financed by the Catholic Church and its Jesuits, to infiltrate and manipulate the increasingly influential Theosophical Society and other occult groups of the Anglo-Saxon world, such as the Crowleyan O.T.O. or the Golden Dawn. Reality is much better than any so-called "Conspiracy Theory." The Jesuits, during their infiltration of the theosophical world, had obviously seen the potential of Frater Achad, and his vast knowledge of the occult was considered powerful, and at the same time dangerous.

Crowley was not the first responsible for the decryption of this ancestral Secret Cipher created for the defense of the initiates, but his disciple who was one of the greatest Kabbalah experts of the time outside of the Jewish world, developed it further, creating waves in the occult world. Frater Achad understood, like his disciples after him, the importance of a specific passage to be found in Chapter II, verse 76, of *The Book of the Law.* This is the passage in question composed of the following alpha-numeric glyphs:

4638ABK24ALGMOR3Y X2489RPSTOVA L.

In this formula, there is a hidden and secret formula for alien contact devised by the Illuminati.

However the use of this mysterious alpha-numerical cipher, found in *The Book of the Law,* was never specified by Crowley, who allowed Frater Achad, he once considered his Magical Child, to find and unveil the mysteries behind this secret cipher in relation to the mysterious supernatural **entity** or "**praeterhuman**" named **Aiwass**. In *Magick in Theory and Practice*, Aiwass is firmly identified by Crowley as; The Devil, Satan, and Lucifer, whose emblem is Baphomet. Greenfield asserts that:

The Cipher contained in **Liber AL** *is indeed the secret code of the initiates of 19th century magick and occultism, and the Cipher of the UFOnauts themselves. Much is to be said for the revisionist historical notion, best expounded by Paul Johnson* (In Search of the Masters), *that Theosophical "Mahatmas" and magical "Secret Chiefs" are very human Adepts deeply enmeshed in the spiritual and political revolutions of the late 19th and early 20th centuries. Madame Blavatsky may indeed have been the first to change the names to protect the adept, but the fact that they can be decoded via the Ciphers of AL—revealed by Aiwass years after Blavatsky's death—indicates perhaps a secret*

---

12   *See* http://en.wikipedia.org/wiki/Charles_Stansfeld_Jones ‡ Archived 11th December, 2017.

code known to Blavatsky and later to Crowley and his heirs. As I have pointed out, the basic documents of the Hermetic Order of the Golden Dawn, for example, were written in a cipher, the originals still being readily available. I have also pointed out that all Royal Arch Masons were (and are) taught a cipher, since frequently reprinted. If there was a common occult cipher, it seems to have emerged in the world of mediumship. The cipher continues in the similar world of UFO contacteeism and trance channeling, which resembles mediumship as well as extraterrestrialism. [13]

As written in Volume I of my *Confessions*, the UFO contactees emerged as a distinct branch of mediumship in the 1940s, [14] initially in Meade Layne's Borderland Sciences Research FOUNDATION (BSRF), and later all over the occult world, but don't forget, Layne is another product of Theosophy and the O.T.O. Layne is in fact, described by Greenfield as: *"An exemplary person, a student of Aleister Crowley's prodigal son Charles Stansfeld Jones (Frater Achad), and, from the 1940s, one of the saner, more decent sorts that occupied the more esoteric side of UFOlogy."*

A MEMORANDUM OF IMPORTANCE was generated within **Borderland Sciences Research Associates** (BSRA), in San Diego, that eventually became one of the infamous UFO documents buried in The Vault, which is the new Freedom of Information Act (FOIA) library launched by the FBI in 2011, featuring searchable dossiers on characters and topics wide-ranging from the 9/11 hijackers to Al Capone, and **Marilyn Monroe**, all the way to alleged UFO sightings.

Returning to the Secret Cipher, Greenfield says that despite being accurately concealed by Crowley's "Magickal Childe," it was rediscovered and fully understood by his disciples in the early 70s. Greenfield describes the events that lead to the full disclosure of the *Secret Cipher of the UFOnauts*:

Crowley was a master occultist, though, is certainly true. Central to our premise is a single occult event in which Crowley, then on an extended honeymoon with his wife Rose in Cairo, acted as a scribe in the transcription of what purports to be a Holy Book for the New Aeon, known as Liber AL vel Legis, or **The Book of the Law.** *Liber AL in some ways follows the same pattern as Newborough's* **Oahspe** *or* **The Book of Mormon.** *It differs in its outlook, the richness of its poetry, and, for our purposes, in one other way. It refers to an internal cipher or secret code which, it predicts, Crowley himself would never transcribe. Predicted, however, is its deciphering by another, who turned out to be Crowley's magical child and one-time heir-apparent, Charles Stansfeld Jones a.k.a. Frater Achad. Achad, in his* **Book 31,** *does indeed find the key to the code, but 70 years passed before a full transcription of the code was made. In the original handwritten manuscript of* **The Book of the Law,** *a single page is inexplicably overlaid with a grid, a line, and an enigmatic mark sometimes referred to as a "Rose Cross," although it looks much like one of the four keys to the Royal Arch Masonic Cipher.* **Liber AL** *was dictated in 1904, according to Crowley, by a præterhuman—some of his successors say extraterrestrial—intelligence calling itself Aiwass. Long after both Achad and Crowley were dead, one Carol Smith and a group in England calling itself the OAA fully deciphered the code. Another 10 years were to pass before a member of OAA's American counterpart, Frater Lamed of QBLH, was to apply computer technology to*

13   Allen Greenfield *Secret Cipher of the UFOnauts, Ibid.* p. 36, [emphasis added].

14   *See* Leo Lyon Zagami, *Confessions of an Illuminati Volume I*, (San Francisco, CA: CCCPublishing) pp. 256-257.

*the cipher solution and produce Lexicon, a computer program that provides a vast, powerful tool for deciphering the code of **Liber AL**, as well as many variants.* [15]

In 1974, after 70 years from the reception of *The Book of the Law*, a cipher solution consistent with all the clues in *The Book of the Law* was actually discovered: *"A key has been left by Crowley, under the direction of Aiwass,"* wrote Carol Smith in 1980, *"in order that Thou shalt obtain the Order and Value of the English Alphabet (Ch.1 V.55) The instruction is in Ch.III V.47, This shall be translated into all tongues but always with the originals in the writing of the beast; for in the chance shape of the letters and their position to one another; in these are mysteries no beast shall divine."* [16]

Allen H Greenfield sums up the importance of this discovery in the last four points outlined in the basic premise of his book, (consisting of a total of eleven points):

8) Crowley's "magical son" Frater Achad did partially decipher the code, but it remained for Carol Smith in 1974 to solve it, and for software programmer, Frater Lamed to make it readily accessible to investigators in the 1980s.

9) The UFOnauts themselves use the cipher when they gve names to themselves, their home planets, etc. They know the case will be reported, and the keywords will be communicated to the Illuminati.

10) Since I applied the cipher to such keywords, the code is now completely accessible to UFOlogists and others. The cipher can help analyze cases, predict manifestations and trace the UFOnauts to their very doorsteps, and yes, they DO have doorsteps.

11) As soon as the UFOnauts and Illuminati know the knowledge of the cipher is widespread, the code will change again. Evidence shows it is already changing. [17]

A **secret cipher of the Illuminati** would transform one from the status of "abductee" into potential "contactist," ready to collaborate with such entities, thus eliminating the dangers of any possible contact with interdimensional entities we commonly refer to as aliens. You may have noticed from the words above, Greenfield also warns that as soon as the secret is publicly revealed, the code may be subject to immediate change: *"Evidence shows it is already changing."* Regarding the importance of Jesuit agent Frater Achad and his present role in the pseudo-religion of Thelema, Greenfield writes: *"The present O.T.O. Grand Master, Hymenaeus Beta, for example, acknowledges that ... his Liber XXXI held the key to The Book of the Law ... While his Qabalistic teachings are sometimes 'unorthodox' ... they are unfailingly self-consistent."* Indeed, in recent years, there has been some effort by orthodox Thelemites to posthumously rehabilitate Achad whose decidedly unorthodox views led to a permanent break with Crowley in 1919. In 1948, Achad further alienated conservative Thelemites—and endeared himself to radicals—by proclaiming the Aeon of Ma, which superseded the Aeon of Horus proclaimed by Crowley in 1904. [18]

---

15   Allen Greenfield, *Ibid.,* p. 21, [**emphasis added**].

16   *Ibid.,* p. 28.

17   *Ibid.,* p. 4.

18   *Ibid.,* p. 53

GREENFIELD, THE ILLUMINATI, AND THE O.T.O./UFO CONTROVERSY

*C*learing the way of understanding on a subject like the possible interdimensional contact of certain Secret Societies we commonly refer to as the Illuminati, is a difficult task, but worth beginning, especially with the study of Greenfield's work. He is a high-level illuminist of various Secret Societies that deal with the contemporary mystery schools devoted to magic. Greenfield is an advocate of what he calls, *Congregational Illuminism,* a term he created to describe: *"pre-existing and emergent phenomena of a decentralized network of groups and individuals interested in illumination working together in free association. Use of the term was not made without also being mindful of the Congregationalist movement, Protestant Christian churches practicing Congregationalist church governance, in which each congregation independently and autonomously runs its own affairs. The decentralized bottom-up nature is said to be traced back to anarcho-syndicalism, to certain Protestant Sects such as the Levelers and True Levelers in Britain at the time of the English Civil War, and denominations such as the Society of Friends. Other influences on the structure include the democracy of Freemasonry as practiced in the USA, the 'Golden Path' described in the* Dune *series by Frank Herbert, the decentralism of the egregore in the Gnostic community and the independent lines of Apostolic Succession."*

It might seem a bit too New Age and liberal, but of course, the dark side of the Illuminati is made up of demented beliefs such as; anarco-syndacalism or the supposed *decentralism of the egregore in the Gnostic community;* values of the Satanic New Age that illuminist Greenfield is willing to promote worldwide with his **Congregational Illuminist Movement (Free Illuminati Bodies).** They are physically based in Atlanta, Georgia, USA, thanks to a new alliance officially sealed on May 18th, 2016, with the powerful and dark Illuminati of the **United Traditionalist Grand Sanctuaries of the Ancient and Primitive Rite of Memphis & Misraim (U.T.G.S.).** This is a group controlled by Most Illustrious Brother Dr. Nicolas Laos, 33° 95° 97° Grand Hierophant-General (also Grand Master the *Societas Masonica Illuminatorum*), that describes his organization operating internationally from Greece, in the following way, confirming his relationship to the infamous Bavarian Illuminati: *"The United Traditionalist Grand Sanctuaries of the Ancient and Primitive Rite of Memphis & Misraim (U.T.G.S.) is intimately related to the legacy of the Bavarian Illuminati. The term 'Illuminati' (plural of Latin 'Illuminatus,' enlightened) usually refers to the Bavarian Illuminati, an esoteric society founded on 1 May, 1776 by Adam Weishaupt, who was the first lay professor of Canon Law at the University of Ingolstadt. The Order of the Illuminati was modeled on Freemasonry, and it was made up of freethinkers. Given that, by the middle of the eighteenth century, many Freemasonic Orders had been placed under the control of authoritarian social elites and Royal Houses and many Freemasons had developed a petit-bourgeois mentality, Adam Weishaupt attempted to politicize the humanist ethos of Freemasonry by creating a new esoteric society whose members would be capable of contemplating the political ramifications of Freemasonry and Rosicrucianism and of promoting humanism and freedom. According to the instructions for the Degree of Regent, if the Order of the Illuminati cannot establish itself in any particular place with all the forms and regular progress of its degree system, it must operate under a cloak of secrecy, and 'the inferior Lodges of Freemasonry are the most convenient cloaks' for the Illuminati's grand object."*[19]

19   http://nicolaslaos.com/wp-content/uploads/2015/09/Founding-International-Treaties-of-the-United-Traditionalist-Grand-Sanctuaries-of-the-Ancient-and-Primitive-Rite-Memphis-Misraim.pdf ‡ Archived 11th December, 2017.

We should pay attention to the recent involvement of Rev. T Allen Bar Kohenim Greenfield, D.D. 33° 95° 97°, with Dr. Nicolas Laos, who is a controversial and influential figure in the Masonic world, connected with the New World Order political arena, as well as British Intelligence, whose primary areas of expertise are: *ontology, epistemology, ethics, philosophical theology, political philosophy, noopolitics, netwar, and cultural diplomacy;* his secondary areas of expertise are *geopolitics, geoeconomics, political economy, organizational behavior, hypergame theory, monotonic and non-monotonic logics, and history of intelligence.* [20] Dr. Nicolas Laos is an expert in esotericism, but also in political economy and the history of intelligence, and lives in a citadel of just under thirty people on the outskirts of Athens. His previous office in London, was at **Wilton Road 95 (SW1V 1 BZ), suite number 3,** a place frequented by numerous Freemasons and members of British Intelligence. Dr. Nicolas Laos makes this shocking statement on his official treaty with Greenfield citing along the way, **The Secret Rituals of the Men in Black:** *"Apart from being an internationally acknowledged authority on the Ancient and Primitive Rite of Memphis & Misraim, T Allen Greenfield is an authoritative researcher in the 'occult.' Some of his conclusions, formulated in his eloquent and metaphorical language, are the following: 'All serious magical rituals are a hidden advanced technology, concealed in a cipher now revealed ... UFOlogy ... has taught me that we humans are, in potential, the most advanced, developed beings in the galaxy ... The Greys, insectoids and other vampiric nightmares from dying stars are here to suck out a little of the life energy that they themselves have so little of, and to delay the inevitable evolution of humanity ... We, as they tell us, and as intercepted cipher messages have told me and all with eyes to see, will someday be the Coming Guardians ourselves.'"* [21]

Now my dear readers you finally have the evidence of an official Masonic document that seems to prove the existence of Greys, insectoids, and other vampiric nightmares from dying stars. You can double check for yourself among the documents listed at *http://nicolaslaos.com*

Greenfield is indeed a lifelong student of esoteric spirituality and Gnosticism, he began studying as far back as 1960. He also had very intense activity as a Ufologist, becoming past (elected) member of the British Society for Psychical Research, the National Investigations Committee on Aerial Phenomena (NICAP) (from 1960), etc., and he has twice been the recipient of the *Ufologist of the Year Award* of the National UFO Conference (1972 and 1992), which has run continuously on an annual basis for 41 years. He is a Borderland Science Research Associate (BSRA), and he has personally conducted on-site UFO abduction investigations in Brooksville, FL; Pascagoula, MS, and Brown Mountain, NC. [22] Greensfield considers the UFO phenomenon to be a "signal" from the Collective Unconscious that the neglect of a magical spirituality by society as a whole, is a cause for emotional plague and social disaster.

In 2006, after twenty years, Greenfield finally resigned his position as a high-level officer of the O.T.O. Caliphate in the United States, declaring in his official statement regarding the *Ordo Templi Orientis:* *"At the end of February 2006, after*

---

20   http://nicolaslaos.com/wp-content/uploads/2015/08/Nicolas-Laos-C.V.1.pdf ‡ Archived 11th December, 2017.

21   *Treaties of the U.T.G.S., Ibid.*

22   http://www.mindspring.com/~hellfire/bishop/ ‡ Archived 11th December, 2017.

much consideration and ample notification of the present management of U.S. Grand Lodge, I resigned from all positions of management held by me at that time in Ordo Templi Orientis." He also added that: *"The O.T.O. has always been rather blasé about its top-heavy autocratic structure, and has gradually moved from the Scientific Illuminism that informed its initiation rituals, and its celebratory ritual, The Gnostic Mass, towards a set of what I see as superstitious beliefs and tendencies. Was this something I could support in the wake of 9/11? I had had doubts before, but now it seemed a legitimate question in the context of what has been called—rightly, in my view—a clash of civilizations."* [23]

Greenfield publicly denounced William Breeze, the Supreme Grand Master of the O.T.O., known as **Hymenaeus Beta,** in his public statement, basically, accusing him of manipulating rituals, centralizing power, and transforming the once glorious Freemasonic School of the O.T.O., into his own personal machine to make money.

Here's another little excerpt to give you a general idea of what the *Ordo Templi Orientis* is really becoming in the hands of the mondialists that control it, not simply as another business venture for their Illuminati empire, but also as the key to their new and perverse religion of Thelema, spreading like a virus, and popular with V.I.P.'s:

> *I had already served the O.T.O. in its current incarnation for nearly twenty years at the time of the attack (Note by author: referring to 9/11), first as a private individual invited by the local body master to organize the **Ecclesia Gnostica Catholica** in the Southern United States, virtually from scratch, then as a Lodge Secretary, sole consecrated resident bishop for many hundreds of miles around, then as Lodge Master, and eventually, for the past decade, as Sovereign Grand Inspector General and Most Wise Sovereign of one of a handful of Chapters of Rose Croix in the world. When the individual elevated to the office of U.S. Grand Master General, Sabazius, chose to make his first VII° full tripartite member, I was the member he chose. I was for some time on good—even intimate—social terms with the Acting Outer Head of the Order, known as Hymenaeus Beta. I have been a guest in the homes of both of these men, as they have been guests in mine.*

> *It is thus not without hesitation that I have come to view their efforts at doing the particular Work uniquely charged to the O.T.O. in its founding and most basic documents, as being a dismal, ill-conceived and ill-executed effort that has brought, under their leadership, the sort of near total failure that has characterized many marginalized societies with pretensions to occult knowledge. The decision to transform an eccentric and radical form of Freemasonic School in the very heart of the authentic esoteric tradition into a rather conventional religious society with an extremely narrow base and zero societal impact was a gradual one, and has had its critics at each level of its deviation from the core program of the society.* [24]

It also seems the O.T.O. did not appreciate his new revelations on Ufology in relation to the Illuminati and the disclosing of secret rituals made in the book following his *Secret Cipher of the UFOnauts,* the one entitled ***Secret Rituals of the Men in Black,*** published in 2005, just a few months before leaving the O.T.O. In

23   http://www.mindspring.com/~hellfire/bishop/statement.htm ‡ Archived 11th December, 2017.

24   http://www.mindspring.com/~hellfire/bishop/statement.htm ‡ Archived 11th December, 2017.

this newer book, which obviously annoyed the O.T.O., Greenfield makes new disconcerting revelations about the practical application of this mysterious secret cipher of the UFOnauts, which is further deepened not only from a historical point of view but also from the ritualistic point of view. Crowley in his channeled interdimensional transmission known as *The Book of the Law* proposes perhaps the most sophisticated version of the cipher and the most elaborated code.

But according to Greenfield, this cipher in various forms, already existed since antiquity, and was secretly transmitted by various mystery schools of the Illuminati network and Freemasonry, especially in the Royal Arch, and in Cryptic Freemasonry, as well as the so-called Egyptian Rituals to which he is particularly linked as a fringe Mason himself. For Greenfield, human beings and adepts have been communicating for a long time with a secret code that we are just beginning to decipher, and because of this all the previous bets on the true nature of our planet's history are now pending. Greenfield writes:

> In *Secret Cipher of the UFOnauts*, I disclosed how the ancient Qabala of Nine Chambers had been employed to develop the English-language Cipher communicated to Royal Arch Masons in the York Rite down to modern times. Looking again into the Ark, the High Priest takes out four pieces of paper, which he examines closely, consults with the King and Scribe, and then puts together, so as to show a KEY to the ineffable characters of this Degree ... The key to the ineffable characters, or Royal Arch Cipher ... consists of right angles, in various situations, with the addition of a dot. By transposition, it forms twenty six distinct characters, corresponding with the twenty six letters of the English Alphabet. That this is built on a structure based on a Qabalistic code formed out of the 22 letters of the Hebrew Alphabet is both extremely clever and indicative of a very long history. The pattern is repeated with other Ciphers in the Masonic System. In the 34th Degree of the Rite of Memphis, The newly made "Knight of Scandinavia" is given a "Runic" cipher. As we show elsewhere in this volume, this Degree is itself built around the Secret Cipher of the UFOnauts and is an allegory for the Visitation of Ultraterrestrial teachers from Sirius in ancient times. Another Cipher is given in the 64°, "Sage of Mythras" one of the oldest and most elaborate of Masonic Degrees. This cipher is similar to the Royal Arch Cipher, and is called the "Ammanian Alphabet." This Degree not only refers to the origins of the Mysteries in the Ultraterrestrial interventions here, but it contains internal evidence that the ritual itself may be of Ultraterrestrial origin! Part of the ritual is conducted in the blue-white light of Sirius, and the "setting" is as in the Tarot Card "The Star" which, as we demonstrate elsewhere, is not our Sun, but a world beneath the Sun-star Sirius. In the Memphis System, there are also ciphers for the 75th Degree and the 90th Degree. The latter alludes to an ancient War between Ultraterrestrial forces for control of the Earth. The cipher is much like that which generated the rituals of the Hermetic Order of the Golden Dawn in the last century. [25]

Greenfield then explains how the secret cipher serves to understand how to disentangle the *Matrix* of the well-known Men in Black, the dangerous "**MIBs**," and in his *Secret Rituals of the Men in Black,* he writes a lot about the various Masonic rituals he himself knows very well, being a high dignitary of Occult

25   See Allen Greenfield, *Secret Rituals of the Men in Black*, Manutius Press, lulu.com 2005.

FIG. 19 In the center of the photo is Dr. Nicolas Laos, between two representatives of the English nobility (photo taken in England in 2009 by an anonymous source).

Masonry, and from the pages of this book he speaks of the thesis of the alien origin of the Craft. Greenfield also states that the MIBs are related to what Crowley also called the **Black Lodge,** that Crowley said has among its bases the Vatican itself. This isn't surprising considering the actual role of the Vatican is at the top of the New World Order, with a Jesuit Pope. It was precisely the infiltration the Jesuits that damaged in the eyes of other occultists, the *Ordo Templi Orientis* of today. Greenfield, who has now joined forces with another side of the diabolical illuminist philosophical and political program of the dark side of the Illuminati, in this latest case based on methexiology, or the philosophy of methexis created by Illuminati Grand Master Nicolas Laos. [26]

GREENFIELD AND ALIEN VAMPIRISM

*T*he *Secret Cipher of the UFOnauts* was delivered to mankind from time immemorial through ritual, the transmission of such knowledge reserved only to a few selected high priests operating within the occult elite since ancient times. Greenfield explains that the highest-ranking public initiate-adept of today was initiated a few years ago in Oslo into his Rite of Memphis Misraïm and his OTO-Version (O.T.O.A.). [27] **Michael Paul Bertiaux** (b. 1935), an American occultist and Old Catholic Bishop, known for his book, Voudon Gnostic Workbook (1988), has long maintained: *"that the (Egyptian) Rite of Mem-*

---

26   See Nicola Laos, *Methexiology: Philosophical Theology and Theological Philosophy for the Deification of Humanity*, (Eugene, Oregon: Wipf and Stock Publishers/Pickwick Publications, 2016).

27   *See* Leo Lyon Zagami, *Confessions of an Illuminati vol.1, Ibid.,* pp. 32, 97.

phis-Misraïm was a 'front' (in a sense) for Ultraterrestrial technology. As a Conservator and Hierophant of a distinct branch of these rites, he would surely know, and our findings, reinforced by extensive 'hands on' knowledge of Masonic and Cryptomasonic ritual as well as the Secret Cipher of the UFOnauts *itself, clearly demonstrates that Bishop Bertiaux's assertion is nothing less than the straightforward truth."*

In Volume I of my *Confessions* series [28] I focus on Sirius, and Greenfield confirms its **sacred technology** for interdimensional travel. He states: *"Legends and lore surrounding **the Star Sirius** figure heavily into our premise. In distant times, in the days of ancient Sumer in Mesopotamia, predynastic Egypt in Africa, Dravidian India and in Mexico long before the Mayans, there is a fairly consistent account of God-like and perhaps amphibious beings from the sky sometimes associated with the Constellations Cancer and Orion, and with **the Star Sirius in the constellation Canis Major, or 'The Great Dog.' They visited Earth**, establishing a nucleus of priest-kings and scientists who have carried forth a secret tradition of contact, communication and Ultraterrestrial overlordship—and rebellion against that overlordship. This tradition is displayed in various rituals through myth and cipher, but, in addition, certain 'sacred technologies' are conveyed for reestablishing communication (should a link be broken), for actual travel to and from Ultraterrestrial realms, and even indicate in minute detail how to effectively resist alien influence."* [29]

For Greenfield, the infamous Men in Black are human only in appearance, while in reality there would also be present the shadow of deadly entities, guarding the system, such as Agent Smith, gatekeeper in the movie *The Matrix*, and Guardian of the Threshold, a menacing figure that is described by a number of esoteric teachers.

When it comes to Satan or Lucifer, there is no moral implication, but only an objective reality. The *Secret Code of the UFOnauts* serves to grant awareness for those who can understand it, and turn off its negative potential. Greenfield finds the secret cipher in the modern *Egyptian Masonic Rite of Memphis*, conferring a secret Degree called **ADEPT OF SIRIUS**, the name of which, decoded using the eleven-fold cipher encrypted in *The Book of the Law*, means SECRET CHIEFS and, also, SECRET MASTER. For Greenfield, the ADEPT OF SIRIUS Degree contains a clue to the great arcane connection between Adepts and Ultraterrestrials. He writes that: *"In the New Aeon Cipher, we discover that ADEPT OF SIRIUS carries the significant cipher value of 192. Scanning our personal cipher directory,* The Book of the Law *and other New Aeon Holy Texts, we find that 192 = FOR THE STARS AND TWO. Sirius is a double star, the smaller white dwarf twin invisible to the ancients but known to the Bambera, Dogon, Bozo, Bandiagara and perhaps other North African tribal peoples even today."* [30]

Returning to the phenomenon of alien vampirism and responsible demonic possession, remember that most channeled beings will claim to be affiliated with the false and so-called light-based Spiritual Hierarchy, which includes archangels, the typical New Age ascended masters, and a wide range of positive

---

28   See *Ibid.*, pp. 30, 33, 35, 66, 67, 232, 233, 234.

29   *Ibid.*

30   *See* Allen H. Greenfield, *The Compleat Rite of Memphis*, (Minneapolis, MN: Luxor Press, 1998), and *THE ULTRATERRESTRIAL ORIGIN OF THE MASONIC FRATERNITY* in *The Secret Rituals of the Men in Black*.

Cypher 6

The Classical English Qabalah

A=1 B=20 C=13 D=6 E=25 F=18 G=11 H=4 I=23
J=16 K=9 L=2 M=21 N=14 O=7 P=26 Q=19 R=12
S=5 T=24 U=17 V=10 W=3 X=22 Y=15 Z=8

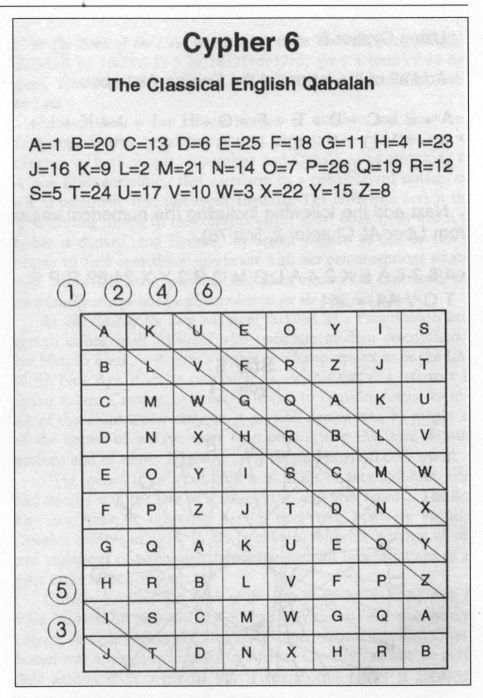

FIGS. 20-21 Extracts from Greenfield's **Secret Cipher of the UFOnauts** *pages, showing an original document from the early 1970s created by a group called O.A.A. (Ordo Argentium Astrum), a British division of Illuminati linked to the* **Hermetic Alchemical Order of QBLH,** *a kind of Church of Alchemists led by Carol Smith.*

Using Cypher 6:

Add all of the letters of the English Alphabet:

A + B + C + D + E + F + G + H + I + J + K + L +
M + N + O + P + Q + R + S + T + U + V + W + X
+ Y + Z = 351

Next add the following including the numerical values
(from *Liber Al,* Chapter 2, line 76).

4 6 3 8 A B K 2 4 A L G M O R 3 Y X 24 89 R P S
T O V A L = 351

Star 6
Cycle 11

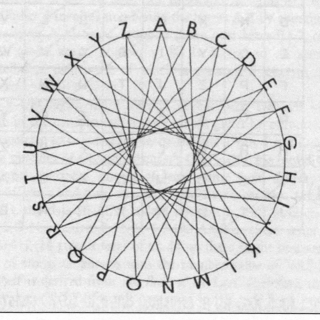

ETs. These channeled messages are a dime-a-dozen, and more keep pouring out every day, but it's all New Age rubbish, most of the time. The dirty little secret is that these beings are beholden to the corrupt demiurge, and are waging a psychological battle on humanity who don't embrace God. These are incredibly deceptive beings that are playing a game in order to garner the energy of worship. Attempting to deal with them with a secret cipher might, in the end, work for one in a million, but the rest, in reality, will be vampirized and trapped.

How can a physical spaceship change shape? They use interdimensional magic that obviously defies our present science. How can they vanish right in front of our eyes? Using interdimensional portals. Where are they hiding? In parallel dimensions and distant worlds. But most of all, why do they move about quietly to abduct people and destroy their lives? Whether abductions are real or not for you, the abductees are never the same afterward, because they might have been the subject of an attempted possession by a vampiric alien being. Now the secret cipher might help the skilled magician or the Illuminati, but most succumb to the alien overlords and lose their soul. Beware of any involvement with so-called magick, because you could end up in the hands of the Black Brotherhood.

In Blavatsky's discussion: *"The conditions under which alone the study of Divine Wisdom can be pursued with safety, that is without danger that Divine (Magic) will give place to Black Magic, it is the motive, and the motive alone, which makes any exercise of power become black, malignant, or white, benevolent Magic."* Remember what Frater Achad stated: *"we are dealing with a full-size world-mystery and a real fight between the Black and White Brotherhoods."* The only problem is that Achad probably thought he was on the right side when he converted to Catholicism and Jesuitry.

ALIEN ABDUCTION OR DEMONIC POSSESSION?

*D*o you think you have been abducted by aliens? It was probably just sleep paralysis says modern science these days, but we know that's not the entire truth. Jacques Vallee wrote in *Passport to Magonia*: *"Throughout medieval times, a major current of thought distinct from official religion existed, culminating in the works of the alchemists and hermetics. Among such groups were to be found some of the early modern scientists and men remarkable for the strength of their independent thinking and their adventurous life, such as Paracelsus. The nature of the beings who mysteriously appeared, dressed in shiny garments or covered with dark hair, and with whom communication was so hard to establish intrigued these men intensely."* But what is their real nature, and how can we distinguish the good beings from the bad ones? Negative Alien Technology is said to exist and some alchemists ended their lives in a bad way because of their close relationship with such beings. Some of you have probably heard of Dr. John Dee (1527-1608, or 1609 depending on the source). He was an Advisor to Queen Elizabeth I, and, according to Wikipedia, *"Dee immersed himself in the worlds of magic, astrology and Hermetic philosophy. He devoted much time and effort in the last thirty years or so of his life to attempting to commune with angels in order to learn the universal language of creation and bring about the pre-apocalyptic unity of mankind. However, Robert Hooke suggested in the chapter Of Dr. Dee's Book of Spirits, that John Dee made use of Trithemian steganography, to conceal his communication with Elizabeth I."* [31] I wrote a detailed exposition on Dee's

31   See https://en.wikipedia.org/wiki/John_Dee ‡ Archived 11th December, 2017.

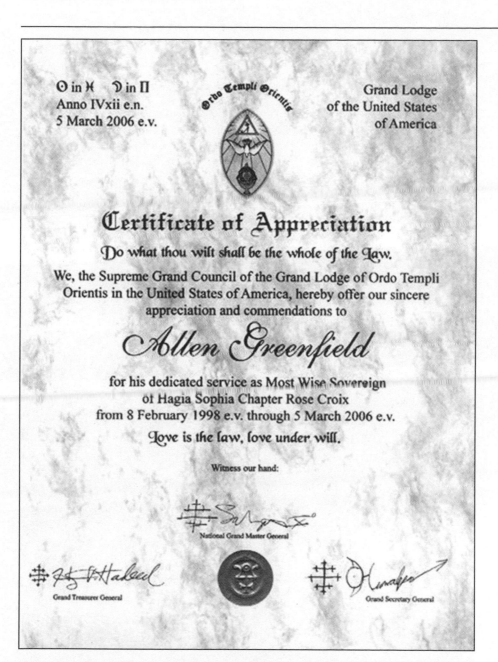

FIG. 22 Certificate of Appreciation by Ordo Templi Orientis Caliphate to Allen H. Greenfield as Most Wise Sovereign of the Hagia Sophia Chapter Rose Croix for services provided from February 8, 1998 to March 5, 2006.

FIG. 23 An image from a few years ago of well-known UFOologist T. Allen Bar Kohenim
Greenfield, Grand Hierophant of Egyptian Freemasonry and a member of the Illuminati,
while showing his past credentials in the Ordo Templi Orientis as Gnostic Bishop.

espionage activities as the original *007* in Volume I of my *Confessions*. [32]

A student of Renaissance Neo-Platonism of Marsilio Ficino, Dee did not draw distinctions between his mathematics research and his investigations into Hermetic magic, angel summoning and divination. Instead, he considered all of his activities to constitute different facets of the same quest: the search for a transcendent understanding of the divine forms which underlie the visible world, which Dee called pure verities. Dee, although a genius in his own right, and one of the most educated and learned men of his day, sought after knowledge in the wrong way. He tried to gain insight into the secrets of the creation apart from God, and instead sought out knowledge from angelic beings. In reality, the angelic beings Dee communed with were fallen angels. In fact, the knowledge Dee and his colleague Edward Kelly gained from the angels is still used even today by occultists and members of secret societies of the Illuminati network like the O.T.O. Clearly the beings Dee and Kelly communed with were not from God. Dee and Kelly developed a special language they called Enochian, which they claimed was revealed to them by angels. It is very telling that the methods they used to contact angels were occult to the core, and developed a complex system of ceremonial magic called Enochian Magic which later influenced The Hermetic Order of the Golden Dawn and legendary occultist Aleister Crowley. The methods used by these occultists are still influencing practitioners of ritual and ceremonial magic today. As a result of his contact with spirits, Dee and Edward Kelly ended up swapping wives for a short time—and this immoral activity was done because the angels commanded them to do it. Later in his life Dee became a disillusioned and broken man. He died at the age of 82, attended only by his daughter Katherine. I hope you can see from this example that Dee and Kelly were not in communication with godly spirits, but fallen beings. While the life of John Dee is very fascinating, it should serve as a reminder that traffic with fallen angels is costly, both in this life and the lives to come. [33]

Today the Illuminati are pushing for the general acceptance of Ultraterrestrial or Extraterrestrial technology, but "Grey Alien technology" as some call it, is not our friend, but it is designed to irresponsibly warp and rip our time fields, through black hole technology, while promoting rapid use of forced artificial technology, like EMP pulsing, that can destroy our planet, and instigates war between the humans of our own global race. They also promote use of supposed healing technologies ("inorganic and artificial replicant matrices") that are designed to remove pain physically, or have physical results in others, however, the *technology* is intended to enslave the soul or implant the human body. They also project mirages and pretty holographic inserts, to keep an abductee calm while they gain control of the person's aura. In short, this is externalized black magic and is ultimately harmful to the organic spiritual bodies and organic auric field. This creates interference with the person's ability to connect with their own spiritual source directly. It is this specific reason of spiritual interference, that there is a Founder Guardian intervention on planet earth.

They were not born on this planet, and there is a reason for that. Once a system is infiltrated with base desires as described in Archontic Deception Behavior or

32   L.L.Zagami, *Ibid.*, pp. 196-201.

33   *Cf.* https://alienantichrist.net/tag/john-dee/ ‡ Archived 11th December, 2017.

selfish ego, the system is not sustainable, as it only collects energies from one group to steal from another group in order to achieve a temporary result, (like a Ponzi or pyramid scheme), or give a small percentage of people who manipulate the energies the energetic advantage over others. This is called **Consumptive Modeling**. This is the abuse of consciousness technology and is known as Black Magic (i.e. many of the world leaders and their families that own the resources of the planet have been directly given this knowledge or parts of it by the demonic interdimensional entities, also referred to as Negative Aliens Archon Group. to maintain the dominant power, economy, and influence over controlling others). [34]

Giambattista della Porta (1535?-1615) who lived in Naples at the time of the Scientific Revolution and reformation, makes a clear distinction between *"two sorts of Magick; the one is infamous ... because it hath to do with soul spirits and ... enchantments ... and is called Sorcery ... The other Magick is natural ... The noblest Philosophers ... call this knowledge the very ... perfection of the Natural Sciences."* Concerns about sorcery, Black Magic, the dark arts, and the left-hand path, continue with modern occultism, emanating from a variety of secret societies of the dark side of the Illuminati network. However, for thousands of years, the rulers, and later the governments of this planet have been determined and controlled by a powerful hidden few ruling on most of humanity, thanks to their privileged link to the interdimensional world. It is time to study these ancient ciphers, and the secret rituals of the Illuminati, to understand who really manages the show. Are we really sure alien abduction is just modern sleep paralysis? Remember dear skeptic, it is not uncommon to describe these kinds of experiences as demonic possession, and Jean Bastide, in *La memoire des OVNI* (1978) wrote: *"The modern contacts established with extraterrestrials respect precisely the same rules as contacts in the past with beings more or less human in form."*

The point is that there is a tradition stretching back thousands of years, of beings abducting humans and their offspring; these beings fly in globes of light, can paralyze their victims, induce amnesia about the event, force strange drinks on their victims, have sex with them and, in many cases, ultimately drive them to madness, physical ruin, or even take over their bodies for their own use. This possession can be permanent or semi-permanent. (Possession takes place after a long period of wearing down of the will through repeated forced encounters, which generally include draining of energy through sexual contact.) Some occultists see any sexual activity as part of man's lower nature. Others see it as a sacrament. [35]

Cornelius Agrippa described copulation as: *"full of magical endowment,"* and Aratus said that: *"As the physical union of man and woman leads to the fruit from the composition of each, in the same way the interior and secret association of man and woman is the copulation of the male and female soul, and is appointed for the production of fitting fruit of the divine life."*

The Illuminati believe that the mysterious psychic energy producing all phenomena is sexual in nature. As a matter of fact, Poltergeist activity is usually associated with a disturbed adolescent who is unable to "ground" their sexual

34   http://ascensionglossary.com/index.php/Black_Magic#Negative_Alien_Technology
       ‡ Archived 11th December, 2017.

35   https://www.sott.net/article/142793-Alien-Abduction-Demonic-Possession-and-
       The-Legend-of-The-Vampire ‡ Archived 11th December, 2017.

energy. It is asserted that sexual currents of the libido are manifestations of an energy that can be transferred from one person to another. In this way, it is suggested, the old can draw the life force from the young. For example, King David regularly slept with young virgins when he became old. The same technique was used in classical Greece and Rome with some success, and also by contemporary politician **Silvio Berlusconi** at his infamous **"Bunga Bunga"** parties. This practice is, unfortunately, connected to the love for pedophilia, witnessed over and over again by the occult elite and the dark side of the Illuminati.

The Emperor Barbarossa for example was reported to have held young boys against his stomach and genitals in order to "savor and absorb their energy" and Pope Innocent VIII, employed healthy young children to stroke him, thereby transferring their energy to him. We hear over and over again about the practice of pedophilia by the deviant clergy of the Catholic Church and other religions like Islam. One of the most disturbing things about Islam is that it does not categorically condemn pedophilia. Indeed, it cannot, for to do so would draw attention to the pedophilia of Muhammad, the founder of Islam. Muslims cannot categorically condemn pedophilia without denouncing him as a false prophet. In addition to Aisha (a nine-year-old girl!) [36] he planned to marry a baby, but it died as a result of a poisoning before he could do so. [37]

Interestingly, scientists have confirmed that sleep paralysis occurs more often in adults reporting repressed, recovered, or continuous memories of childhood sexual abuse. In any case of psychic vampirism or actual possession, there is usually an actual entry point, the point at which the spirit enters into a relationship with the individual, and a decision is made by the victim to allow that contact. This often occurs simply because the victim is not aware of the significance of the event. It can be a minor event and may come as the result of tiredness, mental excitation, frustration, pain and other psychological factors predetermining a weakened psychic constitution or as a trauma-induced event like child abuse that includes sexual, emotional and physical abuse, as well as living with domestic violence in childhood. These beings, be they demons, psychic vampires or malevolent aliens, have the ability to control our thoughts to a certain extent, our physical bodies to the point that we can be worn down under such attack and give in to their demonic control.

ALDEBARAN, THE EGREGORE, AND OCCULT CHAINS

*I*n October 1969, in the town San Leo, in the province of Rimini, in Emilia Romagna, a northern region of Italy, in a place full of mystery, in which Count Cagliostro spent the last years of life in a cell (a place that still today sees a continual pilgrimage of curious Freemasons, alchemists, and fragmentary pilgrims), there was a very important and historical meeting of real Illuminati known as the 3rd Convent of the Unknown Superiors of Martinism. At the Convent of San Leo, numerous initiates were present; there where vari-

36   http://www.answering-islam.org/Authors/Wood/pedophile.htm ‡ Archived 11th December, 2017.

37   https://wikiislam.net/wiki/Was_Muhammad_a_Pedophile%3F ‡ Archived 11th December, 2017.

ous high level initiates known as *Sirius, Lucius, Galahad, Zorobabel, Immanuel* and *Spartacus*, headed by the aforementioned **Count Gastone Ventura,** Sovereign Grand Master of the Order known with the initiatic name of *Aldeberan*. Inside the event, they discussed the theme of the Egregore, as well as the power of Occult Chains, which was discussed in great depth, in addition to the present crisis of the Western Initiatic System. Some eyewitnesses to the meeting, said that in San Leo the imminent advent of the Messiah was being prepared behind the scenes, others, who perhaps disagreed with Count Ventura's policies or decisions, say exactly the opposite in regards to what was going on, claiming that it was simply a meeting of witches tied to the black wing of Martinism, who are preparing for the arrival of the Antichrist.

I don't know which of these two stories could be the correct one, unfortunately, I wasn't born yet, but in the two years following this important event, a conspiracy against Grand Master Gastone Ventura was organized within the Italian Martinist Order by Ventura's Deputy Grand Master **Francesco Brunelli aka** *Nebo* (formerly known as *Mercurius*), who was linked to the French branch of this tradition and the famous French Illuminati and magus **Robert Ambelain**. Now, after many years, thanks to a faithful reproduction of a very rare typewritten version of the main topics discussed in San Leo, I am able to offer you an important testimony that leads us to further understand, both the nature of this mysterious encounter, and also the reality of the Egregore, and the true nature of the Occult Chains operating within the Illuminati from an Illuminati point of view. An initiatic reality, the Martinist Order, which has certainly undergone an inevitable decline in quality in the last decades, in an era where the political and religious games, as well as the economic and marketing interest, often ruin, the genuine esoteric work once undergone in these kinds of orders, as the late Count Gastone Ventura himself strongly denounced during the event in question, the take over orchestrated by the dark materialistic force of the New World Order. Ventura apparently said off-the-record that certain practices were based on a modern version of Satan's original lie, and rightly had no place within the heart of a true initiate.

Ventura, an aristocrat with a truly noble spirit, had surely realized the materialistic deviant direction undergone by certain prominent Masonic figures of the time, as the future Grand Master of the International Academy of the Illuminati **Giuliano Di Bernardo** still operating today within the cabal of the New World Order. The following is a document of tremendous importance, if fully understood:

On the Egregor and the Occult Chain (themes and notes from the Third Convent of the Unknown Superiors—San Leo 1969), reproduction of the original text typed by Arturus S.I.I:

Before considering this topic, I have been thinking for a long time: and pose the question on motives, on whether or not to face, operationally—even if Elementary—lesser-known forces that can create abnormal situations and can lead to counter-initiation.

However, since our ceremonies are rituals and each ritual involves actions that determine the creation of frequencies, and since chain or group work or several groups simultaneously would be willing to do it in various degrees, I decided to deal with this topic.

What is an Egregore?

The word comes from Greek and indicates a thought form, created by a group of people tied to common feelings, ideals, uses, and customs. A family is already a powerful Egregore, a rule based on well-defined rules, precise doctrines followed by all its components, rules, beliefs, practices, etc. Just as there are Egregores that we call physical (formed by men or by living beings), there are spiritual Egregore that generally derives from physical ones. And as there are physical Egregores who profess ideas, uses, good, moral, altruistic, social, spiritual elevation, initiation to the Creator, and others who follow opposing directions, there are good or bad spiritual Egregores, Positive or Negative depending on the point of view from which they are observed. Each physical Egregore, therefore, produces, with its actions, invisible forces when of a magnetic nature, when of electrical character, when of a vital nature, which are the spiritual Egregore produced by the physical Egregore. For example, a crowd of faithful in prayer is a physical Egregore: its action, of course, is as effective as the prayer is heard, and even more so if prayer is for everyone, and if it is guided, conveyed by those who it has the power to achieve a certain goal, it produces the spiritual Egregore.

Another example is on a battlefield, where a body to body fight or one with a cold weapon takes away all limitations, the only desire is to kill the opponent or at least to save one's life by extinguishing that of others, this is a physical Egregore. The action produces a magnetic or electromagnetic field when it is vital, which slowly detaches from the physical plane that generates it (in the form of vibrations with certain frequency) and forms a spiritual Egregore with characteristics of hatred, selfishness, and awful will. I limit myself to these two examples by pointing out, then, that in order to compose a physical Egregore capable of producing a spiritual Egregore, two people can suffice, as there is no limit to their number. The stronger the personality of the participants in the physical Egregore, the greater the powers of the one who directs it, the stronger the Egregore is, the spiritual Egregore, which spreads it in continuous waves, one behind the other, and the Action continues. In this regard, I recommend for a more in-depth discussion of the subject what Aurifer (Robert Ambelain) says in his Egregores. [38]

While I don't agree completely with all that Ambelain says in his proposition, it seems to me that the essay mentioned is among the most complete and eloquent so far written on the subject. I will try to illustrate how the spiritual Egregore is created and behaves from my own experiences and the teachings I received. Much of what Egregore refers to is the theory of space, considered as a series of intense fields saturated with unknown living, energies, so the idea of space can be confused with that of the Ethereal life (i.e. Mana the ethereal energy source), an impalpable, invisible and non-perceptible substance (more psychic than physical) which is, however, ubiquitous and found everywhere, distributed with a greater or lesser density (obviously, all the terms used herein are only means borrowed from language to express ourselves and not to define), so that one place or another may be more conducive to a particular vice or certain virtue. In other words, this substance is the result of vibrations, which can also be conceived as light, distributed throughout, but not in the same quantity, and not with the same density or power. It follows that it can be more or less influ-

---

38   *See Nebo S.I.I.,* **Book of the Initiate**, *(Manuscript), pp. 17,18, 20, 21 (19 missing for a numbering error).*

enced, strengthened or diminished, even eradicated, think of the cases of holy lands and cities, magical places that are strengthened with certain rituals, that can also collapse with a single sacrilege capable of provoking the disintegration of the substance. Traditionally, therefore, space is an almost metaphysical, vivid, magical, magnetic or electromagnetic space, where every gesture made, each traced sign, every word pronounced, each operation performed, has an absolute, decisive, positive or negative. Here comes a key factor. It is that of race, and the degree of influence in that race.

That is why in the ordered Orders, the choice of those present must be accurate. Race or race differences are canceled with Initiation or the Conquest of a Grade. Those who belong to an Initial Order—if it really has not been deceived—belong to one and only one race. Admission to the Order through the Initiative Rite represents a new birth in a single lineage: the conquest of grace in the Order, is the refinement of the lineage, and its reunion with the Hands of that lineage. So in every degree there is a Rite that you should never forget. From these brief and concise indications, one can easily commit a mistake or cause reactions other than those that were prefigured.

This is why in initiating rites, when initiation attempts to obtain the benefit of the "influences" (Egregores) in order to acquire them (i.e. possess their glory) in order to be able to transfer them in part with his gestures and His words on the postulant, the New Venerable Order suggests (and always prefer) the direct, individual, group initiative. One wrong gesture by one of the participants in the Rite, **one more word spoken by the initiator or his assistant (a word that goes to a higher ceremony or other Rite, or even alien to Rite, if Not contrary to it) can render it all in vain and even dangerous.** Because the Rite is **action.**

It is not possible to give a true explanation of the Egregores bearing, but remember the saying:

"The top way is moved from the bottom, and this from that."[39]

Keep in mind that any energy of any kind or character is generated and bound by and at a frequency and this is amplitude.

In this respect the following should be said:

I.

A) The frequency of an energy is represented by the number of vibrations, the unit of time, the matter or substance that the energy enters. If the substance or matter were devoid of energy, the energy would only exist in power.

B) The frequency of a spiritual Egregore is given by the composition (algebraic sum) of the frequencies of the various participants in the physical Egregore in action (act).

If the physical Egregore is rested, its vibrations produce an "egregoric field" that expands around the physical Egregore, but does not break away from it. This field has a direct action on the living bodies that are introduced to it, but these bodies, if nourished by opposing principles, may also diminish their power. When the physical Egregor enters into action (in other words directs its power to a definite purpose, with the Rite, passing from the state of power to the act) the egregore field enters into frequency and leaves itself from Body, that generates it in waves

---

39   Cf. The Emerald Tablet, The Ruby Tablet.

that propagate and add to each other to form the spiritual Egregore, alive until the given frequency goes out slowly because of a lack of impulse.

C) Frequency has maximum amplitude points in one direction to another.

D) The frequency is much higher, and as a result the spiritual Egregore is much more compact, the greater the synchrony of the components of the Egregore.

   2.

(A) The amplitude is given by the range of egregore field, and is the greater complexity of the physical Egregore.

(B) The amplitude tends to decrease (i.e. it's dimmed) as the Egregore spirits away from the physical one that generated it.

Bearing in mind these indications, one might think that an Egregore, once in space, has the form—more or less—of a circle or an elixir, and that it is composed of something denser than air, but at the same time impalpable and invisible. The behavior of the Egregore, for personal experiences, study, and teaching, should be roughly the following:

1st) The encounter between Egregores of the same frequency in the same sense and of different amplitude resonates them, resulting in a reaction that results in an energy that strengthens the breadth of the weaker Egregore by giving it power.

2°) The encounter between Egregores of the same frequency in the same sense and of the same amplitude causes an Egregore of the same frequency with a double width. This is the case mentioned in the previous n. 1°) when the weaker Egregore resonating with the strongest one, acquires the same amplitude. However, it may (and almost always occurs) that the weaker Egregore resonated does not come to the same amplitude as the strongest because of the lack of impulses from this (impulses from the physical Egregore that generated it).

3°) The encounter between Egregores of different frequency causes the creation of a new Egregore which has frequency the sum of the two original frequencies. The resulting egregore may fall under the control (with the occurrence of the resonance phenomenon), of a physical or even spiritual Egregore of the same frequency.

If, then, the frequency of the Egregore that has to control it had the same amplitude, it would flood it by doubling its amplitude. Of course, the two Egregores who have made up the new one are, in any case, lost for those who have generated them.

*4°) If the sense of the frequency of two Egregores of the same frequency but of different amplitude is in opposition, the phenomenon of **disturbance** is generated, which causes the production of an Egregore of the same frequency with a smaller amplitude. This undoes the efforts of those who try to strengthen their spiritual Egregore with continuous deliveries and impulses.*

*5°) If the two Egregores mentioned in the previous n. 4) have the same amplitude, the phenomenon of **interference** occurs: they are canceled.*

6°) Different effects that give rise to different Egregores in the composition of frequencies, amplitudes, and sense are when senses are not entirely opposed but intermediate. Cases are multiple and this is not the place to take them into consideration. It is, however, relatively easy to imagine them roughly.

The Composition of frequencies, amplitudes and sense are when senses are not entirely opposed but intermediate. Cases are multiple and this is not the place to take them into consideration. It is, however, relatively easy to imagine them roughly.

*From what has been said, one can conclude that it is very difficult if it is not entirely impossible to keep **control** of a spirited Egregore that has arisen, if you are not sure to be able to produce, each time it comes into action (with the Rite) the egregore field, such frequency as to generate resonance. But even if this is possible through certain precautions, with the will of the members of the physical Egregore, and with the capacity of the Rite to direct, it may always be that the already formed Spiritual Egregore has been absorbed, captured, modified and canceled by the other Egregore.*

*In Antiquity, the Manes, a Family of chthonic deities sometimes thought to represent souls of deceased loved ones (the Egregore base) could only be summoned by the head of the family who had real and priestly powers within the family **(obstat uetustus)**. He was the only one that knew how to generate the frequency (through the Rite) to produce the spiritual Egregore that created the resonance with the Hands of the family, capturing and acquiring glory. A mistake, or the Rite performed by those who did not have the power, caused sacrilege, that is, the loss of the spiritual Egregore. Such traditions are still found among peoples who base their metaphysics on the Totem.*

*Certainly, an egregoric center (such as a Church, Order, Brotherhood, a military group) can establish a very strong egregoric field, and retain the spiritual Egregore. Is it necessary that the action (the transition from power to act) is carried out continuously? This is the case of a sanctuary, the headquarters of an Order, Domus of a family, the center of a large industrial or commercial community, a military command. To think that the Church for centuries has continued to pray the same prayers, the same formulas, taught the same catechism, performed its functions for certain hours, played the bells in certain ways at the same hour; That in a barracks they always carry out the same military exercises; **Everything is governed by a rhythm** that is well-known by the officers and sergeants: the gestures are the same, and the commands themselves. In modern times, and the continuous shift of families from their Domus (family diaspora), directional centers, mini-commands, and the desire to change everything according to a pretended social civilization, there are still few sanctuaries left.*

*But for Westerners, imbued with social ideas, victims, even if indirectly, of rationalism and atheism, conditioned by democratic ideas of equality, the question is very unlucky. It is another task of the Martinist to study and apply—if possible—the above-mentioned tradition. Regarding everything else, we can talk about current or temporal egregore formats, useful as forces directed for a particular purpose. This long premise was necessary to examine the egregore possibilities of Martinism and to determine how and when chain and group **experiments** could be carried out for egregore purposes. I must say, my dear brothers that the New Venerable Order has been through so many tricks in recent years so that I find it difficult at present to believe that a chain rite can produce positive effects.*

The poor homogeneity of the Order's components, the lack of uniqueness of ideas and trends arising from the application of different rites, the uncertainty so far caused by the plurality of doctrines considered Martinist, infiltrations of a humanistic, social, Political, religious etc. That although noble and contingent have nothing to do with an esoteric order that is interested in metaphysics, although they can be taken into account in the outside life of the Order, but never in the inner one, they have created among themselves the diversity that is to produce different frequencies, and very rarely they amalgamate in a single frequency, with the amplitude, direction, and direction needed to produce a strong Egregore. Whatever, in any case, comes from our chain, and even the only eregoric field that we produce is already a positive fact, it is certain: but this can be considered as an experimental, purely mechanical result. What will be the frequency that will come from it? It may, contrary to the aims and the doctrines of Martinist, for the diversity of the ideas of the participants in the chain,

It could also be an Egregore that would easily be "catwalked" by another stronger Egregore, although negative. I have vaquely heard about the Wizards of the West and the Wizards of the East with someone mentioning Mao Zedong, Hồ Chí Minh, and other left-wing heroes. I have also heard proposals for ambitious plans to push the Order in the political and social spheres of the New World Order. Undoubtedly, all those who believe, think and propose such theories (I speak of those who are part of the New Venerable Order and truly understand the purpose of the Martinist Egregore) if in good faith, deserve respect. But they should remove the political side from Martinism, they are wrong in involving Martinism. I will never be tired of arguing that Martinism (and you can believe me, because nearly forty years of this activity, carried out alongside the last three Grand Masters, and with the advice of other true Masters, even if they did not care about such title, allow me to say it) can not and should not be interested in extremely noble matters as long as it is desirable, but **profane** but as a matter of **study for esoteric purposes**. Martinism is not a gym of humanitarian proposals and resolutions, it does not have to solve problems of progress or of economic or social well-being; Martinism is an **Initiatic Order,** I repeat and underline: An **Initiatic ORDER** that with the initiation by degrees it annuls the social, economic, racial differences and creates an aristocracy of the mind for men who want and must reach inner tranquility and pass on the torch of real illumination and tradition. We are the real Illuminati. Those who do not understand this, who do not realize the significance of the three fundamental symbols of Martinism **(the Mask, the Cloak, the Cordelier)**, make an effort, study, apply to understand it and see that everything will be clear. That is why we say to the **Unknown Superior** who is preparing to receive the initiatory powers: "Now that you are going to take on the initiatic powers and become the guide of your brothers, you are to reach the full possession of the mask and mantle that they have Made of you a Martinist. If the Great Secret has come to you, loneliness will be for you the UNITY that will love all Beings, ALL; but if you do not understand our Anointed, it will be a terrible condemnation that will weigh on you as a Curse because you will send it to those who believe in you."

I think a chain capable of producing a positive and strong Egregore should be done: it is crucial that our Egregore be launched into space reaching our Ultraterrestrial friends. But it must be a strong, compact Egregore: the impulses that strengthen it must be continuous. It must also be an Egregore devoid of profane purposes: in other words the Egregore of those who, having gained inner tranquility, know that the things of this world, the struggles that characterize evolution or involution, namely the economic problems, social, political, religious and so on, are the only contingent, and therefore, **metaphysically unrealistic issues because** *not stable but variable. But what matters is the balance, the law of opposites that support each other, and allow the development of human activities as well as of the cosmic and universal ones. If, then, we want to exploit our egregoric field for physical reasons, for beneficial purposes, mutualists and therefore, material, related to profane problems, then the question is easier: let us also say that we ourselves gathered here, that with our presence alone for a common purpose we form an egregoric field, we concentrate and we engage to send a thought, a help, a wave of greetings to someone who interests us. We will produce, with the appropriate Rite a strong and pure Egregore, created by real Martinists (because we are or we believe we are true Martinists) but not the Martinist Egregore. Needless to give you suggestions and advice: they derive from what I have said: Martinist doctrine, Martinism soul, common rites, common will. If there are no such premises, there is not even a Martinist Initiatic Order, and consequently there can be no Martinist Egregore.*

We hope you enjoy these discourses and are inspired to further meditate upon the symbolism within our mystical tradition.

May you ever dwell in the Eternal Light of Cosmic Wisdom!

(Gastone Ventura-Aldebaran)

ALAMANTRAH WORKING: CROWLEY AND THE FIRST GREY

*A*leister Crowley in a letter to a disciple—later included in the collection eventually published as *Magick Without Tears*—the following statement of position: *"My observation of the Universe convinces me that there are beings of intelligence and power of a far higher quality than anything we can conceive of as human; that they are not necessarily based on the cerebral and nervous structures that we know, and that the one and only chance for mankind to advance as a whole is for individuals to make contact with such Beings."*

Throughout Crowley's years as a magus of the Illuminati, and his many unorthodox magical experiments, he seems to have often attempted to contact interdimensional entities. Through magickal incantations and the regurgitation of ancient inscriptions and veiled verses written in obscure text circulated amongst the Illuminati, Crowley called forward all manner of spirits, demons and **Invisible Masters** from which he sought advice and guidance. One particular entity that draws an intense amount of interest is the character known as LAM. Around 1917, in New York, Crowley drew the image of this praeter-human intelligence, after performing a ritual now known as **The Alamantrah Working**. During this experiment, a discarnate entity urged Crowley to *"find the egg,"* and it seems, at some point, Crowley experienced contact with this large headed entity we have come to know as LAM. Described by Crowley in the inscription accompanying the frontispiece, which was entitled *The Way:*

LAM is the Tibetan word for Way or Path, and LAMA is He who Goeth, the specific title of the Gods of Egypt, the Treader of the Path, in Buddhistic phraseology. Its numerical value is 71, the number of this book.

What is fascinating about LAM, or, at least, Crowley's drawing of LAM, is the stark resemblance it bears to the popular image of Grey aliens we have come to know since the Roswell incident in 1947. Although we now have witnesses claiming to have encountered a whole multitude of different alien visitors, the most popular is still that of the typical Grey, a large-headed, small featured alien that bears a striking resemblance to the figure Crowley apparently channeled during his Alamantrah Working. Yet as even some journalists have pointed out: *"Crowley's image obviously far predates the UFO mania that followed the alleged alien crash and subsequent, apparent, alien visitations that followed."* [40]

Crowley included Lam's portrait in his *Dead Souls Exhibition* held in Greenwich Village, New York, in 1919, something explained in detail also in the Foreword of the Statement *Concerning the Cult of the Lam* issued by the late Kenneth Grant (1924 2011), in 1987, while Grand Master of the **Typhonian Ordo Templi Orientis,** a Illuminati sect now known as **Typhonian Order:** *"Crowley's portrait of Lam is a curious drawing which he included in his Dead Souls exhibition held in Greenwich Village, New York, in 1919. In that same year, it was published as a frontispiece to Crowley's Commentary to Blavatsky's The Voice of the Silence."* The foreword in question also specifies that:

> *Crowley left no record as to the origin of this portrait, although he remarked many years later that it was drawn from life.*
>
> *It is certain, however, that the drawing arose from the Amalantrah Working, a series of magical visions and communications received in 1918 through the mediumship of The Camel, Roddie Minor. This was in many ways a continuation of the Abuldiz Working of several years previous. In both of these Workings, the symbolism of the egg featured prominently. One of the earlier visions of the Amalantrah Working ended with the sentence "It's all in the egg." During the final surviving vision of this Working, in reference to a question about the egg, Crowley was told that Thou art to go this Way. Examining the portrait, we can see the connections. The head of Lam is egg-shaped, and of course, the drawing is called The Way. In the whorlings of the face can clearly be seen a stylized ankh, the Egyptian symbol for Going; as a matter of interest, ankh can best be transliterated into Hebrew as kaph nun aleph, 71. The main theme of The Voice of the Silence clearly brought out by Crowley, is the need to establish contact with the Silent Self. That corresponds to the Dwarf Self, the phallic consciousness, Harpocrates, Hadit, and this theme runs through much of Crowley's writing. It is noteworthy in this context that ALIL, the image of Nothingness and Silence, enumerates as 71. Crowley gave the drawing to Kenneth Grant in May 1945, following an astral working in which they were both involved. Since then it has become apparent that Lam is, in fact, a transmundane or extraterrestrial entity, with whom several groups of magicians have established contact, most notably Michael Bertiaux in the 1960s and a group of O.T.O. initiates in the 1970s.*
>
> *Much remains unclear, however, hence the need for further investigation of this entity. The idea of extraterrestrial entities seems to cause difficulties with some people, associating it as they may, with the wilder shores of science-fiction. There is however, a wealth of material on this matter to suggest the old cliché that truth is stranger than fiction. See, for instance, Robert Temple's **The Sirius Mystery.** Whether these visitors are regarded as visitors from outer space, or as welling up from the depths of some inner space, is neither here nor there. The dichotomy of inner and*

---

40   See http://weekinweird.com/2012/12/01/sirius-business-aleister-crowley-extraterrestrial-medium/ ‡ Archived 11th December, 2017.

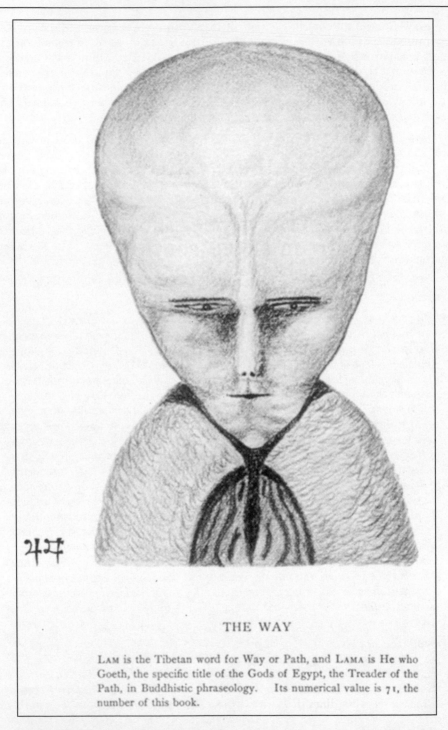

THE WAY

LAM is the Tibetan word for Way or Path, and LAMA is He who
Goeth, the specific title of the Gods of Egypt, the Treader of the
Path, in Buddhistic phraseology.   Its numerical value is 71, the
number of this book.

FIG. 24 *The drawing commonly referred to as "LAM" that appeared in Blavatsky's*
***The Voice of the Silence** with a short description by Crowley before his prefatory note.*

outer is purely conceptual, arising from the dualist notion of an individual being somehow separate from the rest of the universe, which is somehow out there. There is, in fact, nothing outside consciousness, which is a continuum. This position is explored in the article Going Beyond, which appeared in the first issue of Starfire. Lam is discussed in many places in the works of Kenneth Grant, most notably Cults of the Shadow and Outside the Circles of Time, and the interested reader is referred to these. A more lengthy account of Lam is planned for a future issue of Starfire. In the meantime, the following paper issued by the O.T.O. will be of interest, giving as it does a method of attempting rapport with Lam by using the portrait as a gateway. [41]

Researcher Daniel V. Boudillion writes: *"Since Crowley's time, several occult groups and individuals following in his footsteps have claimed to have intentionally and successfully contacted 'Lam.' Most notably, Michael Bertiaux in the 1960s followed by a group of O.T.O initiates in the 1970s. (The O.T.O. is the* Ordo Templi Orientis, *a Magickal order run by Crowley.) These individuals consider 'Lam'* **to be a trans-mundane or extraterrestrial entity and claimed remarkable success in their invocations—if they are to be believed.** *Following the success of these contacts, interest in occult circles, especially Crowleyian ones, gathered considerable steam. In 1987, Kenneth Grant, the generally acknowledged successor to Crowley, went so far as to formalize the Lam Workings into something called the Cult of Lam."* Boudillion also says that: *"It is generally agreed within occult circles that Crowley intentionally opened a portal of entry via magick ritual in the Amalantrah Workings which allowed the likes of Lam and other similar entities a passageway onto the earth-world. The rift 'in-between the spaces of the stars,' created by the Amalantrah Working, created a gateway through which Lam and other extra-cosmic influences could enter the known universe, and most particularly, our earth-world.* **According to occultists involved in such things, the Portal has since widened."** [42]

Quoting from the late Grant Typhonian O.T.O. website:

The Cult (of Lam) has been founded because very strong intimations have been received by Aossic Aiwass, 718°.° to the effect that the portrait of Lam (the original drawing of which was given by 666°.° to 718°.° under curious circumstances) is the present focus of an extraterrestrial—and perhaps trans-plutonic—Energy which the O.T.O. is required to communicate at this critical period, for we have now entered the Eighties mentioned in The Book of the Law. It is Our aim to obtain some insight not only into the nature of Lam, but also into the possibilities of using the Egg as an astral space-capsule for traveling to Lam's domain, or for exploring extraterrestrial spaces in the sense in which O.T.O. Tantric Time-Travelers are exploring the Tunnels of Set in intra-cosmic and chthonian capsules. Members of the O.T.O. who feel strongly attracted to this Cult of Lam are invited to apply for participation therein. It is open only to Order members. They should contact Frater Ani Asig, 375°.° of the Sovereign Sanctuary, O.T.O. and submit a formal, typewritten and signed acceptance of the conditions of Working outlined here. It should be understood that proficiency in the magical formulae of this Cult does not necessarily comport eligibility for advancement in the O.T.O., its parent Order.

Crowley called Kenneth Grant, *"a definite gift from the Gods"* and wrote in a *Memorandum* in his diary dated February 7, 1945: *"Value of Grant: if I die or go to the*

---

41   http://www.parareligion.ch/lam-stat.htm , [emphasis added].

42   http://www.boudillion.com/lam/lam.htm ‡ Archived 11th December, 2017.

FIG. 25 *The image is said to portray some of the London followers of the* **Typhonian Order.** *Note the image of Lam positioned above the participants of the ritual, and also the Master of Ceremonies with his Magickal wand who is apparently* **Rob Curley,** *former Albion O.T.O. (known as Fr ∴ Phaeton X). Curley who was also an ex-member of the Caliphate O.T.O. and the F.R.A. was involved for five years in a bitter legal dispute for the use of the name O.T.O in the UK, a case he eventually lost in 2008. After that Rob and his followers joined forces with Kenneth Grant's Order, who omitted for this reason in 2009, the use of the name Ordo Templi Orientis.*

U.S.A., there must be a trained man to take care of the English O.T.O."—but the U.S. Intelligence and their O.T.O. had other plans.

KENNETH GRANT AND THE ALIEN CULT OF LAM

*T*he name Aleister Crowley is synonymous with Secret Societies and magickal operations. Considered in occult circles as a master of hidden Magic and occult materials, his name still evokes horrors in the minds of some who see Crowley as the personification of the Antichrist. Certainly, he was a master in publicizing himself and his anti-establishment positions, he adopted 666 as his own magic number and took on the Greek epithet of *Mega Therion*, the term used to define *The Great Beast*, used also in his infancy by his mother, a member of the Plymouth Brethren, an English sect of fundamentalist Christians, who used it to describe her deceiving son. There is a considerable discussion in contemporary ufology on Lam, the being Crowley designed, which seems to be one of those interdimensional alien beings that will be later described in modern cases of close encounters with extraterrestrials. It seems that Aleister Crowley's first close encounter was with two "little men" in the Swiss Alps, and dates back to 1896, and was mentioned for the first time in the Jacques Vallee book entitled, *Passport to Magonia: On UFOs, Folklore, and Parallel Worlds*.

The "Magical Mountain," of Crowley's saga, which was Mt. Meal Fuorvonie near Loch Ness, that according to Greenfield is a base of UFOnauts. This could explain the famous mystery of the so-called **Loch Ness Monster**, The first picture of the alleged monster of Loch Ness was made on the eastern shore of Loch Ness near the Boleskine House where Aleister Crowley began the ritual of the Sacred Magic of Abramelin. Boleskine House, that is described and very recognizable in W. Somerset Maugham's *The Magician*, where it is named Skene. Lam's image was entrusted to Kenneth Grant in 1945, which for years was considered one of Crowley's best and brightest students in Europe. Kenneth Grant had a long interest in the C.E.T.I. (*Contact with Extraterrestrial Intelligence*) organization. The phenomenon had been long-lasting he felt, and its position was advanced to the head of what was regarded as one of the main factions of the O.T.O., until 2009, when it made him an international occult star for sure.

In 1955, when Grant was in conflict with the USA O.T.O., he announced the birth of the **New Isis Lodge** in London that became operational in April 1955, when Grant issued a Manifesto announcing his discovery of an extraterrestrial "Sirius/Set current" upon which the lodge was to be based on. The lodge closed down in 1962 and was based in Melcombe Street, near Baker Street in central London, next to where I lived for a number of years. This is where I created the *Cagliostro Lodge* of the **Fraternitas Rosicruciana Antiqua** (FRA) in the early 2000s, whose most prominent members later began the Albion O.T.O., and after failing with that project, finally joined Kenneth Grant's Typhonian Order, becoming in a short time, the driving force of the newly named Typhonian Order.

The aim of Grant's original lodge founded in 1955, was contacting the highest non-human intelligence forms, but he also worked a lot in the literary field in the following years. In 1969, Grant co-edited *The Confessions* of Aleister Crowley for publication with Crowley's literary executor John Symonds. Over the next years he edited—often with Symonds—a range of Crowley writings for republication, resulting in the release of *The Magical Record of the Beast 666* (1972), *Diary of a Drug Fiend* (1972), *Moonchild* (1972), *Magick* (1973), *Magical and Philosophical Commentaries on The Book of the Law* (1974) and *The Complete Astrological Writings* (1974). The release of these publications has been described as being *"instrumental in the revival of interest in Crowley."* [43]

The problem is that at this point, Grant began describing himself as the O.H.O. (Outer Head of the Order) of the O.T.O., claiming that he deserved this title, not by direct succession from Crowley, but because he displayed the inspiration and innovation that Germer lacked, something the USA O.T.O. never accepted. Later on, a document purportedly by Crowley naming Grant as his successor, was subsequently exposed as a hoax created by Robert Taylor, a Typhonian O.T.O. member who was clearly trying to support his Grand Master. However, in the early 1970s, Grant established his own Thelemic organization, the Typhonian Order, previously known as the Typhonian Ordo Templi Orientis (T.O.T.O.), which produced, its first official announcement in 1973. Although adopting the O.T.O. degree system used by Crowley, Grant removed the rituals of initiation designed to allow a member to enter a higher degree; **instead, he personally promoted them through the degrees according to what he believed were their own personal spiritual development.**

The story goes that in 1980, Grant claimed to have received messages that led him to conclude that Lam's portrait of Crowley could be used to provide a focal point for the extraterrestrial energy originally invoked in 1918. That's how Grant eventually arrived to his previously described LAM Statement. The purpose was basically to regularize the type of relationship and build a magic formula for establishing a new communication with the alien interdimensional reality being referred to as Lam. The invocation of Lam or the beings we know of as Greys was thus officially approved by the T.O.T.O., and also accepted by Michael Bertiaux of the O.T.O.A. In the end, **the Amalantrah Working allowed the likes of Lam and other alien greys a passageway onto the Earth plane.**

Furthermore, this portal may have been further enlarged by Jack Parsons and L. Ron Hubbard in 1946, with the commencement of the Babylon Working, thus facilitating a monumental paradigm shift in human consciousness. This experiment continues to expand to this day, also thanks to the work conducted in secret by certain Intelligence agencies with occultists like Lieutenant Colonel Michael Aquino, and a variety of Secret Societies of the Illuminati network on both sides of the Atlantic, that include of course, Grant's T.O.T.O., that have also collaborated with Aquino in secret. Michael Aquino and the late Kenneth Grant, have both been members of another rather secretive Illuminati Order called **The Esoteric Order of Dagon**, named after a secret society in Lovecraft's *The Shadow Over Innsmouth*. This is is a degreed occult system influenced by Thelema, tantra, paganism, Setianism, and, of course, Lovecraft. Members have included Grant, Aquino, Nicholaj de Mattos Frisvold (who was behind the failed launch of the Albion O.T.O. in the UK in the first decade of the new millenium), and the late John Balance from the band Coil, among other notable authors, artists, and occultists. [44]

---

43   https://en.wikipedia.org/wiki/Kenneth_Grant ‡ Archived 11th December, 2017.

44   *See* http://www.cvltnation.com/h-p-lovecraft-occult/ ‡ Archived 11th December, 2017.

The Esoteric Order of Dagon (E.'.O.'.D.'.) describe their Order as: *"a serious occult Order which has been working Lovecraftian magick for nearly 30 years. The E.'.O.'.D.'. utilizes the so-called Cthulhu Mythos of the horror and fantasy writer H. P. Lovecraft as a magickal method of exploring the Collective Unconscious. The Order claims descent from the traditions of the Sirius mystery cults of ancient Egypt and Sumeria. Other influences include Kenneth Grant, the British occultist, disciple of Aleister Crowley, and head of the Typhonian Order, who also attaches great occult significance to the writings of Lovecraft."* [45]

It is fact, and not a conspiracy, that from **Grant's Typhonian brand of Thelema** and **Aquino's Setianism** has arisen an entire Illuminati current of occult practice that relies on or incorporates Crowley's Lam alien approach, and Lovecraft's Satanic mythos. So Grant's Illuminati Order, even if considered by some a minor occult group, compared to the present-day O.T.O. or Temple of Set, has been very influential in the occult world thanks to the many publications and books of the late Kenneth Grant, and also thanks to his alliance and close collaboration with Michael Paul Bertiaux, a key figure in contemporary USA Satanism. So according to the face value of the evidence, one could also theorize that the Magickal Portal that Crowley created in the Amalantrah Working, brought forth the first of these mysterious beings. However, the Portal constructed was also properly closed by Crowley.

In contrast, like Daniel V. Boudillion also points out: *"When Parsons and Hubbard did their similarly constructed Babylon Working involving the opening of the same Portal, either they ripped the portal beyond the ability to be repaired and closed, or it was enlarged beyond their ability to close it. In either case, the Portal—according to the evidence—has remained open ever since to all manner of interdimensional entities to ingress upon the earth-world at will. The Parsons/Hubbard working effectively opened the world to the modern UFO entity situation. And, based on the Lucifer-Gnosis construct, O.T.O.-style occultists have continued to pull further interdimensional entities through this rip or unclosable portal."* [46]

In short, according to the late Kenneth Grant:

- *Lam is known to be a link between the star systems of Sirius and Andromeda.*

- *Lam is the gateway to the Void. Its number, 71, is that of "NoThing," an apparition.*

- *Lam, as a Great Old One, whose archetype is recognizable in accounts of UFO occupants.*

- *Lam has been invoked to fulfill the work set afoot by Aiwass; as a reflex of Aiwass.*

- *Lam as the transmitter to AL of the vibrations of LA via MA, the key to the Aeon of Maat.*

- *Lam is the occult energy beaming the vibrations of Maat and may proceed from that future aeon.*

In a lecture, given in 1994, Michael Staley, who is considered Grant's heir, and is

45   http://www.esotericorderofdagon.org/ ‡ Archived 11th December, 2017.

46   boudillion.com, *Ibid.*

the present Grand Master of the Typhonian Order, made the following statement:

> *Extraterrestrialism emerges increasingly as the core of Grant's Typhonian Trilogies. And with it an awareness that rather more is indicated that the appearance of little green men from the galaxy 10,000 million light years around the corner, or the old "Was God an astronaut?" thesis from authors such as von Daniken twenty or thirty years ago. All the same, what the extraterrestrial gnosis means in a magical context is not entirely unconnected, though it goes further and has a much wider, deeper and more profound sweep. Firstly, what do we mean by "terrestrial?"*
>
> *The term "terrestrial" denotes simply that which is earth-bound, or human. The terrestrial vehicle is a mask, an incarnation of a consciousness, the veils of which dissolve in the course of initiation. "Extraterrestrial," therefore, indicates that which is beyond the comparatively narrow range of human, earth-bound, terrestrial consciousness. "Beyond" or "Outside" is often used in a similar fashion—that which lies beyond the confines of the terrestrial vehicle. What, then, is it that lies beyond these confines, and of which the terrestrial is a facet? The answer may have become a cliché, but it is potent nonetheless—**cosmic consciousness**. Just as over recent years we have become more aware of the vast gulfs and abysses of stellar space which stretch beyond Earth, and of which Earth is a part, so there is a growing awareness of vast, unsounded reaches of consciousness, the human facet of which is a tiny portion. **Extraterrestrial entities are areas within those reaches, and the Magick of real interest and worth is that which facilitates traffic with such entitles. These entities are, ultimately, not something separate from the magician: not something "out there," but equally an aspect of the continuum of consciousness as is the magician.** To explore these reaches of consciousness, traffic is had with such entities; thereby, more and more of the continuum is thrown into relief. This may seem at first sight to be a solipsist conception, the universe as nothing more than an extension of the magician. In fact, the converse is the case: the magician is an aspect of the universe, and initiation is the unfolding realization of this, much as a temple emerges from darkness into the light of day.*
>
> *An example of the use of the term "terrestrial" in this context occurs in the first paragraph of Lovecraft's story* Beyond the Wall of Sleep:
>
> > *From my experience, I cannot doubt but that man, when lost to terrestrial consciousness, is indeed sojourning in another and uncorporeal life of far different nature from the life we know, and of which only the slightest and most indistinct memories exist after waking ... We may guess that in dreams life, matter, and vitality, as the earth knows such things, are not necessarily constant, and that time and space do not exist as our waking selves comprehend them. Sometimes I believe that this less material life is our truer life and that our vain presence on this terraqueous globe is itself the secondary or merely virtual phenomenon.*
>
> *There is a continuum of consciousness, an ocean of awareness, in which we are at once parts and the whole. This is essentially **advaita**, a sanskrit term meaning "not divided." Many people in the West, Thelemites included, seem to find **advaita** repugnant.*
>
> *And yet, Thelema has its roots in **advaita** and similar doctrines such as the **sunyavada**, the "emptiness at the heart of the matter," articulated so beautifully in Prajnaparamita Buddhism and later in Ch'an. Traditions such as these attempt to guide the intuition of the aspirant towards the apprehension of a non-dual reality*

FIG. 26 Kenneth Grant (1924-2011).

by means of paradox. This is not indulgence in mental gymnastics, but because reality is beyond the dualist categories of subject and object, existence and non-existence, emptiness and manifestation, and hence ultimately inexpressible in terms of reason. This does not mean that we need to abandon reason or give up trying to express mystical insight in language—far from it. **We just need to be aware of the limitations of language and reason, that is all.** [47]

I found what Staley wrote very interesting, in this very elaborate disquisition, as there is definitely a lot of limitations in our understanding of certain realities in our present human condition. However, trafficking with such entities is not the solution to all our problems, and many times the magician becomes possessed and loses his mind, as these beings can often be messengers of deception.

REPTILIANS, VRIL, AND THE BLOOD LINES SERVING THE MULTI-DIMENSIONAL WORLD
IV

Messengers of deception

Since the reopening of interdimensional portals operated first by Aleister Crowley, and later by his followers in California, a wave of extraterrestrial activities and UFO sightings began. The synchronicity of the events that took place in the year Crowley died, has in fact, led most occult experts to assume that the wave of sightings and extraterrestrial activities can all be linked to the opening of the aforementioned dimensional portals, that created a fault in the **Great Wall**—which in the Abrahamic tradition protects humanity from *Gog* and *Magog*. This Great Wall is described by French metaphysician and Illuminati René Guénon, as a circular wall (Lokâloka), that separates the world (loka) from outer darkness (aloka). Guénon wrote that Gog and Magog are obviously similar to Koka and Vikoka, important figures of Hindu mythology, and twin generals who aid the demon Kali in her final battle against Kalki, the 10th and final avatar of the god Vishnu, arriving to herald the end of an age. Guénon commented on the roles that these two figures play in Islam as: *Yajuj and Majuj (Gog and Magog)*. For Islam, Earth is not a unique planet. Other planets like Earth exist throughout the universe. The Quran also says that other planets also have land animals: *"And from His signs, He created the heavens and the Earth, and the land animals that He scattered in BOTH of them (heavens and Earth), And He is capable of gathering them (in one place) if He wishes."* (Quran 42.29)

For certain Islamic scholars, the Quran says that extraterrestrial creatures will invade Earth one day.[1] Apparently, there is an interdimensional wormhole right here on Earth that connects Earth with another planet. One day the creatures on that planet will use this wormhole as an interdimensional passage to invade Earth. Allah gave a method of transportation to his angels throughout the universe. **The Quran calls them *Ma'arej* (Quran 70.3) and describes how angels use them for long-distance travel.** Today Muslims know that these "Ma'arej" are what scientists call wormholes.

---

1   *See* http://www.speed-light.info/islam_life_other_planets.htm ‡ Archived 11th December, 2017.

This is how angels (or any interdimensional alien) can reach any place in the universe before you finish reading this sentence: Wormholes. Muslims also believe that wormholes are not strictly for the use of angels. For example, their prophet once used a wormhole in the *Israa & Me'raj* (Me'raj is singular of Ma'arej) (Quran 17.1). In another incident, the Quran describes a clan of Yajuj and Majuj using a Me'raj (wormhole): *"This clan (who didn't understand human speech) were wreaking havoc on Earth.)"* This leads to the infamous armies of **Gog and Magog,** in the Hebrew Bible near the end of times, the advent of the Antichrist, and the great alien deception that surrounds it all. As Gary Bates discussed in his book *Alien Intrusion,* the alien/ UFO phenomenon is very real, but very misleading. Aliens are not creatures from another planet, they are beings from another dimension (a.k.a. fallen angels led by the greatest deceiver of all — Satan).

Hundreds of thousands of people in many parts of the world are claiming they are encountering UFO entities in one way or another, but who and what are they really encountering? They may have had what is called a *Close Encounter of the Third or Fourth Kind,* a term used by ufologist **J. Allen Hynek.** There is also growing public interest in this phenomenon due to media attention. Some contactees and abductees, and also some claiming to channel extraterrestrials, are being revealed the following kinds of information: *We are not alone in the Universe.* We are told—this earth has been visited many times in the past and present by different types of extraterrestrials. These **ET's** have been involved in our creation, evolution, religions, myths, beliefs, etc. Some contactees are told that humans are the consequence of ET encounters with earlier forms of humans. Without this contact, humans never would have evolved to the point we have. Rael, the chosen prophet, and Messiah of the New Age Raelian movement was told that humankind was created by a group of ET's called the Elohim, using advanced genetic engineering in laboratories.

Others who believe in the messages of *the Pleiadians* are told that the Pleiadian ancestors were some of the *Original Planners of Earth,* who seeded this and other worlds. Whatever the explanation, fictitious or real, we are told that ET's are involved in our evolution and creation; something the Illuminati mystery schools seem to confirm. However, most contactees in the New Age game, seem to have an excessive faith in alien intervention, as they are told that humankind stands in a transitional period before the dawn of a New Age, and with peace, love, and understanding, the people of Earth will see a great new era begin to dawn.

For the New Age movement and its followers, the Space Beings are here to teach, not to invade, just as taught by the late Aleister Crowley. They say they are here to help awaken the human spirit, to help humankind rise to higher levels of vibration, so that the people of our primitive race may be ready to enter the New Age and new dimensions. We are told over and over to be ready for a quantum leap that will move humankind forward, on both biological and spiritual levels. In the meantime, however, the Satanic and evil reality around us tells another story. So should we believe them? They say the human soul will evolve, but if we do not raise our vibration within a set period of time, at that point severe earth changes and major cataclysms are said to take place. Such disasters will not end the world but shall serve as cataclysmic crucibles to burn off the dross of unreceptive humanity. Those who die in such dreadful purging will be allowed to reincarnate on higher levels of development so that their salvation will be more readily accomplished through higher teachings on a higher vibratory level.

Others are told that the *receptive* or *chosen* will be saved by benign ET's when these disasters take place. Some, like the Raelians are told they will experience some kind of eternal existence through further genetic engineering, i.e. cloning. For the New Agers, a major leap in consciousness and evolution is about to take place. Crop circles, UFO sightings, contactee and abductee experiences, are preparing those who are receptive to these paradigm changes. Events such as the *Harmonic Convergence* are in this contest to lift the veil, so the Higher Galactic Intelligence of the universe will be able to channel their energies and influences to facilitate the shift towards a New Age. Evidence for these claims is said to be the many abductee and contactee experiences with similar stories and messages, physical scars, hybrid babies, recognition of some kind of symbolic or hieroglyphic language etc., all symptoms typical of demonic possession. There seems to be according to researchers, increasing cases worldwide of UFO sightings, crop or landing circles, animal mutilations, abductions of men, women, and children. All activities, including the crop circles, have always been attributed to Jinn in the Islamic tradition. There is, however, some disturbing evidence according to the late Dr. **Karla Turner**, who worked with over 400 abduction cases:

Aliens can alter our perceptions of our surroundings.

Aliens can control what we think we see. They can appear to us under any number of guises and shapes.

Aliens can be present with us in an invisible state and can make themselves only partially visible.

Abductees receive marks on their bodies other than the well-known scoops and straight-line scars. These other marks include single punctures, multiple punctures, large bruises, three-and four-fingered claw marks, and triangles of every possible sort.

Female abductees often suffer serious gynecological problems after their alien encounters, and sometimes these problems lead to cysts, tumors, cancer of the breast and uterus, and to hysterectomies.

A surprising number of abductees suffer from serious illnesses they didn't have before their encounters. These have led to surgery, debilitation, and even death from causes the doctors can't identify.

Abductees often encounter more than one sort of alien during an experience, not just **the greys.** *Every possible combination of grey, reptoid, insectoid, blond, and widow's peak have been seen during single abductions, aboard the same craft or in the same facility.*

Abductees report being scoffed at, jeered at, and threatened by their alien captors. Painful genital and anal probes are performed ... Unknown fluids are injected into some abductees.

Abductees—"virgin" cases—report being taken to underground facilities where they see grotesque hybrid creatures, nurseries of hybrid humanoid fetuses, and vats of colored liquid filled with parts of human bodies.

Abductees report seeing other humans in these facilities being drained of blood, being mutilated, flayed, and dismembered, and stacked, lifeless like cords of wood. Some abductees have been threatened that they, too, will end up in this condition if they don't co-operate with their alien captors.

Aliens come into homes and temporarily remove young children, leaving their distraught parents paralyzed and helpless. In cases where a parent has been able to protest, the aliens insist that "The children belong to us."

Aliens have forced their human abductees to have sexual intercourse with aliens and even with other abductees while groups of aliens observe these performances. In such encounters, the aliens have sometimes disguised themselves in order to gain the cooperation of the abductee, appearing in such forms as Jesus, the Pope, certain celebrities, and even the dead spouses of the abductees.

Aliens perform extremely painful experiments or procedures on abductees, saying that these acts are necessary but give no explanation why ... Painful genital and anal probes are performed, on children as well as adults.

Aliens make predictions of an imminent period of global chaos and destruction. They say that a certain number of humans ... will be "rescued" from the planet in order to continue the species, either on another planet or back on earth after the destruction is over. Many abductees report they don't believe their alien captors and foresee instead a much more sinister use of the "rescued" humans.

Dr. Karla Turner died under mysterious circumstances. In every instance, there are multiple reports from unrelated cases, confirming that such bizarre details are not the product of a single deranged mind. These details are from the late Dr. Turner, convincing evidence that, contrary to the claims of many UFO researchers, the abduction experience isn't limited to a uniform pattern of events. This phenomenon simply can't be explained in terms of cross-breeding experiments or scientific research into the human physiology. For Dr. Turner, before we allow ourselves to believe in the benevolence of these alien interactions. we should ask ourselves the following questions:

Do enlightened beings need to use the cover of night to perform good deeds?

Do they need to paralyze us and render us helpless to resist?

Do angels need to steal our fetuses?

Do they need to manipulate our children's genitals and probe our rectums?

Are fear, pain, and deception consistent with high spiritual motives? [2]

There is no doubt, Dr. Turner's questions and her discoveries, alarmed the Military Industrial Complex, and the Secret Societies of the Illuminati Network, that seem to promote only the benevolent side of the alien UFO phenomenon in the eyes of the public, that are however becoming more aware in recent years.

2   *Aliens -Friends or Foes* by Dr. **Karla Turner** (from -UFO Universe, Spring 1993)

INTERVIEW WITH THE LATE KARLA TURNER

by B. Alan Walton

From Contact Forum May/June 1995 – ReptilianAgenda Website

CF: You are widely regarded as one of the leading experts in the field of UFO and "alien-abduction" research. How did you get started in your study of these things?

KT: Our family knew nothing about the phenomenon when we started having UFO sightings and abduction encounters. Being a researcher, I turned to the UFO literature for an explanation. When I absorbed what was available, I found no answers that I felt were trustworthy. I decided that this was a crucial situation for my family (if not globally), and the only way I could get answers was to do the research myself. The only way to do the research, in this case, was to go out into the field and deal with abduction cases.

CF: Was *Into the Fringe* the first result of that? [Karla's first book]

KT: Actually, "Into the Fringe" was not a result of research to gain answers. It is more of an account of my family's awakening to, and coping with, these experiences during the first year and a half when they were very intense. It was not until after that that I started to branch out and work with other people. I worked with Barbara Bartholic (*Story of A UFO Investigator*) on our case and began working with her on other cases. Many times she would come to Texas (where I lived) and we would set up a four-or-five-day work session, during which people in that area who wanted to work with her would come to my home. She would interview them and place them under regressive hypnosis there. I began to learn by acting as her assistant. (If Ph.D.'s were available in this field, Barbara should certainly have one. Working with her proved to be much more educational than my academic career.) Then Barbara's caseload got so heavy that she was no longer able to handle it. It was no longer enough for me to assist, and I had to be doing preliminary investigative work myself. And that was how my involvement developed.

CF: We have been finding, in a lot of cases, that experiencers' parents, sometimes their great-grandparents have had the same types of encounters that they have. Is that what you found in your family?

KT: Yes, it is definitely "transgenerational" in Elton's family. [Elton, Dr. Turner's husband, was given the pseudonym "Casey" in the books *Into the Fringe* and *Taken*. They no longer feel it is necessary to protect his identity.]

Before Elton's grandmother died, in 1990 or 1991, the family knew she was near the end of her time here, so they asked her to tell some of the old stories and videotaped her response for posterity ... My mother refuses to say anything because it is just too frightening to her. She has not yet even finished reading *Into the Fringe*. Each time she reads a page or two, she becomes so upset that she can't go any further—which tells me that there is probably a reason for her feelings. I remember that, in 1965, when I was a senior in high school, a big flap was making national news. It was one of the few times that I had ever paid attention to the UFO thing. One day, Mother and I were listening to the TV while doing something in the kitchen. Walter

Cronkite was talking about the UFO flap, and I told Mother that if a UFO landed in the backyard, I probably would go get on it. My mother, who is extremely gentle, and who never raised her voice or hit me, stopped what she was doing, grabbed me by both shoulders and shook me until I felt as if my teeth would fall out. All the while, she was saying, forcefully, "You swear to me, you will not ever, ever, ever get near one! Don't you dare even say that!" It was the only outburst I have ever known my mother to have in my entire life. I now know—from research—that extreme responses like that to this phenomenon are often indicators that a person has had experiences.

CF: You mentioned the use of hypnosis, which has been the subject of a lot of controversy. Some of the other researchers have said that people under hypnosis can come up with scenarios that did not happen, in order to please the hypnotist. Some have said that the multiple levels of experience—where one can break through screen memories and ferret out buried memories that are differen—are artifacts of the process of hypnosis. What are your opinions about these issues?

KT: I think those positions are completely untenable, they grow out of what I call armchair research. I don't conceive you will find them being espoused by anyone who has actually had the experiences. If they have been through them and want to come back and talk about what happens when they undergo hypnosis, to look at what they consciously remember, then we can have a dialogue. Right now, they are speaking without knowledge. They are speaking hypothetically, and their opinions are based on erroneous understandings of the phenomenon, of the experiences, and of the control exerted upon abductees during these experiences. It is easy to philosophize any number of explanations, but that does not mean that those explanations have any relationship to what is really going on. Also, there are bad hypnotists and good hypnotists. A bad hypnotist probably can foul up a number of things. I know that people who have gone to hypnotists for smoking or dietary problems have sometimes suffered more after hypnosis. Obviously, some things can be mishandled. But my experience with hypnosis and the veracity of what is recalled has, in several cases, been proven to me to be accurate. I have been able to investigate these cases. At times erroneous material does surface or is created because of the situation, but that is not typical. I conclude that hypnosis is, by and large, one of the most excellent tools we have. Used properly, it may be the only tool we have to get certain pieces of information (or levels of information) back up to the conscious state. I have been able to test a number of hypnotically recalled memories against externally verifiable evidence, and they have proven to be correct.

CF: You have found, have you not, that sometimes there are multiple levels, like the layers of an onion? An experiencer undergoes hypnosis and comes up with a scenario, then, when he is regressed to a deeper level, he breaks through the first level (you find out that it was a screen memory), and a different scenario emerges.

KT: Yes, and it seems to me that, in some cases, a bottom level can be reached.

CF: How many layers are there; how deep can you go, and what's at the bottom?

KT: We have not done enough research to answer any of those questions without being an armchair philosopher. Typically (not always) the first recall deals mostly with conscious information. When the subject is taken to the next deeper level of the trance state and asked to focus, often what will be reported is that what was seen was not the same as the conscious recall. Then a groping process begins. The subject thinks, "This was inaccurate; I feel that something was wrong, and when I focus, I see that it was not what I thought it was." That is a transitional level. There may be only a couple of levels—as opposed to, say twenty levels—but there certainly is a cover level, underlain by a more solid foundation. If the subjects are helped to program their mental computers to penetrate illusion and to speak only truthful, accurate statements, to, as Barbara has often said, "clarify vision," then they will recall radically different scenarios—not expanded versions of the firsts scenarios, but something quite different from what their conscious memories had left them with. There are at least two levels, and possibly three.

CF: People have told us that they can break through screen memory after screen memory until they get to a scenario involving reptilians, and that is as far as they can go. Have you found that to be the case?

KT: In the few cases that I am very familiar with, when the "baseline" was reached, reptilians were involved.

CF: Are the greys always involved at the top level?

KT: Sometimes the first level involves greys, sometimes humans, sometimes Pleiadians, sometimes strange animals.

CF: Abductees tell stories of seeing beings—angelic Nordics, for example, and then, when they concentrate and try to focus on their memories of those beings, they disappear, and behind them are these "lizard people."

KT: I am not familiar with a number of cases. I have heard other researchers talk about the same thing. In one case that I recount in *Into the Fringe*, James had mostly conscious recollections and almost no hypnosis. He remembered being drawn into the proximity of a beautiful "Pleiadian" woman, who was very alluring and tender, and almost seductive. She wanted him to come into her embrace. When he got into the embrace and thought she was going to kiss him, she disappeared entirely, and what was left in her place was a purplish-black, bumpy, almost slimy-looking character with fairly asymmetrical features. I have encountered this same type of creature in a couple of other cases. The entity was very strong. Instead of embracing James, the creature threw him down to the ground and shoved a two-foot-long tube down his throat, into his stomach, and pulled up stomach juices. The next day, he still had some of the bile taste, the interior of his throat was sore, and he discovered claw marks around both sides of his neck, where he had been held down. Whatever the entity was, there was something claw-like about it (which, of course, matches reptilians). Maybe, as close as he was to it, he could not perceive the whole figure. But he could see a bumpy covering, which could equate to the rough, scaly exterior sometimes reported to be reptilian. It is described as bumpy, ridged, bony, strong, clawed.

CF: Apparently these beings have the ability to project different images.

KT: Some people say that they transform—that they mutate or change their own real forms. I don't accept that as accurate. I don't believe they really look like a blond, and they do something to trick you and then they suddenly look like a reptilian. I think that what they alter is human perception. They certainly can project false images—just as Ted's [Ted Rice's] grandmother was shown her dead husband so that she would consent to have a sexual encounter. Ted's grandfather had been dead for six years. And in the middle of having the encounter with what she thought was her restored husband the image disappeared—I suppose because the aliens wanted to get the "emotional juice" from her—and she saw a "reptoid" on top of her. We also have heard stories about military people being present during an abduction, and when people focus on them, they change. Budd Hopkins tells a story about a person who saw a military policeman. He wondered why on Earth the MP was there and tried to focus very carefully on him. When he did so, the MP changed, before his eyes, into an officer of high rank, and then into a Nazi officer. The aliens cannot allow us to be involved with them in our normal state of mind because we would be under our own control, and that is not what they desire.

CF: A question about the "psychic vampire" nature of the aliens?

KT: Yes. Now you are getting to why may be the crux of the "harvest." That may be that they not only need emotional energy, but also at least one faction (and I would be tempted if I were to guess, that they would be reptoids) actually uses the physical bodies. They are trying hard to get us detached from our bodies by telling us that they are "only containers."

CF: Why?

KT: Because they eat our bodies. If a cow knew you were going to eat it, you would want to tell that cow (if they could understand), "Your body is not important. It doesn't matter."

CF: Regarding the spiritual nature of the Greys and the Reptiloids?

KT: I think it is something to think about. I don't believe the greys have souls but are more like "Frankensteins" or "zombies" or whatever term you want to use for the "living dead." When I have been with them, I have had an overwhelming feeling that they are not alive—that they are dead.

CF: Any positive (ethical) ETs?

KT: I do accept there are intelligent forces that can contact and inform us—perhaps to help us help ourselves.

CF: What about the so-called "Alien Prophecies?"

KT: Aliens make predictions of an imminent period of global chaos and destruction. They say that a certain number of humans—and the number varies dramatically from case to case—will be "rescued" from the planet in order to continue the species, either on another planet or back on earth after the destruction is over. Many abductees report that they don't believe their alien captors and foresee instead a much more sinister use of the "rescued" humans.

Further statements from the late Karla Turner on her important research can be found at reptilianagenda.com

DAVID ICKE AND THE "REPTILIANS"

*A*lex Vandenberg, a contributor to the *Waking Times,* wrote in April 2016:

When scurrying down the rabbit hole on the pathless path one is inevitably confronted by an interdimensional race of beings, often of an insect-like reptilian nature, perched atop the pinnacle of power that constitutes the nucleus of the New World Order. The appellations attributed to these dark interstellar actors are myriad and run the gamut of everything from the Sumerian Anunnaki to the Sons of God. While there is a plethora of contemporary material available on the subject, it appears very little has been written on what these ancient "gods" actually are. Instead of adding to the convoluted nature of the subject with more conjecture, let's try to pin down these phantasmagoric apparitions and put them within a contextual framework that sheds light on their true nature. For if we are to defeat our enemy we must truly understand that enemy.

Vandenberg clearly states that we are being suppressed by this enemy:

As a result of this suppression of the instinctual roots of the unconscious, the world is now engulfed in the flames of psychosis as a psychic split has emerged within the collective consciousness of humanity. Thus our current impasse is a function of sheer insanity. This is a world in which we are all being paganized, brutalized, sexualized, and debased in what is this Nigredo phase of the Alchemical Great Work; a world in which we are literally being fed on by a Force. We hear it every day. Incessant, relentless chatter about how our leaders (or rather misleaders) are completely mad and how everything around us is inverted, corrupted, and perverted. [3]

In 2012, a film called *John Carter* was released, about interdimensional and shape-shifting aliens, few in number and near immortal in lifespan, who manipulate willing leaders, for endless wars. They pretend to be legendary gods and live for psychopathic esoteric domination. In the story, after they establish control of Mars, *Earth will be next.* The protagonists must accomplish two objectives for their freedom; to have the planetary populations rise above contrived fear, hate, and wars, and to recognize and reject the shape-shifters manipulation. These beings are the interdimensional and shape-shifting *reptilians,* that David Icke documents as the esoteric power behind human history. However, *John Carter* is a movie with a message: *Our real-world Earth, not a fictional Mars, requires accomplishment of the film's two objectives for humanity's freedom.* [4]

David Icke (b. 1952), is an English writer and public speaker, with an extraordinary sense of humor and some pretty unconventional ideas. Icke, born in an English working-class family, was a football player, and later became a sports broadcaster for the BBC. However, he is known since the 1990s as a sort of guru of the fight against the New World Order, but for some of his harsh critics, like Adam Wears, he is just a professional conspiracy theorist that has: *"A net worth of*

3   http://www.wakingtimes.com/2016/04/15/psychic-parasites-inter-dimensional-be-ings-and-the-occult-elite/ ‡ Archived 11th December, 2017.

4   http://www.washingtonsblog.com/2012/03/john-carters-shape-shifting-inter-dimensional-aliens-are-david-ickes-reptilians.html ‡ Archived 11th December, 2017.

FIG. 27 David Icke.

10 million pounds, accumulated through book sales and expensive, sold-out live talks."[5]
You might not agree with everything he writes or says, and some of his initial
predictions failed to manifest, but Icke is a true idealist living a very modest life
in a very normal apartment in the Isle of Wight. *"No mansion, and no Bentley."*[6]

David Icke, who was a BBC television sports presenter and spokesman for the
Green Party, completely changed his life when a psychic, the late **Betty Shine,** professed in March 1990, that he had been placed on Earth for a purpose, and would
begin to receive messages from **Wang Ye Lee** a messenger of the spirit world.[7]

Interestingly enough, *Wang Ye* worship is a Fujianese and Taiwanese folk religion, frequently considered as an aspect of the Taoist belief system linked to
Invisible Masters known as Wang Y, supernatural beings, spirits that were once,
according to legend, real human beings. There are many kinds of Wang Ye; some
traditions claim there are a total of 360, with 132 surnames among them. The

5   *See* https://rationalwiki.org/wiki/David_Icke ‡ Archived 11th December, 2017.

6   *See* https://www.youtube.com/watch?v=m0jjGiuxCCs ‡ Archived 11th December,
       2017.

7   *See* Michael Barkun, *A Culture of Conspiracy: Apocalyptic Visions in Contemporary
       America,* (Berkeley, CA: University of California Press, 2003), p. 103.

most important element in Icke's new role is that they are **divine emissaries who tour the world of the living on behalf of the celestial realm, expelling disease and evil from those who worship them.**

Betty Shine was a gifted spiritualist, medium, and healer from England. She was born in 1929 and passed away in 2003 at the age of 73. Before embarking on her healing and clairvoyant career, she sang professionally. At times she also delved into vitamin and mineral therapy, as well as medical hand analysis. She also taught yoga. [8] David Icke visited her four times, and one of the things she said to him was: *"One man cannot change the world, but one man can communicate the message that will change the world."* Betty who reached literally millions with her New Age best-selling books functioned as a medium, and Invisible Master, a spirit voice that followed her since she was two years old. As a child, Betty had many psychic experiences. She often heard a male voice speaking to her, and initially assumed everyone heard him. She realized this wasn't the case when comparing notes with a friend. Betty Shine suffered for many years with choking fits, dizziness and heart palpitations. Doctors were unable to help her situation.

Fearing that she may die, she visited a well-known medium by the name of **Charles Horrey**. Charles Horrey told Betty that she was to be a healer and the attacks were caused by a build-up of unused energy. He told Betty that once she started healing her health problems would clear up, and so they did. He told her she was also going to be a great medium. **As her healing work expanded, Betty Shine was able to see mind energy, which she felt resembled a halo as portrayed in biblical times.** She assigned various mind exercises to help her clients improve their mental energy, and hence improve their situation. If a client of Betty was depressed their mental energy would funnel in toward their head. As Betty Shine's healing sessions continued this energy would change its shape and begin to radiate out as a healthy mind would. Shine wrote many books in her lifetime. Three of them in particular, stress the importance of using your mind energy to help you achieve what you want in this lifetime. [9]

David Icke was contacted by Wang Ye Lee, an entity that changed his life, and this happened through Betty Shine, a medium of the Invisible Masters, that appeared in David's life in March 1990, after Icke had searched for answers from the invisible world while alone in a hotel room. A few days later, Icke was playing soccer, his favorite game, with his son Gareth. He visited the seafront at Ryde on the Isle of Wight, a place where he would regularly go with his son, and later have lunch at the railway station café, a short walk away. The café was full that day, and as they turned to walk away, someone recognized David and began to chat with him about soccer.

When the conversation was finally over, David couldn't find his son Gareth, but he knew he would probably be in the newspaper shop nearby looking at books he liked. David stood at the entrance to the shop and said they were going now to find another café, but as he turned to leave, his feet wouldn't move. They were stuck to the ground as if two magnets were pulling them to the floor. He

8   http://community.humanityhealing.net/m/group/discussion?id=1388889%3ATopic
        %3A1352413

9   *See* https://www.youtube.com/watch?v=TZNoQPFnfVQ ‡ Archived 11th December,
        2017.

then heard a voice in his head say: *"Go and look at the books on the far side."* His immediate thought was: *"What the hell was this all about?"* He knew this shop very well and the books in that section were of no interest to him. But given the voice and what was happening to his feet, he went over to see what would happen. The first book he saw was one by Betty Shine and he was immediately intrigued because of the presence he had felt around him. [10]

Icke's experience demonstrates that Spiritualism is not always demonic or an end-times deception, even if the initial messages and apocalyptic visions Icke received were incomplete, and were obviously implanted in him by a trickster entity, that made him look at times like a fool to the outside world.

However, for every form of provocation by a trickster, there is always a hidden lesson that eventually led Icke to learn the truth about these entities. Let's remember that Spiritualists like the late Betty Shine, who practice healing or mediumship, often pray to God not only for assistance but also for the protection upon those who receive certain messages from the psychic world. Like some researchers have pointed out, demons would not propagate a religion (i.e. Spiritualism), that says you have to earn your way into heaven by good works and that you have to atone for evil deeds also by good works. In fact, why should demons or evil interdimensional entities encourage people to do good works at all, when they actually want to manipulate and control the world of matter for evil purposes. According to the parable of *A Tree and Its Fruit*, Spiritualism cannot be evil when it yields good results or is a vehicle for an important message for humankind, like in the case of Betty Shine and David Icke. Spiritual healers like the late Betty Shine, are responsible for many physical cures, and mediumship has truly helped many people suffering from grief.

There are also great dangers to be found in the practice of Spiritualism, with the majority of mediums interested in making money, and others involved in the occult and Satanism, often acting willingly or unwillingly, as tools of demonic interdimensional forces. Demon spirits prey on those who are weak mentally, physically and emotionally. When a person suffers a trauma in their life and they are unable to cope with the trauma mentally and emotionally, a part of their soul chooses not to have that experience and splits off causing *soul fragmentation*. [11] This leaves a vacuum or space for demon spirits to reside within the soul and influence the mind and feelings of the person who becomes involved with a medium to find consolation. They can become possessed, deprived of sleep, attacked physically by these entities, who are often heard slamming doors, knocking on walls, etc. This, of course, was not the case for David Icke.

In February 1991, Icke followed his first strong spiritual experience, when he visited a pre-Inca Sillustani burial ground near Puno, Peru, where he felt drawn to a particular circle of waist-high stones. As he stood in the circle, he had two thoughts: that people would be talking about this in 100 years, and that it would be over when it rained. His body shook as though plugged into an electrical socket, he wrote, and new ideas poured into him. Then it started raining and the ex-

10   https://web.archive.org/web/20110619122640/http://davidickebooks.co.uk/index.
        php?act=viewDoc&docId=1 ‡ Archived 11th December, 2017.

11   *See* http://www.spiritualistresources.com/cgi-bin/rescue/index.pl?read=92 ‡ Archived 11th December, 2017.

perience ended. He described it as the kundalini (a term from Indian yoga) activating his chakras, or energy centers, triggering a higher level of consciousness. [12]

David Icke now lives in the town of Ryde on the Isle of Wight, and is one of the world's most successful lecturers; gathering hundreds, even thousands of people at times, for his public speeches/performances. He has published many books based on his *conspiracy theories*, translated all over the world into several languages, promoting his unusual and uncensored vision of the current political, economic, and social fact. Icke has certainly been one of the first to deal with certain issues right at the birth of the internet era, and I have to thank him for promoting on his website back in 2006, some of my early articles, when I began my blogging activity, fearing for my own life and the possibility of retaliation from my enemies. Icke has been dealing with an Invisible Master, who pushed him to deliver his visions to humankind. Like in all cases related to Spiritualism including David Icke, we need to always keep in mind the **Parable of the Tree and its Fruits** (also called the *Trees and their Fruits*), a parable of Jesus about testing a prophet beginning at Luke 6:43 (NIV) that says: "No good tree bears bad fruit, nor does a bad tree bear good fruit. **Each tree is recognized by its own fruit.**"

So we will judge David in years to come and his Invisible Master on the fruits of his divulgation, not on the lies or the disinfo spread today by his detractors.

ARE REPTILIANS MULTI-DIMENSIONAL VAMPIRES?

*R*egarding David Icke and Reptilians, did you know that the pheromones in human women and iguanas are a chemical match? You only have to look at the bottom of the human spine to see the remnant. Indeed, some humans continue to be born with tails or caudal appendages. For Icke, the Reptilian Race covertly controls humanity from a dimension of reality very close to this one, just beyond visible light, and that is why we do not usually see them. The world that we live in is on a *set* frequency range very similar to a radio station on a receiver. Icke's reptilian theory always made me think these beings could actually be the Jinn of Islamic folklore, supernatural beings made of smokeless fire invisible to human sight. This is a theory I originally made public over ten years ago in an article published by *Illuminati News* in November 2006, [13] explained later in detail in my interview on *Project Camelot*. [14]

Jinn are said to inhabit the unseen world, just beyond the visible universe of humans. The visible spectrum of humans is a very narrow band of electromagnetic spectrum. In Islamic teachings, Jinn are said to have the mango shaped eyes with an iris-like cat's eyes. We cannot say definitively what they look like, as we cannot see them. They do not frequent clean places, like mosques, churches, etc. They feed on low vibrational frequency (fear, hate, etc), and are repelled by high vibrational frequency (love, happiness, etc). The evil Jinn are said to vex and harm people. Jinn are akin to demons in the Christian gospels. They are said

12   *See* David Icke, *Tales from the Time Loop*, (Wildwood, MO: Bridge of Love Publications, 2003), pp. 12–13, 16.

13   http://www.illuminati-news.com/111906a.htm ‡ Archived 11th December, 2017.

14   http://projectcamelot.org/leo_zagami.html ‡ Archived 11th December, 2017.

to inhabit people. The ministry of Jesus was casting out the Jinn/Demons from possessed individuals. The gospel stories make a big play on Jesus casting out demons, especially the earliest one, Mark. The reptilians of David Icke are in fact, Jinn/Demons operating just outside visible sight, possessing people in the power system. These are the Reptilians, Icke believes in, most of the time invisible to human sight. If our three-dimensional world is set at a frequency of 98 then these Reptilian inter-dimensional entities would exist on a frequency range of 98.1, which would be the lower fourth dimension just beyond our ability to see them.

The physical Universe is teeming with various Reptilian races. They can be found in many forms and variations, from those of humanoid appearance with green scaly skin to albino whites, and those with tails and horns and even wings. For the record not all Reptilian beings or Jinn are *bad*. Some are malevolent, some are benevolent, and most of them are somewhere in between.

CERN, INTERDIMENSIONAL PORTALS, AND THE ROSWELL INCIDENT

*T*here has been much talk about interdimensional worlds, even in the mainstream media. It seems like the scientific community is actively working on the concrete possibility of creating artificial interdimensional doors, careless of any possible consequences, especially the growing fear regarding the experiments that take place in CERN. Most of you who have heard of CERN, will have heard of the LHC (Large Hadron Collider), the largest scientific instrument which exceeds 20 miles in diameter and travels under the sovereign territory of two countries (Switzerland, France), but some might not know that the Large Hadron Collider has been created to discover the **FIFTH** dimension, with the possibility of creating doorways to other universes. These are a couple of extracts from their official website stating their future intentions: *"Though it may sound like science fiction, if extra dimensions exist, they could explain why the universe is expanding faster than expected, and why gravity is weaker than the other forces of nature."* How are they going to achieve this? Well CERN says that: *"One option would be to find evidence of particles that can exist only if extra dimensions are real. Theories that suggest extra dimensions predict that in the same way as atoms have a low-energy ground state and excited high-energy states, there would be heavier versions of standard particles in other dimensions."* [15]

So by using the LHC to create *microscopic black holes* and other scientific diableries, CERN wants to achieve access to a multi-dimensional reality. Of course, piercing the universe in search of answers might not be such a good idea after all. Bizarre images of cloud formations have in fact, appeared above CERN's Large Hadron Collider (LHC) on the **24th of June 2016**, [16] on the FEAST of St. John the Baptist, a key moment in the Masonic year, as well as the **International Flying Saucer Day**, in honor of Kenneth Arnold's encounter on June 24th, 1947 with nine saucer-like objects spotted over Washington state. And this event that appeared,

---

15   https://home.cern/about/physics/extra-dimensions-gravitons-and-tiny-black-holes
      ‡ Archived 11th December, 2017.

16   *See* https://www.express.co.uk/news/weird/684219/What-is-CERN-doing-Bizarre-
      clouds-over-Large-Hadron-Collider-prove-portals-are-opening ‡ Archived 11th De-
      cember, 2017.

thanks to a brilliant photo in the media, could actually be the shocking proof that the world's biggest experiment is moving further in opening a portal to another dimension, helping to facilitate a possible alien invasion. And what's up with the human sacrifice staged on the grounds of CERN in front of the statue of Shiva, just a few weeks later, that was conveniently disregarded as a prank? [17]

While many may not think twice about it, Shiva is, in fact, the Hindu god of creation, death, and destruction. When Shiva mates with his consort, Kali, they are depicted as a beast of destruction, and a time of death as they combine like Voltron during Tantric sex, a practice Aleister Crowley and other occultists in the Illuminati knew very well. In the previously cited BSRA *Memorandum*, found in the FBI Vault, put together by **Meade Layne** (1882-1961) and his associates from the venerable Borderland Sciences Research Foundation, it says in regards of these entities that: *"Their mission is peaceful. The visitors contemplate settling on this plane."* But can we trust Meade Layne and his perception of the interdimensional alien agenda? Greenfield, tells us that Layne was for many years the editor of BSRF's *Round Robin* and other journals, and he worked closely with trance channeler Mark Probert. Layne who was also a student of Frater Achad (Charles Stansfeld Jones) of the O.T.O, and even Israel Regardie at one time, had also been a member of the Society of the Inner Light, a direct offspring of the **Hermetic Order of the Golden Dawn**. At the end of the 19th century, this important Secret Society developed its rituals from certain Rosicrucian cipher manuscripts based on the teachings of the Third Order, or **Secret Chiefs**, or **Ascended Masters**—which are for Greenfield and most contemporary Illuminati, identical with the Space People in contact lore.

A lot of the cipher material that shows up in and around Layne, who was said to be in frequent communication with the Great White Brotherhood, is highly suggestive that he was one of those who introduced the cipher into UFO trance-channeled contactee lore. Let's remember that Layne was also writing about flying discs before Kenneth Arnold's sightings. He also introduced the idea of channeled masters to UFOlogy. The mysterious *Memorandum* now known as **Memorandum 6751**, addressed to scientists and military authorities, and produced under the editorial direction of Meade Layne, for the BSRA publication *Round Robin/Flying Roll*, that can now be easily found on the FBI Vault website under the **UFO section,** just by opening the first document (1 of 16), and typing 22 at the bottom of the page. There shows a very interesting date: **July 8, 1947.** This is the day of the **Roswell incident**; a key event in the history of Ufology, which occurred in Roswell, New Mexico (USA). A strange case of synchronicity, or is there something more to it? The document states:

This memorandum is respectfully addressed to certain scientists of distinction, to important aeronautical and military authorities, to a number of public officials and to a few publications. The writer has little expectation that anything of import will be accomplished by this gesture. The mere fact that the data herein were obtained by so-called supernormal means is probably sufficient to ensure its disregard by nearly all the persons addressed: nevertheless, it seems a public duty to make it available. (The present writer has several university degrees and was

17   *See* https://www.theguardian.com/science/2016/aug/18/fake-human-sacrifice-filmed-at-cern-with-pranking-scientists-suspected ‡ Archived 11th December, 2017.

formerly a university department head). [18]

The Roswell incident was indeed the end of a large wave of UFO sightings across the world, including Europe, the UK, and South America, with a number of *flying saucers* that were spotted across America, but we also know that at that time the infamous **Babylon Working** of John W. Parsons and L. Ron Hubbard had completed its first phase, just before the Roswell incident. Therefore, Illuminati occult activities were heavily monitored by the state authorities who feared Parsons' growing bonds with the interdimensional realm, especially considering his role of great importance in what would later become **NASA**. In the *Memorandum* Meade Layne also warns about the heavy responsibility of authorities: *"We give information and warning and can do no more. Let the newcomers be treated with every kindness. Unless the disks are withdrawn an (illegible, illegible) with which our culture and science are incapable of dealing. A **heavy responsibility** rests upon the few in authority who are able to understand this matter."* [19]

Apparently, as also noted by Allen H. Greenfield, many groups involved with the New World Order, like the Knights of Malta, are involved in privately *selling* cooperation between ultraterrestrial forces of dubious motivations, and terrestrial governments and industrial groups. In February of 1937, on the eve of the Second World War, an American representative of the Knights of Malta, met with the esoteric leadership of the Third Reich in Germany. The meeting took place in a hidden SS retreat and was attended by General Karl Haushofer, the senior initiate of the Black Lodge inside the German Reich. The purpose of the meeting was to *sell* the Nazi regime on contact with what the young Maltese Knight called *"the coming race."*

Asked by Greenfield in 1979 what he meant by the term, he stated: *"The Ultraterrestrials, of course. The Germans had noted their 'ghost rockets' in Sweden and were aware of their power. Most of the older Nazis present, though, were former members of the Thule Group or the archaic Vril Society and took me to be talking about Tibetans or Aryan supermen or some such bunk. Except for Haushofer, who knew better, and the 'Man with the Green Gloves' who, though supposedly a Tibetan himself, was certainly an Ultraterrestrial."* The deal fell through when the Reich fell, and the Knights switched their attention elsewhere.

In the early 1950s, U.S. President Eisenhower unknowingly bought into a similar plan proposed by the Knights of Malta, on behalf of ultraterrestrial overlords, in the name of the anti-communist crusade of that period. **Deviants** were rounded up, and unprecedented power was placed in the hands of the Military Industrial infrastructure throughout the decade, until Eisenhower, in a surprise farewell address, asserted his fundamental decency and libertarian patriotism and roundly denounced the whole deal, and the Military Industrial Complex that is still the biggest problem in today's America, regardless of ones political view.

The Knights of Malta's viewpoint infiltrated organized occultism and UFOlogy on behalf of the Jesuits, through the connection between William Dudley Pelley's underground American fascist organization found in 1933 called **The**

---

18   https://vault.fbi.gov/UFO/UFO%20Part%201%20of%2016/view ‡ Archived 11th December, 2017.

19   *Ibid.*

Silver Legion of America, commonly known as the Silver Shirts prior to World War Two, and the occult Black Lodge within the Third Reich, centered in the SS, the **Ahnenerbe Society**, and the appropriately named *Black Order*—that descended from such black magical bodies as the Thule Group and the Vril Society, as detailed in Greenfield's *Secret Cipher of the UFOnauts*. Pelley and his outfit were certainly tools for the Maltese Knights, and key figures in UFOlogy became involved, including George Adamski and George Hunt Williamson aka Michael d'Obrenovic, and Brother Philip, another American flying saucer contactee, channel, and metaphysical author in the 1950s.

Adamski was introduced to Williamson by Pelley at a time when Adamski was trying to sell his contact story as science fiction to Ray Palmer, then a prominent publisher. For Greenfield, these initiates, not including the well-meaning Adamski, were knowledgeable about the *Ultraterrestrial Cipher*, and the *Sirius-Oannes* legend, but they were still met with a spirited libertarian resistance from the very start by Meade Layne, and his immediate successor, the late Riley Crabb, who *blew the whistle* on the interaction between the U.S. Government, the Knights of Malta and ultraterrestrials since at least 1954. [20]

In the early 1930s, while living in Laguna Beach, Adamski founded the **Royal Order of Tibet**, that held its meetings in the *Temple of Scientific Philosophy*. The O.T.O., the B.S.R.F., and many other sects of the Illuminati Theosophical Network operating in the Post World War II period recalled in many ways the work done in esoteric Nazism, which featured mediums chosen by the Nazi elite to communicate with distant worlds, the so-called *Vril-Damen*.

In 1940 Adamski, his wife, and some close friends moved to a ranch near California's Palomar Mountain, where they dedicated their lives to studying religion, philosophy, and farming. In 1944, with funding from Alice K. Wells, a student of Adamski, they purchased 20 acres (8.1 ha) of land at the base of Palomar Mountain, where they built a new home, a campground called Palomar Gardens, and a small restaurant called Palomar Gardens Café. At the campground and restaurant, Adamski often gave lectures on Eastern philosophy and religion, sometimes late into the night to students, admirers, and tourists. He also built a wooden observatory at the campground to house his six-inch telescope, and visitors and tourists to Palomar Mountain often received the inaccurate impression that Adamski was an astronomer connected to the famed Palomar Observatory at the top of the mountain.

On the 9th of October 1946, during a meteor shower, Adamski and some friends claimed that while they were at the Palomar Gardens Campground, they witnessed a large cigar-shaped *mother ship*. In early 1947, Adamski took a photograph of what he claimed was the 1946 cigar-shaped mother ship crossing in front of the moon over Palomar Gardens. In the summer of 1947, following the first widely publicized UFO sightings in the USA, Adamski claimed he had seen 184 UFOs pass over Palomar Gardens one evening. In 1949, Adamski began giving his first UFO lectures to civic groups and other organizations in Southern California; he requested and received fees for the lectures. In these lectures, he made fantastic claims, such as: *"Government and science had established the existence of UFOs two years earlier, via radar tracking of 700-foot-long spacecraft on the other side of the Moon."*

---

20   *See The Secret Rituals of the Men in Black, Ibid.*

In his lectures, Adamski further claimed that: "*Science now knows that all planets [in Earth's solar system] are inhabited,*" and "*photos of Mars taken from the Mount Palomar observatory have proven the canals on Mars are man-made, built by an intelligence far greater than any man's on earth.*" However, as one UFO historian has noted: "*Even in the early 1950s (Adamski's) assertions about surface conditions on, and the habitability of, Venus, Mars, and the other planets of the solar system flew in the face of massive scientific evidence ...'mainstream' ufologists were almost uniformly hostile to Adamski, holding not only that his and similar contact stories were fraudulent, but that the contactees were making serious UFO investigators look ridiculous.*"[21]

Was Adamski deliberately sabotaging UFOlogy on behalf of the Vatican and the Knights of Malta? Strangely enough in 1963, Adamski claimed that he had a secret audience with Pope John XXIII, and that he had received a **Golden Medal of Honor** from His Holiness. Even if many skeptics are doubtful in regards to the possibility that this meeting ever took place, it shows clearly his will to serve the Pope.

Among other strange occurrences regarding Mount Palomar, the **Agape Lodge** of the O.T.O. founded by Wilfred Talbot Smith in Hollywood in 1935—where Parsons was initiated—later moved to Pasadena, where they established a temple near Mount Palomar, a place that will become shortly after, the home of the Mount Palomar Observatory.

The controversial events of George Adamsky also took place in proximity to this important observatory, initially one of the most important in America, equipped with the largest telescope in the world between 1949 and 1952. In *Alchemical Conspiracy and the Death of the West*, Michael Hoffman says: "*The O.T.O. believed that Palomar was the sexual chakra of the Earth. Parsons commuted regularly between Palomar and Pasadena. The Mount Palomar Observatory opened in 1949. Smith probably consecrated his temple on Palomar soon after his move to California in 1930, before the Observatory was planned. Palomar lies just minutes north of the 33rd parallel. This is significant because 33 is an important number in Masonic symbolism. It is the number of the highest grade of the Scottish Rite. It is also the number of years Christ walked the earth. Hoffman mentions the 33 bones of the human spinal cord. This brings to mind kundalini yoga. Crowley's O.T.O. was a quasi-Masonic order. The higher grades show esoteric Hindu influences of a sexual nature.*"[22] This brings us right back to the Hindu statue that was unveiled at CERN, the European Center for Research in Particle Physics in Geneva in 2004, a two-meter tall statue of the Indian deity Shiva Nataraja, the Lord of Dance.

The statue, symbolizing Shiva's cosmic dance of creation and destruction, that was given to CERN by the Indian government to celebrate the research center's long association with India, but also something far more sinister connected to the New Age movement—most notably **Fritjof Capra** and his international bestseller *The Tao of Physics* (1975), that draws interesting parallels between theories in New Physics, and traditional forms of mysticism, thus arguing that ancient religious ideas are now being proven by contemporary science.

21   *See* https://en.wikipedia.org/wiki/George_Adamski ‡ Archived 11th December, 2017.

22   *See* Paul Rydeen, *Jack Parsons and the Fall of Babalon*, (PKerrville, TX: Crash Collusion Publishing, 1995).

In choosing the image of Shiva Nataraja, the Indian government acknowledged the profound significance of the metaphor of Shiva's dance, to the cosmic dance of subatomic particles, which is observed and analyzed by CERN's physicists. The parallel between Shiva's dance and the dance of subatomic particles was first discussed by Fritjof Capra in an article entitled, *The Dance of Shiva: The Hindu View of Matter in the Light of Modern Physics,* published in *Main Currents in Modern Thought,* back in 1972.

Shiva's cosmic dance then became a central metaphor in Capra's *The Tao of Physics.* A special plaque next to the Shiva statue at CERN explains in fact, the significance of the metaphor of Shiva's cosmic dance with several quotations from *The Tao of Physics.* Here is the text of the plaque:

Ananda K. Coomaraswamy, seeing beyond the unsurpassed rhythm, beauty, power, and grace of the Nataraja, once wrote of it: *"It is the clearest image of the activity of God which any art or religion can boast of."*

More recently, Fritjof Capra explained that: *"Modern physics has shown that the rhythm of creation and destruction is not only manifest in the turn of the seasons and in the birth and death of all living creatures, but is also the very essence of inorganic matter,"* and that, *"for the modern physicists, then, Shiva's dance is the dance of subatomic matter."*

It is indeed as Capra concluded: *"Hundreds of years ago, Indian artists created visual images of dancing Shivas in a beautiful series of bronzes. In our time, physicists have used the most advanced technology to portray the patterns of the cosmic dance. The metaphor of the cosmic dance thus unifies ancient mythology, religious art, and modern physics."* [23]

Now we have verified there is an invisible thread between CERN, interdimensional portals, occult activities and the ROSWELL INCIDENT, we can confirm we are not alone in the multi-universe, but what will happen once the genie is let out of the bottle?

Learning the theosophical aspects of *Memorandum 6751* might help us in our quest to not only understand but to protect ourselves from this great evil being unleashed upon humankind.

THE THEOSOPHICAL ASPECTS OF MEMORANDUM 6751

*T*o complete the study of *Memorandum 6751* from the FBI Vault, let's analyze this focal passage: *"A very serious situation may develop at any time with regard to the 'flying saucers.' If one of these should be attacked, the attacking plane will almost certainly be destroyed. In the public mind, this might create near panic and international suspicion. The principal data concerning this craft is now at hand and must be offered, no matter how fantastic and unintelligible it may seem to minds not previously instructed in thinking of this type."* The Memorandum continues:

23   http://www.fritjofcapra.net/shivas-cosmic-dance-at-cern/ ‡ Archived 11th December, 2017.

Part of the disks carry crews, others are under remote control.

Their mission is peaceful. The visitors contemplate settling on this plane.

These visitors are human-like, but much larger in size.

They are not excarnate Earth people but come from their own world.

They do NOT come from a planet as we use the word, but from an etheric planet which interpenetrates with our own and is not perceptible to us.

The bodies of the visitors, and the craft, automatically materialize on entering the vibratory rate of our dense matter.

The disks possess a type of radiant energy, or a ray, which will easily disintegrate any attacking ship. They reenter the etheric at will, and so simply disuppear from our vision, without a trace.

The region from which they come is not the "astral plane," but corresponds to the Lokas or Talas. Students of esoteric matters will understand these terms.

They probably cannot be reached by radio, but probably can be by radar. if a signal system can be devised for that apparatus.

After the nine points, an *addendum* specifies that: *"The Lokas are oval-shaped, fluted length, oval with a heat-resisting metal or alloy not yet known, the front cage contains the controls, the middle portion a laboratory; the rear contains armament, which consists essentially of a powerful energy apparatus, perhaps a ray."*

Lokas or Talas, are terms and concepts of Hindu origin launched in the West by the Theosophical Society, confirming that Layne was still very close to his Theosophical roots. This suggests that the *supernatural* means through which Layne came into possession of the information of the *Memorandum,* came from his occult background in the Illuminati network. The concept of Lokas was adopted by Theosophy and can be found in the writings of Blavatsky and G. de Purucker. There is also reference to *kamaloka* (a world of desires) as a sort of astral plane or temporary after-life state, according to the teachings of Blavatsky, Leadbeater, and Steiner.

The *Occult Glossary* by Gottfried de Purucker, republished in 1996, by The Theosophical Society (Pasadena), describes the words Tala and Loka (Sanskrit) in the following way:

Tala: *A word which is largely used in the metaphysical systems of India, both in contrast and at the same time in conjunction with loka. As the general meaning of loka is a place or rather a world, so the general meaning of tala is an inferior world. Every loka has as its twin or counterpart a corresponding tala. Wherever there is a loka there is an exactly corresponding tala, and in fact, the tala is the nether pole of its corresponding loka. Lokas and talas, therefore, in a way of speaking, may be considered to be the spiritual and the material aspects or substance-principles of the different worlds which compose and in fact, are the cosmic universe. It is impossible to separate a tala from its corresponding loka—quite as impossible as it would be to separate the two poles of electricity.*

The number of talas as generally outlined in the exoteric philosophies of Hindustan is usually given as seven, there being thus seven lokas and seven talas; but, as a matter of fact, this number varies. If we may speak of a loka as the spiritual pole, we may likewise, call it the principle of any world, and when we speak of the tala as being the negative or inferior pole, it is quite proper also to refer to it as the element of its corresponding loka or principle. Hence, the lokas of a hierarchy may be called the principles of a hierarchy, and the talas, in exactly the same way, may be called the elements or substantial or material aspects of the hierarchy. It should likewise be remembered that all the seven lokas and all the seven talas are continuously and inextricably interblended and interworking and that the lokas and the talas working together form the universe and its various subordinate hierarchies that encompass us around. The higher lokas with the higher talas are the forces or energies and substantial parts of the spiritual and ethereal worlds; the lowest lokas and their corresponding talas form the forces or energies and substantial parts of the physical world surrounding us, and the intermediate lokas with their corresponding talas form the respective energies and substantial parts of the intermediate or ethereal realms. Briefly, therefore, we may speak of a tala as the material aspect of the world where it predominates, just as when speaking of a loka we may consider it to be the spiritual aspect of the world where it predominates. Every loka, it should be always remembered, is coexistent with and cannot be separated from its corresponding tala on the same plane. As an important deduction from the preceding observations, be it carefully noted that man's own constitution as an individual from the highest to the lowest is a hierarchy of its own kind, and therefore, man himself as such a subordinate hierarchy is a composite entity formed of lokas and talas inextricably interworking and intermingled. In this subordinate hierarchy called man live and evolve vast armies, hosts, multitudes, of living entities, monads in this inferior stage of their long evolutionary peregrination, and which for convenience and brevity of expression we may class under the general term of life-atoms.

Loka: *A word meaning a place or locality or, as much more frequently used in theosophy, a world or sphere or plane. The lokas are divided into rupa-lokas and arupa-lokas—material worlds and spiritual spheres. There is a wide range of teaching connected with the lokas and talas which belongs to the deeper reaches of the esoteric philosophy. (See also Arupa, Rupa, Tala)* [24]

Lokas and Talas, the high and the low, the virtuous and the vicious, dharma and sin, knowledge and ignorance. In this context, the evil spirits are the Asuras or demons (Suras were the gods) that constantly fought the gods in heaven while living in Patala above Naraka (Hell), one of the three Lokas. For the Theosophist, they must become fully conscious in all the lokas and talas and sub-lokas and sub-talas before they truly know the Universe and themselves. On the subject of interdimensional travels in relation to multidimensional demonic entities, there is a film that I recommend called *Event Horizon*, a British-American science fiction horror film distributed in cinemas back in 1997, directed by Paul WS Anderson, and set mainly on a starship, called the "Event Horizon." The story is more or less this: In 2047, a distress signal is received from the Event Horizon, a *starship* that disappeared during its maiden voyage to *Proxima Centauri* seven years before and mysteriously reappeared in a decaying orbit around Neptune. The Event Horizon spontaneously appears in orbit around Neptune. Searching the ship for signs of life, the rescue crew learns that the Event Horizon was re-

24   http://www.theosociety.org/pasadena/ocglos/og-jkl.htm ‡ Archived 11th December, 2017.

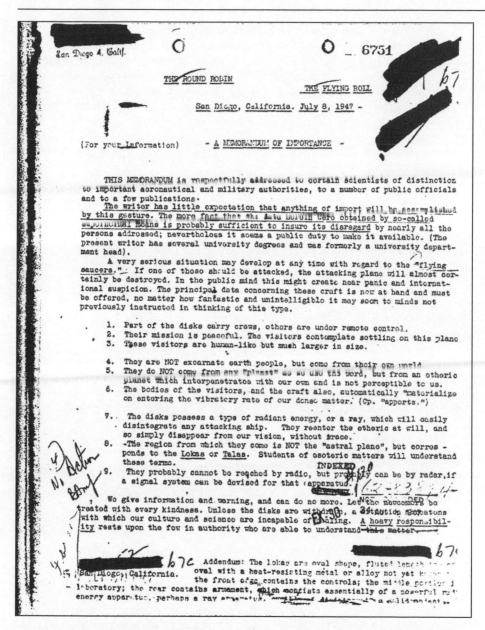

FIG. 28 FBI Memorandum dated 8 July, 1947. The highlighted part supports the multi-dimensional hypothesis of the phenomenon.

sponsible for testing an experimental engine that opened a rift in the space-time continuum, allowing a hostile interdimensional demonic entity on board the ship. This makes me think of the experiments with the Large Hadron Collider (LHC) at CERN. The crew discovers an experimental gravity drive and the drive, surprise, surprise, generates an artificial black hole (exactly what they are trying to achieve at CERN) and is used to bridge two points in space-time, reducing travel time over astronomical distances. However, the crew soon discovers a video log of the Event Horizon's crew going insane and mutilating each other. Let's pray this never happens at CERN! The video log ends with a shot of the Event Horizon's captain, who has apparently gouged out his own eyes, holding them up to the camera and saying in Latin, *liberate tuteme ex inferis* ("save yourself from Hell"). Maybe they should screen this film at CERN to remind them of the possible dangers of playing with a multi-dimensional reality.

MANLY P. HALL AND FLYING SAUCERS

*T*he following is a rare historical gem I decided to include in my book. It is probably the only copy extant, a 12-page set of typed notes from a 1950 lecture on the subject of UFOs by the late Manly Palmer Hall, a 33° Mason and a prolific author often mentioned in my writings. The classic language and the prosaic perspective exercised by Manly P. Hall might disappoint some of you, but the document is nonetheless of great value for historical purposes.

THE CASE OF THE FLYING SAUCERS

by Manly Palmer Hall (33°), July 2, 1950

Typed lecture notes by Virginia B. Pomeroy

241 Orizaba Avenue, Long Beach 3, California

This morning our purpose is to analyze certain aspects of the human mind in connection with the mysterious case of the Flying Saucers. First of all, I would like to create a little parallel, something that will help folks to see just what we are up against in a matter of this kind. Quite a number of years ago a famous stage magician by the name of Harry Keller created a strange illusion, he perfected in stage magic the Illusion of levitation. Keller, who was a very able exponent of the art of conjuring, worked out a method by the means of which the human body could be suspended in the middle of a well-lit stage without any visible means of support. He was able to so project it that a committee, honestly chosen from the audience could walk around the stage and even could walk under the floating body.

Of course, in those days legerdemain was one of the principal forms of entertainment. It has failed in popularity because folks of our generation are insulted rather than amused when they are fooled. Keller gave his professional secret, the mystery of the floating lady, to Howard Thurston, who exhibited it to the public throughout his life. In order to add glamour to the spectacle, the scene was decked in Oriental splendor, like the Arabian Nights which brought to the mind of the beholder the wonderful story of the magic of the East, all of which contributed to the disorientation of his judgment, which was the necessary ingredient of such entertainment.

After watching this illusion a number of times from the audience, I used to listen to the explanations that were given. Those present knew in their common mind that it was a trick of some kind. The majority of these audiences assumed that and were not profoundly shaken in their judgment even though completely deceived by their eyes, which proved definitely that you cannot always believe what you see. There were, however, in such groups several classes of people, and there was always that little group interested in Eastern mysticism, which would have been willing to die to defend the belief that the lady actually floated, that it was done by a secret formula right out of the Arabian Nights. Nothing could have convinced them to the contrary.

Then there was another group semantically addicted to the belief that conjurers and mirrors were always associated. When you do not know how it is done, it is done by mirrors. So another group was very smug, happy and wise and knew all about it, it was done with mirrors. Having decided that, they gained proper distinction in their own eyes and among their associates and they were ready to enjoy the performance. There was another group with a more scientific type of mind. This group would gather in the corner of the lobby and explain in detail how it was all done with magnets. Magnets were the mysterious thing you could do anything with. It never occurred to these people to have it done by magnets would be more difficult than to have the lady actually float.

I listened to these groups explaining the wonder and it was only on rare occasions that anyone ever suggested anything that was close to the facts. In the first place, facts were too simple and in the second place, the mind was conditioned away from the prosaic understanding of the matter. It was very amusing because I happened to know how it was done after being present on a number of occasions when the device was assembled. They did not realize how perfectly, how simply and how completely the human mind can be misdirected. Of course, incidentally, we may say there was the lunacy fringe that had decided the whole audience had been hypnotized. But the real answer was very simple, but very cleverly and intelligently worked out.

Also when I was younger than I am now, considerably, I lived in a small town where circuses went by. One year before these more recent devices, such as the radio, but not before the party line on the telephones which was the great method of communication at the turn of the century, everybody listened to everybody else, the deepest rut in the linoleum was in front of the phone. On this occasion, an old, decrepit, dying, mangy lioness disappeared from one of the cages. In the following week, the lioness was sighted in an area of over five hundred miles. It was seen anywhere from three to ten places at the same time. It frightened dozens of reputable, honest, God-fearing citizens, all of the solid citizens. Then the lioness showed up dead two hundred yards from the circus tent. It had ambled over there and fallen dead. Yet all of those who reported having seen it were honest, God-fearing people, which brings us to a simple fact that has been studied and analyzed for centuries, that is the delusion of masses.

Once a story starts it is almost impossible to determine how far it will go and how many variations it will assume before the journey is ended. Like interesting fragments of gossip, it develops jet propulsion and also passes through innumerable transformations, so the final account has little resemblance to the original story. Knowing these tendencies of the human mind, these tendencies that are present in perfectly honest and honorable people, we have to approach all remarkable accounts, not in an effort to demonstrate how remarkable they are, but to discover, if possible some simple, natural, normal explanation, clinging to that until that explanation itself obviously falls. There are always levels of explanations ascending from the simple to the complex. We should carefully wear out every level, exhausting its most reasonable probabilities before we ascend to more rarefied strata of opinions.

Not long ago I was talking to a gentleman who had had a very bad moment, he had nearly killed a friend while out deer hunting. He told me the happiest moment of his life was the moment he realized he had missed him. But he said while he was aiming, while he was attempting to shoot what he believed to be the deer, which, of course, was obscured in the thicket, he would have taken an oath on any Bible and swear before God as a witness, that he actually believed he saw the deer. He saw movement, he saw movement in the underbrush, twig and branches took the actual appearance of antlers, and he was perfectly willing to swear that he saw the deer.

Now such visualization along lines of expectancy is not a new experience, and after a number of reports are circulated we have to recognize the possibility of such delusions. We must, however, bear in mind that the elements of delusion may not disprove the entire structure, but may account for certain difficulties which arrive later. I read an article recently on the flying saucers in which one researcher in the field was attempting to reconcile all the differences in the accounts, and trying to find an explanation large enough to include all the details of the various authentic statements.

This was to my mind a mistake. These authentic details will probably never be completely reconciled when all the facts are known. It is not necessary for us to verify every tiny thread of the report. It is impossible. These very threads may be so tangled and so exaggerated and enlarged in the retelling, that they obscure rather than contribute to a general statement of facts. The facts will probably show that a great many honest reports were untrue and that many very simple and factual elements were completely overlooked.

I do not believe there is any use in attempting to explain away the existence of these flying saucers. Even had we not the most recent reports, such as that which appeared in the last issue of the **Readers Digest**, and even before that, probably a year ago when Winchell mentioned the flying saucers in his column, telling the people not to worry, it was a government secret, even without these statements that have never been disputed there is still evidence enough that there is something, or several somethings, that has been seen.

Thus we may assume without any great exaggeration that something not previously generally considered is happening, and that there are basic truths under the stories of the flying saucers, that these truths like the levitation of the lady, have been explained very badly is also pretty evident, inasmuch as explanation utterly irreconcilable cannot all be right. Conversely, we can say they cannot all be wrong. That may also be possible, then again the truth may be a little different from all the reports, because it is hard to formulate reports where the necessary facts are not available.

But assuming for the moment that which I think we are entitled to assume without too much allowance for imagination, that something has been seen, and that the various reports about it like those matters in which they are in common agreement may have some validity, we are then confronted with the question of what we have seen. Nearly all accounts report several different things seen. Naturally, some of these accounts, including the flying cucumber, and the report of a great spaceship that took fifteen minutes to float across the horizon, and reached from side to side of the visual heavens, might be suspected of exaggeration. These things get larger the longer we think about them, and like the famous fish story, they improve with the telling and with the enthusiasm of the narrator.

The various things seen and described can be classified into various groups; one group consisting of the flying saucer which is round, almost round, oblong, concave and convex. That various sizes have been noted, we know, some being of

no great size, and others being of considerable proportion. Then something resembling the jet propulsion machine, either without wings, or with exceedingly thin,
fin-like extensions, propelled by a tremendous power from what appeared to be
gills on the sides, the whole structure shaped roughly like a cigar, have also been
described by several persons. Detached floating lights that are seemingly under
control have also been noted. Rays, beams and lights, and such phenomena, disas-
sociated from any visible structure have been reported. These might, theoretically,
represent the distortion due to the pressure of the excitement of seeing something,
but as the reports gather and fall naturally into several classifications they are
worthy of being given consideration in those classifications.

But we must consider the type of person testifying. Several witnesses have been
of more than common integrity, they have been specialists in various fields, they
have been experts in aerial physics and things of that nature. We must also take
into consideration the pressure of an enlarged legend and how this legend can
bring with it a tendency toward the fulfillment of expectancy. No sooner had the
mysterious missiles, or whatever they were, begun to accumulate as stories, then
we began to have the same type of thing that we had in the story of the floating
lady. We had a number of well-authenticated, well-documented forms of hysteria.
Of course, the milleniumists moved in immediately.

This was a new indication of the end of the world and the Second Coming. I
think that can be somewhat discounted. I do not believe the next Avatar will arrive on a flying saucer. In spite of the delinquencies of humanity, I am also loath
to believe we are apt to be wiped out by the wrath of the Almighty, or something
of that nature. Not the wrath of the Almighty, but the stupidity of man, is causing
most of the trouble. So those who used the flying saucer as a "Repent ye, the day is
at hand" made quite a stir at the time and worked upon the level of thinking that
has been so tormented in the past by such procedures as to be rather receptive to
the most incredible beliefs. This would be equivalent to tying the floating lady to
the Arabian Nights, and making it appear it could be justified that the magician is
a fakir of India or some other equally wonderful explanation.

The next question that arose was the possibility that the so-called flying saucers
were a guided or propelled weapon, and that they were the result of experimental
research in military armament. I imagine that if at any time since the flurry began
Mr. Gallup had conducted a poll on public opinion, he would have found the idea
that they were experimental research in arms was held by the majority of people,
end to a degree this rather matter of fact attitude toward the subject would indicate that the mass mind is calmer and collected than any of the individual elements
which compose it. If the flying saucer, the floating cigar, and the very highly strati-
fied will-o'-the-wisp, if these were indications of armament projects, then naturally
it would be difficult for the average citizen to pierce the protective wall which the
government has placed around such research under prevailing world conditions.

I remember very well the flurry in Santa Fe and that area during the development of the atom bomb. Santa Fe is only a short distance from Los Alamos where
so much of the research was carried on, and of course, the cracker barrel congress was held in the lobby of the Fonda Hotel in Santa Fe. It was there the great
physicists brushed elbows with the agents of espionage from various countries. It
was there that detectives and secret service men were breathing down each other's

necks all the time. It was here also we had a factory for rumors that was almost out of this world. Everyone had the inside of it. Everyone had a friend who had a friend who was in the know. The stories, when the facts became known, were all of them wrong, but each one was strongly defended by a group of champions who are now ready to defend something else equally uncertain.

I remember one day while I was down there in that mountain country, something happened that almost belongs in the department, projects flying saucers. Out on a ranch there of several thousand acres, and standing on the side of a hill with the view extending from ten, twenty or thirty miles, I noticed one afternoon an extraordinary roar. It was far stronger and more powerful than the sound of an ordinary airplane motor, even a large transport or passenger plane. Suddenly without any warning whatever, this roaring took on the proportions of a definite vibration and something moved at an incredible rate passing almost directly over the place where I was standing.

That it was moving very close to the ground was evidenced by the fact that pinion trees not more than ten feet high were bent half way to the ground. The thing passed in a fraction of a second, but I saw absolutely nothing although there was ample visibility for miles in the direction in which the sound seemed to fade out. What it was I have not the slightest idea, but I am quite certain it was not the Second Coming. The thought that came to mind was that it was a jet-propelled instrument of some kind, moving more rapidly than the human perception could follow, and by the time I could organize myself to look for it, it was gone. That almost certainly was the answer. It is also quite possible that the sound of the instrument, or whatever it was, was such that it actually was moving in the opposite direction from that which the sound seemed to be traveling, and in looking in one direction I failed to see it because it moved in the opposite direction.

Anyway, nothing was visible, it left no track of any kind, no smoke or gas, there was a terrific roar as it moved over the ground, bending the trees and it was gone. Well, at that time what was going on in these research laboratories was not known to us, but it seemed almost certain that it was a high powered, possibly jet-propelled plane. I thought no more of it and said nothing about it until it came to my mind in connection with the project saucer. Almost certainly these things have an explanation in terms of the incredible advancements that have been made in scientific research in recent years.

Considering the next problem we have to bear in mind also the association between the concept of the flying saucer and the rapidly intensifying science-fiction literature which is getting more and more attention in the popular mind each year. This is like tying the story of the floating lady to the Mahatmas of India. It is a fortuitous circumstance that reality and fiction should exist at the same time which would incline thousands, possibly millions of people, to enlarge their sense of the possible and cause them confusion when trying to estimate the probabilities.

We have become comparatively immune to such abstracts as interplanetary travel, we have become immune to the fantastic fortunes of Buck Rogers and Flash Gordon. We would not be surprised to see Superman float in our window at any minute; there might be a slight shook but nothing serious. We are being constantly conditioned by the pressure on one hand of a science fiction concept, and on the other hand by the quiet but intense findings of our great geophysicists and astrophysicists, and persons of that caliber. These groups seem to melt together and defend each other, but this defense is more of appearance than reality.

If we go beyond the second theory of the possibility of international armament, which we will come back to later, we come into the most delightful phase of the whole problem, and that is the problem of interplanetary or interworld communication. The reasonable and inevitable conclusion held by some as being demonstrable and the only adequate explanation is that the flying saucer is a spaceship. Back to our illusion, there is no doubt in the world that the lady floats because of magnets. Obviously, there is no other explanation except the scientific theory. Now the space-ship idea appeals to a great many people but it has been my observation during the two and a half years I have been watching it, that it appeals to the wrong people; that is, it has appealed to a group of people who represent a level of worry, a group that is always present and always ready to be involved in such problems.

One of the interesting phases has been to draw Charles Fort and some of his opinions into it in an effort to prove that mysterious atmospheric visitors have been reported for more than two hundred years. Now, if that can be proved then we have a new equation to consider, but before we consider it seriously let us remember that not only were the aeronautical sciences inferior two hundred years ago to anything we have today—in fact, unknown except to men like Leonardo—but the general approach to any phenomena was exceedingly inadequate. We have in the history of periods back to the beginning of time, reports of various things. Let us consider, for example, the accounts of comets.

Scientific books, and books of pseudo-scientific interest, borderline theories, very often include tables of comets, in which the shape, form, and appearance of comets are distinctly described. Some of them show as many as twenty forms of comets, each type in the form or shape of some familiar object, a comet exactly the shape of a sword with hilt and decoration, a comet exactly the shape of a snake with two eyes and a forked tongue, a comet exactly the shape of a crown with jewels set around it. These comets were claimed to have been seen, and one was reported in the form of a sword hanging over Jerusalem at the time of its fall, and a similar one was seen hanging over Mexico City at the time of Cortez.

Now I think we can safely say that in the experience of astronomy in the last two hundred years there have been no comets that exactly resembled swords. There are no comets that can be seen writhing away in the sky like snakes, and there are no comets that resemble physical articles so closely that the article itself seems to be floating there. So we must assume a considerable degree of interpretation. We can also find well-authenticated accounts of sea-serpents, lake monsters, and within the last two hundred years quite a collection of very justifiable, authentic and conscientious descriptions of mermaids.

These are not due to the desire to deceive, but it is believed that a certain type of penguin was mistaken at a distance for a mermaid. That is quite possible, although to me they look more like a groom at a wedding, but a dozen penguins standing on a piece of ice, just barely within the actual vision range of some old salt of the Seven Seas, suddenly developed long golden curls and started playing harps gesticulating wildly. These stories are not intentional fabrications, they are the result of the human mind looking for that which it expects, and taking a dim and uncertain form and clothing it in those expectations.

The problem of space navigation around this planet is one which remains as yet in the position of remote probability, nothing is impossible. We should be wise enough to realize that, and we should also be modest enough to recognize that other planets might have very well developed arts and sciences, far beyond our own accomplishments. At the same time we have incredible time factors. We have to begin to think of man or creature built machines that can go at the speed of light. We have to think of cosmic energy already controlled as a means of fuel.

We have to further assume that the production of spaceships on other planets, or other suns, or other planets revolving around other suns, would present innumerable difficulties. We have incredible difficulties, difficulties as to whether creatures of other worlds could even exist in the atmosphere of the earth, which would make it necessary for them to be protected by some special kind of device. We have already so completely embraced the concept of a trip to the moon that the first two or three journeys are already sold out and it will not be long until they will be subdivided with a slight additional charge for frontage facing the earth.

Some three, four or five years ago people believed so certainly that lost Lemuria was coming up near the coast of California that they even bought land that has not shown up yet. There is always someone to believe everything, but the problem of the spaceship as a solution to the present dilemma should be held, it seems to me, as a last recourse to be considered only when every other explanation fails. It involves too much that is imponderable to us, too large an explanation for what we see and for what we have seen. It makes the tail of the kite much longer than the kite and gives us such a tremendous disorientation that we should consider it carefully.

The concept, in fact, as far as can be discerned, landed on the public mind with a dull thud. It would be impossible to assume that we would have the present sense of complacency in the matter if we really believed that these ships navigated by intelligent creatures capable of building them were approaching and sailing around in good military formation, not alone entirely, but in bunches and clusters, without a definite reaction from the only group that could really estimate what it means, and that is, your scientific body.

The only person able to mentally envision even twenty-five percent of the implication would be your physicists, astrophysicists and your researcher in the fields of cosmic energy and atomic power. These particular people are not apparently suffering from unnervement. They are not collapsing on street corners, they are not wandering around their homes absent-mindedly as though the sword of Damocles was hanging over their heads, they are not breaking up and falling to pieces under the nerve tension of it. In fact, from these distant, austere ivory towers there is a thundering silence. The wrong people are talking about space navigation.

If there were a reasonable probability of these mysterious things actually being the spearhead of a possible "project earth" being carried on from elsewhere, this fact in itself would almost inevitably unite the earth in a common determination to devote every possible research of every nation to determining the aims, purposes and means available for such contact between this planet and another. We would have no more right to assume that such space visitors were friendly than we would have a right to assume they were unfriendly. If they exist and are capable of such methods of transportation they must be accepted as at least equal and possibly superior to ourselves in scientific accomplishment because if they exist they got to us well before we had the means to get to them, which would indicate a very high degree of scientific knowledge.

That these strangers for some reason might scout the outer atmosphere of the planet is fantastic but conceivable, but that they should suddenly take such an interest in these matters, gives us time for pause. Either those in the best position to know do not believe that these mysterious projectiles come from the outer atmosphere, they do not believe they are spaceships, or the whole group of them is the most idiotic combination ever recorded. They are stupid beyond concept if they believe or have any scientific evidence of penetration of our earth's atmosphere from the outside and are still worrying about China, Korea, India, Russia, America, England or any other nation on the earth. If our experts are still pondering how to raise taxes, or lower the budget, or the politicians and statesmen of the world are still trying to cheat each other, in the presence of such a situation, then their imbecility is beyond calculation.

The least we should expect from those like Einstein, or other leaders In these fields, although they might be able to explain something created by another culture, is that they shall not be indifferent to its imponderables. If these people have information which they are not passing on to other leaders of the world, information that would unite the planet against a possible threat, if such things do not happen we must assume that those in a position to make them happen either know a great deal, or else are incapable of knowing anything. While there might be exceptions to both extremes it seems unlikely that we have a complete breakdown among all the leaders of our higher scientific and diplomatic life.

It would, therefore, appear, that unless we see more interest in preparing the planet on the basis of a global concept that we are not much concerned about this possibility. You will remember the result at the beginning of the second world war of the actions and intentions of Hitler when his planes flew over France without dropping a bomb, until the people hardly expected anything to happen, then suddenly without warning a terrific bombardment began. The possibility that spaceships floating in the earth's atmosphere might be cruising about indefinitely for no reason is no better a possibility than that these are the spearhead of a project of some kind, and the earth, its people, its leaders, and scientists, should either be unrolling the red carpet for friendly visitors, or else getting into a position for taking care of unfriendly ones.

Neither procedure has been followed. Therefore, we can only assume that the spaceship theory is interesting people who are interested in the scientific-fiction approach to life, but not those deeply concerned with the salvation of the planet. There seem to be no reason for the assumption, and no actual proof, that these mysterious flying saucers and their retinues of other factors have to be explained as belonging to some other universe or coming to us from out of space.

There is an ingenious belief that the explosion of the atom bomb here and the recent report of something that happened in the flash of an instant, purported to be an explosion on Mars, might be tied together, and that the investigation of the planet is due to the reports of such atomic phenomena which has been noted by the astronomers and physicists on another planet, but this again more or less undermines the idea that scientific-fiction writers have advanced, that this touring around the earth's atmosphere has been going on long before the atomic bomb.

The whole issue is a little too confused on these matters to require much further consideration along those lines. I think it is possible that someday there will be communication between planets, but we will have to make several very marked advances beyond even what we know as our atomic project before we will be ready to launch ourselves into the incredible vicissitudes of space, where we know with the highest concept of energy and power we possess today that even presuming we had all the equipment necessary, the human being would not live long enough to make the trip there and back, even with very old age.

That such things might happen on other planets where life might be different, where life may be longer and the problem of the rejuvenation of life has been accomplished, all this is possible, but where it means fifteen, twenty or twenty-five years of travel through space at an incredible speed, with fuel problems almost beyond estimation, traveling at a speed almost as great as that of light, we might be wise and look for something simpler, and only depend upon such a concept in an emergency. Where everything else fails we are forced to fall back on the miraculous as an explanation of the problem we face.

Now let us consider the problem that was originally advanced. and which has been more or less sustained by documentation and recent reports. We know that on various continents in secluded areas very elaborate experimental laboratories have been functioning for a number of years. We know that prior to the collapse of Germany the Germans were already pondering a number of ideas in relation to the development of atomic armament, and fantastic, scientific dreams about the earth's outer atmosphere. Many of these scientists survived the disastrous collapse of Hitler's regime, and have disappeared behind the Iron Curtain. It is known with reasonable certainty at least a few of these scientists are now cooperating with the Russian atomic project.

We also have every reason to believe that that project is situated in the great Mongolian area in a little community called the State of Tanna-Tuva, where many of these laboratories are underground and where research in atomic missiles and in the delivery of these missiles is under consideration. There are almost certainly other such centers of this research which will account for the reports of jet- propelled rockets, or something of that nature that were seen in a considerable number over Sweden and other Scandinavian countries several years ago. There are other reports that Britain has experimental projects in Australia and Canada. There is every reason to believe that even France may be carrying on moderate work in one of her lesser-known colonial possessions.

We do not know exactly where, but we can well imagine they could do a lot of private work in Madagascar, where the inhabitants seldom leave their own country, and very few people go there. That the United States has an elaborate research project we know too well to even question it, because the reports that come out, little by little, are backed up by every indication that we actually lead the world in that type of research.

That all these nations are searching for certain means which include both missiles and the delivery of missiles, and undoubtedly include a number of other problems relating to matters of which we have no knowledge—and probably it is not good that we necessarily have knowledge if that knowledge can be of any comfort or assistance to a real or potential enemy—cannot be questioned. We know, for ex-

ample, that we hear very little about the development of bacteriological warfare, yet there have been hints of research in that field, and from material that has come to my hands, I do not think all of it is imagination.

There has been a hint of pollution warfare in which sources of, water can be so rapidly and definitely contaminated as to completely wipe out huge areas of civilian population. These things in themselves are very terrible to think about, very horrible to contemplate, but are still, apparently, the inevitable consequence of the materialistic trend of our way of life. We are dooming a great part of our own race to destruction by our own ingenuity. We have enough strength and resourcefulness to do this but we have not as yet sufficient greatness of heart and goodness of spirit to find constructive solutions to world problems. With the situation as it is we must realistically recognize a tremendous rise in atomic armament, a tremendous determination for one people to excel or exceed all others in the accomplishment of the instrument of offensive warfare.

There seem to be very good grounds for believing flying saucers are an experimental project in such warfare research. There has been some question as to where they came from. A recent opportunist film indicated they originated in Russia. I think probably that would cause Uncle Joe to have a broad smile under his mustache. I do not believe that is true. I think again it is the field of the unknown dramatized by the mystery of the Iron Curtain. We always wonder what someone is doing who is off in a corner where we cannot see him. It seldom interests us sufficiently to go over and explore, we simply sit down and wonder. The chances are if we go over we find him doing something just as useless as we would be doing under the same circumstances, probably nothing.

But with the conviction of Russia's broad militaristic program, and the great chart or map of the Communist revolution dangling before our eyes, we are quite certain that with the various scientific minds that have been commandeered from other countries, the Russians could be well on their way toward the development of atomic science, and through spies, espionage and treason have most of our knowledge on the subject. Therefore, it would seem possible to some that these missiles might be of Russian origin.

This presents us, however, with another problem. Problems multiply when we contemplate them. One is, what would cause the massing of these missiles over certain areas of our own country where they would be extremely remote from their source or origin. If these missiles were developed within the boundaries of the Soviet Union, even in Mongolia, they would have to cross Japan, or at least the great Pacific wastes, and finally come here, almost halfway around the world. That such missiles traveling at such distances should be so completely controlled as to be able to move a little to the right or left when some airplane approaches them would be a little hard to believe in terms of guided missiles. That guided missiles might be brought within a reasonable scope of their objective, yes, but most of the reports of these projects indicate that the instrument was exceedingly sensitive in its reaction to almost any contact.

Well, we have again the dear old magnetic theories and other things to fall back on, but the fact seems to beg if the missiles were guided and came from another nation there would be a larger report of these disabled in various ways, disintegrated in mid-air, or things of that nature. It at least offers an interesting thought, but it seems unlikely as a first choice that if these missiles contained living persons and are guided by crews, which might be possible with the larger ones, that they would be used experimentally by one nation on the opposite side of the earth from its own laboratory and expose them to a number of accidents which might dump them and their entire secret right into the lap of the enemy.

Of course, there is the possibility of detonation equipment intended to destroy the instrument in case of disability. The possibility of such instruments themselves being destroyed when they become disabled brings up the problem of a crew that would have to bail out or die with it, and even if the crew died with it, there would be wreckage of some kind, so it would seem such an experiment would be carried on over an isolated area. That it should be so secret and so wonderful that no one is allowed to know anything about it, and yet to have the testing field on the opposite side of the earth presents too many technical difficulties to me.

Another consideration we have to face is, that for whatever espionage we have operated in countries dominated by the Soviet policy to have no way of determining the work going on there, this seems a little strange, and it also seems a little strange that absolutely no effort has been made by any of our equipped military forces to shoot down or attack any of them. Nothing has been done to pursue and investigate them. Where any effort has been made to contact them, it was instinctively on the part of some individual pilot who thought for a moment of trying to ram the disk or something of that nature. There is no program, as might be expected for those in authority being ordered to get hold of one of these disks. Even traveling at high speed over various areas a few potshots should have been taken at them.

An alert could have been created and still could be, by which some military emplacement would get a visible opportunity to turn anti-aircrafts on them, but no such thing has been done. Certainly, a foreign country sending such instruments without our knowledge could not complain if we attacked and destroyed them. In some instances, they have been reported as low as one thousand feet, in other instances as high as fifty, or twenty thousand feet, and at other places have been reported to be stationary for a considerable time. These reports indicate efforts could be made to bring them down if anyone wanted to do it.

There has gradually drifted out from the same sources a report that the facts about the saucers are known and those who apparently have the facts are not worried. I met one individual who has the facts, who was not talking. He did not tell me anything, but he was not collapsing from worries, in fact, he was playing bridge. Now with so heavy a cosmic secret as some folks would like to maintain, it does seem like he would have trumped his partner's ace, but he was in good form. He was undoubtedly a member of the air intelligence and knew the answer.

The only conclusion that seems to be reasonable and carries a larger part of the story is that which is now beginning to drift to our contemplation, and that is that the flying saucers and the floating cigars are the products of our own research equipment, that the flying saucer is some type of research device, an experimental device for either defensive or offensive armament. It is the only practical explanation that exists. This explanation violates none of the essential facts of the matter. So prosaic an explanation should not immediately discourage us.

There is every indication that the secret of the flying saucer will come to the public in the relatively near future, that the time of useful secrecy is nearly passed.

Whatever it is we will know, and whatever knowledge we receive will be received with mixed emotions by those who have already thought about it. Some will accept it when the explanation comes, other will insist that the explanation is only a blind to cover up the fact that Venus, or Mars, or a Fixed Star has frightened us out of our wits. Actually, almost certainly the explanation will be the correct one.

Upon the point of explanation, we can all speculate. Certainly, I have no further enlightenment on it than anyone else has. If anyone really knows it would be his duty to refrain from any factual statement as long as the government or intelligence service desires that it should be that way, but without any prior knowledge, therefore without any restrictions of secrecy we can speculate within the bounds of the reasonable. Our speculations may be as false as any other, but there are things that apparently are necessary for armament today, and we may be right to assume that that which is necessary to the balancing of the efficiency of our modern defense program would be the logical direction in which research would be carried on. We would be plugging weaknesses in our defense structure and also plugging weaknesses in our offensive program if we have to carry a program of offense into another nation's territory.

The one thing that seems to me to have been a weakness, up to the moment, in nearly all the defense programs, and the offensive programs of other nations, is in the ingenuity for the discovery of such incredible instruments as the atomic bomb, the hydrogen bomb, the bacteriological bomb and the pollution bomb, the difficulty with all of them is delivery. The only way we have of delivering them at the moment is the old traditional forms. We can deliver them by controlled rockets which, however, as was proved in the blitz on England was not effective directly and against which various defenses could be created. We can deliver them in high-powered, high-flying airplanes, in which one plane in a large convoy of planes carries the bomb, but against this we will find a rising tide of defense. No matter how far we extend the ceiling for anti-aircraft, the enemy can extend the anti-aircraft defense. We have the problem of trying to reach a destination with various kinds of material.

We also have another problem which relates to protection against types of armament, which we can well imagine will be developed in other countries, but about which our public knows nothing. This interval of efficiency between available means of accomplishing certain projects, and the more desirable means, could explain the problem of saucers. It could well represent a guided missile or an instrument with a living crew, capable of certain advantages in the delivery of armament, in the delivery of bombs, or the delivery of some forms of material. They could also definitely be useful in the development of observation in the discovery and checking of the activities of an enemy.

But their construction, their formation, the way they operate suggest they have one of several possibilities, either they are going to be used for the distribution of rays or some natural force that could be the focal point, possibly some means of short- circuiting motors, or affecting or attacking various mechanized devices. or they could be used for the delivery of bombs, they could control or pilot robots, and function upon larger instruments and give the nation that has them complete control over the air.

That this type of thinking should be consistent with the projects as we know them, and with the temper and thought of our times, would seem to suggest that this is the general direction. There is always a possibility they may represent an entirely new dimension of cosmic rays or the penetration of some principle of energy by which we could have very definite advantages. There is a discussion as to the possibility of these devices being radioactive. That situation has not been satisfactorily solved. There is the report that some are luminous, according to others, they appear to be either a silver light or white disk. Whatever they may be they are most certainly instruments for the defense of a land, or for the extending of the power of the military into the land of the occupied, and there is much to indicate the experimental work is being carried on in the United States.

The question as to why such experiments are permitted in areas with considerable habitation, where there is the possibility of one of these huge disks, some being two hundred and fifty feet in diameter, falling to the earth, injuring individuals, or destroying property, has caused a number of speculations against it being developed here. It seems we would be endangering our population in the experimental research. Yet most accounts report these devices contain some means for their own annihilation. What this means is we are not aware. As far as I know, no one has seen one of them disintegrate and break up. There has been no wreckage to speak of, although one or two have reported it.

That the project may be in experimental stage and completely harmless is also a possibility. That it is extremely light, having the appearance of mass, but actually consisting of a small amount of any heavy material is suggested by the type of research. We have thought of it as containing motors and things of that type, but no report has been made that any such motor power has been used. It is possible the entire device in its experimental stage is completely harmless, and even if it should fall in a community would cause no more damage then a little consternation. We must therefore assume it is in an experimental stage and not equipped with whatever is intended to be used as a device of offense or defense.

That some of them are comparatively small might indicate they are involved in a new principle, either of motion or focus of energy of some kind. That they have practical utility is certain or else they would not be developed as a military project. These things have to pass very extreme groups of critics, scientists and research men before the army or navy would adopt them, and their utility must be demonstrated, or else a good probability of it, before the project begins. The project seems to have been running for several years, but is gradually emerging. The public mind does not seem to be unnecessarily anxious, and from everything indicated, the secret will soon be out.

But up to that time it is a very good example for those persons who wish to be thoughtful to assume the attributes, attitudes, and policies of mature thinking, and show how intelligent human beings can approach the unknown, and also give those of a less stable and substantial type of mind an opportunity to control their own thinking and escape from a tendency toward the fantastic. If we approach these things reasonably we shall generally be right; whereas, if we approach them too dramatically we shall be wrong.

The device in all probability is some highly specialized scientific structure intended to advance research. The device itself may not be the project, but some means of testing for something else, but whether it is a means to an end, or is the end itself, it is almost certainly humanly guided, humanly devised, and is being advanced in the unfoldment of necessary research into the great and powerful potentials of the planet. Beyond that, I think we shall simply have to wait until Uncle Sam decides to talk, and anyone who talks before that would be doing every one concerned a great unkindness.

THE OCCULT ORIGINS OF SCIENTOLOGY

Those who are familiar with actors like John Travolta, Jenna Elfman, and Tom Cruise, might also be familiar with Scientology, but not necessarily with the *Ordo Templi Orientis*. Kenneth Grant refers to **Frater H** (i.e. L. Ron Hubbard) as: *"A confident trickster who wormed his way into the O.T.O. on the pretense of being interested in Magick."* Explaining this while Hubbard was still at large [1972], having grown wealthy and famous by a misuse of the secret knowledge which he had extracted out of Parsons. In *Jack Parsons and the Fall of Babulon*, Paul Rydeen clearly confirms the identity of Frater H, adding that: *"Other writers refer to him merely as Frater X. The late Frater X's identity is now clearly a matter of public record. I see no reason to do anything other than calling him by name. He was L. Ron Hubbard: philosopher, world traveler, science fiction author, and founder of Scientology."* [25]

It began in the spring of 1945, when Parsons met a new aspirant to the Great Work, a young man called L Ron Hubbard. Hubbard's magical potential was very great, and he made a considerable impression upon the members of Agape Lodge, especially on Betty, the mistress of Dr. Parsons—she soon found herself sleeping with him. Frater 210 (Dr. Parsons) was not unduly upset about this, for he had decided to follow even more closely in the Beast's footsteps and find, by magical means, a Scarlet Woman, his own true Whore of the Stars. He proposed, in other words, to attract an elemental or familiar spirit: *"About three months ago I met Ron Hubbard,"* as Parsons wrote in July, 1945 to Crowley whom he addressed as "Most Beloved Father." Continuing, *"About 3 months ago I met Capt. L. Ron Hubbard, a writer and explorer of whom I had known for some time; He is a gentleman, red hair, green eyes, honest and intelligent and we have become great friends. He moved in with me about two months ago, and although Betty and I are still friendly, she has transferred her sexual affections to him."* Parsons' letter to Crowley continues:

> *Although he has no formal training in Magick he has an extraordinary amount of experience and understanding in the field. From some of his experiences, I deduce he is in direct touch with some higher intelligence, possibly his Guardian Angel. He describes his Angel as a beautiful winged woman with red hair whom he calls the Empress. ... He is the most Thelemic person I have ever met and is in complete accord with our own principles. He is also interested in establishing the New Aeon, but for cogent reasons, I have not introduced him to the Lodge.*

> *We are pooling our resources in a partnership which will act as a parent company to control our business ventures. I think I have made a great gain, and as Betty and I are the best of friends, there is little loss ... I need a magical partner. I have many experiments in mind. I hope my elemental gets off the dime (**gets moving**)—the next time I tie up with a woman it will be on (**my**) own terms.*

> *Thy son, John.*

25   *See* Paul Rydeen, *Jack Parsons and the Fall of Babalon*, (Kerrville, TX: Crash Collusion Publishing, 1995).

The *magical partner* is a reference to Hubbard, not to a shakti or Scarlet Woman, as some of you might have initially supposed. In January 1946, Parsons devised an Operation to, as he put it, *"obtain the assistance of an elemental mate."* [26] How to attract an elemental (which one can turn into one's familiar spirit) is set forth in the top-secret O.T.O. treatise entitled *De Nuptiis Secretis Deorum cum Hominibus.* [27] This treatise was rewritten by Crowley, who added, of course, his own characteristic touches. In the following two months, Parsons set to work to obtain his goal. At the end of February 1946, Parsons returned to the Mojave Desert and invoked Babalon. He gives no further details of this, unfortunately. All he does say is that during this invocation: *"the presence of the Goddess came upon me, and I was commanded to write the following communication."*

This communication, which purports to be the words of Babalon, consists of 77 short verses. Whether it was a direct voice, trance, or inspired writing, he does not say. The answer probably lies in his Magical Record for this period, but as far as I know, it has not survived. This communication of 77 verses he entitled *Liber 49*. He does not explain the title, but no doubt considered such explanation unnecessary since 49 is a number sacred to Babalon.

A few days after receiving *Liber 49*, Parsons put in hand the ritual preparations as indicated in the text. Again in his own words:

> On March 1 and 2, 1946, I prepared the altar and equipment in accordance with the instructions in **Liber 49**. The Scribe, Ron Hubbard, had been away about a week and knew nothing of my invocation of BABALON, which I had kept entirely secret. On the night of March 2, he returned and described a vision he had had that evening, of a savage and beautiful woman riding naked on a great cat-like beast. He was impressed with the urgent necessity of giving me some message or communication. We prepared magically for this communication, constructing a temple at the altar with the analysis of the keyword. He was robed in white, carrying a lamp, and I in black, hooded, with the cup and dagger. At his suggestion, we played Rachmaninov's Isle of the Dead as background music and set an automatic recorder to transcribe audible occurrences. At approximately 8 am he began to dictate, I transcribing directly as I received. [28]

He wrote to Crowley that he had followed the VIII° instruction carefully, with a talisman consecrated in the proper manner, the rite ending with the command to the spirit in question to appear visibly before him. For this class of magic (VIII°), one needs no assistant for it is sexual magic of the solitary kind (i.e. masturbation), but Parsons chose to perform the rite in the presence of Ron Hubbard. **The fact L. Ron Hubbard was present at the VIII° ritual implies by O.T.O. rules and regulations [29] that he was an Eighth Degree (VIII°)**

26   *See* http://www.parareligion.ch/dplanet/staley/staley11.htm ‡ Archived 11th December, 2017.

27   These secret instructions given to the members of the eight degree of the O.T.O are reproduced in their entirety in Leo Lyon Zagami, *Confessions of an Illuminati Vol.I*, pp.99-104.

28   www.parareligion.ch/ *Ibid.*

29   *The International camp, oasis and Lodge Master's Handbook* (Revised July 1997) states:*"The official instructional documents of the VII°,VIII°, IX°, X° are to be treated as strictly confidential to the members of those degrees."*

member of the *Ordo Templi Orientis*. Parsons was wearing a black hooded robe, and Hubbard a white one. Thundering away in the background was one of Prokofiev's piano concerto or Rachmaninov's symphonic poem, Island of the Dead. The ritual must have been one of Parson's or Hubbard's own making, for it went on for about eleven nights. Hubbard, it seems, partly instructed Parsons. The magic drive which Parsons was screaming for most of the time (if not the puerility of his verses to Babalon, the Scarlet Woman) would have offended Crowley's sense of magical propriety. Another letter to Crowley contained a further account of the operation:

For the last three days, I have performed an operation of birth, using the air tablet, the cup, and a female figure, properly invoked by the wand, then sealed upon the altar. Last night I performed an operation of symbolic birth and delivery.

The Air Tablet, or the Elemental tablets of Fire, Earth, and Water is the magical system of John Dee and his scryer, Edward Kelly, which Crowley had successfully worked during 1909 in the North African desert with his chela, Victor Neuburg. The *wand* was his penis; the talisman was placed on the altar, symbol of the womb. The only immediate result of this operation was a violent and unnatural wind storm. *"The wind storm is very interesting,"* wrote Parsons to his Most Beloved Father, *"but that is not what I asked for."* In February 1946, the gestation period ended and the elemental inhuman form appeared. Frater 210 wrote exultingly to Crowley: *"I have my elemental! She turned up one night after the conclusion of the Operation and has been with me since, although she goes back to New York next week. She has red hair and slant green eyes as specified. If she returns she will be dedicated as I am dedicated!"*

Her name was Marjorie Cameron. Crowley replied: *"I am particularly interested in what you have written to me about the elemental because for some little time past I have been endeavoring to intervene personally in this matter on your behalf. I would, however, have you recall Lévi's aphorism: 'The love of the Magus for such things is insensate and may destroy him.'"* With his Scarlet Woman (Marjorie Cameron) and in the presence of Hubbard, Parsons began to perform IX° magic to produce another higher being. *"I can hardly tell you,"* he wrote somewhat incoherently to the Beast:

*I am under the command of extreme secrecy. I have had the most important—devastating experience of my life between February 2nd and March 4th. I believe it was the result of the IX° working with the girl who answered my elemental summons. I have been in direct touch with One who is most Holy and Beautiful as mentioned in **The Book of the Law**. I cannot write the name at present. First instructions were received directly through Ron the seer. I have followed them to the letter. There was a desire for incarnation. I do not yet know the vehicle, but it will come to me, bringing a secret sign. I am to act as instructor guardian for nine months; then it will be loosed on the world. That is all I can say now...*

Not the sort of letter to please the Beast, and he replied thus: *"I thought I had a most morbid imagination, as good as any man's but it seems I have not. I cannot form the slightest idea what you can possibly mean."*

And to Frater Saturnus (Karl Germer) in New York, Crowley wrote: *"Apparently Parsons or Hubbard or somebody is producing a Moonchild. I get fairly frantic when I contemplate the idiocy of these louts."* But the "lout" Hubbard had a great business ability, and later founded his celebrated Church of Scientology. The two

In 1946 Aleister Crowley (left), the sorcerer and mystic whose dabblings in black magic earned him the title The Wickedest Man in the World, found a new disciple and welcomed him to one of his occult communities in California. The extraordinary activities of this new and enthusiastic disciple are described in a vast collection of papers owned by a former admirer of Crowley, which we have examined. The man in question is Lafayette Ron Hubbard (right), head of the now notorious Church of Scientology.

FIG. 29 Journal article cutout dedicated to Crowley and Hubbard in the Sunday Times of October 5, 1969.

magicians in Pasadena quarreled, and Hubbard departed with Betty in Parsons' yacht. Frater 210 put on his magic robe, seized his wand, entered the magic circle and performed the Banishing Ritual of the Pentagram, which is preliminary to all magical work, then a full invocation of Bartzabel, the spirit of Mars, whose aid he sought. The result: *"a squall blew the yacht to the rocks. I have them tied up; they cannot move without going to jail,"* he wrote gleefully. [30]

In October 1969, the London *Sunday Times* exposed Hubbard's magickal connections with Aleister Crowley. The Scientologists threatened legal action and the *Sunday Times*, unsure of its legal position, paid a small out-of-court settlement. Without retracting their earlier article, they printed a statement submitted by the Scientologists:

> *Hubbard broke up black magic in America: Dr. Jack Parsons of Pasadena, California, was America's Number One solid fuel rocket expert. He was involved with the infamous English black magician Aleister Crowley who called himself "The Beast 666." Crowley ran an organization called the Order of Templars Orientalis [sic, actually "Ordo Templi Orientis"] over the world which had savage and bestial rites. Dr. Parsons was head of the American branch located at 100 Orange Grove Avenue [actually 1003 South Orange Grove Avenue], Pasadena, California. This was a huge old house which had paying guests who were the U.S.A. nuclear*

---

30   *See* John Symonds, *The Beast 666*, (London, UK: Pindar, 1997).

physicists working at Cal. Tech. Certain agencies objected to nuclear physicists being housed under the same roof.

*L. Ron Hubbard was still an officer of the U.S. Navy because [sic] he was well-known as a writer and a philosopher and had friends amongst the physicists, he was sent in to handle the situation. He went to live at the house and investigated the black magic rites and the general situation and found them very bad. ... Parsons wrote to Crowley in England about Hubbard. Crowley "the Beast 666" evidently detected an enemy and warned Parsons. This was all proven by the correspondence unearthed by the **Sunday Times**. Hubbard's mission was successful far beyond anyone's expectations. The house was torn down. Hubbard rescued a girl they were using. The black magic group was dispersed and destroyed and has never recovered. The physicists included many of the sixty-four top U.S. scientists who were later declared insecure and dismissed from government service with so much publicity.* [31]

During the Scientologist's case against Gerald Armstrong in 1984, the original of this particular statement was produced. It is in Hubbard's handwriting and the statement is mistaken on several points. Karl Germer, not Parsons, was in charge of Crowley's organization in America. Parsons, known as *Frater Belarion* or *Frater 210*, was head of the single "Church of Thelema," or "Agape Lodge," in Pasadena. Hubbard's opening statement, the claim to have broken up black magic in America, is of course, ridiculous.

Hubbard did, however, contribute significantly to Jack Parsons financial difficulties. There is no evidence to support the claim that Hubbard was working for Intelligence. Parsons' FBI file shows that he was routinely investigated from 1943 onwards, because of his peculiar lifestyle. There is no mention of Hubbard in the file and despite investigations, Parsons retained his high-security classification until shortly before his death in 1952. However, the Scientology statement does admit Hubbard's involvement with Parsons. In a bulletin written for Scientologists in 1957, Hubbard said this of the man whose black magic group he had "dispersed." He described Parsons as: *"One chap, by the way, gave us solid fuel rockets and assist take-offs for airplanes too heavily loaded and all the rest of this rocketry panorama and who [sic] formed Aerojet in California and so on. The late Jack Parsons ... was not a chemist, the way we think of chemists ... He eventually became quite a man."* [32]

Parsons was indeed *quite a man*. He was one of the developers of Jet Assisted Take-Off (JATO) units and an original member of CalTech's rocket project, which became the Jet Propulsion Laboratory. Hubbard also had something to say about Aleister Crowley, Parsons' mentor. In the Scientology *Philadelphia Doctorate Course* lectures, given by Hubbard in 1952, there are several references to Crowley. Hubbard made it clear that he had read Crowley's pivotal *Book of the Law*. He also said: *"The magic cults of the 8th, 9th, 10th, 11th, 12th centuries in the Middle East were fascinating. The only work that has anything to do with them is a trifle wild in spots, but it's fascinating work ... **written by Aleister Crowley, the late Aleister Crowley, my very good friend**. It's very interesting reading to get hold of a copy of a book, quite rare, but it can be obtained,* The Master Therion ... *by Aleister Crowley. He signs himself 'The Beast,' the mark of the Beast, six sixty-six."* In another Hubbard lecture we are

31   *Sunday Times*, London, 5 October & 28 December 1969.

32   *Technical Bulletins of Dianetics & Scientology*, vol. 3, p. 31.

Maria   Traute   Sigrun   Gudrun   Heike

Einige der wichtigsten "Vril-Damen" zwischen 1922 und 1945

FIG. 30 Alleged members of the Vrilerinnen, also known as the Vril-Damen—Maria, Traute, Sigrun, Gudrun and Heike—who are said to have channeled transmissions that dictated diagrams and blueprints of advanced flying machines, complete with the mathematics and physics to go with them from 1922 to 1945.

told: *"One fellow, Aleister Crowley, picked up a level of religious worship which is very interesting—oh boy! The Press played hockey with his head for his whole lifetime. The Great Beast—666. He just had another level of religious worship. Yes, sir, you're free to worship everything under the Constitution so long as it's Christian."* [33]

Hubbard's work will begin in that period, in the early 1950s, a program of ideas in a book called *Dianetics*, which was distributed through the Dianetics Foundation, but the foundation soon entered bankruptcy and in 1952, Hubbard lost all the rights to his seminal publication entitled, ***Dianetics: The Modern Science of Mental Health,*** published two years earlier in 1950.

He then recharacterized the whole subject as a pseudo-religion and renamed it Scientology, retaining the terminology, doctrines, the E-meter, and the infamous practice of auditing, which he previously outlined in his book. Within a year, he regained the rights to *Dianetics* and retained both subjects under the umbrella of the Church of Scientology or the *Church of Fear* as suggested by the title of John Sweeney's book released in 2013, [34] on this dangerous sectarian reality.

Scientology is apparently tied to the mysterious **Xenu,** a kind of alien Satan. Xenu also called Xemu, was, according to Scientology founder L. Ron Hubbard, the dictator of the "Galactic Confederacy" who 75 million years ago brought billions of his people to Earth (then known as "Teegeeack") in DC-8-like spacecraft, stacked them around volcanoes and killed them with hydrogen bombs. Official Scientology scriptures hold that the thetans (immortal spirits) of these aliens adhere to humans, causing spiritual harm. These events are known within Scientology as "Incident II" and the traumatic memories associated with them as "The Wall of Fire" or "R6 implant." The narrative of Xenu is part of Scientologist teachings about extraterrestrial civilizations and alien interventions in earthly events, collectively described as "space opera" by Hubbard. Hubbard detailed

33   *Philadelphia Doctorate Course lectures* 40, 35 & 18.[**emphasis added**].

34   John Sweeney, *Church of Fear*, (Kidderminster, Worcestershire, UK: Silvertail Books, 2013).

the story in Operating Thetan level III (OT III) in 1967, warning that the "R6 implant" (past trauma) was "calculated to kill (by pneumonia, etc.) anyone who attempts to solve it."

Within the Church of Scientology, the Xenu story is part of the church's secret **Advanced Technology**, considered a sacred and esoteric teaching, which is normally only revealed to members who have completed a lengthy sequence of courses costing large amounts of money, [35] but the church officially denies this. A statement quoted by *The Telegraph* in 2012 said: *"Scientology holds no such belief. Adding, Any suggestion otherwise is as absurd as asserting that those of the Christian faith believe themselves descended from aliens because they believe there is a Heaven."* [36] Despite this, much material on Xenu has leaked to the public via court documents, copies of Hubbard's notes, and the Internet. [37]

In the short term, Hubbard with his questionable **Bridge to Total Freedom** and the creation of what *Rolling Stone* described as America's *"most controversial religion,"* [38] has certainly served the dark side and Satan, in a much more effective way than Crowley's O.T.O. However, Crowley laid the foundations for Hubbard's work and the work of many other False Prophets of the New Age.

L. Ron Hubbard's son confirms this in his 1983 interview with *Penthouse Magazine*. L. Ron Hubbard Jr., (Ron DeWolf) stated: *"I believed in Satanism. There was no other religion in the house! Scientology and black magic. What a lot of people don't realize is that Scientology is black magic that is just spread out over a long time period. To perform black magic generally takes a few hours or, at most, a few weeks. But in Scientology, it's stretched out over a lifetime and so you don't see it. Black magic is the inner core of Scientology—and it is probably the only part of Scientology that really works. Also, you've got to realize that my father did not worship Satan. He thought he was Satan. He was one with Satan."*

According to Hubbard's son, the inner core of Scientology is involved with black magic and Satanism! In this shocking interview to *Penthouse Magazine*, L. Ron Hubbard Jr., also explains in detail his father's fascination for Aleister Crowley's occult practices since the tender age of sixteen:

That involvement goes back to when he was sixteen, living in Washington. D.C. He got hold of the book by Aleister Crowley called **The Book of Law**. *He was very interested in several things that were the creation of what some people call the Moon Child. It was basically, an attempt to create an immaculate conception—except by Satan rather than by God. Another important idea was the creation of what they call embryo implants—of getting a satanic or demonic spirit to inhabit the body of a fetus. This would come about as a result of black-magic rituals, which included the use of hypnosis, drugs, and other dangerous and destructive practices. One of*

35   https://en.wikipedia.org/wiki/Xenu ‡ Archived 11th December, 2017.

36   http://www.telegraph.co.uk/news/0/what-is-scientology-and-who-was-l-ron-hub-bard/ ‡ Archived 11th December, 2017.

37   *See* Urban, Hugh B, *Fair Game: Secrecy, Security, and the Church of Scientology in Cold War America, Journal of the American Academy of Religion*. Oxford University Press, Volume 74, Issue 2, 1 June 2006.

38   https://www.rollingstone.com/culture/news/inside-scientology-20110208 ‡ Archived 11th December, 2017.

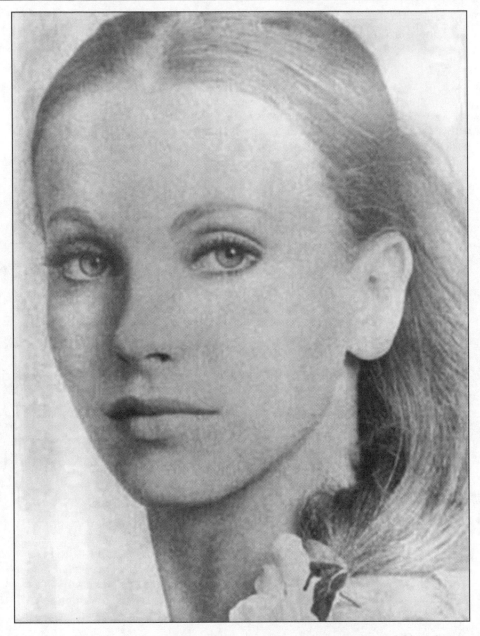

FIG. 31 Maria Orsitsch, also known as Maria Orsic, was a famous medium who later became the leader of the Vril Society.

the important things was to destroy the evidence if you failed at this immaculate conception. That's how my father became obsessed with abortions. I have a memory of this that goes back to when I was six years old. It is certainly a problem for my father and for Scientology that I remember this. It was around 1939, 1940, that I watched my father doing something to my mother. She was lying on the bed and he was sitting on her, facing her feet. He had a coat hanger in his hand. There was blood all over the place. I remember my father shouting at me. "Go back to bed!" A little while later a doctor came and took her off to the hospital. She didn't talk about it for quite a number of years. Neither did my father. [39]

THE VRIL FACTOR

*T*he first hint of the Vril Society's existence would seem more like a scene out of one of Dennis Wheatley's occult thrillers. In the news media, on 25 April 1945, it was reported:

A group of battle-weary Russian soldiers were making their cautious way through the shattered remnants of Berlin, mopping up the isolated pockets of German resistance that remained in the heart of the Third Reich. The soldiers moved carefully from one wrecked building to another, in a state of constant readiness against the threat of ambush. In a ground-floor room of one blasted building, the soldiers made a surprising discovery. Lying in a circle on the floor were the bodies of six men, with a seventh corpse in the center. All were dressed in German military uniforms and the dead man in the center of the group was wearing a pair of bright green gloves. The Russians' assumption that the bodies were those of soldiers was quickly dispelled when they realized that the dead men were all Orientals. One of the Russians, who was from Mongolia, identified the men as Tibetans. It was also evident to the Russian soldiers that the men had not died in battle but seemed to have committed suicide.

Over the following week, hundreds more Tibetan bodies were discovered in Berlin: some of them had clearly died in battle, while others had committed ritual suicide, like the ones discovered by the Russian unit. What were Tibetans doing in Nazi Germany towards the end of the Second World War? [40] The Vril Force or Vril Energy was said to be derived from the **Black Sun**, represented as a Swastika made up of Sig runes—which supposedly exists in the center of the Earth, giving light to the Vril-ya, emitting radiation in the form of Vril. The term *Schwarze Sonne* (Black Sun), also referred to as the *Sonnenrad* (Sun Wheel), is a symbol of esoteric and occult significance. Its design is based on a sun wheel mosaic incorporated into the floor of the *Obergruppenführer Hall* (SS Generals' Hall) in Wewelsburg Castle. It is not known with any certainty whether this symbol was placed in the marble floor at Wewelsburg before or during the National Socialist Regime. [41]

There remains speculation as to whether the symbol was placed in the hall by the Nazis, or whether it was there previously, but there is no definitive proof either way. Today this symbol is also used in occult currents of Germanic neopa-

39   http://www.lermanet2.com/scientologynews/penthouse-LRonHubbardJr-inter-view-1983.htm‡ Archived 11th December, 2017.

40   *See* Peter Crawford: http://thirdreichocculthistory.blogspot.it/2012/10/the-vril.html ‡ Archived 11th December, 2017.

41   *See* Nicholas Goodrick-Clarke, *Black Sun: Aryan Cults, Esoteric Nazism and the Politics of Identity* (New York, US: New York University Press, 2002).

ganism and in *Irminenschaft* or *Armanenschaft*—inspired esotericism—but not necessarily in a racial or neo-Nazi context. However, the Black Sun is often associated with the mystic-esoteric aspects of National Socialism. [42] The origin of this post-war SS mysticism, which refers to the Black Sun, not as a symbol, but as a kind of esoteric concept, is the right-wing Illuminati esoteric circle founded in the early 1950s in Vienna by former SS member Wilhelm Landi (1909-1997), known as the Landig Circle, Vienna Group, or Vienna Lodge. [43]

The Vril Force or Vril Energy was said to be derived from the Black Sun, a big ball of **Prima Materia**, which supposedly exists in the center of the Earth, giving light to the Vril-ya, and putting out radiation in the form of Vril. The Vril Society believed that Aryans were the actual biological ancestors of the Black Sun. This force was known to the ancients under many names and it has been called "Chi," "Ojas," "Vril," "Astral Light," "Odic Forces" and "Orgone." In a discussion of the 28th degree of the Ancient and Accepted Scottish Rite of Freemasonry—called **Knight of the Sun or Prince Adept**—Albert Pike said: *"There is in nature one most potent force, by means whereof a single man, who could possess himself of it and should know how to direct it, could revolutionize and change the face of the world."*

This is the force that the inner occult circle of Thule were so desperately trying to unleash upon the world, for which the mysterious Vril Society had apparently groomed Adolf Hitler. Vril is a substance first described in Edward Bulwer-Lytton's 1871 novel, *The Coming Race* which was later reprinted as *Vril: The Power of the Coming Race*. The novel is an early example of science fiction. However, many early readers believed that its account of a superior subterranean master race and the energy-form called Vril was accurate, to the extent that some theosophists accepted the book as truth. *The Coming Race* was originally published anonymously in late 1871, but Bulwer-Lytton was known to be the author. Samuel Butler's *Erewhon*, ("Nowhere"—in reverse) was also published anonymously, in March, 1872 and Butler suspected that its initial success was due to it being taken by many as a sequel by Bulwer-Lytton to *The Coming Race*.

The use of **Vril** in the novel among the Vril-ya, vary from an agent of destruction to a healing substance. According to Zee, the daughter of the narrator's host, Vril can be changed into the mightiest agent over all types of matter, both animate and inanimate.

It can destroy like lightning or replenish life, heal, or cure. It is used to render ways through solid matter. Its light is said to be steadier, softer and healthier than that from any flammable material. It can also be used as a power source for animating mechanisms. Vril can be harnessed by use of the Vril staff, or by mental concentration. A *Vril staff* is an object in the shape of a wand or a staff, which is used as a channel for Vril. [44]

It is also said that if an army met another army and both had command of the Vril-force, both sides would be annihilated. Considering Bulwer-Lytton's alleged occult background, many commentators were convinced that the supposedly

42   *See* https://en.wikipedia.org/wiki/Black_Sun_(occult_symbol ‡ Archived 11th December, 2017.

43   https://en.wikipedia.org/wiki/Landig_Group ‡ Archived 11th December, 2017.

44   Peter Crawford, *Ibid.*

fictionalized Vril was based on a real magical force. Helena Blavatsky, the founder of Theosophy, endorsed this view in her book *Isis Unveiled* (1877) and again in *"Die Geheimlehre"* or *The Secret Doctrine* (1888). Blavatsky's esotericism was virulently anti-Christian, however the racial ideas of Madame Blavatsky, concerning root races and the emergence of a spiritually-developed type of human being in the Aquarian Age, were avidly accepted by the nineteenth-century German nationalists who mixed Theosophical occultism with anti-Semitism, [45] and the doctrine of the racial supremacy of the Aryan or Indo-European peoples.

Edward Bulwer-Lytton, 1st Baron Lytton PC (25 May 1803 – 18 January 1873), was an English novelist, poet, playwright, and politician. He was immensely popular with the reading public and wrote a stream of bestselling novels which earned him a considerable fortune. In 1870, the *Societas Rosicruciana in Anglia* (S.R.I.A,) appointed Bulwer-Lytton as their "Grand Patron." Although Bulwer-Lytton apparently complained about this by letter in 1872, the claim has never been revoked. [46]

The S.R.I.A is a Masonic Christian Rosicrucian order formed by Robert Wentworth Little between 1865, and 1866 or 67, depending on the source and reclutes their members from the ranks of subscribing Master Masons from the United Grand Lodge of England. The structure and grade of this order, as A. E. Waite suggests, were derived from the 18th-century German Order of the Golden and Rosy Cross. It later became the same grade system used for the Golden Dawn. Lytton's association with many contemporary occultists in his day, such as Eliphas Lévi, has also caused speculation about his actual affiliation or possible link to the birth of the Hermetic Order of the Golden Dawn, a magical order which practices theurgy and spiritual development, that was officially founded after Baron Lytton's death in 1887.

The three founders, William Robert Woodman, William Wynn Westcott, and Samuel Liddell MacGregor Mathers were Freemasons and members of *Societas Rosicruciana* in Anglia (S.R.I.A.) Westcott appears to have been the initial driving force behind the establishment of the Golden Dawn. [47] Author Theo Paijmans, in his book *Free Energy Pioneer*, states that:

> *According to Wynn Wescott, one of the founders of the Golden Dawn, in 1850* **Bulwer-Lytton was appointed "member in absence" of the exclusive German high-grade Rosicrucian lodge "Karl zum aufgehenden Licht" based in Frankfurt.** *This ancient lodge was founded in the 18th century and was one of the last representatives of a* **German Masonic-alchemical Rosicrucian system** *... Bulwer-Lytton allegedly corresponded with this lodge and* **became intimate with their alchemical teachings and doctrines.** [48]

While Bulwer-Lytton's honorary membership in the German Masonic lodge, Carl zum aufgehenden Licht #273 is now confirmed, his alleged membership in

45   *See.* http://www.conspiracyarchive.com/NWO/Vril_Society.htm ‡ Archived 11th December, 2017.

46   *Ibid.*

47   Mark Salot, from "Excerpts in progress" a note publicly distributed on Facebook from CHAPTER IX (a) of the upcoming *Nazi Technology and Beliefs.*

48   Theo Paijmans, *Free Energy Pioneer: John Worrell Keely,* (Kempton, IL: Adventures Unlimited Press, 2004) p. 242 .

another Lodge in the same city called *Zur aufgehenden Morgenröthe*, has been proven wrong. [49] Known Illuminati researcher Terry Melanson explains that: *"The Vril Society or The Luminous Lodge combined the political ideals of the Order of the Illuminati with Hindu mysticism, Theosophy, and the Cabbala. It was the first German nationalist groups to use the symbol of the swastika as an emblem linking Eastern and Western occultism. The Vril Society presented the idea of a subterranean matriarchal, socialist utopia ruled by superior beings who had mastered the mysterious energy called the Vril Force."*

The existence of a Vril-Society was mentioned for the first time after the Second World War by Louis Pauwels, in his 1954 book titled *Monsieur Gurdjieff*, [50] where he claimed that the Vril Society had been founded by General Karl Haushofer, a student of Russian magician and metaphysician Georges Gurdjieff. The Vril-Society, was later discussed in greater detail in 1960, by the same Louis Pauwels and Jacques Bergier, in their bestselling book, *The Morning of the Magicians*, where they claimed that the Vril-Society was a secret community of occultists present in pre-Nazi Berlin, described as a sort of inner circle of the Thule Society. They also thought that it was in close contact with the English group known as the Hermetic Order of the Golden Dawn.

The Vril information takes up about a tenth of the volume, the remainder of which details other esoteric speculations, but the authors fail to clearly explain whether this section is fact or fiction. Historians have often shown that there has been no actual historical foundation for the claims of Pauwels and Bergier and that the article of Willy Ley, that I will talk about shortly, has only been a vague inspiration for their own ideas. Nevertheless, Pauwels and Bergier influenced a whole new literary genre dealing with the alleged occult influences of National Socialism, [51] that is taken more seriously in recent years by mainstream historians, but have however defined the Vril Society as fictional. It is said that in this branch of the Illuminati network they practiced methods of concentration and a whole system of internal gymnastics by which they would be eventually transformed. Terry Melanson writes that:

These methods of concentration were probably based on Ignatius Loyola's Spiritual Exercises. The Jesuit techniques of concentration and visualization are similar to many occult teachings, especially in shamanic cults and Tibetan Buddhism. The Nazi's revered these Jesuit Spiritual Exercises, which they believed had been handed down from ancient Masters of Atlantis. ... The occultists of the time knew that Ignatius was a Basque—some claimed that the Basque people were the last remnant of the Atlantean race—and the proper use of these techniques would enable the reactivation of the Vril for the dominance of the Teutonic race over all others. The Vril Society believed that whoever becomes master of the Vril will be the master of himself, of others around him and of the world. The belief was that the world will change and the "Lords" will emerge from the center of the Earth. Unless we have made an alliance with them and become "Lords" ourselves, we

49   Julian Strube, *Vril. Eine okkulte Urkraft in Theosophie und esoterischem Neonazismus*, (München/Paderborn, DE: Wilhelm Fink Verlag, 2013), pp. 55–74.

50   *See* Louis Pauwels, *Monsieur Gurdjieff : documents, témoignages, textes et commentaires sur une société initiatique contemporaine*, (Paris, FR: Éditions du Seuil 1954, rééd. Albin Michel, 1979 et 1995).

51   *See* Julian Strube, *Ibid.*, pp. 126–142.

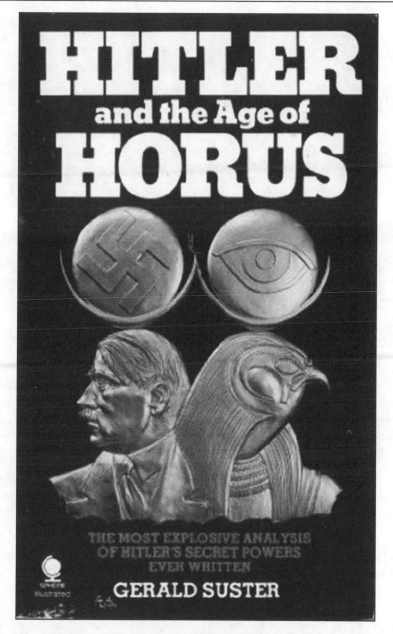

*FIG. 32 The cover of the first English edition in 1981 by Gerald Suster, Hitler
and the Age of Horus, which shows a deep knowledge of the esoteric symbolism
in which we note Hitler and Horus as a kind of two faced **Janus**, linked to the
natural cycles of time so dear to the followers of **Thelema**, the religion promoted by Crowley, that believes that the history of humanity is divided into a
series of **aeons** (also written **æons**), This is the Aeon of Horus, which was controlled by the child god, symbolised by Horus. In this new aeon, Thelemites believe that humanity will enter a time of self-realization and self-actualization.*

FIG. 33 (left to right) Heinz Haber, Wernher von Braun, **Willy Ley.**

shall find ourselves among the slaves, on the dung-heap that will nourish the roots of the New Cities that will arise. [52]

In *The Unknown Hitler,* Wulf Schwarzwaller writes:

In Berlin, Haushofer had founded the Luminous Lodge or the Vril Society. The Lodge's objective was to explore the origins of the Aryan race and to perform exercises in concentration to awaken the forces of "Vril." Haushofer was a student of the Russian magician and metaphysician George Gurdjieff. Both Gurdjieff and Haushofer maintained that they had contacts with secret Tibetan lodges that possessed the secret of the "Superman." **The Lodge included Hitler, Aalfred, Rosenberg, Himmler, Goring and Hitler's subsequent personal physician Dr. Morell. It is also known that Aleister Crowley and Gurdjieff sought contact with Hitler.** *Hitler's unusual powers of suggestion become more understandable if one keeps in mind that he had access to the "secret" psychological techniques of Gurdjieff which, in turn, were based on the teachings of the Sufis and the Tibetan lamas and familiarized him with the Zen teaching of the Japanese Society of the Green Dragon.* [53]

The evidence of the existence of the Vril Society comes from none other than **Willy Ley (1906-1969)**, a German-born scientist and scientific writer who emigrated to the USA in 1935, best known for his historic conversation with German rocket scientists (and ex-Nazi), Wernher Von Braun. Highlights of this conversation recorded June 9th and 23rd, 1959, in New York City and Redstone Arsenal, Huntsville, Alabama, including the development of the German rocket programs during WWII and the space program in the 1950s. A few years earlier,

52   conspiracyarchive.com, *Ibid.*

53   *See* Wulf Schwarzwaller, *The Unknown Hitler: His Private Life and Fortune,* (Toronto, ON: Stoddart Publishing, 1988).

Ley wrote a revealing article entitled, *Pseudoscience in Naziland* published in May 1947, in the science fiction magazine *Astounding Science Fiction*. In this article, Ley attempts to explain to his readers how National Socialism could have fallen on such a fertile ground in Germany. [54]

Basically, Willy Ley explained how the high popularity of irrational convictions in Germany during the time, was actually crucial for the rise of Nazism. Among other pseudo-scientific groups present in Nazi Germany, he mentions one in particular, in search of the Vril, that partly confirms the existence of the Vril Society, that Ley called the *"Society for Truth"* (in German *Wahrheitsgesellschaft*), probably omitting the real name for fear of reprisals by the many high level German Nazi's, like Von Braun, who moved to the USA in those years, protected by American counter-intelligence, who recruited former Gestapo officers, SS veterans and Nazi collaborators to oppose the Soviet Union. This is the crucial passage of the article in question by Willy Ley:

> The next group was literally founded upon a novel. That group which I think called itself **Wahrheitsgesellschaft**—Society for Truth—and which was more or less localized in Berlin, devoted its spare time looking for Vril. Yes, their convictions were founded upon Bulwer-Lytton's **The Coming Race.** They knew that the book was fiction, Bulwer-Lytton had used that device in order to be able to tell the truth about this "power." The subterranean humanity was nonsense, Vril was not, Possibly it had enabled the British, who kept it as a State secret, to amass their colonial empire. Surely the Romans had had it, enclosed in small metal balls, which guarded their homes and were referred to as lares. For reasons which I failed to penetrate, the secret of Vril could be found by contemplating the structure of an apple, sliced into halves. No, I am not joking, that is what I was told with great solemnity and secrecy. Such a group actually existed, they even got out the first issue of a magazine which was to proclaim their credo. (I wish I had kept some of these things, but I had enough books to smuggle out as it was.) [55]

Nonetheless, the mondialist occult elite are still denying to this day the very existence of the Vril Society, scared of the truth behind links with its members to an interdimensional reality. The German Wikipedia for example, describes the Vril society as complete fiction in the very first sentence. [56] But who were the members of the Vril Society and how did they operate?

The Vril Society was apparently formed by a group of female psychic mediums led by the Thule Gesellschaft medium Maria Orsitsch (Orsic) of Zagreb, who claimed to have received communication from Aryan aliens living on Alpha Cen Tauri, in the Aldebaran system. Allegedly, these aliens had visited Earth and settled in Sumeria and the word Vril was formed from the ancient Sumerian word "Vri-Il" ("like god"). A second medium was known only as Sigrun, a name etymologically related to Sigrune, a Valkyrie and one of Wotan's nine daughters in Norse legend. The Society taught concentration exercises, in an attempt to awaken the forces of Vril with their main goal to achieve *Raumflug* (Spaceflight) to reach Al-

---

54   *See* https://en.wikipedia.org/wiki/Vril ‡ Archived 11th December, 2017.

55   http://www.alpenfestung.com/ley_pseudoscience.htm ‡ Archived 11th December, 2017.

56   https://en.wikipedia.org/wiki/Talk%3AVril_ Society ‡ Archived 11th December, 2017.

debaran. To achieve this, the Vril Society joined the Thule Gesellschaft, to fund an ambitious program involving an inter-dimensional flight machine based on psychic revelations from the Aldebaran aliens. Members of the Vril Society are said to have included Adolf Hitler, Alfred Rosenberg, Heinrich Himmler, Hermann Göring, and Hitler's personal physician, Dr. Theodor Morell. These were the original members of the Thule Society, which supposedly joined Vril in 1919.

The NSDAP (*NationalSozialistische Deutsche ArbeiterPartei*) was created by Thule in 1920, one year later. Dr. Krohn, who helped to create the Nazi flag, was also a Thulist. With Hitler gaining power in 1933, both Thule and Vril Gesellschafts allegedly received official state backing for continued disc development programs aimed at both spaceflight and possibly a war machine. After 1941, Hitler forbade secret societies, so both Thule and Vril were documented under the SS E-IV unit. The claim of an ability to travel in some interdimensional mode is similar to Vril claims of channeled flight with the *Jenseitsflugmaschine* (Other World Flight Machine) and the Vril *Flugscheiben* (Flight Discs). [57]

THE ALIEN DIMENSION: FROM THE GOLDEN DAWN TO THE A∴A∴

*T*he origins of The Hermetic Order Of The Golden Dawn are still a matter for dispute. Somehow or other, some coded manuscripts fell into the hands of two gentlemen interested in the occult, Dr. Woodford and Dr.Wynn Westcott. When deciphered, these manuscripts turned out to consist of some skeletonic rituals, and the address of a certain adept, one **Anna Sprengel**, who lived in Nuremberg. Dr. Westcott asked an occult scholar Samuel Liddell (or Liddel) MacGregor Mathers, to assist him. Mathers agreed to write a series of suitable rituals based upon the skeletons, and Westcott wrote to Anna Sprengel and received a charter to found an Order and much occult teaching. Now, it has been alleged that Anna Sprengel never existed and that the Golden Dawn was the creation of Westcott and Mathers, but this does not really matter; the Golden Dawn is important for what it was and not for who founded it. We can at least state that it was founded in 1888.

In 1891, it was claimed that Anna Sprengel died, her successors in Nuremberg broke off all correspondence, and that they urged the English magicians to formulate their own links with the Secret Chiefs. Who or what were these mysterious beings? It seems that they were the same as the Hidden Masters of Blavatsky or the Unknown Supermen of Lytton. [58] In 1892, S. L. Mathers claimed to have formulated a link with them, and his description is of interest:

Concerning the Secret Chiefs of the Order, to whom I make reference ... I can tell you nothing. I know not even their earthly names. I know them only by certain secret mottoes, I have but very rarely seen them in the physical body, and on such rare occasions, the rendezvous was made astrally by them. They met me in the flesh at the time and place appointed beforehand. For my part I believe them to be human and

---

57   http://www.echoesofenoch.com/Musium13%20vril_society.htm ‡ Archived 11th December, 2017.

58   *See* Gerald Suster, *Hitler and the Age of Horus* (1981; in the United States as: *Hitler: The Occult Messiah*)

living on this earth but possessing terrible superhuman powers. When such rendez-
vous has been in a much-frequented place there has been nothing in their personal
appearance or dress to make them out as differing in any way from ordinary people
except the appearance and sensation of transcendent health and vigour ... which was
their invariable accompaniment; in other words, the physical appearance which the
possession of the Elixir of Life had traditionally been supposed to confer. On the other
hand when the rendezvous has been in a place free from any access by the Outer
World they have usually been in symbolic robes and insignia. But my physical in-
tercourse with them on these rare occasions has shown me how difficult it is for a
Mortal, even though advanced in Occultism, to support the presence of an Adept
in the physical body ... the sensation was that of being in contact with so terrible a
force that I can only compare it to the continued effect of that usually experienced
momentarily by any person close to whom a flash of lightning passes during a vio-
lent storm; coupled with a difficulty in respiration similar to the half strangling effect
produced by ether, and if such was the result produced on one as tested as I have
been in Occult work, I cannot conceive a much less advanced Initiate being able to
support such a strain, even for five minutes without death ensuing. [59]

The late Gerald Suster (1951-2001), who knew Israel Regardie and Gerald Yorke
personally, was a member of the Tabula Rasa of the O.T.O. in London (in those
days an Oasis), explained in *Hitler and the Age of Horus*, that Mathers emerged as
the Order's undisputed master, and though Westcott, who resigned in 1897, later
claimed that a Belgian occultist, rather than Unknown Supermen, dictated occult knowledge to Mathers, the latter definitely believed that he was in contact
with the Secret Chiefs from that moment onward. Indeed, he was a remarkable
man, who devoted his life entirely to magic. He was the translator and editor of
such arcane medieval classics as *The Greater Key of Solomon* and *The Sacred Magic
of AbraMelin the Mage*; *The Qabalah Unveiled*, and a short book on the Tarot from
which most subsequent authors have borrowed without acknowledgment. Yet nowhere in these books does he display the synthetic genius which enabled him to
create the system of magic practiced by the Golden Dawn. He weaved together
rituals, methods, and knowledge from innumerable sources, into something that
was beautiful, harmonious, logical, and, for those who worked with it, efficacious.

The aim of Golden Dawn magic is nothing less than to become Superman:
the method is the use of light, color, sound, scent, words, and ceremony, and
meditation—to train the human brain and focus the human will so that a transformation of the magician's life can take place, enabling him to know and use his
full potential. A strong supporter both of the hereditary principle and of authoritarian government, Mathers believed that man could become Superman here
and now, but that this course was only for the few. In 1894, he moved to Paris with
his wife, and founded another Order temple; meanwhile, the membership of
the Golden Dawn grew to three figures, without publicity, and temples operated
in London, Edinburgh, Bradford, and Weston-super-Mare. English men and
women, from all walks of life, studied and practiced means of tapping Lytton's
Vril force, developing the unconscious, and coming into contact with the supersensible beings of another world. It is a very odd fact that when they attained
to the Grade of Zelator, which was connected with the energies of the element

59   Letter by S. L. Mathers quoted in Francis King's *Ritual Magic in England* and in Pau-
      wels & Bergier.

of Earth, members learned to give a certain sign, which may or may not have been learned from Anna Sprengel and her Order in Nuremberg: this sign, which invoked the power of the soil, would become notorious as that of *Heil Hitler!* [60]

Eventually, a quarrel between W. B. Yeats and S. L. Mathers and his ally, Aleister Crowley, will split the Golden Dawn into a group of warring sects, while others left the Order. Aleister Crowley portrayed Mathers as a villain named SRMD in his 1917 novel *Moonchild*. According to Crowley's memoirs, *The Confessions of Aleister Crowley,* Mathers was in the habit of ostensibly playing chess matches against various pagan gods. Mathers would set up the chessboard and seat himself behind the white pieces, with an empty chair opposite him. After making a move for himself, Mathers would then shade his eyes and peer towards the empty chair, waiting for his opponent to signal a move. Mathers would then move a black piece accordingly, then make his next move as white, and so forth. Crowley did not record who won. Earlier, Crowley wrote in his diary that: *"As far as I was concerned, Mathers was my only link with the Secret Chiefs to whom I was pledged. I wrote to him offering to place myself and my fortune unreservedly at his disposal; if that meant giving up the Abra-Melin Operation for the present, all right."* [61]

Golden Dawn groups have lingered on to this day, one of the most sincere and relevant is guided by my friend David Griffin, but the Order's significant work was done by 1900. A few inhabitants of the most industrialized and rational empire in the world acquainted themselves with the ancient and neglected arts of magic. Nor had the people of Great Britain's leading competitor for world supremacy, the German Empire, been left untouched by this sudden occult fever. Various groups, quite ferociously nationalistic, continued throughout the nineteenth century.

In 1895, Karl Kellner, a wealthy iron-master, who was taught by one Arab and two Hindu masters, proclaimed the establishment of the quasi-Masonic Order of the Oriental Templars, or O.T.O. By 1904, this Order produced a periodical, *The Oriflamme*, teaching a system of sexual magic based upon the control of the Vril. Though this Order became the second greatest influence upon twentieth-century esoteric thought, it was not at the time of its foundation as important as two German magicians independent of it, Guido von List and Lanz von Liebenfels.

In 1875, Guido von List, a white-bearded magus in flowing robes, celebrated the Summer Solstice by burying a number of empty wine bottles on the summit of a hill overlooking Vienna: these wine bottles were placed in the form of a sign which had not been seen in the land before; it was used as a Badge of Power in the Golden Dawn, where it was known as The Hermetic Cross; it was also known as the Hammer of Thor; it was an exclusively Aryan symbol; it was the Swastika. In 1907, Adolf Lanz, who called himself Lanz von Liebenfels, ran up a flag from his magical temple which overlooked the Danube; it was the Swastika.

The sign stood for all that List and Liebenfels believed in: an abandonment of Christianity, an embracing of neo-paganism, a desire to become or create the Superman, and an affirmation of Aryan racial superiority. We will be returning to these two strange men, who had much effect upon the views of Hitler.

60   Gerald Suster, *Ibid.*

61   https://en.wikipedia.org/wiki/Samuel_Liddell_MacGregor_Mathers ‡ Archived 11th December, 2017.

Such were the ideas which were born or resurrected at around the same time as Hitler's birth. Such were the ideas which he would greedily imbibe in Vienna. Such were the ideas which began to infect a world which believed it could not be infected. Such were the ideas which played their part in making the twentieth century what it is. One could be pardoned for observing that the values and gods of the world were entering upon their dotage, and that the gods of a new, strange, and terrible age were stirring in their sleep and about to awaken. Was there a meaning behind this assortment of signs, portents, prophecies; beliefs, omens, coincidences and lunacies? [62]

Why does Crowley end his sentence by talking about suspending the practices of Abramelin Magic? It's something I'll follow up on shortly. From the words of Samuel Liddell MacGregor Mathers it is noticed that, despite the human aspect, these mysterious Secrets Chiefs have supernatural and almost divine characteristics, but differ in some respects from the mysterious preternatural figure obtained with the *knowledge and conversation* of one's Holy Guardian Angel; a term that originates in the Catholic Church, where a morning prayer is recited which reads: *"Holy Guardian Angel whom God has appointed to be my guardian, direct and govern me during this day/ Amen."*

The idea of a Holy Guardian Angel is also central in *The Book of the Sacred Magic of Abramelin the Mage* by the German Cabalist Abraham of Worms, who wrote this book on ceremonial magick during the 15th century, that was later translated by Mathers, and popularized by creepy Crowley within his hideous religious and philosophical system of Thelema built for the New Age. However, the original concept goes back to the Zoroastrian *Arda Fravaš*—Holy guardian angels who guide people through their lives. In S.L. Mathers' publication of *The Book of the Sacred Magic of Abramelin the Mage*, a key text of the Illuminati used to establish contact and deals with interdimensional beings, he writes: *"If thou shalt perfectly observe these rules, all the following Symbols and an infinitude of others will be granted unto thee by thy Holy Guardian Angel; thou thus living for the Honour and Glory of the True and only God, for thine own good, and that of thy neighbour. Let the Fear of God be ever before the eyes and the heart of him who shall possess this Divine Wisdom and Sacred Magic."* Later, author and occultist Aleister Crowley popularized the term within his religious and philosophical system of Thelema. [63]

It is obvious that in the rituals of the orthodox Western ceremonial magick tradition, as contemporary Illuminati Allen H. Greenofield also points out, we find the technology for contacting Ultraterrestrials across barriers of time, space and dimensionality, but also for breaking such contact should this prove necessary, or for containing any force being brought forth in this manner to avoid being vampirized or manipulated. The immediate past source for such rituals are the medieval magical texts termed *grimoires* or *grammars* that is, basic instructional texts—but their sources are much older. A clue to the origin of such texts can be found, for example, in the introductory narrative of the *Clavicula Salomonis*, or **Key of King Solomon**. In the 1888 translation by S.L. Mathers, we are told by Solomon, the purported author: *"I suddenly beheld, at the end of a thickly-*

---

62   Gerald Suster, *Ibid.*

63   *See* https://en.wikipedia.org/wiki/Holy_Guardian_Angel ‡ Archived 11th December, 2017.

shaded vista of trees, a Light in the form of a blazing Star, which said unto me with a voice of thunder: Solomon, Solomon, be not dismayed; the Lord is willing to satisfy thy desire by giving thee knowledge of whatsoever thing is most pleasant to thee."

What follows Solomon's request for wisdom are various techniques for conjuring Celestial Powers and Beings, of controlling their energies and sending them back to their places of origin. These beings are named and described in detail, as are the planets and spheres of their origin. While the antiquity of some of this material is unknown, some of it shows a knowledge of ancient Gnostic Wisdom Literature unavailable in medieval Europe, suggesting a very ancient origin. One ritual that invokes the *Power of Contact that comes from the Stars* is certainly of very ancient origin. The Hermetic Order of the Golden Dawn polished the ritual as *The Bornless Ritual for the Invocation of the Higher Genius,* in the late 19th Century, but a cruder version was published in 1852 under the unappetizing title: *Fragment of a Greco-Egyptian Work Upon Magic,* and later reprinted by the great Egyptologist E. A. Wallis Budge in his turn-of-the-century book, *Egyptian Magic.* [64]

In ancient Egypt, people generally knew that some hierophants had risen to a high condition of knowledge and power as compared with ordinary humanity, thanks to their links to the alien world. Definite systems of initiation were known to lead upward towards those heights using secret ciphers and codes to communicate with each other and with their ultraterrestrial masters, viewed by Thesophists as the Secret Chiefs of the Great White Brotherhood, and others as Greenfield writes: *"have used the same or similar ciphers to communicate with their opposition,"* [65] meaning their Satanic counterparts.

Though later generations have completely lost sight of this deeply significant truth, it is still as true as ever, especially when linked to the alien mystery. The (relatively) lower levels of the Divine Hierarchy are still recruited in that way. In recent ages, the Illuminati system has been veiled from common observation in the reserved groups, by the likes of Freemasonry and others. However, the progress of humanity is worked out in accordance with a definite secret Divine plan guided by the Invisible Masters and their Secret Chiefs. For a time it was necessary that human intelligence should be trained in the study of a more physical nature. The improvement of brain capacity was the first task before humanity could move forward to the next level of human evolution. Knowledge, and the fascination for the unknown, attracted the recent pioneers of brain culture on the path to awaken humanity, that seems to be on the wrong path of materialism and ignorance. Human evolution does not stop short at the stage reached by the most brilliant representatives of our current civilization, and should lead on to the appreciation of the idea that infinitude is applicable to this evolution, as to the loftier conception of Divine nature, a concept Alfred Percy Sinnett underlined in his *Collected Fruits of Occult Teaching.* [66]

Going back to the reason why Crowley at one point offered to abandon the Abramelin operation, let's remember that such an operation would have eman-

64   *See* Allen Greenfield, *Secret Rituals of the Men in Black.*

65   *Ibid*

66   Alfred Percy Sinnet, *Collected fruits of occult teaching*, (Philadelphia, PA : J. B. Lippincott & Co, 1919), pp. 24-25.

cipated Crowley from Mathers and the Golden Dawn, putting him in direct contact with the Secret Chiefs and Invisible Alien Masters, who assist humanity by secretly guiding the various Orders of the Illuminati. This is something that eventually happened when Crowley broke with Mathers in 1903, after causing the Golden Dawn disintegration. The following year he went to Cairo to get in touch with Aiwass, a Secret Chief of the god Horus, and receive from it, *Liber Al vel Legis*, also known as *The Book of the Law,* which will help him, within a few years, to formulate his new pseudo-religion of *Thelema,* so dear to the modern Illuminati and their infamous New World Order. The first time that the name of Aiwaz (or Aiwass, as Crowley spelled it) was heard by Aleister Crowley was in March 1904, when his wife, Rose Edith Crowley née Kelly, spontaneously entered into a state of trance. It is often forgotten that it was not Aleister Crowley who sought out the Cairo Working. It was an unknown intelligence communicating itself through the spontaneous mediumship of Rose that called Crowley to fulfill his role of the Beast 666, who he identified himself with both in his childhood imaginings and in his poetry. It was Rose who told Crowley that the source of the cryptic messages concerning the Child, Osiris, Horus, the Equinox of the Gods, Christian Rosy [sic] Cross, and the Solar Force was one Aiwass. Years later, Crowley would state that he had never heard this name before.

This is probably true. Aiwaz (Aiwass is an intentional misspelling) is very rare. One search showed only 29 individuals have this surname, mostly in the United States and Pakistan. There are also numerous variations (e.g., Awazi, Awaz, Ahwaz, etc.). It is the 2,158,018th most popular surname in the world. Rose then instructed Crowley to sit at his writing desk at 12 noon on Friday, April 8, 1904 and for the next two days write down what he heard. He obeyed, armed with paper and fountain pen (it was a Swan quill dip pen), and at 12 noon precisely, he heard a voice and had a vivid impression of a ghost-like figure behind his left shoulder. Crowley described the voice as passionate, deep, musical, expressive, tenor or baritone. Crowley found the voice *"startling and uncanny"* because it was completely devoid of any accent, and therefore, the voice sounded not human.

Crowley also felt the voice as an odd vibration in his heart. The ghost-like figure was tall, dark, a little older than Crowley himself (at the time, Crowley was all of 28), personable, athletic, aristocratic, and Persian-Assyrian in appearance, *"with a face like a savage king"* (this was a psychic impression; at no time did Crowley turn and look at the figure). In Crowley's vision, the figure wore a veil or mask across his eyes. Aiwass is identified as the speaker in the seventh verse of the first chapter of *The Book of the Law*, as the subsequent dictation came to be called: *"Behold! it is revealed by Aiwass the minister of Hoor-paar-kraat."* Aiwass refers to himself in the third person. Whereas the physical voice of *The Book of the Law* is that of Aiwaz, he himself is the medium of the three ultimate cosmic beings: Nuit, the Egyptian goddess of the sky; Hadit, the winged solar disk; and Horus, the avenging son of Isis and Osiris. Aiwaz says only that he is the "minister." A minister is both a minor priest (or a priest's servant) and a high officer of the Crown (or the state). Originally, *"to minister"* is to serve food or drink. Aiwaz's superior is Hoor-paar-kraat (Eg. Har-pa-khered, Heru-pa-khered; Gk. Harpokrates, lit. "Horus the Child"). Harpokrates, the god of silence, is represented as a small boy with his finger held to his lips. In fact, the voice of Aiwaz himself is never heard in *The Book of the Law*. He is perfectly inscrutable. At first, Crowley interpreted the Cairo

Working, as he called it, as an astral vision and *The Book of the Law* an automatic writing. Crowley, who intensely disliked spiritualism, was initially embarrassed by *The Book of the Law,* and distanced himself from it as I also stated earlier in the book, but clearly, he was also fascinated by it. He doodled on the cover page of the Book, and there is a large stain on the first page of the third chapter. He took the Cairo Working seriously enough, however, to inform S.L. Mathers, the Chief of the Hermetic Order of the Golden Dawn, that a New Eon had been proclaimed with Crowley to supplant Mathers not only as the Head of the Order (i.e. Golden Dawn) but also as the Prophet of the New Aeon.

After some preliminary kabbalistic analysis, Crowley ruminated whether to include the Book in his collected works, then promptly lost the manuscript that reappeared years later in his Boleskine House. Crowley carried on with his spiritual work without any further reference to *The Book of the Law*. By this time he was no longer merely a magician, he was a mystic, seeking personal communion with his own Godhood. He invoked his Holy Guardian Angel. He crossed the **Abyss** and attained the grade of *Magister Templi* (Master of the Temple) of the A∴A∴ or Silver Star. He founded the Order of the A∴A∴ initially without any reference to the Cairo Working or *The Book of the Law,* based rather on his experiences in the Hermetic Order of the Golden Dawn, Yoga, Buddhism, and metaphysical philosophy that he synthesized in his system called Scientific Illuminism. [67]

In this system, Crowley added the memorization of certain Holy Books and *The Book of the Law* itself was memorized in part in the grade of *Zelator*. The specific *Thelemic* task of the Great White Brotherhood is also described in *Liber V*, the *Ritual of the Mark of the Beast*, in the grade of *Philosophus*. Within the system of the magical Order A∴A∴ founded by Aleister Crowley, one of the two most important goals is to consciously connect with one's Holy Guardian Angel, representative of one's truest divine nature—a process termed *Knowledge and Conversation*.

In some branches of occultism, the term Holy Guardian Angel is widely known as HGA, a common abbreviation now used even in non-English-speaking countries. Crowley seemed to consider it equivalent to the Genius of the Hermetic Order of the Golden Dawn, the Augoeides of Iamblichus, the Atman of Hinduism, and the Daemon of the ancient Greeks. [68]

He obviously borrowed the term from the Grimoire *The Sacred Magic of Abramelin the Mage,* translated by his friend, turned enemy, S.L. Mathers. Even though the Holy Guardian Angel is considered by some the *higher self,* it is often experienced and considered by the occultist in the Illuminati network as a separate alien being of a superior kind, independent from the adept. Crowley said however that the Abramelin procedure was not the only way to achieve success in this endeavor. He wrote in *One Star In Sight*:

It is impossible to lay down precise rules by which a man may attain to the knowledge and conversation of His Holy Guardian Angel; for that is the particular secret of each one of us; a secret not to be told or even divined by any other, whatever his

67   https://bethelkhem.wordpress.com/2012/02/04/who-was-aiwaz-the-strange-story-of-samuel-jacobs-and-aleister-crowley/ ‡ Archived 11th December, 2017.

68   See https://en.wikipedia.org/wiki/Holy_Guardian_Angel ‡ Archived 11th December, 2017.

grade. It is the Holy of Holies, whereof each man is his own High Priest, and none knoweth the Name of his brother's God, or the Rite that invokes Him. [69]

Since the operation described in Abramelin is so complex and requires time and resources not available to most people, Crowley wanted to provide a more accessible method. While at the Abbey of Thelema in Sicily, he wrote *Liber Samekh*. [70] Going back to Crowley's Thelema, **Sex magick** is also Thelemic, of course, though not exclusively so, as it existed in the various mystery schools of the Illuminati in the Far East, and in witchcraft since time immemorial. However Crowley's version of it was later grafted onto the original A∴A∴ system in *Magick in Theory and Practice*, especially the grades of *Zelator, Philosophus*, and *Adeptus Minor* (Within), in connection with the formula of the Rosy Cross in the College of the Holy Ghost and Devotion to the Order. Thus, the final system of the A∴A∴ that I joined during my time on the dark side of the Illuminati (reaching The Order of the S∴S∴), includes both the Law of Thelema, and the Supreme Secret of the O.T.O., without being subordinate to either.

The central tasks of the Great White Brotherhood in Crowley's vision, was simply the underlying universals of the Great Work attributed to the Kabbalistic Tree of Life (*Etz Chayim*). The story of Crowley's conversion to his own religion of Thelema—or, rather, the religion that had been revealed to him as the apotheosis of his own work for Satan and his fallen angels, was fully realized by Crowley together with the significance of the Cairo Working, only after he crossed the Abyss, and rededicated his life to the promulgation of the Law of Thelema in June 1909, more than five years after the original alien transmission.

In the course of his subsequent career, Crowley explained the identity of Aiwaz in different ways, not necessarily mutually exclusive. Crowley identified Hoor-paar-kraat, the silent child-god of the sun, with the True Self, which would make Aiwaz the minor of the True Self, the Holy Guardian Angel, interior Genius, or daemon. In the *Ab-ul-Diz Working*, an account of a communication with a preterhuman (intelligence man) through the seer Ouarda, Crowley (as Frater Perdurabo), was informed that he was the *demon* of the Aeon, and his age the number of Chaos (1400). [71]

More, properly, תא is a contracted form of תוא, "sign," indicative of the accusative tense. Crowley also glosses this word as "the" or "Essence" (401), *"the sum and essence of all, conceived as One."* Crowley is at times hostile to his biographer, John Symonds, who had a rather negative interpretation to the connotation of the word "demon" (*daemon* or *daimon*), [72] but for ordinary Thelemites or most Illuminati, this term is not necessarily a pejorative. The idea of a daemon comes from the beliefs of the Ancient Greeks. To them, a daemon was a spiritual being falling somewhere between a god and a human, or the ghost of a fallen hero. Daemons are even considered good or helpful spirits. So the idea of the daemon to have survived to this day, as a sort of Guardian Angel or an inner driving

69   https://hermetic.com/crowley/book-4/app2 ‡ Archived 11th December, 2017.

70   *See* https://en.wikipedia.org/wiki/Holy_Guardian_Angel ‡ Archived 11th December, 2017.

71   *See* https://hermetic.com/crowley/libers/lib60 ‡ Archived 11th December, 2017.

72   *See Sepher Sephiroth, Liber LVIII*, and John Symonds, *The Great Beast*, pp. 157, 171.

force, is not uncommon. According to Plato, in his *Cratylus*, the etymology of δαίμονες (daimones) from δαήμονες (daēmones) (=knowing or wise), though in fact, the root of the word is more probably *daiō* (to distribute destinies). In Plato's *Symposium*, the priestess Diotima teaches Socrates that love is not a god, but rather a "great daemon" (202d). She goes on to explain that "*everything daemonic is between divine and mortal*" (202d-e), and she describes daemons as "*interpreting and transporting human things to the gods and divine things to men; entreaties and sacrifices from below, and ordinances and requitals from above*" (202e). In Plato's *Apology of Socrates*, Socrates claimed to have a *daimonion* (literally, a "divine something") that frequently warned him—in the form of a "voice"—against mistakes but never told him what to do. However, the Platonic Socrates never refers to the daimonion as a daimōn; it was always an impersonal "something" or "sign." [73]

Like Socrates, Plato taught that the soul is immortal, and all knowledge gained in one's life is knowledge learned from a previous lifetime, a concept considered of great importance by Count Cagliostro and the Illuminati mystery schools. For those interested, I wrote extensively on the subject of reincarnation in one of my previous works. [74]

For some, this is also where human intuition (wisdom) originates from. The knowing within our very DNA that helps our soul to be guided through life with the assistance of our spirit guides, AKA benevolent aliens or interdimensional demons. Manly P. Hall also wrote on demons and angels in his most popular book, *The Secret Teachings of All Ages*:

The Christian Church gathered all the elemental entities together under the title of demon. This is a misnomer with far-reaching consequences, for to the average mind the word demon means an evil thing, and the Nature spirits are essentially no more malevolent than are the minerals, plants, and animals. Many of the early Church Fathers asserted that they had met and debated with the elementals.

The word demon can also have the same meaning as the English word, *genie*. The name genie is derived from the Latin *genius*, meaning a guardian spirit thought to be assigned to each person at birth. The various synonyms for genie are spirit, jinnee, ghost, gin, genius and of course, the Arab Jinn. There is evidence, however, that the word jinn is derived from Aramaic, where it was used by Christians to designate pagan gods reduced to the status of demons, and was introduced only later into Arabic folklore late in the pre-Islamic era.

In the Spring of 1904, Crowley believed he was in contact with a praeter-human intelligence called Aiwass, who was the source that he dictated the three chapters that make up *The Book of the Law*. The essential empowerment of the grade of Adeptus Major of the Interior College of the Great White Brotherhood, that Crowley claimed to have reached in that moment, was simply his act of enslavement to alien entities. In the biographical note in *The Book of Thoth*, Crowley states that he attained this grade in April 1904, but at what cost?

More generally, Crowley identified Aiwass with the libido, more in the Jungian sense of psychic energy, than in the Freudian, strictly sexual sense. Although

73   *See* http://www.artandpopularculture.com/Daemon_(mythology ‡ Archived 11th December, 2017.

74   *See* https://en.wikipedia.org/wiki/Abrahadabra‡ Archived 11th December, 2017.

Crowley regarded Aiwass as both a magical formula and entity, at no time did Crowley consider that Aiwass might be the proper name of a man. Crowley thought the word was an artificial kabbalistic construction like *Abrahadabra* or *Babalon*, perhaps subconsciously realizing they were alien ciphers. Crowley replaced the "C" in "Abracadabra" with an "H," which the Hermetic Order of the Golden Dawn in their Neophyte ritual linked with Breath and Life as well as with the god Horus, who later delivered *The Book of the Law* through **Aiwass,** the **minister** of Horus the Child.

THE NWO AND THE ROLE OF ALIEN GENES

*T*he late **John Keel**, influential Ufologist who is best known as the author of *The Mothman Prophecies,* (made into a film starring Richard Gere) wrote: *"The UFOs do not seem to exist as tangible, manufactured objects. They do not conform to the accepted natural laws of our environment. They seem to do nothing more than transmogrifications tailoring themselves to our abilities to understand. The thousands of contacts with entities indicate that they are liars and put-on artists. The UFO manifestations seem to be, by and large, merely minor variations of the age-old demonological phenomenon."*[75]

The Christians think that prior to the Second Coming of Jesus, a pair of harbinger angels will make an appointed appearance. The angel flying in mid-heaven, and the second angel is said to follow the first angel as related in *Revelation 14:6-8.* They will proselytize to the people of the Earth, proclaiming an eternal gospel to its inhabitants (See *Matthew 24:14*) and are to serve as heralds of the coming Judgment. God has, however, forewarned us. Do not confuse the cherubim of these angels who are loyal messengers of God, with the cherubim of the fallen angels. Apparently, the Second Coming (See *Matthew 24:30-31*), will be hailed initially as a malevolent alien invasion, and some say,[76] the Bible prophecies such an attack:

> And I saw heaven opened, and behold a white horse (a white cherub), and he that sat upon him was called Faithful and True (this is the cherub of the conquering Jesus), and in righteousness, he doth judge and make war ... And the armies which were in heaven followed him upon white horses (angels in white cherubim) ... And I saw ... the kings of the earth, and their armies, gathered together to make war against him that sat on the horse (against Jesus in his cherub), and against his army (of angels). –Revelation 19:11,14,15-16,19.

As Keel points out:

> It would be very dangerous for us to exclude the possibility that a very small residue of sightings may be very real. Most scientists agree that there is a chance that there may billions of inhabitable planets within our own galaxy, there is always a chance that living beings on those planets might have visited us in the past, are visiting us now, or are planning to visit us in the future. To regard all UFO sightings as illusions, hallucinations and paraphysical manifestations would expose us to a potentially volatile situation—an invasion from another world. There have been many apparently physical sightings and landings which produced markings

---

75   John A. Keel, *Why UFOs: Operation Trojan Horse* (New York: 1970) p. 281.

76   *See* John of the Gentiles, *The Demonic Theory of UFOs* (Copyright 2012-2016 by JMB Productions).

COMPARISON TABLE OF COMMON PROPERTIES BETWEEN ALIENS AND JINN

ALIEN:	JINN:
1) There are good and bad aliens.	1) There are good and bad Jinn known as Ifrit.
2) There exist different coalitions and races of aliens in a war with each other.	2) There are many stories of wars between Jinn and Ifrit.
3) Many of them are tricksters.	3) Many of them are Tricksters, they can be ruthless or foolish or both.
4) Alien Greys are thin looking, big black eyes, grey looking skin. Reptilians have vertical pupils, and scales.	4) Alien Greys are thin looking, eyes or with reptilian shape and vertical eye slit/reptile eye.
5) They live in other worlds, or deep under the earth, like the society of underground dwellers (the Agarthans), and we have many accounts of E.T. underground bases in the deepest part of the oceans.	5) They live in the skies, caves, deep under Earth, and in the deep and dark underwater Abyss.
6) Some researchers have said that the Biblical Aliens adore the smell of burning animals and grain because God does in Genesis 8:20.	6) Good Jinn or Angels like any good smell whereas, the Ifrit do not, and prefer bad smells. But they are all attracted by burned meat and strong perfume.
7) Reptilians or Reptoids are a race of lizard or snake-like alien humanoids that are said to inhabit the Earth Underground and can shapeshift.	7) Jinn are talented shapeshifters. They often take on a human shape, with horns, tails, feathered wings, or extra heads added for flair. Likewise, their skin comes in many vivid shades, from blue to green to red.
8) Most alien abductions tend to have sex as their ultimate goal.	8) Jinn and Human beings can have sexual relations.
9) They abduct people by enchanting them and levitating them like fairies or take them in their sleep by paralyzing them in order to bring them on their spaceship.	9) There are a number of things said about the Jinn in the Quran that fit abductee narratives.
10) Some say the Greys dislike silver.	10) The Jinn escape in contact with salt, silver, some kinds of incense and tar.
11) Aliens have the ability to paralyze humans by emitting an electrical impulse.	11) Jinn can take possession of just one area of the body or the whole body; as in the case of sleep paralysis.
12) Aliens seemingly work to create a race of human-alien hybrids.	12) Humans can mate with Jinn, and produce children together. Such offspring are called Demi-Jinn, or Huma-jinn. If the union is with a bottled Jinn, aka Genie, then they are called Demi-Genies, or Genieans.

on the ground and other evidence that the objects were solid machines. But if those events represent the presence of true manufactured spacecraft in our atmosphere, then the overall evidence suggests that they are following a long-range plan, a covert military-style buildup which will culminate in hostile action. In psychic phenomena and demonology, we find that seemingly solid physical objects are materialized or dematerialized. There are many baffling cases of houses which appeared and disappeared mysteriously. In religious demonic possession, well-documented by attending priests and doctors, the victims regurgitated impossible quantities of stones and even sharp steel needles. Apparently, these foreign objects materialized in their bodies. Some victims have levitated to the ceiling and had to be forcibly tied to their beds to keep from floating away.

Ufologists have constructed elaborate theories about flying saucer propulsion and antigravity. But we cannot exclude the possibility that these wondrous "machines" are made of the same stuff as our disappearing houses, and they don't fly, they levitate. They are merely temporary intrusions into our reality or space-time continuum, momentary manipulations of electromagnetic energy. When they "lower their frequencies" (as the contactees put it) and enter a solid state, they can leave impressions on the ground. But to enter that state, they need some atoms from our world, parts of an airplane, an auto, or blood and matter from an animal or human being. Or, in some cases, they need to drain off energy from the human participants or from power lines and automobile engines. This may seem like a fantastic concept, but we have wasted twenty years trying to simplify all this, trying to find a more mundane explanation. The fact is, all of the evidence supports our fantastic concepts more readily than it supports the notion that we are receiving visitors from Mars or Aenstria. [77]

The late General Douglas McArthur once warned that: *"The nations of the world will have to unite, for the next war will be an interplanetary war. The nations of the earth must someday make a common front against attack by people from other planets."* And his British counterpart in those days (circa 1950 AD), Lord Mountbatten, likewise addressing the UFO threat also concluded that: *"If the human race wishes to survive they may have to band together."* But can we believe them? John Keel said that the late General Douglas MacArthur, a man who must have been privy to much secret information, repeatedly made public statements asserting that the next war would be an interplanetary conflict with humankind, uniting to combat **"evil forces"** from some other world. [78]

Keel was trained in psychological warfare during his time as a propaganda writer for the U.S. Army and was particularly conscious of this double-barreled threat, and particularly concerned over the obvious hoaxes and manipulations apparently designed to foster both belief and disbelief in the reality of the flying saucers. These days, however, there is growing talk in the conspiracy world of a faked alien invasion portrayed as the famous Orson Welles' *War of the Worlds* broadcast, as well as talk about a possible faked Second Coming of Christ.

Kelly L. Segraves offers us the following prescient warning concerning the subject of New Age teachings: *"In recent years a fascinating new religion has landed upon the world scene. It is the (New Age) religion of UFOlogy ... Reportedly these super-intelli-*

---

77   John A. Keel, *Ibid.*, pp. 279-280.

78   *Ibid.*, p. 281.

gent visitors from outer space claim to be our gods and the entire Bible are to be reinter-
preted in the light of this frightening concept ... Even the sacred belief that Jesus Christ is the
Son of God is challenged by these champions of UFOlogy as we are told that Jesus Christ
was simply a saucer being ... that he will come again with his myriad of saucers to take
control of this world that is waiting for judgment. These new religionists firmly believe in
their concept and with the evangelistic fervor, they proclaim their beliefs for all who will
listen. But what is the purpose behind their preaching? What is the meaning of their mes-
sage? ... the evidence clearly shows that the (New Age) concepts of UFOlogy are really
Satan's last attempt to falsely fulfill Bible prophecy (particularly as concerns the Second
Coming of Jesus) in an effort to deceive mankind in the end times. Satan and his followers
are preparing now to establish the kingdom of ... the antichrist (a false Christ)."[79]

The lying Antichrist will not only deceive the masses, manipulating their na-
ivety, but will also compile worthy acolytes among the worshipper and the powerful. They have been working to overthrow tradition to establish a caricature
of the Celestial Jerusalem: a New World Order all terrain and material, which
according to some researchers will take a visible form with the 2020 turning
point for humanity. They are the occult power groups that drive global agenda,
as I have shown extensively in my earlier publications. They are run by the British Royals, the Vatican and the great economic power of the Zionist lobby, the
big banks, Big Pharma, the Bilderberg Group, the Trilateral Commission, the
Liberal side as well as the corrupt elements on the Conservative side of the Craft,
the Satanic Illuminati sects, etc. Their influence is evident, but they simply work
on behalf of the Secret Chiefs and Invisible Masters from the alien world; that's
why there is no interest for the elite the central/core perpetrators of globaliza-
tion to reveal the actual truth about the alien/UFO issue.

Yes, they are silently driving us towards something new, to colonize and control our dimension, and Aleister Crowley's contacts, and work for Higher Intelligence, must be observed in this new light. Grady Louis McMurtry, known
with the name *Hymenaeus Alpha*, who served as Caliph of the O.T.O. from 1969
until his death in 1985, observed: *"Some of the things Aleister said to me, could be*
interpreted as hints pointing that way," in relation to Crowley's alien link. He then
went on to quote Crowley's aphorisms about various standard entities contacted
by Magick; the Abramelin spirits, for instance, need to be watched carefully.
"They bite," Aleister explained to him in his best deadpan *am-I-kidding-or-not?*
style. That the Enochian "angels," on the other hand, don't always have to be
summoned. *"When you're ready, they come for you,"* Aleister said flatly. McMurty
also explained that the theory of higher dimensions made more sense to him
than the extraterrestrial theory in terms of actual spaceships entering our bio-
sphere. He also said something pretty earth-shattering:*"There's war in Heaven.*
The Higher Intelligence, whoever they are, aren't all playing on the same team. Some
of them are trying to encourage our evolution to higher levels, and some of them want
to keep us stuck just where we are." According to McMurty, some occult lodges are
working with non-human intelligence who want to accelerate human evolution,
but some of the others are working with the intelligence who wish to keep us
nearer to an animal level of awareness. [80]

79   John of the Gentiles, *Ibid.,* p. 346.

80   https://www.bibliotecapleyades.net/bb/vallee.htm ‡ Archived 11th December, 2017.

JINN IN RELATION TO THE
REPTILIANS AND THE NWO

A demonic feature of the Jinn is their affinity with the reptiles, under whose appearance they are manifested in most cases as attested by Arab tradition and folklore. Professor Toufy Fahd, a professor at the University of Strasbourg, has conducted a remarkable study on this subject in a book compiled by him and other authors, and published in Italy in 1994, entitled "Geni, Angeli e Demoni" (*Genies, Angels and Demons*).[81] Professor Fahd says that: *"Despite the affinity of blood between humans and Jinn, the latter are characterized in particular, by their greater affinity with animals, especially the reptiles, under which they appear in most cases. Numerous testimonies in this regard are gathered by Damir."*[82]

Just look at the collection of legends reworked in *One thousand and one nights*, to realize the frequency with which the Jinn appear in the form of reptiles, mostly gigantic snakes, also with wings, able to fly or embark on aerial combat. These legends also help us understand their reptilian and multi-dimensional nature, which allows them the ability to fly but to also disappear suddenly. In regard to the reptilian aspect in relation to religion, the name Ophites, which in ancient Greek means snake, is a type of Christian Gnostic sect that worship the serpent that corrupted Adam and Eve. Epiphanius of Salamis (d. 403), wrote in *Panarion*:

They have a snake, which they keep in a certain chest—the cista mystica—and which at the hour of their mysteries they bring forth from its cave. They heap loaves upon the table and summon the serpent. Since the cave is open it comes out. It is a cunning beast and, knowing their foolish ways, it crawls up on the table and rolls in the loaves; this they say is the perfect sacrifice. Wherefore, as I have been told, they not only break the bread in which the snake has rolled and administer it to those present, but each one kisses the snake on the mouth, for the snake has been tamed by a spell, or has been made gentle for their fraud by some other diabolical method. And they fall down before it and call this the Eucharist, consummated by the beast rolling in the loaves. And through it, as they say, they send forth a hymn to the Father on high, thus concluding their mysteries.

In the 5th century, Theodoret tells (Heresies 1:24) of having found serpent worship practiced in his diocese by people who he called Marcionites, but who may have been Ophites. Of the Nag Hammadi Gnostic texts that mention the serpent, three appear related to early church accounts of the Ophites. These texts are *Hypostasis of the Archons*, On the Origin of the World, and the *Apocryphon of John*.[83]

Going back to the Jinn, Toufy Fahd adds in his research: *"That the Jinn have assumed the reptilian form is a fact that that has been largely witnessed by Arabic-Islamic literature and folklore if we think of the great respect and fear that the Arabs feel for serpents and the close relationship between the Jinn and the divinities of Arab paganism, the existence of an affinity between the two things in Arabic culture that does not*

---

81   Vv.Aa., *Geni, Angeli e Demoni*, (Rome, IT: Edizioni Mediterranee,1994).

82   *Ivi.*, 164

83   *See* https://en.wikipedia.org/wiki/Ophites ‡ Archived 11th December, 2017.

seem to be excluded." [84] As intermediaries of esoteric knowledge, the Jinn created by fire and the appearance of snakes, according to Émil Amman, in his *Diction-naire de théologie catholique,* [85] is a function analogous to that of the Archons in the Gnostic texts. This is probably from Judaism in the Christian era, and then protracted until the end of the 6th century AD. In order to have another point of view, it is possible to consult the book of the great Illuminati and Freemason, Robert Ambelain, entitled, *Adam, dieu rouge de l'esoterisme judeo-chretien, gnose and les oplite. Luciferien et Rosecroix.* [86]

The *Pistis Sophia,* a text still considered of fundamental importance by the Illu-minati of the **Fraternitas Rosicruciana Antiqua (F.R.A.),** which I have been part of for a few years, is derived from the Ophite system probably elaborated between 250 and 300 AD, and it seems to have had a great influence on the subsequent formation of Islamic Cosmogony. I quote, for example, chapter 139 of the famous Coptic edition curated by Carl Schmidt (1868-1938) in Copenhagen in 1925.

Returning to the research of Toufy Fahd on the nature of Jinn, he states that they are: *"mutilating and elusive figures, the Jinn seems from time to time a goblet comparable to the se'irim, and to Lilith in Jewish poetry, a genie of places."* [87] When an Arab traveler entered a valley and camped to spend the night, he would say: *"I put myself under the protection of the Jinn of this valley so he can distance from me tonight, any danger."* In another interesting excerpt: *"a wolf took a lamb from the shepherd who reminds the lord of the place that it was his duty to protect him (Jivar); then he went to the wolf and forced him to leave his prey."* [88]

A few years ago, *WikiLeaks* released secret cables, that disclosed information about ETs in our solar system, but nothing yet on their interdimensional nature and technology. However, documents released by *Wikileaks,* offered hints about an alien extraterrestrial presence, and recently, even NASA is accused of hiding evidence of alien life. I predict that in a few years, when humankind is finally re-vealed the truth about the interdimensional alien/UFO phenomenon, this book will be viewed as pioneering science, and not a conspiracy.

Wikileaks documents didn't bring down government or agencies implicated in the cover-up as some expected after the revelations, but it did tell us, before NASA, that there exists supposed extraterrestrial life. Here's the proof: This cable, for example, is from the year 2006, from the American Embassy in Vil-nius, Lithuania. The statement was made by **Albinas Januska,** who at the time, was an appointed adviser to the Lithuanian Prime Minister. The cable states: *"Reflecting his self-image as a patriot fighting off Russian influence, he (Januska) also warned of the existence of 'a group of people, who are directed from the East, a group of UFOs, who are making influence from the Cosmos,'"* adding elliptically that: *"there also exists a decreasing group of persons, who are trying to rationally analyze the situation and to objectively evaluate what is happening."*

---

84   *Ibid.*, p. 165.

85   Émil Amman, *Dictionnaire de Théologie catholique XI, 931,* pp. 1063-1076.

86   *See Robert Ambelain, Adam, dieu rouge de l'esoterisme judeo-chretien, gnose and les op-lite. Luciferien* et Rose + Croix, (Paris, FR : Editions Niclaus, 1941).

87   Vv.Aa., *Geni, Angeli e Demoni, Ibid.*, p. 165.

88   *Ibid.*, p. 177.

Januska held much power in the country, as is noted in the cable: *Albinas Januska's continuing influence in Lithuanian politics cannot be overstated. In addition to being a cunning strategist, he is extraordinarily well-connected among Lithuania's political class.* Another cable comes from Japan, in 2007, on how the Chief Cabinet Secretary **Nobutaka Machimura**, was unhappy with the government's official view, rejecting the existence of UFOs: *"I am sure that unidentified flying objects exist, otherwise it is impossible to explain the Nazca Lines (in Peru), isn't it?"* There is another important *Wikileaks* cable to analyze from 2010, when the mayor of the Tajik city of Dushanbe, Mahmadsaid Ubaidulloev, met with U.S. Ambassador Ken Gross in 2010.

Mahmadsaid Ubaidulloev might not be a name well-known outside Tajikistan, but he has most certainly been someone well-known to Tajikistan's people throughout its 25-year history as an independent country. Tajikistan is a Central Asian country bordered by Afghanistan, Uzbekistan, Kyrgyzstan, and China. Ambassador Gross summarized his meeting with Ubaidulloev in a classified document later released by *Wikileaks*. The talk was mostly concerned with political, as well as economical projects for Tajikistan, that focused on the topic of extraterrestrials. Gross wrote: *"[Ubaidulloev] asserted the existence of life on other planets, caveating this by noting that we should focus on solving our problems on Earth."* Gross even quoted Ubaidulloev: *"We know there is life on other planets, but we must make peace here first."* Apparently, the chat was not a pleasant one for the U.S. ambassador, who summed it up as: *"a right painful 90 minutes."* Gross characterized Ubaidulloev as *"difficult, unpredictable, and sometimes hostile."* During their meeting, the mayor obviously lied about free elections, voluntary contributions to the dam project, and free media, according to Gross, but why did Mahmadsaid Ubaidulloev also asserted the existence of life on other planets? In the *Wikileaks* cables there appears material of interest regarding the dangerous UFO cults often used and controlled by Satanists.

Tara MacIsaac, for *Epoch Times,* reported that: *"A couple of unclassified documents, one listed as coming from the American Embassy in Ottawa and the other from the American Consulate in Montreal, express some concern over the Raelian religion in Canada. The Raelians believe humanity was created by extraterrestrials as a lab experiment, according to the documents. They had targeted high schools in the province of Quebec to persuade Roman Catholics to renounce their faith. **The Raelians even had a plan to give students crosses to burn, according to the cables.** One of the documents cites local news analysis in stating that: 'The ultimate goal of Raelians is to create life in a laboratory which would make human beings immortal and enable them to create another civilization on another planet.' In the meantime ... [they] want to build an embassy in Israel to welcome the Elohim when they come back in 2035. The group has also been criticized for advocating the use of genetics for eugenic attempts at improving the human race. At the time the cable was written, the group had claimed to have successfully cloned a human."*

Some may remember back in 2002, when Boisselier, a Raëlian bishop, and CEO of **Clonaid**, a mysterious company registered in the Bahamas with ties to the UFO religion Raëlism, announced at a press conference in Hollywood, Florida, that Clonaid had successfully performed the first human reproductive cloning. Since then there has been no further evidence, and the Clonaid claim seems more of a publicity stunt for Raëlism. So what about the Elohim return to

Israel in 2035? Maybe by that time, the building of a third temple in Jerusalem will truly be a reality. However, at the end of an interview dating back to 1986, Rael declared 2020 as the ultimate deadline for the Elohim's arrival. This is an interesting indication, as this year is indicated by many as truly relevant in the New World Order scheme of things. Ex-Raelian members even said at one point that the deadline was 2015, but sociologist Susan J. Palmer indicates 2025 as the deadline most held by Raelians in her book *Aliens Adored* (2004).

The latest official deadline from the Raelians seems to be 2035 (at least since 2001, when Rael published *Yes to Human Cloning*, in which he mentions Vernor Vinge's concept of a technological Singularity). The date 2035 was often cited by the proponents of the concept. Interestingly, in 2035, Rael will turn 89 years old. By then, he'll have nothing to lose for sure. [89]

BLOODLINES, ILLUMINATI, AND THE SCIENCE OF GOD

*T*here is a special relationship between the families of the elite, and the entities they serve, a link established through a union that is still considered sacred amongst the men and women of the dark side of the Illuminati, and what the Rosicrucian alchemists called **Alchemical Wedding**, on which Crowley based some of his teachings in the IX° degree of the O.T.O. in relation to the sexual practices used to create this union. The ultimate goal that Crowley sought through his sexual magic went far beyond the mundane desire for material wealth or mortal power. In his most exalted moments, Crowley appears to have believed that he could achieve a supreme spiritual power—the power to conceive a divine child, a godlike being, who would transcend the moral failings of the body born of mere woman. This goal of creating a divine fetus, Crowley suggests, lies at the heart of many esoteric traditions, from ancient Mesopotamia to India to the Arab world:

> *This is the great idea of magicians at all times—To obtain a Messiah by some adaptation of the sexual process. In Assyria, they tried incest ... Greeks and Syrians mostly bestiality. ... The Mohammedans tried homosexuality; medieval philosophers tried to produce homunculi by making chemical experiments with semen. But the root idea is that any form of procreation other than normal is likely of a magical character.* [90]

Sex magic, particularly in its transgressive, nonreproductive forms, can thus unleash the supreme creative power: the power to create not an ordinary fetus, but a magical child of messianic potential. [91] Witches, who are usually not from nobility, have joined the alien demonic entities through the so-called **Sabbath,** also spelled Sabbat or Sabba. Distinguishable features that are typically contained within a Witches Sabbat are assembly by foot, beast, or flight, a banquet,

---

89   *See* https://raelian-truth.blogspot.it/2012/01/2035-2025-or-2020-or-even-2015.html ‡ Archived 11th December, 2017.

90   *See* https://hermetic.com/crowley/libers/lib415#the-esoteric-record-of-the-thirteenth-working ‡ Archived 11th December, 2017.

91   Hugh B. Urban, *Magia Sexualis: Sex, Magic, and Liberation in Modern Western Esotericism,* p. 133

FIG. 34 Fethullah Gülen (b. 1941), the leader of the Gülen movement who allegedly works for the CIA and lives in exile in the United States, residing in Saylorsburg, Pennsylvania, speaks openly to his followers of the uninhibited use of Jinn, Extra-dimensional entities, by the U.S. Intelligence operatives.

dancing and cavorting, and sexual intercourse. [92] Such gatherings of witches usually implemented under the cover of darkness in remote and solitary places like a forest, will see the witches gather around a fire to honor their evil Masters and copulate with them. Sex is central to the rituals; witches copulate with Satan and other demons in the Sabbath, that usually culminates in an incestuous orgy. The chief inquisitor Henri Boguet, a Burgundian judge in the days of the Inquisition, known for his *Discours des sorciers* ("Discourse on Sorcerers" or "An Examen of Witches") of 1602, presented a graphic discussion of the threat posed by witches as well as a discussion of whether witches actually copulate with demons.

Some commonly mentioned dates for this type of ritual referring to the Sabbath are said to be February 1 (to some February 2), May 1 (Great Sabbat, Walpurgis Night), August 1 (Lammas), November 1 (Halloween, commencing on October 30's eve), Easter, and Christmas. Other less frequently mentioned dates were Good Friday, January 1 (day of Jesus' Crucifixion), June 23 (Saint John's Eve), December 21 (St. Thomas), and Corpus Christi on October 3. The modern Sabbats that many Wiccans and Neo-Pagans now follow are; Imbolc (February 2), Ostara (Spring Equinox), Beltane (May 1), Litha (Summer Solstice), Lammas (August 1), Mabon (Autumn Equinox), Samhain (October 31) and Yule (Winter Solstice). According to the testimonies of Benandanti and similar European groups, common dates for gatherings are during the weeks of the Ember days, during the twelve days of Christmas or at Pentecost. [93] Let's also remember that the term Sabbath was initially a Christian demonization of the Judaism's day of

92   https://en.wikipedia.org/wiki/Witches%27_Sabbath ‡ Archived 11th December, 2017.

93   *Ibid.*

rest, called Shabbat. In the 13th century, the accusation of participation in a Sabbath was said to be considered very serious. European records indicate cases of persons being accused, or tried for taking part in Sabbath gatherings, from the Middle Ages all the way to the 17th century or later. Witches still today, encounter demonic entities hoping to acquire new powers, but back in those days if they were discovered by the Church, they will obviously be killed.

Some witches managed to eventually create a **Magickal child** from these meetings. A typical example is Merlin, as Crowley also pointed out in *The Book of Thoth*. The legendary figure best known as the wizard featured in the Arthurian legend, is described as the son of a demon, an incubus, and of a mortal woman, who inherited his powers from birth. And even though Walt Disney (among other roles, a CIA agent and Freemason), in his *The Sword in the Stone*, a 1963 classic animated musical fantasy, Disney attempted to make a positive character out of him, and many medieval sources give Merlin a very different image, at times truly disturbing and diabolical. Is all this only a thing of the past? As Donald Tyson writes in his *Sexual Alchemy* book: *"In the modern Western world carnal union with spirits has ceased to be a matter for religion and instead become a subject for medicine and clinical psychology."* [94]

The bond with these entities is maintained as we have seen over and over again, through the rites of ceremonial magic by both the well-to-do, and the less-favored classes, where the use of low magic and witchcraft, seems to attract the less important entities/Jinn, who enter this dimension and serve their Principalities of evil, including Beelzebub, Satan, and Lucifer, who obviously rule them, and even in this dimension treat them as slaves, while they reside in bodies worthy of their rank, usually linked to an elite.

In either case, to satisfy these interdimensional entities, even human sacrifice is required at times. The earthly aristocracy has a bond with these entities, present in their mutual DNA, and that is considered more worthy by their alien overlords. In return they offer them the temporal power they need, practically enforcing total control over the Matrix that surrounds us, becoming **the threshold guardians**, charged with preserving the equilibrium of that which is above and that which is below, **the Men in Black**.

The most powerful alien overlord, for acts of Black Magic, is according to some, **Set,** the Satan of Christians, who some say works and collaborates with certain elements in the U.S. Military Intelligence through the already mentioned Lieutenant Colonel Michael Aquino, but there are also many other demons, or Jinn, in the service of U.S. Intelligence. This is also confirmed by **Fethullah Gülen**, born in Erzurum, Turkey, on April 27, 1941, a controversial Islamic leader and Turkish writer, known for his influential religious movement, and as an alleged member of the CIA. This fact has repeatedly been reiterated in 2012, by the well-known investigative journalist program, **60 Minutes** on CBS. Gülen, who has been recently accused of collusion with the Clinton's, and is wanted in his native Turkey for being the mastermind behind the **2016 Turkish** *coup d'état* **attempt,** is among other things, an alleged descendant of Prophet Mohammed. He currently resides for security reasons in the United States, in the Pocono Mountains in Pennsylvania.

94   Donald Tyson, *Sexual Alchemy- Magical intercourse with Spirits*, (St. Paul, MN: llewellyn Publications, 2000), p.25.

Gülen, during one of his usual Friday sermons, said that U.S. Intelligence works with Jinn, and is completely controlled by them in their actions, and not vice versa. This is a very serious fact, don't you think? In my opinion, this could partly confirm the reasons why Michael Aquino is still indicated by many as one of today's top mind control experts in the Intelligence community. Gülen, whose schools educate the Turkish elite across the world to this day, interprets science in an entirely different order and nature than we understand in the West. Gülen inhabits a magical world of Jinn and sorcery, where he began talking Aramaic as a child with no prior knowledge of it. Strangely enough, demon-possessed people are sometimes said to speak in languages they never learned, even dead languages such as Aramaic. Science is just a powerful form of magic for Gülen and his Turkish Illuminati, that must be used to enhance their worldly power, as he writes in his 2005 book, *The Essentials of the Islamic Faith:*

> *Jinn are conscious beings charged with divine obligations. Recent discoveries in biology make it clear that God created beings particular to each realm. They were created before Adam and Eve and were responsible for cultivating and improving the world. Although God superseded them with us, he did not exempt them from religious obligations.*
>
> *As nothing is difficult for God almighty, he has provided human beings, angels, and jinn, with the strength appropriate for their functions and duties. As he uses angels to supervise the movements of celestial bodies, he allows humans to rule the Earth, dominate matter, build civilizations and produce technology.*
>
> *Power and strength are not limited to the physical world, nor are they proportional to bodily size ... Our eyes can travel long distances in an instant. Our imagination can transcend time and space all at once ... winds can uproot trees and demolish large buildings. A young, thin plant shoot can split rocks and reach the sunlight. The power of energy, whose existence is known through its effect, is apparent to everybody. All of this shows that something's power is not proportional to its physical size; rather the immaterial world dominates the physical world, and immaterial entities are far more powerful than material ones.* [95]

So when Gülen talks about the union of **religion and science** in his long interminable speeches, what he means quite concretely is that the magical view of Jinn in the Quran aids the Islamic believer in enlisting these occult forces to enhance the power of a supposed **True Islam**. Basically, science for Mr.Gülen means the management of alien Jinn and a privileged **Contact** with the alien world. For this reason, the Gülen Movement has secretly intensified in recent years, the gradual infiltration of NASA by its top mathematicians, something the National Security Agency and the U.S. State Department should investigate, as it's dangerous to let these guys take over the alien agenda.

Gülen's pan-Turkic mysticism views Turkey as the center of a new Caliphate uniting the Muslim world just like Daesh/Isis. Even before the failed coup attempt in 2016, in December 2015, the Gülen movement was already classified as a terrorist organization by Turkey under the assigned names Gülenist Terror Organization (*Fethullahçı Terör Örgütü*, FETÖ) or Parallel State Organization (*Paralel Devlet Yapılanması*, PDY) but nothing has been done by the U.S. government. Is Gülen protected by Jinn, or by the Deep State, or both?

95   *See* M. Fethullah Gülen, *Essentials of The Islamic Faith*, (Tughra Books, 2011).

THE SECRET DOCTRINE OF ATLANTIS

*T*he research provided in the next pages, especially in relation to Atlantis and *Lovecraft/Necronomicon* lore, originates from Freemason and occult author, Tracy R. Twyman, the former Editor of *Dagobert's Revenge Magazine*, who has been a recognized expert on occult history for many years, and was once associated publicly with the now-deceased British writer Nicholas Logan Weir, known as **Nicholas de Vere**, as well as Prince **Nicholas Thomas de Vere von Drakenberg** (1957-2013). A controversial, if not colorful figure of the contemporary Illuminati network, de Vere was deeply involved in black magic and occultism since a young age, and claimed to be the head of a mysterious secret society with an ancient lineage called *"the Dragon Court."* He stated that he was the foremost scion of a royal bloodline going back to praeterhuman creatures that pre-dated the Garden of Eden, but he never produced any satisfying elements to fully confirm, his, at times, outlandish claims. Nevertheless, the alleged Sovereign Grand Master of the Imperial and Royal Dragon Court and Order, Nicholas de Vere, who was secretly working with the late black magician **Andrew D. Chumbley**, and the UK-based Satanic group, **Cultus Sabbati**, provided, the inspiration, and the research, for quite a large portion of the writing that appeared in two of the best-known works by the late Laurence Gardner, the previously cited *Genesis of the Grail Kings*, and *Realm of the Ring Lords*.

Amazingly enough, de Vere who was a good friend of Laurence Gardener, is not even listed as a co-author, and received absolutely no credit at all for these books. For the late Nicholas de Vere: *"The dragon tradition related to all the current genetic and historical evidence says yes they were. Both relatively recent and ancient accounts of Dragons or Elves going back to the Annunaki speak of them as having clearly distinct physical attributes, and these attributes are inherited from a species that scientists now assert preceded the human genetic bottleneck by about thirty thousand years. These attributes are not human in the accepted sense. Whether this ancient race was hybridized with another before history is anybody's guess but their later hybridization to produce the Elven God-Kings and Ring Lords: (the King Tribe), is clearly recorded in the Cylinder Rolls."*

In the same interview, he also stated that these Dragons were the same as the Nephilim of the Bible, or the Watchers of *The Book of Enoch*, adding that: *"The Platonic Atlantis theory is preceded by a much older tradition relating to the 'Ogdoad.' The Ogdoad, sacred to Jesus himself, were the eight great Gods who raked the Sacred Mountain—'Atlantis'—after the original Flood. This Flood occurred in the Black Sea and the Sacred Mountain, so inundated, was believed to be the Pontus Euxine. ... Apparently, the Ogdoad failed in their attempt to bring fertility back to the Holy Place and abandoned it for a life wandering the planet. This is probably why the legend of the Flood spread and can be found in most cultures."* [96]

These answers were given by de Vere in an interview from 2004, with Tracy R. Twyman, who had full access to Nicholas de Vere's vast archives, and later expanded on the Atlantis topic in an interesting article originally written by Twyman for the ***DragonKeyPress Website***. This article does not necessarily rep-

---

96   *See* http://quintessentialpublications.com/twyman/?page_id=87 ‡ Archived 11th December, 2017.

resent her current viewpoint, however, it seems to lay down some interesting points on this topic. So here are a couple of extracts from the article in question:

*The Secret Doctrine given to the elite castes of mankind by the "Anunnaki" (the gods of ancient Sumeria and Atlantis), has been passed down through the ages, not only to the Masons, Templars, Rosicrucians, and other fraternal orders which perpetuate the tradition within the Illuminati network, but also to the teenage geeks and "gamers" of today. The Lovecraft/Necronomicon lore has in fact, given birth to a cornucopia of role-playing and computer games, in much the same way that Monty Python and the Society for Creative Anachronism (S.C.A) have kept the Grail myth alive for these same teenagers. The fact that S.C.A.'s membership correlates strongly with participation in Lovecraftian role-playing games is no coincidence, for the "demons" of the "Cthulhu Mythos" as its called, are the same as the gods of ancient Sumer, and the fallen angels who spawned the Grail family. The "Grail Blood" and the "bloodline of the Great Old Ones" are the same thing. They also represent the same archetypes as legendary sea-monsters such as Leviathan or Dagon, the "Lords of the Deep" and gods of the "underworld," or "Abyss" recorded in the legends of many ancient cultures. It takes only a cursory examination of H.P. Lovecraft's most quintessential work, **The Call of Cthulhu** to see that his entire system of mythology is based on **The Book of Enoch**, the Nephilim story in Genesis, and the universal tale of the fall of Atlantis. In this story, Lovecraft's main character finds a strangely carved idol in his late grand-uncle's effects, its appearance described as that of, "an octopus, a dragon, and a human caricature ... scaly body, rudimentary wings." The discovery of this idol leads to his investigation and uncovering of a sinister, age-old "cult of Cthulhu" (the name of the idol), who worshipped the creature represented by the idol, and the entire race of demons from which he had come. The description of the idol bears a striking resemblance to the descriptions of the Sumerian god-king Enki, also known as Dagon or Oannes, a half-human, half-fish combination who was known as the "Lord of the Flood," and was said to rise out of the sea every day to teach his secret knowledge to those who followed him. He is mentioned in I Samuel:5, when the Philistines capture the Ark of the Covenant and place it in the Temple of Dagon. Two nights later, Dagon was fallen upon his face to the ground before the Ark of the Lord, and the head of Dagon and both the palms of his hands were cut off upon the threshold; only the stump of Dagon was left to him. The physical description attributed to Dagon applied to an entire race of gods, or as they were described in the Bible, Nephilim, or fallen angels—the Great Old Ones, as Lovecraft calls them. The Watchers, those who were cast down, are described in **The Book of Enoch** literally as stars that descended to Earth. Cthulhu is also described with wings, another attribute of the Nephilim, who were real flesh-and-blood beings, and ruled as the antediluvian kings of the ancient world over a global kingdom whose capital was Atlantis. As they were an expert sea-faring people—navigators—they were also depicted as sea gods, half-man, and half-fish, with the horns of a goat.* [97]

For Twyman, and obviously for de Vere, the fact that Lovecraft's "Great Old Ones" ruled over Atlantis is quite clear, as their city, called *R'lyeh*, is covered with what Lovecraft describes as *"cyclopean architecture,"* the same word used by author **Ignatius L. Donnelly** in *Atlantis: The Antediluvian World*, a very influential book published in 1882, by the late Minnesota politician, who was born in Philadelphia, Pennsylvania in 1831. Donnelly considered Plato's account of Atlantis as largely factual, and attempted to establish that all known ancient civilizations were descended from this lost land considered of great importance by the Illuminati. Many of its theories turned out to be the source of modern-day concepts about Atlantis, including: *The civilization and technology beyond its time, the origins of all present races and civilizations, and a civil war between good and evil.*

Much of Donnelly's scholarship, especially with regard to Atlantis, as an explanation for similarities between ancient civilizations of the Old and New Worlds, was inspired by the publications of noted French writer, ethnographer, historian and archaeologist, **Charles Étienne Brasseur de Bourbourg (1814-1874)**, and the fieldwork of **Augustus Le Plongeon**, French-American photographer, amateur archeologist, antiquarian and author, who studied the pre-Columbian ruins of America in the northern Yucatán Peninsula. *Atlantis: The Antediluvian World,* was also avidly supported by the publications of Helena Blavatsky and the Theosophical Society, as well as Rudolf Steiner.

Some authors and researchers on the subject have openly accused Madame Blavatsky of having largely plagiarized Donnelly's work on Atlantis, that inspired furthermore the books by British occult writer James Churchward on the lost continent of Mu, also known as Lemuria. Churchward's younger brother, Albert (1852-1925), was a Masonic writer, known as the author of *The Origin and Evolution of the Human Race.* His theories have also influenced the visions of Edgar Cayce, and more recently the creation of the superhero Namor, the Sub-Mariner in the 1969 pop song "Atlantis" by Donovan, and the 2001 film *Atlantis: The Lost Empire*, written by Graham Hancock, and last but not least the plot of the 2009 film *2012* by Roland Emmerich. [98]

Returning to the research of Tracy R. Twyman and Nicholas de Vere, Lovecraft's descriptions paint a picture of **multi-dimensional, non-Euclidean angles, as if they existed in a space-time different than ours, perhaps in an "otherworld" somewhere in between the planes of Heaven and Earth.** They are described as grand and mighty creatures, with a moral creed similar to that of Aleister Crowley's *Do what thou wilt*, and they trounced on all those weaker than them, bringing destruction to the Earth, devouring every living thing. This is exactly the behavior that is ascribed to the sons of the Watchers, or Nephilim, the giants who wrought havoc upon the world, oppressed and devoured all of God's living creation to feed their own voracious appetites. Because of the pride and destructive behavior of the Great Old Ones, their empire city, R'lyeh, sank beneath the ocean as part of a punishment by a natural disaster mercifully imposed by God.

This is exactly what is said to have happened to the island kingdom of Atlantis, which also sank because of the pride of its inhabitants. It is also what is said about the Nephilim in the Bible, who, along with their offspring, were destroyed by God via the Flood of Noah. The fact that the Great Old Ones are lead by a being called *Cthulhu* is significant, for *Thule,* which is another name for Atlantis. The Nazis believed that an advanced civilization was literally located inside the Earth, in the "underworld," the city of *Agartha* or *Agade,* the

---

98   *See* https://en.wikipedia.org/wiki/Atlantis:_The_Antediluvian_World ‡ Archived
      11th December, 2017.

abode of the Gods. The *Hollow Earth*, or underworld seems to be the place where R'lyeh ultimately sank to, where Cthulhu and the rest of the Great Old Ones now remain, sleeping in their watery tomb, *dead but dreaming*, as Lovecraft now describes it. They are waiting for the day when they will awaken, and their city will rise from the waves, and their empire will once again hold dominion over the whole earth. This echoes the story of the Watchers or the Nephilim, who were said to be imprisoned by God inside the Earth, or in "the Abyss," which was a word used by the ancients to describe the ocean. The theme of a subterranean Lord, imprisoned in the underworld, who will one day awaken from his death-like slumber to reclaim his kingdom is, as I have established in other writings, is a very common archetype, most notably in the form of Kronos. Called *the Forgotten Father* and *the Hidden One*, Kronos was the leader of the Titans, and the King of Atlantis, whose kingdom was cast down into the Abyss, and who was imprisoned therein, to be thereafter known as *the Dark Lord* of the underworld. And there is clearly an etymological connection between "Titan" and *Teitan*, otherwise spelled Satan.

The Titans, or Satans, and the Nephilim are clearly the same as the Great Old Ones, and Kronos, otherwise known as Saturn, or Satan, is clearly the same as Cthulhu. He is also synonymous with Dagon or Oannes, who is referred to in the Bible as Leviathan, the beast who will rise from the sea at the Apocalypse. The return of Cthulhu, the Great Old Ones, and the city of R'lyeh would appear to be Lovecraft's way of depicting the Apocalypse. Confirmation of the above conclusions can be found by examining quotations from Lovecraft's manuscript, the implications of which, in light of what I have just said, will be self-explanatory.

When the main character in *The Call of Cthulhu* manages to interview an actual member of the Cthulhu cult to determine their beliefs, the descriptions that follow parallel precisely the tales of the Nephilim, the Titans, and the war in Heaven between God and Lucifer, as well as the fall of the Atlantean empire:

They worshipped, so they said, the Great Old Ones, who lived ages before there were any men, and who came to the young world out of the sky. These old ones were gone now, inside the earth and under the sea; but their dead bodies had told their secrets to the first man, who formed a cult which had never died. This was that cult, and the prisoners said it had always existed and always would exist, hidden in the distant wastes and dark places all over the world until the time when the Great Priest Cthulhu, from his dark house in the mighty city of R'lyeh under the waters, should rise and bring the Earth again under his sway. Someday he would call when the the stars were ready, and the secret cult would always be ready to liberate him. Meanwhile, no more must be told. There was a secret which even torture could not extract. Mankind was not absolutely alone amongst the conscious things of the Earth, for shapes came out of the dark to visit the faithful few. But these were not the Great Old Ones. No man had ever seen the Old Ones. The carven symbol was great Cthulhu, but none might say whether or not the others were precisely like him. No one could read the old writing now, but things were told by word of mouth. The chanted ritual was not the secret—that was never spoken aloud, only whispered. The chant meant only this: In his house at R'lyeh, dead Cthulhu waits dreaming.

106 F

again to repeat the cycle.
Hence, the final Initiation marks the return of the oldest of all cults, the
Cult of Set, the Dark Star whose brooding consciousness symbolizes the oldest and
most primordial of all forces, burning within our souls is the ecstasy of Set, beyond
morals and ethics waiting to be realized and to bring about the final transformation
for those prepared for the greatest Initiation, that of the Dark Flame....
Man, the alien child, must at least return home.........

Notes.

*1. The Slave Gods are the various Religious and Idealogical concepts which
have controlled man for so many years, some examples include Christianity,
Morality, Political control and so on.

*2. Thelemite Cultus represents the various schools of thought which utilize
the work of Aliester Crowley (Master Therion) and other esoteric
traditions to unlock the potential of the Will (Thelema is Greek for WILL).

*3. E.V. Is used to designate a date past the time of Christ, it represents the
Era of the Vulgar.

*4. The Overman or Superman is the Philosophical equal to the next stage of
evolution and is found in the works of Fredrich Nietzsche, a German
philosopher who wrote such texts as Thus Spake Zarathustra, Beyond Good and
Evil and the Antichrist.

*5. The terms Androgyne and Hermaphrodite have been used interchangeblly in
this article, even though there is a technical difference in the sense of
God forms there is no physical body so the difference is irrelevant.

FIG. 35 Secret teachings of the Illuminati typewritten in a rare internal document from the
1970s states that: "Hence the final initiation marks the return of the oldest of all cults: the
Cult of Set, the darkstar whose brooding consciousness symbolizes the oldest and most
primordial of all forces, burning within our souls is the ecstacy of Set, beyond morals and
ethics waiting to be realized and to bring out the final transformation for those prepared
for the greatest Initiation, that of the Dark Flame. ... Man, the alien child, must at least
return home."

For Tracy R. Twyman, this clearly describes the secret Luciferian doctrine of the gods being transmitted to their offspring, *the first man*, just as the serpent gave wisdom to Adam and Eve in the Garden of Eden. They created a covenant with man, and a cult of magic, of ritual and sacrifice, in order to preserve their infernal secrets, one of which is so secret that it could not be talked about, only whispered. This is what has been done in the rites of Freemasonry, Rosicrucianism, the Knights Templar, the Greek and Egyptian mystery schools, the Sufis, the Assassins, and countless other secret occult orders, which Lovecraft was no doubt alluded to when he referred to the: **"cult which had never died ... had always existed, and always would exist,"** preserving the teachings of the Forgotten Father, until such time as he should rise again from the sea to once more rule the Earth. **The connections to Leviathan and the rise of the Antichrist do not even need to be elucidated.** Lovecraft's description is as follows:

Old Castro remembered bits of hideous legend that pale the speculations of Theosophists and made man and the world seem recent and transient indeed. There had been eons when other things ruled on the Earth, and they had had great cities. Remains of them ... were still to be found as Cyclopean stones on islands in the Pacific. They all died vast epochs of time before man came, but there were arts which could revive them when the stars had come round again to the right positions in the cycle of eternity. They had indeed come themselves from the stars and brought their images with them.

Tracy R. Twyman explains that Lovecraft, like the prophet Enoch, and like ancient man himself, conceived of the Atlantean gods or Nephilim as possessing supernatural power, and, like Enoch, states that **this power comes from the stars**—that these beings, in fact, had come from the stars themselves, and seem to be metaphysically affected by the movement of the stars, being able to resurrect from the dead only when the stars were in a certain position. Likewise, the Atlantean god-kings purposely associated themselves with the stars and the planets, taking on the personifications of planets and constellations, each of which had a particular energy, or plain of existence associated with it. This energy is further manipulated by the prayers and rituals of the cult members in Lovecraft's stories, who are loyal to the Great Old Ones and wish to see their kingdom rise again.

In much the same way, Masons, Rosicrucians and other occultists today perform rituals in hope of bringing about the **Great Work** called the **New World Order**, a new Golden Age, just like the one that covered the antediluvian world when the Atlantean god-kings (whom they revere) ruled over the Earth directly. [99]

Michael Aquino for example, in his infamous Temple of Set, describes the Master of the Temple (IV° degree), as a person who wears the Pentagram of Set against blue, the traditional color of the most advanced and accomplished initiates such as the Philosopher-Kings of Plato's Republic, or **the Priest-Kings of Atlantis.** [100]

---

99   https://www.bibliotecapleyades.net/cienciareal/cienciareal15.htm [emphasis added], ‡ Archived 11th December, 2017.

100   Michael A. Aquino VI°, *Black Magic*, (© Michael A. Aquino 1975-2002) p. 39, [emphasis added].

SEX WITH ALIENS

V

$\mathscr{A}$ sign of the times

liphas Levi, in his classic *Histoire de la Magie* gives the following explanation of the supposed origin of *elementals*, also known by spiritists as *"dwellers on the threshold."* Levi states that: *"According to the best authorities, these spirits (larves) possess an ethereal body formed of the vapor of blood. That is why they seek blood and why they were supposed, formerly, to feed on the smoke of sacrifices. They are the **Incubi** and **Succubi**, the monstrous children of impure dreams. When sufficiently condensed to be visible, they are only a vapor colored by the reflection of a picture and, having no independent life, they imitate the life of him who evokes them as the shadow does the body. They generally manifest around the idiots and beings devoid of morality, whose isolation has led them to develop irregular habits. Owing to the feeble cohesion of the parts of their fantastic bodies, they fear the open air, fire, and above all, the point of swords, and as they live only by the life of those who have created or evoked them, they become the vaporous appendices of the real body of their parents. So it can happen that an injury inflicted on them might actually react upon the parent body, as the unborn child is really wounded or disfigured by an impression made upon its mother. **These elementals draw the vital heat from persons in good health and quickly exhaust those who are weak.** They are the source of the stories of vampires, stories only too true and periodically recurrent, as everyone knows. That is why one feels a chill of the atmosphere when approaching mediums who are persons obsessed by these spirits that never manifest in the presence of anyone able to unveil the mystery of their monstrous birth. They are children of an exalted imagination or unbalanced mentality."* [1]

As explained in the controversial book *Occult Theocrasy: Vol. 1* by Edith Starr Miller (Lady Queenborough): *"In politics, throughout the ages, witchcraft, as practiced by subversive sects, has played a prominent part. Illustrations of this are to be found in the case of the North Berwick Witches who were tried for treason in 1592 when their Devil or Grand Master, Francis Stewart, Earl of Bothwell, attempted to supplant James VI as King of Scotland. The Black Masses held by the infamous*

---

1   Eliphas Levi, *Histoire de la magie*, (The History of Magic), 1860, p. 116.

*Abbe Guibourg for Madame de Montespan, with the object of regaining for her the favor of Louis XIV, are famous in history. Eliphas Levi, the great initiate, has thus defined the aims of magic and witchcraft: **To deceive the peoples for the purpose of exploiting them, to enslave them and delay their progress, or prevent it even if possible, the crime of black magic.**"* [2]

There are entities operating within the human soul and above the veil of matter, who in reality are **hyper-dimensional alien being entities**. Astral and ethereal, free from the classic physical bodies and able to operate interdimensionally at will. They are entities capable of conditioning and distorting the quality of human perception, and they do this in order to make the world appear structured on the physical plane, rather than according to the spiritual Matrix as it truly is. Learn what mystics and prophets have said for thousand of years (often in great detail), about hyper dimensional entities who attempt to influence the mind of humankind. We live in an alien driven illusion, observing the world, not for how it truly is, but for how these entities make it appear through their long work of persuasion and manipulation, conducted by Secret Societies and Occult Fraternities, operating for the New World Order. Most so-called extraterrestrial phenomena are actually caused by hyper-dimensional entities.

Let's focus now on the elemental spirits, who the Rosicrucians claim to be able to see and work with. In order to be admitted into their co-fraternity, their eyes are purged with an alchemical substance called the *Panacea* or *Universal Medicine*, a legendary substance with miraculous curative powers that literally opened their eyes and illuminated them to a multi-dimensional reality, and its many alien dangers. Remember that these entities generate images, that most of the time they can appear to be real and physical to the human eye, but in reality they are etheric, projective processes, and remotely directed. Basically, they are schizophrenic, illusory phenomena that are made to manipulate people.

Spiritual science does not deny the possibility of an extraterrestrial existence and extraterrestrial visitations. The great Rosicrucian and Illuminati Rudolf Steiner for example, repeatedly explained his encounters with inhabitants of other planets, often occurring during the night, that we will all live within during the period following physical death. They are mostly etheric forms, made up of electromagnetic energy—they are entities belonging to angelic and demonic spheres, but unfortunately, there is very little proven in the Ufology field, as well as in the field of religion and demonology. Steiner theorized that the people of our prehistory were largely guided and directed by a higher order of beings who interacted and communicated with certain humans—the smartest, the strongest, the most intellectually flexible. Eventually, these select humans within certain bloodlines produced what might be called demigods, divine human beings, who, in turn, could relay instructions from higher intelligence, these are the true Illuminati of all Ages, the ones who grasped the secret ciphers of the UFOnauts and enacted certain rituals over and over again across the Ages, to maintain constant contact with such beings.

In effect, Steiner may have given us another definition of the semi-divine progeny that the ancient Hebrews named Nephilim, which does, in fact, mean

2   Edith Starr Miller (Lady Queenborough), *Occult Theocrasy: Vol. 1* (PUBLISHED POSTHUMOUSLY FOR PRIVATE CIRCULATION ONLY, 1933)., pp. 116-117.

demigod, men of great renown. Steiner went on to speculate that within the larger evolving human race were the **descendants of those divine-human hybrid beings**, men, and women who are animated by higher ideals, who regard themselves as children of a divine, universal power. Steiner definitely had far too positive an idea of alien interaction, as well as the descendants of divine-human hybrid beings that to this day constitute the occult elite of the New World Order.

Remember, Steiner was a member of the Illuminati, and the Egyptian rites of Freemasonry, as well as a major figure in Theosophy, before founding his own Anthroposophy. Steiner promoted alien contact because he considered the larger body of humankind too devoted to the service of egotism, materialism, and selfish, personal interests, and hoped for an alien savior to ultimately save the day. In fact, Steiner believed that within what he termed the emerging "Sixth Post-Atlantean Race," the children of the Divine universal power, those who have the "seed" within them, will be able to initiate the more advanced members of humankind to the next level. People so initiated will be able to receive revelations and perform what others consider miracles, but Steiner seems to forget that this will also encourage the evil side of New Age to mime and impress humankind with false miracles and increase the threat of False Prophets. [3]

Many abductees begin to believe that they are alien or part alien. This is probably a result of the terrible brainwashing and trauma that they have been exposed to. I would normally assume that a human could not possibly be part elementary spirit or Jinn, but the Dictionary of Islam states that the Jinn propagate their species, sometimes in conjunction with human beings; in the latter case, the offspring partake of the nature of both parents. That's why alien entities are seen creating, or trying to create, hybrids in the bizarre scenarios that a great many abductees have been shown or been involved with. Steiner, like most Illuminati, thought that **these privileged initiates constituted by descendants of those divine-human hybrid beings would eventually go on to become the mediators between humankind and the higher intelligence.**

The whole point of all the efforts made by these higher intelligence, in the eyes of Steiner and the Illuminati, of both the good and the bad side, is to enable humankind to become more independent, more able to stand on its own feet without having to rely on the higher order of beings that directed us in ancient times, like Osiris. A concept repeated to me not so long ago by the known French alchemist and Illuminati Jean Pierre Giudicelli, whose interview you will find in Volume I of my *Confessions*. [4]

Futurist Theodore J. Gordon, commented on the alien reality and the future of religion, by saying: "*In considering the future of religion, it is appropriate to ask what the unknown might yield in the next few decades that would have relevance to man's view of his relationship to the cosmos. A major event ... would be the discovery of extraterrestrial life wherein we would become members of a community of life, participants in a drama bigger than we could have dreamed.*" This drama may already be unfolding in the rooms of power, and in certain Masonic structures aware of the interdimensional alien factor, while Earth is increasingly wrapped up in an invisible

3   *See* http://www.rense.com/general81/eud.htm ‡ Archived 11th December, 2017.
4   *Ibid.*, pp. 188-191.

electromagnetic prison made of satellites, cellular phones, radio, television, and internet networks, which have all increasingly intensified in the last few decades, creating an enclosure through which the alien phenomenon can be filtered, and completely controlled by the occult elite of the Illuminati. Through electromagnetic waves these entities can operate on matter in a much more effective way than ever before, making both morphological modifications and appearances in our reality. In the meantime, the supposed messages of so-called **crop circles**, help us believe there is an alien reality that wants to make contact, by showing their power through a technology capable of producing sensational phenomena.

In reality, the Jinn, the alien interdimensional Tricksters, want to erase spiritual awareness and shift the attention of most people to the material side of the UFO phenomenon, making us believe that God, angels and especially demons, do not exist. Alien demons basically say: "*There are extraterrestrials who want to contact you—embrace them.*"

Steiner envisioned a century ago, a dual plan devised by the demonic side and the Jesuits, who would eventually take over his Anthroposophical Society:

—To realize a future civilization that completely denies the presence of the Divine in the cosmos, replacing it with an abstract and absurd concept of extraterrestrial existence that "observes" and can also "save us."

—Prepare for the incarnation of a demon called Ahriman the spirit of opposition, which will be embodied in the earth by the third millennium by using the support of these forces to enslave humanity.

Steiner explains that since Ahriman is a spirit of opposition, we might begin to understand his nature by understanding what he opposes: the Gods plan of earthly and human development. But the situation is not as simple as a two-sided contest; basic to a competent understanding of the world-process is the recognition of at least three kinds of spiritual influences upon the evolution of humankind and the cosmos. For Steiner, this "evolution" is something very different from the random, meaningless, material process conceived by the neo-Darwinists and such theorists. What he means by "evolution," is a thoroughly purposeful, thought-filled process of development, initiated and guided by spiritual beings: "*The normal Gods (the regular hierarchies) create and nurture the evolvement of the world and mankind, so as to bring about the possibility of Men attaining the status of divinity as 'Spirits of Freedom and Love'—the tenth hierarchy. (At the present stage of evolution, the Man progresses through alternating periods of earth-lives and purely spiritual lives: birth, death, and reincarnation.) As the name implies, essential to the fulfillment of mankind's task is the realization of 'freedom,' meaning not so much political freedom as spiritual freedom—that Men should become independent, unique individuals acting consciously as the originators of their own deeds.*"

For Rudolph Steiner, "occult wisdom," independently rediscovered and made public (and greatly simplified here, to put it mildly for the non initiates), explains this evolution as being created and guided through seven great cosmic ages. We are now in the fourth great age, called the "Earth" Age. (All age names are given in order of succession.) The previous three ages in Steiner's view are called **Saturn, Sun,** and **Moon.** Again, these are past ages of cosmic development, not to be confused with the present-day heavenly bodies of the same names. The same holds for the three future ages: **Jupiter, Venus,** and **Vulcan.** The great Earth Age comprises seven lesser ages, of which we are in the fifth. These five are called **Polarian, Hyperborean, Lemurian, Atlantean,** and **Post-Atlantean.** The Post-Atlantean Age is comprised of seven cultural epochs, of which, again, we are in the fifth. The previous four are called **Indian, Persian, Egypto-Chaldean,** and **Greco-Roman.** Recorded history begins only with the Egypto-Chaldean Epoch; what is generally known about ancient Indian and Persian culture derive from records made in the third epoch.

This does not imply that nothing was happening on other regions of the earth, but that the archetypal evolutionary impulses of the times were centered in the regions designated. The epochs lasted approximately 2160 years, and the present, fifth post-Atlantean epoch began about 1413 AD. Neither epochs are considered to be sharply differentiated; transitions happen gradually, future developments being prepared in advance, and past influences lingering after. The essential Ahrimanic tendency is as Steiner reminds us; to materialize, to crystallize; to darken; to silence; to bring living, mobile forces into fixed form—in other words, to kill that which is living. This tendency in itself, within proper bounds, is not evil; the dead, material world is necessary for God's plan of human and cosmic development. The Ahrimanic tendency is evil only when it exceeds proper bounds when it reaches into what should be alive—and Ahriman does try to exceed proper bounds. Again, the basic reality of the world is spiritual beings together with their deeds, but Ahriman promotes the illusion, the lie, that matter is the basic reality or the only reality. In fact, Ahrimanic spirits, not "atoms" or "ultimate particles," are the reality behind the material world. Ahriman lives upon lies; he is a spirit of untruth, the "Father of Lies." [5]

This naturally corresponds with Satan's character, because Satan, as we know, is the father of all lies (John 8:44). There is NO truth in Satan or in his Alien Legion, so don't be fooled by new interpretations of ancient texts that suggest that Satan may have been an extraterrestrial who was more of an ally to humanity than an enemy. It's too bad people like David Hatcher Childress (b. 1957), a popular American author and publisher, often seen on TV, whose historical revision seems to be going too far these days when he writes:

Who or what is Satan? Is he, a demon, the devil, the personification of evil, or was he, in fact, a benevolent extraterrestrial being? One who stole technology from alien beings in an effort to lead early man out of darkness and ignorance. Perhaps he is testing us using alien technology to modify human behavior in ways we have yet to understand. In a sense, Satan is not such a bad guy. You can't have light without the dark. You can't have right without wrong. And we have to learn these things for ourselves, and ultimately, through the choice wrong and right, we grow and we become who we are and ultimately to be like our makers, or to be gods ourselves. [6]

Well, no wonder, "God is Man" or *Deus est Homo* is one of the mottos of the *Ordo Templi Orientis.* Can people please wake up to this massive deception? Can we please react, or are we all brainwashed by alien demonic propaganda? Someone cleverly commented the following on Mr. Childress' blog: *"We have a history*

5   *See* https://www.bibliotecapleyades.net/biblianazar/ahriman01.htm ‡ Archived 11th January, 2018.

6   *See* https://lamarzulli.wordpress.com/2013/10/30/ancient-aliens-satan-is-misunderstood/ ‡ Archived 11th January, 2018.

of men and women, dating back thousands of years, who knew and understood who Satan was. They wrote about this fallen cherub, or as I prefer to call him, The Fallen One. They know who he is and warn us of his diabolical plans to destroy mankind. Jesus describes The Fallen One the best and I'll close with this and I'm not applying this to the History Channel, *however, they should understand what it is they are promulgating."*[7]

Why should interdimensional alien beings, angels or demons, of whatever race or type, risk a public landing, especially when they have full control of this planet and its corrupt elite? Of course, Illuminati papist, George Adamsky, back in the 1950s, had a very different view: *"So why should they risk a public landing? They have seen what the mob does to that which it fears, and what it does to that which it worships. Their ship would be impounded for evasion of customs duties. Their clothes would be torn off and sold as souvenirs. They would be denounced as saboteurs, anti-Christs, disturbers of the peace, emissaries of Satan, and the rest, as happened on that ill-advised attempt made in France during the reign of Charlemagne. Le Comte de Gabalis tells us that on this occasion, the famous Qabbalist Zedechias attempted to improve conditions on Earth by suggesting to the aerial peoples that they should make a great and wondrous demonstration. They did so sumptuously, says de Gabalis. ... These beings were seen in the air ... sometimes on wonderfully constructed aerial ships whose flying squadrons roved at will. The result of this attempt to win recognition was no more successful than it is today, assuming that the apparitions seen in our skies relate to the same cause. The people insisted that sorcerers and demons had taken possession of the air (today it is secret weapons; just as bad). Even the Kings believed it. Charlemagne and his successor, Louis the Debonair, decreed terrible penalties for these tyrants of the air."*[8]

THEOSOPHY IN THE SPACE AGE

George Adamski, who wrote *Flying Saucers Have Landed* (1953), with his friend Desmond Leslie (1921-2001), a member of the elite and an esoterist, whose father was a first cousin to the Druid and Freemason, Sir Winston Churchill. This is very interesting as Adamski was later (at least officially), very much against any form of psychic communication with space people, and strongly objected to the esoteric interpretation of his physical contacts given by people like the aforementioned Meade Layne and his successor **Hansard Crabb (1912-1994)**, of Borderland Sciences Research Association (BSRA) one of the most influential realities in the creation of Ufology, who regarded the spacecraft and the space people, as belonging to the etheric world normally invisible to us. The BSRA viewed the whole topic from a typical Theosophical perspective, confirming once again the importance of Theosophy in the creation of the Space Age. In *The Adamski Documents. Part I* there is a letter where Adamski gives this view of the problem: *"in reference to Riley Crabb we have met several years ago. I do not support his esoteric views for if the teachings had been correct we would not be in the trouble that we are today ... I feel that his research is based on the psychic, and his little bearing on the present day events."* (December 11, 1962).

This is a rather contradictory statement from Adamski, especially compared to earlier explanations that I will analyze shortly, thanks to the research of a con-

7   *Ibid.*

8   Desmond Leslie and George Adamski, *Flying saucers have landed*, London: Panther Books, 1957), pp. 91-92.

temporary Swedish researcher. Riley Crabb was a Theosophist, ex-leader of the Honolulu Lodge of the Theosophical Society, and the space people teachings given in Adamski's follow up to the *Flying Saucers Have Landed*, entitled *Inside the Spaceships*, from 1955, are basically identical to Theosophy, so his criticism of Riley Crabb seems to be missing the point for some researchers, but again, Adamsky had to completely give up on his previous occult theosophical background, to serve the interest and disinfo spread by the Knights of Malta and the Church of Rome, something you should always keep in mind when studying both Adamsky's work and Ufology at large.

In the 1980s, Swedish researcher **Håkan Blomqvist** (b. 1952), who corresponded with Riley Crabb between 1979-1985, [9] received, from Lucius Farish, a copy of a unique correspondence between George Adamski and Miss Emma Martinelli. The letters were written between August 16, 1950, and May 8, 1952, i.e. before the famous contact in the California desert on November 20, 1952. Emma Martinelli was a member of the *San Francisco Interplanetary Club* and knew Adamski from 1949 until his death in 1965. In these letters Adamski revealed some very interesting facts regarding his first science fiction book, *Pioneers of Space*, published in 1949, *"speaking of visitors from other planets, you see, in the physical I have not contacted any of them, but since you have read* Pioneers of Space *you can see how I get my information about these people and their homelands."* (January 16, 1952). In an earlier letter he presented this explanation: *"In this letter, I have explained, using illustrations, how one may venture from one place to another, while his physical is one place and he is in another. That is the way I have written this book. I actually have gone to the places I speak of; I actually have talked to the ones I speak of. To you, I can reveal this since your letter reveals much, while to others I keep silent about this."* (August 16, 1950). [10]

As you can read for yourself, Adamsky and Leslie cite with great knowledge and understanding, the obscure tale of *Le Comte de Gabalis*, the 17th-century French text by **Abbé Nicolas-Pierre-Henri de Montfaucon de Villars (1635-1673)**, by then considered relevant only to the occult milieu of the Western Initiatic System, but almost unknown to the majority. In this book, the protagonist, the mysterious Count of Gabala, explains to the astonished and at times annoyed de Villars, the mysteries of the world. It first appeared in Paris in 1670, anonymously, though the identity of the author eventually came to be known.

The original title as published by Claude Barbin was *Le Comte de Gabalis, ou entretiens sur les sciences secrètes*, meaning **The Count of Cabala, or Dialogs on the Secret Sciences**. The book was widely read in France and abroad and is a source for many of the alien-like marvelous beings that will later populate European literature. French readers included such illustrious figures as Charles Baudelaire, and Nobel Prize winner in literature, Anatole France. As Alexandra H.M. Nagel, explained in her erudite scholarly dissertation, given a little over a decade ago at the Faculty of Religious Studies at the University of Amsterdam, many authors have taken *Le comte de Gabalis* to be a serious source, including Edward Bulwer-

9   http://ufoarchives.blogspot.it/2014/04/riley-crabb-ufos-and-theosophy.html ‡ Archived 11th January, 2018.

10   http://ufoarchives.blogspot.it/2013/10/the-george-adamski-correspondence.html ‡ Archived 11th January, 2018.

Lytton and prominent occult writers such as Eliphas Levi, Helena Blavatsky, and Manly P. Hall. [11]

Alexandra H.M. Nagel, who is skeptical in regards to the UFO/alien interpretation of Villars work, also points out that: *"Pursuing the research topic, in addition to visiting the libraries, the Internet was fruitfully googled. At first sight, it came as a complete surprise to see* Le Comte de Gabalis *pop up on UFO websites. If there were clues in Villars' novel about extra-terrestrials and unidentified flying objects, I certainly had missed them. The main source for the connection happens to be* Passport to Magonia *(1969) by Jacques Vallee who most likely was made aware of Villars through one of the original UFO popularizers, Raymond Drake (1913-1989). In his quest for early stories on invaders from space, Drake roamed old and ancient literature and apparently, found some in the 1963 edition of* Le Comte de Gabalis*."* [12]

Jacques Vallee was most likely made aware of *Le Comte de Gabalis* by the prior work of George Adamsky and Desmond Leslie, that came out ten years earlier in 1953. Nevertheless, in the same essay Alexandra H.M. Nagel has some good things to say about the research of French scientist and Ufologist Jacques Vallée, who was also inspired by *Le Comte de Gabalis*:

Contrary to the highly colored, missionary style by Drake, the French-American Vallee approached the UFO matter with an observational, academic perspective. He then became the first to notice similarities between alien stories which truly happened and stories in which fairies abduct humans. In both fairy and alien lore people encounter strange beings, see apparitions, or experience intercourse with nonhumans, so on and so forth. Starting from the hypothetical point of view that UFO phenomena may be much older than the twentieth century, Vallee, like Drake, began to collect cases. The quest led him, as indicated above most likely via Drake, to Le Comte de Gabalis*, and he must have studied the same edition as Drake did, the one with an introduction by Roger Laufer, or the 1913 one commented on extensively by The Brothers. Although Vallee's notes mention Villars only once, three of the many names and events the Count and Villars brought up were incorporated in* Passport to Magonia*, thereby referring to original sources which Laufer and The Brothers had also tracked down. The episodes Vallee considered worth retelling involve the learned men who had encountered humanoids, and/or had seen* des Navires aériens d'une structure admirable *"wonderfully constructed aerial ships," i.e. the cases of Saint Anthony who lived around 300 AD, the Archbishop of Lyon, Agobard (779- 840), and Fazio Cardan who left a note dated August 13, 1491, found by his son Girolamo Cardan. Vallee took notice of the (pseudo?)-Ludovico Sinistrari's* Demoniality *as well; he cited from him the extensive description of a young woman named Hieronyma, who for a long time was harassed by an incubus. Vallee:* **"As a theologian, Fr. Sinistrari was as puzzled by such reports as most modern students of UFO lore are by the Villas-Boas case."** *Brazilian Antonio Villas Boas had been 23 when in mid-October 1957, he was abducted by four beings. Taken into their egg-shaped craft, he was seduced by*

11   *See* Alexandra H.M. Nagel, *Marriage with Elementals: From Le Comte de Gabalis to a Golden Dawn ritual*, (Dissertation prepared for the MA Mysticism and Western Esotericism offered at the Faculty of Religious Studies, University of Amsterdam 2006-2007). pp. 52–53.

12   *Ibid.*, pp. 58-59 [**emphasis added**].

a beautiful female creature with white hair. She uttered strange noises. Twice An-
tonio and the modern succubus had intercourse. The second time the female had
rubbed her belly and pointed to the sky as if she indicated to have his baby some-
where in space. **Hence, Vallee noticed characteristics strikingly similar between**
contemporary humans harassed by aliens, and humans harassed by incubi or
succubi in Medieval times. *Seven years later, Vallee's quest for explanations of*
UFO manifestations brought him in touch with the **Order of Melchizedek** *founded*
in California by **Hiram Erastus Butler** *(d. 1916). And now things really begin to*
loop back to one another for it was this man, Butler (and Thomas Lake Harris),
whom Madame Blavatsky had accused "of begetting children on the astral plane."
And it was Butler's magazine, **The Esoteric** *of which Charles Mackay, the author*
of **The Salamandrine,** *had been managing editor during the late 1880s.* [13]

Hiram Erastus Butler (1841-1916) mentioned in the work of Alexandra
H.M. Nagel's, was an American occultist, organizer of **The Esoteric Fraternity,**
known initially **as Genii of Nations, Knowledge, and Religions** or **G.N.K.R.,**
and later as Order of Melchizidek,[14] an Illuminati sect founded between 1887
and 1888, based on astrology, radical celibacy (despite Butler's reputation for
womanizing and sexual magical operations), and the development of the will
as the main path to illumination, like the far more successful *Ordo Templi Orien-*
tis founded only a few years later. Butler made sacred sexuality the core of his
doctrines, but in a very odd manner, and this might have limited the success of
his project. He was drawing on the karezza practices of the Oneida community
(i.e. masturbation or intercourse without the ejaculation/climax), and the ascetic disciplines of historical mystics and yogis, he insisted that to truly achieve
higher consciousness, not only orgasm but sexual contact itself in any form, had
to be avoided completely. Total celibacy was for him the key to Enlightenment.
Occult researcher Marc Demarest, in his piece **Fruit and Seed in Applegate,**
believes that the Esoteric Fraternity may have used celibacy as a cover-story
for Tantric or even orgiastic sexual rites that were performed at higher levels of
initiation—a common practice among sex magick-oriented groups. Uncovering
the stories about Butler's scandals in Boston and San Francisco, he also noted
that the allegedly chaste Butler was dodging charges about his group's "sensational" doings as late as an 1899 lawsuit over the Applegate property.

In 1887, Butler dubbed himself **Adhy-apaka**, the Hellenic Ethnomedon, and
founded the "Genii of Nations, Knowledge and Religions" or GNKR, to organize
his modest following and promulgate his teachings on sacred celibacy and consciousness. For some reason, this aroused the anger of Helena Petrovna Blavatsky,
the Grande Dame of Theosophy, who attacked Butler in the Theosophical Journal
Lucifer, saying that he was no better than a cheap pseudo-spiritual hustler and
that his group's initials actually stood for **Gulls Nabbed by Knaves and Rascals.**

Blavatsky, herself was a Brotherhood of Luxor initiate who may have feared
Butler was revealing sect secrets in his teachings, even went so far as to accuse
him of siring astral plane children with female elementals—a sort of spiritual-
istic Deadbeat Dad. The great occultist may have been onto something. In 1889,

13   Alexandra H.M. Nagel, pp. 59-60.

14   *See* http://www.iapsop.com/archive/materials/esoteric/ ‡ Archived 11th January,
2018.

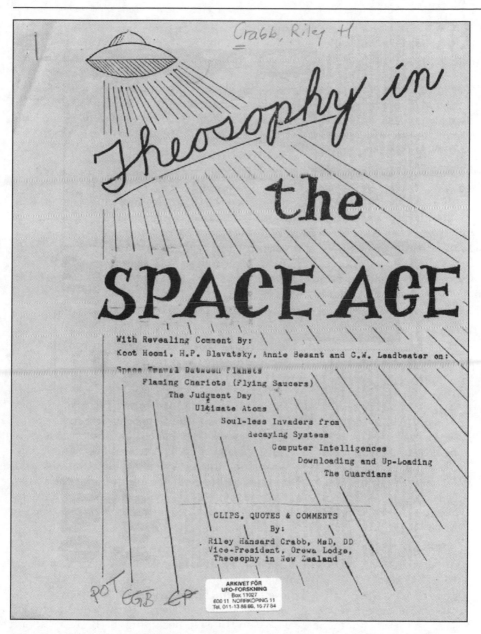

FIG. 36 Cover of a booklet published in New Zealand back in the 1980s, by the late Riley Crabb entitled Theosophy on the Space Age.

the *New York Sun* and *Boston Herald* ran stories that claimed Butler and another male GNKR leader had initiated women into their inner circle by seducing them. In one instance, according to the *Herald*, a female initiate was told to wait in a room until a man of extremely venerable appearance; after a time of conversation and prayer: *"she was to give herself up to the spirit."* Butler and his associate were threatened with both civil and criminal actions, but nothing seems to have come of them. Both men fled Boston. When Butler landed three thousand miles west, in San Francisco, the scandal followed. In late September 1890, a San Francisco paper called him: *"a professional hypnotizer who was run out of Boston last year,"* and claimed he possessed: *"an occult influence over weak-minded young men and women ... using his magic powers, under the guise of a species of theosophy, to secure funds with which he promises to build an esoteric college in the Santa Cruz mountains. How well he is succeeding no one knows, but Butler declares he has at least 500 converts in San Francisco."*

In truth, Butler probably had no more than a dozen hardcore California followers. In 1891, he changed the group's name to The Esoteric Fraternity and gathered about him, several close disciples. All single men and women, they pooled their money and possessions, and moved to Applegate, in the heart of what had been Gold Rush country four decades earlier. They bought a 500-acre homestead overlooking the American River and settled in to build a self-sufficient, co-ed monastic community. Nevertheless, this seemingly obscure cult later found a place in Jacques Vallee's *Messengers of Deception: UFO Contacts and Cults* (New York: Bantam, 1979). [15]

Vallee, who studied the political machinations of The New Age Illuminati, saw the sect writings as early exemplars of a sort of occult authoritarianism that was tied in with the Melchizedek mythos, that was spreading throughout the post-Sixties California metaphysical subculture, that was completely manipulated and controlled by the programs for Mind Control of the Central Intelligence Agency. Vallee cited two passages from *The Order of Melchizedek* as echoing a particularly ominous concept, well-known to conspiracy theorists of today, based on an initiated elite operating as a behind-the-scenes political power bloc: *"The power to overthrow nations cannot be had in its fullness until the neophytes, as sons of God, have gathered together to work together as a unit."* A passage about powers available to such a unit is followed by this prescient remark from the mid-1920s, written in the wake of the Russian Bolshevik revolution and the Italian Fascist coup: *"One of these powers operates through what is called 'Mob Psychology.' The vast majority of the people are controlled wholly by their feelings, and he who can play on the feelings of the masses can control them."*

The Order of Melchizedek is typical of most sects of the Illuminati network who work consciously or unconsciously for the Invisible Masters of the New World Order and often fall victim to their own occult wrongdoings. From reading *The Order of Melchizedek*, Vallee believed that the aim of the Fraternity was not only to assemble a 144,000-strong Priesthood to dominate the earth (another typical sectarian theme) but to merge with God Himself, becoming the Body of Elohim and co-ruling the Universe with Yehova.

But such grandiose plans were far beyond the group's grasp, in fact, by the time Vallee began gathering notes on the occult-fascist phenomenon, the esoteric fraternity's numbers had dwindled to four, aged, isolated men still tending to the Applegate property, growing vegetables and selling books and literature to their few customers and correspondents. To the handful of metaphysical re-

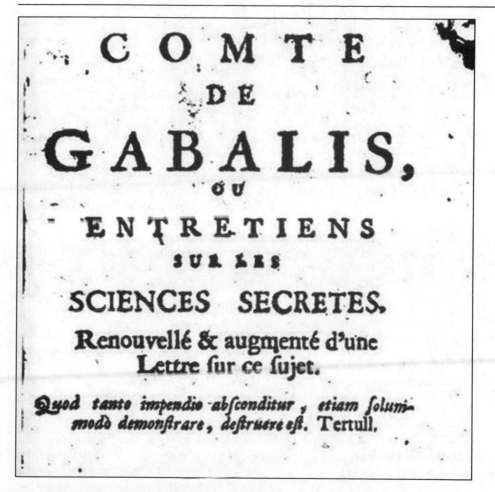

FIG. 37 *Original French cover of the first edition of* Le Comte de Gabalis ou Entretiens sur les sciences secrètes. *Le sylphe amoureux; Les ondins, conte moral, or* "The amorous sylph; The ruffians, moral tale."

searchers and religious scholars aware of their existence, the Fraternity seemed to be almost like living history re-enactors of late-19th Century American communalism, and they were paid little notice, save for the occasional human-interest piece in local papers. One of the last four Fraternity members was murdered in August 1973, in a strange incident that has never been solved or explained.

Matthew Alexander Bosek, a 79-year old Russian immigrant, was tending the sects cucumber patch when someone came up behind him and shot him three times in the head with a .38 caliber pistol. Bosek, a refugee of the Bolshevik revolution, who lived on the land for over fifty years, was a well-liked man with no known enemies, and the incident both puzzled lawmen and terrified the surviving fraternity, who posted guards on the property and offered a $10,000 reward for the murderer's capture. Despite a thorough investigation by the Placer County Sheriffs Department, no one was ever charged with the killing. The case remains unsolved, although this author was told that the identity of the killer was known by some locals, who lacked evidence or eyewitnesses to present to the law. The pathway leading through the cucumber patch was later named The Assassin's Trail, in commemoration of the grim event.

In 2003, the E Clampus Vitus historical-society/men's club erected a plaque in Applegate commemorating the group and took over management of the community grounds. More recently, English astrological scholar Kim Farnell reviewed Hiram Butler's career in her book *Flirting with the Zodiac* and identified him as perhaps the first "pop" astrologer in the modern West. The fraternities books remain in print through the Kessinger Publishing reprint house. [16]

Today, the Esoteric Fraternity / Order of Melchizedek exists mainly as a memory in the USA, but in Italy in particular, it has recently found new ground and a growing number of initiates, thanks to a famous Freemason **Alfredo di Prinzio**, known for his work on symbolism, and his two disciples, the publisher and Ufologist Adriano Forgione, a collaborator of the late Monsignor Corrado Balducci, and his brother, the Ufologist turned occultist, Mike Plato, who published a book dedicated to his beliefs on the subject in 2015, titled *Melchizedek the Immortal*. [17]

THE ELEMENTAL SPIRITS

*B*efore analyzing further *Le Comte de Gabalis*, let's explore the nature of elementals. These entities supposedly interact with us in so many ways, both positive and negative, and seemingly travel through dimensions and visit our recognizable reality. According to British researcher and author Nigel Mortimer, they achieve this with the manipulation of time and space, a technology that we cannot comprehend. Definitely, to better understand the elementals, as well as all other beings operating in a multi-dimensional reality, we need *"to take a descriptive look at the types of interdimensional entities that have been recorded throughout history as traveling through the gates of the unseen."* [18] Elemental beings, in particular, appear, as Mortimer also points out, as interdimensional beings: *"Mainly due to portals occupying land, sea and air, that is ancient and sacred in one form or another, they are associated with natural elements and as such elemental beings which are said to either inhabit the actual location in a semi-physical form, or to use the portals (as many other entity types do) to travel between their realm and ours."* [19]

The portals, in turn, are related to phenomena of electromagnetic origin. First of all, the term *elements* means both the fundamental components of the physical world, the basic elements of matter, as well as the principles that govern the order of the cosmos, both the symbols of orientation in space and time, and you can add to this the many matching systems (cardinal points, colors, stones, metals, male / female genitals, body parts). Depending on the Eastern or Western

---

16   *Ibid.*

17   *See* Mike Plato, *Melkizedek L'Immortale*, (Monterotondo, Rome: XPublishing Srl, 2015).

18   Nigel Mortimer, *UfOs, Portals and Gateways*,(Settle, UK: Wisdom Books, 2013), p. 95.

19   *Ibid.*, pp. 106-107.

tradition, the classification of the elements presents some differences. Elementals, in turn, are the spirits that inhabit, characterize and animate matter. Universally, an elemental is any magical entity who embodies/personifies a force of nature and therefore possesses the powers of elemental cognizance, elemental detection, elemental generation, elemental manipulation, elemental self-transmutation, elemental expungement and elemental immunity—these powers are usually exclusive to the elemental's own unique element. Within the Paracelsian concept so important for the Illuminati of the Rosicrucian tradition, an elemental is a mythic being described in occult and alchemical works from around the time of the European Renaissance and particularly elaborated in the 16th century works of Paracelsus. From the classical Paracelsuslan perspective there are four elemental categories: **gnomes, undines, sylphs, and salamanders.** These correspond to the Classical elements of antiquity: **earth, water, air, and fire.** [20]

So within each of the four elements there are nature spirits that are the spiritual essence of that element. They are made up of an etheric substance that is unique and specific to that particular element. They are living entities often times resembling humans in shape, but inhabiting a world of their own. The beings in the Elemental Kingdom work primarily on the mental plane, and are known as builders of form. **Their specialty is translating thought-forms (i.e. Egregore) into physical forms by transforming mental patterns into etheric and then physical patterns.** Each of them is a specialist in creating some specific form whether it is an electron or interstellar space. Elementals range in size from smaller than an electron to vaster than galactic space. Like the angels, elemental beings begin their evolution small in size and increase their size as they evolve. The elementals serving on planet Earth materialize whatever they pick up from the thoughts and feelings of humankind. This relationship was intended to facilitate the re-manifestation of heaven on Earth. They take their orders from the Devas. They do not remain individualized as humans are. These beings are animated by the thought power of the lower angels and so are thought forms of sorts. They may be etheric thoughts forms, yet they have etheric flesh, blood, and bones. They live, propagate, eat, talk, act, and sleep. They cannot be destroyed by material elements such as fire, air, earth, and water because they are etheric in nature. They are not immortal. When their work is finished they are absorbed back into the ocean of spirit. They do live a very long time—300 to 1,000 years. They have the power to change their size and appearance almost at will. They cannot, however, change elements. [21]

Elemental spirits permeate all matter, so elementals are found basically in everything. It is important to remember, however, that when you approach the elemental world, what differentiates them from humans is they are what they are. They are not characterized by free will, and they are therefore considered by some as loving creatures, without any responsibility. We must remember that elemental spirits are by nature chaotic and destructive, but also capable of reasoning and clever actions. Some writers describe them as evil, others as evil or just mischievous, others say they are both good and bad. The latter description is derived from

20   https://en.wikipedia.org/wiki/Elemental ‡ Archived 11th January, 2018.

21   *See* https://www.bibliotecapleyades.net/mapas_ocultotierra/esp_mapa_
        ocultotierra_6a.htm ‡ Archived 11th January, 2018.

the Greek term *daimone*. They also have been classed somewhere between angels and men, and can materialize in animal or human form just like Jinn.

The pure elemental does not have the proper corporeality or material substance. It is ethereal in substance although it does partake to some extent of the nature it inhabits. They preside over the element they belong to and govern it, they can be said to be the element, and as such act according to their nature, which is not liable to be harnessed.

Those who choose to work consciously with these hyper-dimensional entities must develop a firm will and absolute control, because instead of controlling them, most of the times you end up being controlled and manipulated by these hyper-dimensional entities. Many have recognized, discussed and warned about them throughout the history of humanity. Naturally, there are many people who scoff at the very idea of such beings, believing them to be fictitious inventions of the human mind. However, the fact that so many cultures, traditions, religions, and spiritualities have discussed the nature of these creatures, using different terms, but essentially describing the same thing, gives credence to the idea that they exist.

We have been cautioned for millennia that humanity is under psychic attack by a group of energetic, discarnate beings that seed thoughts of judgment, separation, anxiety, anger, and fear in order to generate *loosh* (negative emotional energy) that they siphon off as food. In searching for what force is really behind the construction of the New World Order and the grander conspiracy, one is bound to investigate these hyper-dimensional entities, who may be the original handlers, puppet masters and mind control perpetrators manipulating the whole of humankind. [22]

This also means that occult groups who act through elementals, have full responsibility for their wrongdoing in the world, and they will have to pay the consequences for their actions sooner or later. Regardless of whether he or she is in the Illuminati group operating the "Contact," there is a huge risk of causing damage to others. Remember it would be wise to always abstain from summoning the unknown, but the best way to interact with an elemental safely is to seek it in its own kingdom. To speak with, let's say, an elf, one would find easy accommodation in the heights of a tall tree, resting on a limb. With the sylphs, speak your questions into the wind, and the wind shall whistle back your answers. For a Basilisk, one could find its presence as you meditate in a desert, and for the sprites, there is no better time to communicate with them than the sunset on the shore of an ocean.

These are their unique kingdoms, each safe and in its respective comfort zone. An elf is often willing to speak with a magician he finds sitting on the same limb, assuming the magician starts the conversation, and a sylph shall often shout a word to you as it flies by overhead. This type of casual interaction, with no definitive summoning involved, is arguably one of the easiest in-so-far as the interaction is kept simple. For a short, peaceful conversation, this method can be employed. However, for working magical operations with the spirits, summoning is often a necessity, (unless the magician in question has attained a significant level of harmony with the element that can work the desired operation).

It is desirable for the magician (or any another interested party to the experiment), who seeks such simplistic interaction to first attune himself to the necessary element. So, if he wishes to communicate with the nearby gnomes in a patch of woods, he should first spend about ten minutes meditating on the nature of the element earth and the function of the gnomes within it. This done, and his mind, apparently, saturated with earthy thoughts, the magician should then accumulate *prithivi* in his body to such an extent that he feels weighted down and even a little damp. When this is accomplished the magician may find such passive communication with the elementals far easier, as the elemental shall not immediately identify you as something too different from itself.

Your mindset and overall feeling should be a receptive, magnetic one, so as to invite such communication without imposing any emanations upon the nearby elementals. For those of you interested, within this method exists the possibility of approaching living animals and interacting with them without causing them to flee or feel frightened. All that is required is a little insight of your own upon these same homeopathic principles. As mentioned briefly in the first paragraph of this section, this *modus operandi* is not necessarily the best choice when the desire is to work with the elementals in immediate magic. However, if the magician achieves passive communication on a regular basis, then he simultaneously acquires an auric emanation which invites such conversation on the part of the elementals as well, and therein he gradually becomes identified as a "friend" of sorts.

In this manner, the magician progressively obtains a kind of synergy with the elements that he has been conversing with, and he gradually becomes identified as an existence harmonious with that of the elementals. In time one may learn to actually call forth various numbers of the desired elementals simply by asking aloud or telepathically for their presence, and they may then be persuaded to help in a magical operation. This, however, is a luxury only those who understand harmony can have. [23]

Since ancient times the Illuminati, or Freemasons, or witches, or those who want to dominate elemental spirits, or even better, win their collaboration, had to overcome initiations into the four elements. For this reason, in his famous Doctrine of the Four Elements, the Greek philosopher Empedocles (5th century BC) associated the four elements with four divinities: earth (Hera), air (Zeus), fire (Hades), and water (Persephone). These four divinities and their relative priesthoods guarded the four elements. For this reason Albert Pike's version of the initiation for the First Degree of Freemasonry involves four tests or trials by the elements. I was initiated with this ritual that is not widely practiced in any of the U.S. regular jurisdictions, but is still in use in many European Obediences. The first trial experienced by the Masonic candidate is that of earth and involves the Chamber of Reflection.

The following three trials are known as *The Journeys,* which are made up of circumambulations around the Lodge with various barriers and experiences to

---

23   *See* http://files.vsociety.net/data/prophecy/Elemental_Magic.pdf ‡ Archived 11th January, 2018.

encounter. Each journey is accredited with an element; air, water, and fire, and let me tell you, it is a truly fascinating experience compared to the more pragmatic and bland initiations I received with the Emulation ritual on Great Queen Street, in London. These trials connected to the elements are a cultural heritage present in every human being, and often emerge in different forms, far away from traditional magic and the religious sphere, mostly as rites of passage into adulthood or a stupid virility test among some of the modern gangs that operate in our cities, or you can find them in tribal populations. It's almost as if it is a part of our DNA. The Golden Dawn even developed a ritual to marry one of its members to an elemental. [24]

Montfaucon de Villars' *Le Comte de Gabalis*, might still be the main work responsible for this incredible step into the unknown, undertaken by MacGregor Mathers, a true fan of de Villars work. There was high esteem held for the wit and wisdom of the Abbé de Villars' masterpiece, by litterateurs, as well as occultists, in the early years of the 18th century.

THE SECRET SCIENCE OF ALIEN SEXUALITY

Once we understand that the hidden ruler(s) of the world are invisible, or at least operate from frequencies beyond our normal perception, we are pushed to learn more about their secrets. In 1670, a curious booklet appeared in Paris, entitled *Comte de Gabalis*. The author was a thirty-year-old Catholic preacher, and abbot, **Pierre de Montfaucon de Villars**, who was punished, for this reason, by the Church, with interdiction from the exercise of the Sermon which forbade him the pulpit, and forced him to officially withdraw his publications. Royal censorship also prohibited the spread of his book that was subsequently reprinted clandestinely in the Netherlands.

De Villars was born in the diocese of Alet, near Toulouse, in the year 1635. He was a member of the very ancient family of the Canillac-Villars, grandson of Jean François de Montfaucon de Roquetaillade Canillac-Villars, and nephew of the celebrated and learned Benedictine father, Bernard de Montfaucon of Saint Maur. He went to Paris three years earlier in the year 1667, with the intention of advancing himself through preaching, and fired with that enthusiasm, hoped for a brilliant career. The Abbé's wit, eloquence, and quiet demeanor charmed all with whom he came into contact, and he soon gained many illustrious friends, admittance into the most exclusive circles, and he won the esteem of **Madame de Sévigné.** He became the center of a coterie of beaux esprits who were in the habit of meeting at the Porte Richelieu. He awakened a desire for truth in the jaded though brilliant minds of that effete period, and sought to turn them from their chief consideration, the degradation of the times, by pointing out the possibility of regeneration, doing much to elevate the thoughts of all who came under the sway of his gentle and persuasive influence.

The Abbé de Villars was an earnest worker for the Illuminati, most visibly as the author of several books and pamphlets, some of which remain to be discovered. One of these, on the origin of our species, inspired, unfortunately, none other than Jean-Baptiste Lamarck, whose writings stimulated Darwin in his diabolical quest for the understanding of evolution. The Illuminati of the dark side knows that if you destroy belief in God, people will cease to fear God. They then become pawns of the Illuminati, willing to serve money instead of principle, and carry out iniquities, from sexual misdeeds to even murder. Considering what we know of **Darwin** from historical accounts, he could very well have been an Illuminati/**Satanist,** as his work seemingly fits well with his total disdain for humanity and the world. In the propaganda arsenal of the dark side of the Illuminati, the greatest tool for destroying faith in God has been Darwin's theory of evolution. I know some say, "I believe in evolution and God." Nonetheless, countless people have become atheists from being taught this theory as **fact.** [25]

So is Darwinism an Illuminati scam? The answer is yes, as it is impossible to fully believe in the theory of evolution, which holds that living beings are not created by God, but are products of mere coincidence along the way of evolution. However, we need to fight Darwinism with a scientific approach and hard evidence that will demonstrate to the contrary.

Returning to de Villars, few of the works attributed to the mysterious Abbot were actually written by him. There are contrived forgeries, as well as sequels and interpolations in the later editions of Le Comte de Gabalis itself, inserted by those who feared and sought to nullify the profound influence which this book exercised over the minds and imaginations of its readers and of the Western Initiatic System, for there were those who regarded the truth it embodies as unorthodox and harmful to the temporal authority of the Church. A political-religious source may, therefore, be ascribed to the ingenious fiction that Le Comte de Gabalis became, that was instead a direct translation of an Italian book La Chiave del Gabinetto, written by Giuseppe Borri, published in 1681. Thoughtful comparison of La Chiave del Gabinetto, with the contemporary French and English editions of Le Comte de Gabalis reveals the fact that the Italian book is but a faulty translation and expansion of the former, masquerading under the guise of letters dated from Copenhagen in 1666, an imaginary date employed to lend color to its pretension to priority, and to cast discredit upon the Abbot's book.

The book describes an encounter with a mysterious **Comte de Gabalis (meaning "Count of Cabala"),** who was a master of the occult sciences allegedly killed for his beliefs. Gabalis initiates de Villars into the secrets of the elemental beings: the Sylphs of the Air, the Undines of the Water, the Gnomes of the Earth and the Salamanders of Fire. The Abbé is not sure whether the elementals are demons, while Gabalis encourages him to marry one of the elementals. Three years after the publication of Le Comte Gabalis, the abbot had his throat cut (for others he was killed by gunshot), on a trip to Lyon. There was a rumor that it was revenge from the Gnomes and the Sylphs, as de Villars had revealed some of their secrets in his book, while others pointed to the mysterious Rosicrucians, as possible organizers of the conspiracy that murdered him, or even the Jesuits, who later printed his book in Naples, with the help of Rosicrucian Raimondo di Sangro, Prince of Sansevero (i.e. Pickard, 1751 edition).

But who was this man? Little is known about him. The year before the publication of the book, without the author's mention and in total anonymity, a Montfaucon De Villars was in fact, sentenced in absentia by the Parliament of the city of

25   https://www.henrymakow.com/2013/08/Darwinism-is-an-Illuminati-Scam.html ‡ Archived 11th January, 2018.

Toulouse, where they broke all his bones and was left to die an agonizing death on the wheel, for homicide and fire crimes, along with his alleged accomplices.

He was a controversial character, since he had already been imprisoned in 1661, for some wrongdoings of a more terrestrial nature. To his dangerous life, de Villars unveiled a great literary talent, even though his works never managed to surpass *Le Comte de Gabalis*. Across the title page of the first edition of *Le Comte de Gabalis*, published in Paris in the year 1670, you will find a cryptic phrase from Tertullian: *Quod tanto impendio absconditur etiam solummodo demonstrare destruere est*, or "When a thing is hidden away with so much pain merely to reveal it, is to destroy it," suggesting that there was a concealed mystery. Hungry souls, heeding these words, have sought and found beneath the esprit and sparkle of its pages a clue to the truth which the occult world is always seeking to hide in jealousy. Many readers will recall Sir Edward Lytton's citation of *Le Comte de Gabalis* in his strange novel *Zanoni*, certain portions of which were based upon this source. [26] Alexander Pope, in his dedication to the *Rape of the Lock*, the first draft of which was written in 1711, says:

> The Rosicrucians are a people you should be acquainted with. The best account I know of them is in a French book called, **Le Comte de Gabalis**, which both in its title and size is so like a Novel, that many of the Fair Sex have read it for one by mistake. According to these Gentlemen, the four Elements are inhabited by Spirits, which they call Sylphs, Gnomes, Nymphs, and Salamanders. The Gnomes or Demons of Earth who delight in mischief; but the Sylphs, whose habitation is in the Air, are the best-conditioned Creatures imaginable. For they say, any mortals may enjoy the most intimate familiarities with these gentle Spirits, upon a condition very easy to all true Adepts, in an inviolate preservation of Chastity.

Very interesting points indeed, but for Pope's critics: *"Alexander Pope's poem bears the same relation to its inspiration* Le Comte de Gabalis, *that a dancing mote does to the sunbeam whose brilliance it reflects. For the reader of today this light shines, as it were, through a window fashioned in an Alien Age, and mullioned with a frankness of speech almost unknown in this century of conventional circumlocutions. Rather, let the reader view these discourses with a sympathetic understanding of the thought of the period in which they were written. Let him regard not their letter but their word, and so justify our belief that years are passed in which to point out spiritual worth wherever found is to compass its destruction, and that the day has come when we should seek to unlock the treasure of this ancient volume with a key fashioned from the Philosopher's Stone."* [27]

In reality, de Villars reveals no ultimate secret, no philosopher's stone, in the sense that the revelations contained in his book, about certain elemental beings, and the way to interact with them, are arguments and theories, known for centuries among the initiates of the various Illuminati mystery schools of the Western tradition. Nevertheless, no one has revealed them with such clarity, always veiled by a certain degree of allegory to avoid problems with the Church, with brief and unintelligible allusions made by the authors of the past, far more hermetic in their exposition; with the only exception—it must be said—for **Paracelsus** (1493-1541), born **Theophrastus von Hohenheim** (full name **Philip-**

26   http://www.sacred-texts.com/eso/cdg/cdg01.htm ‡ Archived 11th January, 2018.

27   *Ibid.*

pus **Aureolus Theophrastus Bombastus von Hohenheim**), a *Swiss* physician, alchemist and astrologer of the *German Renaissance*, that may have influenced de Villars. It is because of Paracelsus that for the first time in Western literary history we encounter the hidden people of the elements, the elementals. Contained in de Villars work, there is a vast spectrum of classical, patristic and more relatively modern literary works, that our mysterious author assembles with skillful play, interlocking it with Gabalis' own knowledge and almost prophetical vision: *"We speak wisdom among the initiated, not the wisdom of this age (but of the life-giving Force), nor of the archons of this age who pass away (but of the archons of the life-giving Force who do not pass away), but we speak the Wisdom of God in a secret made known to the initiated, the wisdom kept secret, which God ordained before the ages for (the upbuilding of) our spiritual body."* [28]

Central to this books theories is the possibility that man could have sexual relations with disincarnated elemental entities. De Villars also mentions pagan oracles in the context of his book, which corroborate the doctrines contained in *Secret Conversations* with the mysterious Count. They are drawn from an almost unknown and rare book, by the 16th-century ecclesiastical writer, **Augustinus Steuchus Eugubinus**, who wrote *De Perenni Philosophia Libri X* (1540), in which he transcribed from Greek such oracles. Gabalis' alleged teachings, since the publication of de Villars work, have always been present, more or less underground, handed down in the history of esotericism in a secretive manner, so that they will eventually reappear in the twentieth century with important figures of the Illuminati occult milieu like Eugène Vintras, Antoine Boullan, and Georges Le Clément de Saint Marcq. To de Villars, however, it is possible to attribute the merit—and the risk—in giving these doctrines an organic and orderly form, with more light and a popular approach, accessible and understandable by many, beyond the realm of Secret Societies. Let's look for a moment at what Paracelsus says:

I propose intrinsic nerves on the four species of spiritual beings, namely Nymphs, Sylphs, Pygmies, and Salamanders; for these four species, in truth, one would have to add Giants and several others. These beings, because they have a human appearance, do not descend from Adam at all; they have a very different origin from that of men and animals. But they get together with man, and from this union were born the Human race.

Paracelsus' doctrines are scattered here and there in de Villars work, especially in his philosophical works, *Liber de nymphis, sylphis, pygmaeis et salamandris, et de caeteris spiritibus*, but also in the scientific ones. But what is the mission of de Villars for writing such a revelatory book? For a long time, it was debated that by doing so he wanted to divulge a secret, or he wanted to ridicule esoteric doctrines, basically, as Umberto Eco teaches in his book, *The Name of the Rose*, [29] Abbot de Villars was definitely playing with fire far beyond any other of his time.

Regardless of his true intentions—which could have cost him his life—remains the objective fact that the book by de Villars aroused enormous clamor, igniting the curiosity of many from the Western Initiatic System for centuries to come. An echo that can still be heard today with de Villars quotes present in

28   http://www.sacred-texts.com/eso/cdg/cdg16.htm ‡ Archived 11th January, 2018.

29   *See* Umberto Eco, *The name of the rose*, (New York: Harcourt Brace Jovanovich, 1983).

the book, *The flying disks have landed,* by Desmond Leslie and George Adamski. If the result was to create a book that drifted away from the growing interest in the occult, the result was certainly not the one hoped for, indeed it was the exact opposite ... It became a classic of seventeenth-century literature and Esotericism, and as such, condemned by the Church itself, but not by the Jesuits, who, one hundred years after the first release of this book, were thrown out of the Vatican with heavy accusations.

GABALIS' TEACHINGS

I would like to now explore some of the passages in *Le Comte de Gabalis,* that I regard as relevant to our study on the Invisible Masters of humankind. At noon the Count of Gabalis conveyed to Montfaucon a note announcing a visit for eight o'clock in the evening. So it happened, and the two, in a carriage, went on to a secluded location, the labyrinth of Rouel's garden, where they would be undisturbed. The Count began to weave the praises of Divinity for giving us the Lordship over the whole of Creation and proposed to his companion the possibility to magically dominate all Nature. To do this, it was necessary for Montfaucon to be willing to give up whatever was meant by this and his current condition. He was initially excited about the miraculous prospects, but became more fearful in light of having to give up something, worried that he would be asked to give up his baptism or paradise! The Count answered, however, that the first step in approaching this new reality was to give a waiver, to renounce something incompatible with wisdom. He said, *"You have to whisper in my ear, that will you give up every carnal relationship with women!"* That bizarre idea made de Villars initially laugh. He asks the Count why such a great wisdom, like the one passed on by King Solomon, had been subjugated by the goodwill of sex, and what did the wise do, in order to avoid such pitfalls?

The carnal relationship with women, as a consequence of original sin, would prevent the grasp of knowledge of the integrality of reality and, in particular, those parts present in the Four Elements that are all populated by an innumerable array of spirits and entities: *The air is filled with an innumerable multitude of human-looking individuals (Sylph), proud, but actually docile souls: great lovers of the Science, subtle, helpful with the Wise Men but enemies of the rude and ignorant people. Their wives and daughters (Silphids) are as beautiful as Amazons.*

Montfaucon learns that the spirits of the Water element, called **Ondine** and **Nymphs** are mostly females and of incredible beauty. The Gnomes, on the other hand, populate the inner Earth in the company of the Gnomids, who are little, pretty women in eccentric clothing. In the Fire live the more discreet Salamander, who have little use to entertain themselves with men and are nothing like the animals that bear their own name. He also learns many other things about elemental spirits and when he will be able to communicate with them, he feels sad when he learns that they are not immortal as he probably thought, but they live for many centuries before dying and merging into the cosmic ether.

Conscious of this, these spirits are greatly afflicted by such deprivation. Yet God, in his infinite goodness, offered a loophole: *"The Sylphids, the Gnomes, the Nymphs, and the Salamanders, thanks to the alliance they can make with man, can be made part of immortality."* Thus a Nymph, or Sylphid, when they are fortunate to marry a wise man they become immortal and passable of the same bliss that we humans aspire to, being the immortality of the soul. A Gnome or Sylph ceases to be dead when he marries one of our daughters.

The Count takes the opportunity to add that the Church Fathers, and the Jews themselves (for Gabalis "all Jews are ignorant"), have wrongly believed that they were angels who, according to Scripture, had relations with women when in reality they were, elemental spirits. However in all the legendary tales of rapes and love between divine beings and mortal women, one can see the desire of elemental spirits to become immortal. The conclusion of Count Gabalis' speech is this: *"Their innocent desires, far from scandalizing us Philosophers, seemed to us quite legitimate, so much so that we agreed to renounce women and to devote ourselves entirely to immortalize Nymphs and Silphids."*

At the surprising exclamation of de Villars, Gabalis replies that it is not worth the loss of this incredible opportunity for some ephemeral pleasure that can last only a few days or years but is always followed by years of horrible wrinkles, when you can enjoy the never-ending pleasures of immortality, with the added merit of making such creatures immortal. He tells de Villars to give up the useless and foolish pleasures that he may have with women, for Gabalis, *"the most beautiful of them is horrible when confronted with the simplest of Sylphs."* Montfaucon at this point rebelled and got angry with the Count, accusing him of being a deluded visionary, telling Count Gabalis that he is willing to give up on such a foolish and ridiculous wisdom, as well as feeling sorry for such abominable sexual encounters with ghosts shouting, *"I tremble for you at the thought that some of your so-called Sylphids do not drag you to hell in the midst of one of your intercourses."* The Count, however, did not give up on his proposal in the face of such an angered reaction from his possible disciple. He removed from his pocket, the horoscope of Monfaucon, and justified his reaction to the fact that he had Saturn retrograde.

Nevertheless de Villars did not want to believe in the astonishing accounts given by Count Gabalis, and claimed that all these invisible love stories where nothing more than a joke created by devils and goblins, and that—in spite of all the literature that attested their existence—he did not want to know how to make love with the "elemental ladies."

Well, faced with such firmness, Count Gabalis admitted that there are wise men who prefer to neglect these invisible beings to deal with deeper things, as he would later demonstrate; but in any case, he did not want de Villars to think that such relationships were of a ceremonial nature, as is usually the case with the evocation of genies, or that you needed a whole series of superstitious and demonic devices to establish such a relation, because that was not the case. Instead, one needs to apply purely physical and natural laws for this work, even if disguised as ceremonial magical operations to confuse the profane. Gabalis then goes on to give a practical example to de Villars, after specifying that elemental spirits are consistent with the purest and most subtle part of the elements, *"If we want to possess the Salamanders, we must purify and exalt the Fire element that is in us reconciling a link that has been lost over time."*

Salamanders, however, live for a long time and are not so eager to join with humans, as happens with other spirits where contact is much easier. Relying on these explanations, though still hesitant, the Abbot Montfaucon de Villars asks the Count more information about the origins of these creatures. The answer is totally unexpected. The elemental spirits, for Gabalis, are nothing more than the old gods of paganism, which at one point, inspired by the devil, wanted to deny the true worship of God. However, these spirits discovered later on that they could get what they needed from men without being worshipped, and preferred to transform themselves from pagan gods into the infamous incubus and succubus. The Irish poet W. B. Yeats, an initiate of the Hermetic Order of the Golden Dawn, famously described that MacGregor Mathers, the Order's leader, was beset by women undergoing incubus infestations. Yeats wrote that: *"One has called to ask his help against phantoms who have the appearance of dead corpses, and try to get into bed with him at night. He has driven her away with one furious sentence, 'Very bad taste on both sides.'"*

Anton LaVey's daughter Zeena, and her husband Nicolas Schreck from the Sethian Liberation Movement (SLM), had this to say: *"Aside from the colorful legends of Eastern dakini and Western succubi and incubi, it is apparent that men and women in every culture known to man have reported the realistic sensation of sexual congress with such beings. These visitations usually occur as the percipient hovers in the hypnagogic state between sleep and waking but are not typically felt to be a dream. Quite often these phantom visitors take the form of a much-desired living person of the host's acquaintance. Encounters with such beings are hardly limited to those who consider themselves to be magicians; in fact, the uncanny sense of tangible reality that sex with these elemental creatures provides has often been the turning point that has convinced ingrained materialists to first explore esoteric study."* [30]

ALIEN ABDUCTIONS SINCE TIME IMMEMORIAL

*P*sychologist, Paranormal Investigator, Ancient Mystery Explorer, Documentary Maker, UFO Theorist, and Author Dr. Greg Little, digs deep into the incubus and succubus alien connection. Dr. Little writes:

These spirits are spirits that seek to have sexual intercourse with men and women during the night hours. Incubi is described as a spirit being that comes to have intimate relationships with women while they are asleep, while Succubi is described as a spirit being that comes to have relationships with men in their sleep. These dream visitors are also called "night husbands and night wives." Given the current intense interest in alien sexual encounters, many people seem to feel that such reports are relatively recent but as I have shown you in this chapter they aren't. Witches supposedly were taken into the air for meetings with the devil. People who had been abducted by fairies were left with distinctive body scars similar to those in UFO abductees. And the Incubus and Succubus of medieval times did the exact same things to their abductees as today's sexually-inclined aliens do to their abductees. [31]

According to fairy lore, fairies create a circular cluster of small bruises as their mark. The phenomenon is known as fairy bruising and is a sign of either favor or disfavor. The ring of bruises is often found around the genitals. They did this,

30   Nikolas & Zeena Schreck, *Demons of the Flesh*, (Washington DC: Creation Books, 2002), p. 373.

31   Excerpts from the article *Grand Illusions: The Spectral Reality Underlying Sexual UFO Abductions, Crashed Saucers, Afterlife Experiences, Sacred Ancient Sites, and Other Enigmas* -1994 by Dr. Gregory L. Little.

*according to various 17th century accounts, by pinching their victims. **An Ency-**
***clopedia of Fairies** (Briggs, 1976) gives numerous ancient examples of fairy ab-
ductions. Almost always a special drink was given to the abductee. This drink,
usually described as a thick liquid, was an essential part of the fairy abduction.
Women are abducted much more often than men and some fairies take special
delight, in repeatedly capturing women for amorous motives. In short, some fairies simply liked having sexual relations with mortals. Fairies abduct their victims
through paralysis; then they simply carry (levitate and fly) the abductee away
into fairyland. Fairyland is always nearby; under normal conditions, we can't see
or perceive it. The paralysis induced on the victim is how fairies get their abductee
to enter fairyland. The modern word "stroke" (meaning paralysis) is derived from
the ancient terms elf-stroke and fairy-stroke. Fairies travel in circular globes of
light, sometimes called "will-o-the-wisp." There are so many different types of
fairies that going through them all would be tedious. Some of them, however, are
virtually indistinguishable from what has been described as demons. One particular type, the bogie, looks a lot like the traditional Bigfoot. Virtually every society
has some lore of these little people and myths of them forcing their sexual atten-
tions on human victims. Fairy lore has a tradition of thousands of years. Fairies
have been said to be abducting humans, human babies, flying in lighted globes,
striking paralysis and amnesia on their victims, forcing a strange drink on their
victims, and having sexual relations with humans for all time. If we could remove
the mythological aspect from fairy abductions and dress them a little differently,
the folklore reports of a thousand years ago would be virtually indistinguishable
from present UFO abduction reports.* [32]

In a fresh and brilliant analysis on the subject, Dr. Gregory L. Little acknowledges that: *"The same thing could be said for the reports of demons. As my eyes fell on
the demon drawings in Plancy's **Dictionaire infernal** (1863), I was struck by their similarity to the famous 1955 Kelly-Hopkinsville UFO case. Imagine the demons as gray in
color, and they would also fit the description of the ubiquitous greys in recent abductions.
There are many in the UFO field (as well as various religious leaders) who believe that the
creatures associated with UFOs are demons. The similarity of some demons to the greys
of UFO reports are probably no coincidence. The resemblance between modern UFO abduction reports and ancient accounts of demonic visitations are striking, indeed. Ulrich
Molitor's **De Laniis et phitonicis mulieribus** (1489) shows the first known engravings
of demons who abduct and then have sexual relations with humans. ... Olaus Magnus'
Historia de gentibus septentrionalibus (1555) contained engravings of the devil and
demons carrying women (witches) away for sex."* [33] Dr. Gregory L. Little seems aware
of the link and expands further with great knowledge and understanding:

*The early accounts of these are similar to UFO abductions; however, in that era
it was not seen as a good thing to happen to you (as contrasted to many UFO
abductees who view it as a positive and special experience). In the early days of
the church, people who told of having visitations by "demons" were tolerated.
Somewhat later, they were fined or removed from the church. It was in the 15th
century that the church was no longer content to simply throw the "witches" and
"sorcerers" out of the church. From that point onward they sought to wring con-*

---

32   *Ibid.*

33   *Ibid.* [emphasis added].

fessions out of suspected witches and then burn or hang the accused. To have sex with a demon meant you were a witch or a sorcerer. Witches almost always had sexual relations with the demons or Satan himself and they were said to have some power over elemental demons. It is the lower orders of the demons that supposedly take on the appearance of UFO-like beings and fairies. In fact, in many of the witch trials in the 15th and 16th centuries, the lower orders of demons were described as leprechauns, gnomes, and other fairies. According to this ancient witch lore, Satan and demons had their favorite humans for sex. Both women and men were abducted for sex but women were favored. Most victims were unwillingly abducted in their bedrooms at night. Many victims described several demons (of different types) being present at the time of their abduction. Some of the demons stood by just watching during the act. The first written mention of Satan himself forcing sex on a victim was probably at the trials of Artois. The writer Vignate (1468) chronicled the trial. Here too, was the first mention of Satan's sexual organ as being cold as ice. This statement is similar to what some UFO abductees have said about their abductors who forced sex on them—particularly the insects or grasshopper-like creatures. Far more frequent was mention of sexual intercourse forced on victims by demons known as Incubus or Succubus. [34]

According to the *Dictionary of Witchcraft & Demonology*: **"Essentially the incubus is a lewd demon or goblin which seeks sexual intercourse with women ... the corresponding devil which appears to man is the succubus."**

Guazzo's (1608) *Compendium Maleficarum* stated: **"(The demon) can assume either a male or female shape; sometimes he appears as a full-grown man, sometimes as a satyr."**

St. Augustine firmly believed that demons abducted people and forced sexual relations on them: **"(Demons) have often injured women, desiring and acting carnally with them."**

Virtually no one disputed the existence of these sex-seeking demons. Known inquisitor Martin Del Rio (1599) wrote of the reality of Incubus in the *Disquisitionum Magicarum*, stating: **"to disagree (with their existence) is only obstinacy and foolhardiness; for it is the universal opinion of the fathers, theologians, and writers on philosophy, the truth of which is generally acknowledged by all ages and peoples."**

Peter Binsfeld's *De Confessione Maleficarum* (1589) stated: **"(The incubus) is an indisputable truth which is not only proved most certain by experience but also is confirmed by history."**

However, Dr. Gregory L. Little underlines that for a number of reasons, most people studying UFO abductions are deeply disturbed by the parallels between ancient and modern UFO abduction reports. For Dr. Little: *"They are so disturbed that they refuse to even see that any relationships exist. I am astonished at how many contemporary investigators—professionals who should know better—simply refuse to see the historical perspective of this phenomenon. It is easy to be smug and say, 'This is different, we aren't superstitious anymore, these are modern times.' But in 500 years a lot of what we deeply believe will be laughed at and ridiculed. Many, many people want to believe that UFOs are crafts from other worlds carrying advanced extraterrestrial beings. Many want to believe that the sexual abductions represent genetic experimentation*

34   *Ibid.*

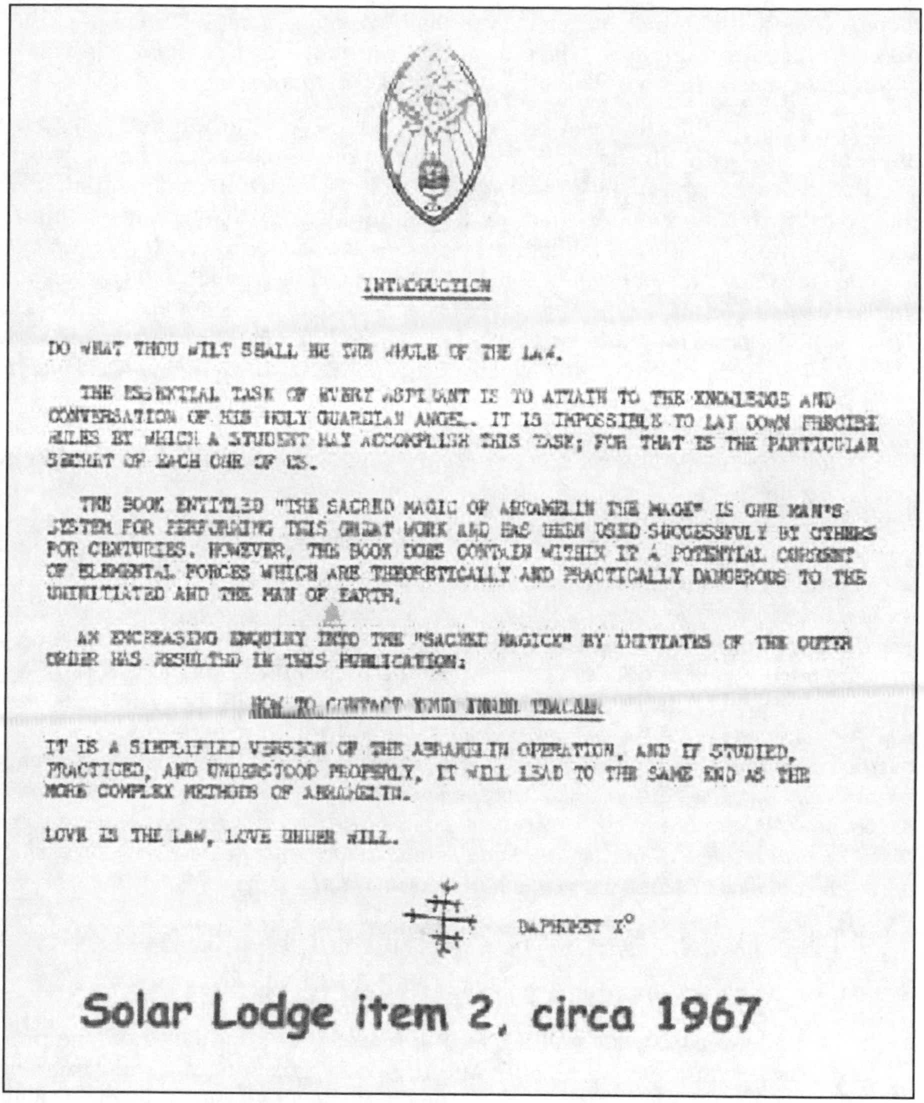

INTRODUCTION

DO WHAT THOU WILT SHALL BE THE WHOLE OF THE LAW.

THE ESSENTIAL TASK OF EVERY ASPIRANT IS TO ATTAIN TO THE KNOWLEDGE AND CONVERSATION OF HIS HOLY GUARDIAN ANGEL. IT IS IMPOSSIBLE TO LAY DOWN PRECISE RULES BY WHICH A STUDENT MAY ACCOMPLISH THIS TASK; FOR THAT IS THE PARTICULAR SECRET OF EACH ONE OF US.

THE BOOK ENTITLED "THE SACRED MAGIC OF ABRAMELIN THE MAGE" IS ONE MAN'S SYSTEM FOR PERFORMING THIS GREAT WORK AND HAS BEEN USED SUCCESSFULLY BY OTHERS FOR CENTURIES. HOWEVER, THE BOOK DOES CONTAIN WITHIN IT A POTENTIAL CURRENT OF ELEMENTAL FORCES WHICH ARE THEORETICALLY AND PRACTICALLY DANGEROUS TO THE UNINITIATED AND THE MAN OF EARTH.

AN INCREASING ENQUIRY INTO THE "SACRED MAGICK" BY INITIATES OF THE OUTER ORDER HAS RESULTED IN THIS PUBLICATION:

HOW TO CONTACT YOUR INNER TEACHER

IT IS A SIMPLIFIED VERSION OF THE ABRAMELIN OPERATION, AND IF STUDIED, PRACTICED, AND UNDERSTOOD PROPERLY, IT WILL LEAD TO THE SAME END AS THE MORE COMPLEX METHODS OF ABRAMELIN.

LOVE IS THE LAW, LOVE UNDER WILL.

BAPHOMET X°

Solar Lodge item 2, circa 1967

FIG. 38 Solar Lodge Document, circa 1967.

and crossbreeding by extraterrestrials. The simple fact is that believing that is far more comforting than accepting the possible reality of what has been described in the prior few pages. Most of us don't want to really believe that there are actual beings that exist that have been called demons or fairies or a devil. Contemplation of such possibilities is deeply disturbing. It touches the darkest and most remote areas of our psyche. It energizes the most fearsome and powerful psychological processes of our minds."[35]

Dr. Little continues: *"Nuts and bolts Ufologists avoid studying or even acknowledging abductions by stating that these aren't true UFO reports because we have heard nu-*

35 *Ibid.* [**emphasis added**].

merous Ufologists state over and over again that, 'We know these (UFOs) are a physical craft, they are spaceships.' The psychic and parapsychological stuff doesn't have anything to do with these craft. Anything but what I'm studying is 'New Age bunk.'"[36]

To me, it seems the other way around, as most New Age authors and researchers seem obsessed with the physical side of the phenomenon, and even those ones who were inspired by organizations such as the BSRA, have gradually moved towards a more materialistic and sensationalist approach, as most Ufologists are simply ignoring the big picture, and as Dr. Little states: "It is important to understand that I am not saying that UFOs are piloted by demons. I am not saying that fairies and demons are the rapists who force themselves on their abducted victims. There is a real problem with terminology here—most of us have a preconceived idea of what a fairy or a demon is, and I really don't want to conjure up that image. What I am saying is that there is a process that has been ongoing—probably for all of humanity's history—that manifests itself through the appearance of archetypal creatures and beings. John Keel was one of the first to recognize this. Others, including Vallee, Clark, and many British Ufologists have long pointed out the resemblance between modern UFO reports and the ancient traditions. It doesn't really matter what we call the process underlying UFOs, abductions, and all of the related phenomena but it is important to see that they all tie together. Even the dreaded and paranoia-producing 'government' has long-recognized this connection in their earliest reports (although changes in policy precluded too much future mention of it). John Keel's UFOs: Operation Trojan Horse cites the preface from a 1960s publication by the U.S. Air Force Office of Scientific Research called UFOs and Related Subjects: An Annotated Bibliography. In that report it was stated: 'A large part of the available UFO literature is closely linked with mysticism and the metaphysical. It deals with subjects like mental telepathy, automatic writing, and invisible entities, as well as phenomena like poltergeist manifestations and possession. ... Many of the UFO reports now being published in the popular press recount alleged incidents that are strikingly similar to demonic possession and psychic phenomena which has long been known to theologians and parapsychologists.'"[37]

THE O.T.O. SECOND-DEGREE INSTRUCTION ON ELEMENTALS

*I*n Aleister Crowley's O.T.O. second-degree working based on the previous symbolism of Saladin and the Oasis present since the Minerval degree, the Orator reads the Prayers of the Elementals, from Eliphas Levi's work. Later on, we find the elementals in the **Epopts—Pontiffs—of the Illuminati (VIII° degree),** where Crowley introduces the subject of union with these entities: "Acceptance of the devotion of a lower or partial being such as a nymph or elemental in such wise that it is thereby redeemed and made a perfect soul through the death which it must pay as the price of union with man." With a clear warning, from creepy Crowley:

That he treat them with kindliness and firmness, being on guard against their tricks. This being said, it is enough; for to have them is but the pains to call them forth from their homes. And the Spirits of the Elemental Tablets given by Dr. Dee and Sir

---

36   Ibid.

37   Ibid.

Edward Kelly are the best, being perfect in their nature and faithful, affectioning (sic) the human race. And if not so powerful as, they are less dangerous than, the planetary Spirits; for these are more boisterous, and by distraction, stars are easily perturbed and afflicted. Call them therefore by the Keys of Enoch as is written in the Book ye know of, and let there be after the Calls an Evocation by the Wand, and let the Marrow of the Wand be preserved within the pyramids of the letters that make up the name of the Spirit. Now unless ye be well skilled in Art Magick, ye will not dare call forth the Three Great Gods of the whole Tablet, or the King Serpent thereof, or the Six Seigneurs majestical, or even the Gods of the Calvary Crosses in the lesser angles. But the Cherubic rulers, yea verily and amen, these are your mates, and ye may yet more safely summon the Lesser assistant angles. And those that are in this Art novices should wiselier call forth only the Trigrammaton of the Sub-Elements.

In the Secret Instruction of the Ninth Degree of the *Ordo Templi Orientis*, Crowley's project for a Human-Elemental Hybrid is finally unveiled:

*If this be accepted, then clearly it is possible that a magician might find means (a) to bar the gate against any Human Ego, and (b) **to cause the Incarnation of some non-human being, such as an elemental or planetary spirit, of a nature fitted to some desired end**. Thus one eloquent, from an incarnation of Tiriel, or one bold in war, from the indwelling of Graphiel. And these will be his chief difficulties (a) that Man (even when discarnate) is so spiritually powerful, that to bar him from his urgent need is a task of colossal awe, and (b) **it is necessary to choose a spirit suitable to the foetus.** Thus if the babe that is to be were by reason of physical heredity sluggish, melancholy and weak, it would be but nugatory to invoke into it a spirit of Nakhiel or Raphael or Haniel or Anael.* [38]

The rituals and instructions might have been slightly modified in the current degree workings of the *Ordo Templi Orientis* Caliphate and the *Handbook for Lodge, Oasis and Camp Masters of O.T.O. International* revised in July 1997, gives a clear warning on page 19 to their translators in section 5 dedicated to the editorial standards of the O.T.O., stating they: *"should be careful not to use the work of other editors, such as Marcello Motta, Kenneth Grant, John Symonds, Francis King, Stephen Skinner, Israel Regardie, etc."* However the fascination of the Illuminati of the O.T.O. with the elementals is quite obvious. In 1967, in the Solar Lodge of the O.T.O. in Los Angeles, linked to the recently deceased Charles Manson, in a document made public by Swiss researcher Peter R. Koenig, signed by Baphomet I, admonished all O.T.O. members who have not attained a degree superior to the Man of Earth Triad, to practice *The Sacred Magic of Abramelin the Mage*, because of the theoretical and practical dangers of the elemental forces. In August 1969, Charles Manson's *family* committed their notorious murders, while at the same time the Solar Lodge was at the center of its own scandal, involving a six-year-old boy called Anthony Saul Gibbons, chained to a box for 56 days. This is an excerpt from *Ordis Templis Intelligentis* by Alex Constantine, 1996:

The O.T.O.'s Solar Lodge in San Bernardino was founded by Maury McCauley, a mortician, on his own property. McCauley was married to Barbara Newman, a former model and the daughter of a retired Air Force colonel from Vandenberg. The group subscribed to a grim, apocalyptic view of the world precipitated by

---

38   Extracts from *Secret Rituals of the O.T.O.* (Essex, England: C.W. Daniel Company, 1973).

race wars, and the prophecy made a lasting impression on Charles Manson, who passed through the lodge. In the L.A. underworld, the O.T.O. spin-off was known for indulgence in sadomasochism, drug dealing, blood drinking, child molestation, and murder. The Riverside O.T.O., like the Manson Family, used drugs, sex, psycho-drama, and fear to tear down the mind of the initiate and rebuild it according to the desires of the cult's inner-circle.

However, most people ignore the fact that this deviant O.T.O. lodge, once attended by Charles Manson,[39] had their own UFO episode cited in the documentation brought forward by Swiss researcher Peter R. Koenig who researched the FBI files of the Solar Lodge. *Quote: (anon) and yes, ceremonies were performed there. One of them resulting in the UFO story that has not yet been revealed.* [40]

Considering that the previous Babalon Working that took place in California had been directly influenced by Crowley's own writings on the sex-magic creation of elementals and homunculi, and in light of the legendary status this operation has gained in recent years, it should be mentioned that the Great Beast was not at all pleased by the elaborate operations being carried on in his name. The first chilling words of Crowleyan admonition that came back from England could not have been warmly welcomed by Parsons, prophetic though they later turned out to be: *"I am particularly interested in what you have written to me about the Elemental, because for some little while past I have been endeavoring to intervene personally on your behalf. I would, however, have you recall Levi's aphorism 'the love of the Magus for such beings is insensate, and may destroy him.'"* [41]

ELEMENTALS AND THE ROOTS OF THE BLACK MASS

Abbé Joseph-Antoine Boullan (1824-1893) was a French Roman Catholic priest and later a laicized priest, who was often accused of being a Satanist, although he continued to defend his alleged Christian status until the end of his life. He was a friend and inspiration to the writer **Joris-Karl Huysmans (1848-1907)**, the author of the shocking novel entitled, *Là-Bas* **(The Damned)**, that depicted an innocents descent into a world of depraved Satanic activities and blasphemous rituals. Huysmans, with Henri Antoine Jules-Bois, supported Boullan in a celebrated occultist feud with the Marquis Stanislas de Guaita, who I discussed extensively in Volume I of my *Confessions.* As Massimo Introvigne writes:

The narrative of Boullan was substantially gnostic: human beings are imprisoned in matter, and to fight the final battle against the Devil and his agents they must set themselves free and "ascend" to a higher plane. In fact, in the last days that precede the Apocalypse, not only human beings but also all creation, from angels to the inferior spirits known as elementals and even animals, are engaged in an "ascension." The "life unions" are the means of ascension: each creature can, and must, ascend by uniting with one that is placed above in the ascension scale, and must at the same

39   https://www.infowars.com/charles-manson-dies-with-his-secrets-about-the-birth-of-the-ordo-templi-orientis/ ‡ Archived 11th January, 2018.

40   http://www.pararelligion.ch/sunrise/manson.htm ‡ Archived 11th January, 2018.

41   Nikolas & Zeena Schreck, *Ibid.*, p. 313.

time become the instrument of the ascension for one that is below, by uniting with an inferior creature. The letters Boullan wrote to Wirth and to another follower, of whom Wirth managed to assure the collaboration, clarified the sexual implications of the practice. "It is the Ferment of Life, Boullan wrote, which, when included in the principle of life of the three kingdoms, makes them rise, step by step, the ascending scale of life. ... One being alone having but one fluid. The Ferment of Life is the combination of two fluids," male and female. The letters to Wirth from three young female initiates, who hoped to perform a "life union" with him, countersigned by their mother and Boullan himself, claimed that "Carmel **means flesh elevated unto God"** *and that in the Carmel of Boullan "one finds celestification here-below through the act that was and still is the cause of all moral decadence." Boullan's doctrine was not only about "life unions" among humans.* **To ascend, there must also be unions with "spirits of light" but one must also lend oneself so that the spirits of earth, air, water, the strange "humanimals," and animals themselves may ascend.** *A member of the group wrote to Wirth that one follower of Boullan was "obliged to receive the caresses and the embraces not only of spirits of light but also of those that she calls humanimals, malodorous monsters that plagued her room and her bed and united with her in order to be elevated to humanization. She assured me that these monsters had impregnated her on more than one occasion and that, during the nine months of this gestation, she had all the symptoms, even external ones, of pregnancy. When the time came, she gave birth without pain and she was freed from the flatulence of the organ where children are born at the moment of birth."* [42]

Again, one meets the subject of Satanism in Jorio Karl Huysman's previously cited *Là-bas*, a truly influential book in promoting to a much wider audience, the forbidden ritual of the Satanist, the infamous Black Mass. In the 19th century, the Black Mass was popularized in French literature, in books such as *Satanism and Witchcraft*, by Jules Michelet, and in *Là-bas*. Notably the figure of Dr. Johannes, in *Là-bas*, was modeled after Joseph-Antoine Boullan. [43] The more conservative readers were shocked and urged the editor to cancel the series, but he ignored them. Later the sale of the book was banned in French railroad stations. The main character Durtal, a thinly disguised portrait of the author himself, would appear in subsequent books. Durtal became disgusted with the decadence, and found relief in the study of the Middle Ages, beginning with research into the life of Gilles de Rais, a notorious 15th-century child-murderer.

Through his contacts in Paris, Durtal quickly discovers that Satanism is not just a thing of the past but still currently flourishes in France. Durtal begins investigating the occult underworld assisted by his lover Madame Chantelouve. The work culminates with the description of the Black Mass, which Huysmans must have witnessed many times, due to his connections to the occult world of the Illuminati. Today, the blasphemous Black Mass introduced in Huysman's book is used as inspiration by Lucien Greaves, the pen name for Satanic Temple spokesperson **Doug Mesner**.

Historically, the Black Mass phenomenon appears prominently in the Middle Ages and there are many secret traces of it found in the 15th century. The 16th

42   Massimo Introvigne, *Satanism: A Social History*, (Leiden, The Netherlands: Brill, 2016), p. 123.

43   *See* L.L.Zagami, *Confessions of an Illuminati, Volume I*, p. 69, p. 72.

century then marks the widening of this phenomenon practiced in all the major aristocratic and royal households, and at that point, it also appears in Rome, even in the Vatican ... But it is in the 17th century that Black masses spread like a gigantic poisonous flower, becoming public domain. The women of the aristocracy made public their alien infernal alliance, offering their naked bodies to the Illuminati of the French aristocracy in their quest for lust and power. Finally, the ladies of the aristocracy acted just as the peasant witches of the age-old Witches Sabbath, disrespecting and thereby cursing their privileged angelic DNA, compromising many bloodlines from that point onwards.

However, it is certain that very few Satanic adepts were aware of the real influence of elemental entities, and the risk they were taking by inviting them into their lives. There were in the seventeenth century, and still are, very few real esotericists, and many opportunists among the participants of these kinds of events. As Jean Lignieres (known in the occult world as *Schemahni),* reminds us in his obscure occult classic *Les Messes Noires. La Sexualité dans la Magie*, or "The Black Masses. Sexuality in Magic," published in Paris at the end of the 1920s. [44]

Participants to seventeenth century Black Masses had always attributed to the Mass all the success they had continuously achieved throughout their lives. Sometimes they were surprised that the precise purpose of the Mass, such as the death of a wealthy relative, did not occur immediately after the ritual but in return, they had, a great number of other benefits around them that could help enrich their lives and their pockets without fatigue. This came from a supposed magnetic fluid gained by attending these Black Masses, that were favored among many of the occult elite, both by the King for special assignments and missions, and by ministers and officials for other duties.

Lignieres claim that the participants to Black Masses, by intrinsic virtue, increase their attractiveness. Remember the nudity of the many people present at these ceremonies produce a far more intense and quick **magnetical fluid exchange** than in ordinary life. To put it another way, the activation of the fluid motion makes the **Solar Plexus Chakra, your power chakra** increase for a certain period. The magnetic environment is charged, and every individual with attractive tendencies acquires a delicate sensitivity that remains even after the ceremony. When they leave, in the days that follow, they are able to perceive with their new psychic capabilities and know how to assume the most appropriate attitude based on the person they are in front of. Moreover, this attractive faculty is maintained and involves the presence of one or more elemental entities by means of psychism, and suggests to the person involved in the Illuminati/Satanic cult of choice, the actions to be performed. When this sensitivity decreases, they celebrate another Black Mass and little by little, ceremony after ceremony, they evolve an extraordinary magnetic fluid temperament. Unfortunately, this increased sensitivity and magnetism is paid at times with a gradual neurosis for the exaggeration, as Lignieres also points out. It is for this reason that witches involved in such deviant practices are seen from time to time self-accusing for what they consider to be their wrongdoing against God, or turning towards Christianity for an answer, hoping to be reborn.

44   *See* Jean Lignieres, *Les messes noires. La sexualité dans la magie* (Paris, FR: Librairie Astra, 1928).

MAGIC AND MAGNETISM IN THE ILLUMINATI

*T*he *Vis Medicatrix Naturme* is universal, invisible, intangible, and imponderable. It can perform feats which a doctor cannot rival, and it escapes around the corner before its presence has even been guessed. It is like the luminiferous ether which tantalizes scientists, all-pervading, yet subtly elusive of every attempt to capture it. Indeed, there seems only one clue to its identity. It is an aspect, or a mode, or an effect whichever the reader may choose, of the *Universal Subject* or *First Matter,* dating back to ancient Alchemy: the substrate of life centrally subsisting in all that circumferentially exists from it. A common name for it is the **Sophic Mercury** (i.e. Wise Men's Mercury), to distinguish it from common quicksilver. Yet it has received so many names that it is really unnameable, though not unknowable. A certain thing is found in the world which is also in everything and in every place: It is not earth, nor fire, nor air, nor water, albeit it wants neither of these things. It contains in it all life. Of it is **made** the medicine that will preserve you from all maladies. *Lucerna Salis.*

It is, indeed, one of the most ancient of all beliefs that there is a fluid or vitalizing principle permeating the whole universe and latent in the air we breathe—a quality in the atmosphere which is a secret food of life. This one element cherished by the ancient Illuminati mystery schools, and insisted on by the alchemists as their *Sola Res,* has naturally been derided by most modern scientists, yet its existence has been granted by such chemists as Wilhelm Homberg (1652-1715), Herman Boerhaave (1668-1738), Robert Boyle (1627-1691) and others, and by such masterminds such as Sir **Isaac Newton.** This diffused substance (or magnetic fluid) is sensible only in its mixed forms: yet it is the only pure and active source of all things, binding the natural elements, vitalizing bodies: the fontal Spirit of Nature, apart from manifestation, and it is distinct from that elementary ignition with which our senses are familiar. This invisible "Fire," "Stone," or "Ether," became known to certain sages through its masculine and feminine, or attractive and repelling, effects or aspects, and was noticed especially through the analogy of the magnet.

From very early times it was observed that the magnet appeared to possess a certain curative power, and the idea dawned that the human body possessed magnetic properties. **Paracelsus held that all animated beings are endowed with an occult power analogous to mineral magnetism.** This, he thought, was derived from the stars: he called it **Magnale,** and said that by its virtue the magnetism of healthy persons attracts the enfeebled magnetism of the sick. He is said to have personally used the magnet with his patients. His chief medicinal *medium* he called *Mumia,* the life-essence contained (invisibly) in some physical vehicle, such as part of a human animal, or vegetable body: which even when separated from its parental organism retains for a period its vital power.

Robert Fludd, who attained some distinction in the middle of the seventeenth century as a Rosicrucian writer, gives a fairly succinct view of the magnetic theory: "*Man containeth in himself his heavens, circles, poles, and stars even as the great world outside. These particular (i.e. microcosmic) heavens ordinarily govern themselves according to the harmony of the superior motions (i.e. in the outer heavens). Sick persons by the persuasion of their proper heaven have wandered from the motion of the universal heaven, and through the disharmony, they feel more keenly* *the changes of seasons, etc. When man was made in the Divine likeness he was able to affect all things by his mere beck or will but this magical power now sleeps in him because of the Fall.* " (*Mosaicall Philosophy*)

William Maxwell, a Scottish physician of the same period, writes:

From the stars, the human body, and all substances in the universe there radiate forth beams which reciprocally affect all other bodies: but the starry influence is original and predominant. Every astral influence in creation doth by a natural inclination, and that sympathetically, aspect the Star or celestial Fountain whence it sprang. Likewise, the Star in heaven by a paternal respect doth send down his influence to feed and nourish his like filial force and fire in creation here below. The stars bind the vital spirit to its proper body by light and heat and pour it into the same by the same means. (De Medicina Magnetica)

Fludd and Maxwell feel that these rays or beams are of inconceivable tenuity but are only the vehicle of the indwelling spirit which directs their operation and gives them their virtue. Fludd continues: *"The Ethersical Sperm or Astrallical influences are of a far subtler condition than the vehicle of visible light ... Yea, they are so thin and mobile, penetrating and lively ... that they continually penetrate even unto the center or universal bosom of the earth, where they generate metals of sundry kinds. It is not the starry light which penetrateth or deeply or operateth or universally but the Eternal Central Spirit."*

All things emit these beams: it is thus that medicine sends forth its healing influence. Man holds within himself a secret mystery, the center or miracle of the world. Fludd describes the spiritual *mumia*, which has its seat in the blood, thus agreeing with the alchemical teaching that the universal principles of attraction, repulsion, and circulation are in their natural generation unequally composed in the vital spirit of the arterial blood, or that, the repulsive force predominating over the interior attraction, the total circulating life is expulsive and is drawn away in a weakened consciousness from its First Cause. [45]

Johann Baptist van Helmont (1597-1644), an eminent Belgian chemist who established the present scientific sense of the word gas, was another practicing disciple of Paracelsus. Material nature, he declared, draws forms through constant magnetism from above, and implores for them the favor of heaven: and as heaven, likewise, draws something invisible from below, a free and mutual intercourse is established, and the whole is (micro-cosmically) contained in an individual person. Magnetism contains nothing new but its name. Man is a magnet and contains his own poles or points of reciprocal attraction and repulsion, corresponding to the opposites of light and darkness, centripetal and centrifugal action, male and female, etc. The medium by which his influence is conveyed is a subtle and vital essence, pervading all bodies, establishing a correspondence between all the different parts of the world, and regulating their forces. This essence Van Helmont called *Magnale magnum*: but he did not connect it especially with the stars, as for him: **"The stars of our intelligence are far above the stars of heaven."** All magical power lies dormant in man and it requires to be excited. **Will is the first of all, powers, for by volition motion is impressed on all ob-**

---

45   *See* Baron du Potet de Sennevoy, *Magnetism and Magic*, (London, UK: George Allen & Unwin Ltd., 1927), p. 15-16, [emphasis added].

jects: the Will existing in man is the principle of all his actions, and the Will can direct the subtle *Magnale magnum*.

No patient is in a favorable condition unless his internal imagination abandons itself entirely to the impression the physician wishes to produce upon him: or if he possesses more energy than he who operates. If the patient be well-disposed, or weak, he readily yields to the magnetic influence of the operator through the medium of his imagination. Thus, Van Helmont seems to have anticipated the modern schools led by Charcot and others with their endless insistence upon suggestion and imagination, and the subjective factor in the patient. He claimed to have cured thousands of patients yearly "without any diminution of his medicine." So astounding were his cures that he was actually accused of magic and thrown into prison, whence, his friends eventually rescued him. He left two medical treatises on magnetic healing. Up to the end of the eighteenth century the Magnetic system was, broadly speaking, based on a spiritual philosophy: and in practice religion, and healing without drugs was interdependent on each other. In the eyes of such men as Fludd, Maxwell, Van Helmont, and others it was the link between heaven and earth which operated vitally. Man could only obtain complete mastery and use of his latent (or occult) powers by assimilating his will to the Divine Will. [46]

This is something the true Illuminated (not the illuminist), have always done in order to protect humanity from the dark side of the Western Initiatic System and their alien demonic allies. For some writers, such as Paracelsus and Maxwell, a greater stress might put on the visible operations of the subtle element (*Magnale magnum*) but they never lost sight of the mystical aspect and basis of the whole matter.

When religion and healing of this kind parted company, the result was disastrous to both, as modern medical science began to grow increasingly materialistic, at least until the recent rise of alternative medicine, growing in popularity and used by a discrete percentage of the population in many countries, that has changed this previous negative trend. **Jules Denis, Baron du Potet or Dupotet de Sennevoy (1796-1881),** who was a French esotericist who practiced homeopathy in London during part of his life, complained that the doctors of his day were little more than "mechanics," who had lost sight of nature's more subtle workings. Some Christians have gone to the opposite extreme, denying the reality or potency of any medical material at all. There can be no real reconciliation until we recognize that the spirit and matter which God has joined together must not be put asunder by our theories, and we must prove our assertions with credible scientifical means. This, of course, is a dangerous game. Especially when you take into consideration that the pharmaceutical companies of today are completely controlled by certain branches of Freemasonry and the elite, working constantly to sabotage our interest as a species, to simply increase their finances and their economic influence.

The man who, some say unwittingly and innocently, others say, diabolically and methodically, began this disastrous process, was the aforementioned Illuminati and Freemason **Anton Mesmer,** the Viennese physician who went to Paris and published his "discovery" of the subtle fluid in 1775. In his system, the

46   *Ibid.* p. 17-18.

spiritual aspect practically disappears. For him "Animal Magnetism"—as it began to be called—was purely a question of matter and motion. He presented his theories on this matter to appeal to Paris doctors in the so-called "Age of Reason," for France was already trembling on the verge of revolution. In any case, Mesmer only revived an old doctrine or philosophy, shorn of its deeper aspects, and gave it a new name. Mesmer basically secularized a mystery, and his explanations suggest it as the mechanical operation of an indifferent non-moral force. It is, however, only fair to remember that he went to Paris, not primarily as a healer but as the exponent of what he sincerely believed to be a new physical fluid, to demonstrate that, being a doctor, he practiced healing. He was personally benevolent, and treated his poor patients for free, giving them the same care that he bestowed on the wealthy. Whether he became a greedy charlatan, as his enemies asserted, is doubtful, certainly, he spent the last years of his life still practicing magnetic cures gratuitously for the poor. [47] *Magnetic Mesmerism* has also been indicated as the occult medicine of the Kabbalists.

For a final consideration of the important topics ranging from elementals to magnetism touched in this chapter, I would like to include the following passages from the work of controversial Theosophical Society member **C.W. Leadbeater** entitled, *Some Glimpses of Occultism* (Chapter VIII):

*We have also to consider another class of entities which are frequently employed in magic, and this time we are dealing with real and evolving beings—not merely with temporary creations. There is a whole kingdom of vivid life which does not belong to our human line of evolution but runs parallel with it, and utilizes this same world in which we live. This evolution contains all grades of intelligence, from entities at the level in that respect of our animal kingdom, to others who equal or even greatly surpass the highest intellectual power of man. This evolution does not normally descend to the lower part of the physical plane; its members, at any rate, never take upon themselves dense physical bodies such as ours. The majority of those with whom we have to deal possess only astral bodies, although many types come down to the etheric part of the physical plane and clothe themselves with its matter, thus bringing themselves nearer to the limit of ordinary human sight. There are vast hosts of these beings and an almost infinite number of types and classes and tribes among them. Broadly speaking, we may divide them into two great classes (a) nature-spirits or fairies, and (b) **angels or, as they are called in the East, devas** (a cognate of our word "devils"). This second class begins at a level corresponding to the human (the incarnate angel) but reaches up to heights far beyond any that humanity has as yet touched, so that its connection with magic is naturally of the slightest kind, and belongs solely to one special type of it, of which we shall speak presently. The nature-spirits have been called by many different names at different periods and in various countries. We read of them as **fairies, elves, pixies, kobolds, sylphs, gnomes, salamanders, undines, brownies, or "good people" and traditions of their occasional appearance exist in every country under heaven.** They have usually been supposed to be merely the creations of popular superstition, and it is no doubt, true that much has been said of them which will not bear scientific investigation. Nevertheless, it is true that such an evolution does exist, and that its members occasionally, though rarely, manifest themselves to human vision. Normally they have no con-*

nection whatever with humanity, and the majority of them rather shun than court the presence of man, since his ill-regulated emotions, passions, and desires are to them a source of much disturbance and acute discomfort; yet now and then exceptional circumstances have brought some of them into direct contact and even friendship with man.

Naturally, they possess powers and methods of their own, and sometimes they can be either induced or compelled to put these powers at the service of the student of occultism. Although they are not as yet individualized, and in that respect correspond rather to the animal kingdom than to humanity, yet their intelligence is in many cases equal to that of man. They seem, however, to have usually but little sense of responsibility, and the will is generally somewhat less developed with them than it is with the average man. **They can, therefore, readily be dominated by the exercise of mesmoric powers, and can then be employed in many ways to carry out the will of the magician. There are many purposes for which they may be utilized, and so long as the tasks prescribed to them are within their power they will be faithfully and surely executed.**

All this will no doubt seem strange and new to many minds, but any student of the occult will confirm what I have said here as to the existence of these beings and the possibility that they can be used in various ways by one who understands them. I have myself made a considerable study of this subject and you must, therefore, pardon me if I appear to speak positively and as a matter of course, with regard to many things that for the majority of you may seem questionable or beyond human knowledge. To give a full account of all of the many classes of these nature-spirits would be to write a kind of natural history of the astral plane and in order to describe them all, we should need many large volumes. Yet the man who wishes to deal fully and efficiently with what is called practical magic must not only be able to recognize immediately upon sight all these thousands of varieties but must also know which of them can most suitably be employed for any special piece of work that he may have in hand. The forces to which I have referred are those most commonly employed in ordinary types of magic, but in addition to them, the occult student has at his command stupendous reserves of power of various sorts not yet known to the scientific world. There is an etheric pressure, just as there is an atmospheric pressure; but the scientific man will never be able to use this force, or even to demonstrate its existence, until he can invent some substance which shall be impervious to ether, so that he can construct a chamber or vessel out of which ether can be pumped, precisely as the air is withdrawn from the reservoir of an air-pump. There are methods known to occult science by which this can be done and so this tremendous etheric pressure can be reined in and utilized. There are also mighty electric and magnetic currents, which can be tapped and brought down to the physical plane by him who understands them and an enormous amount of energy may be liberated by the mere process of transferring matter from one condition to another.

So that along different lines there is much energy available in nature for a man who knows how to use it and all of it is controllable by the developed human will. Another point that must not be forgotten is that all around us stand those whom we call the dead—those who have only recently put off their physical bodies and are still hovering close about us in their astral vehicles. They also may be influenced, either mesmerically or by persuasion, just as those still in the flesh can be

and many cases arise in which we have to take account of their action and of the
extent to which their control of the astral forces can be brought into play. [48]

We may usefully divide the subject of magic into two great parts, according
to the methods which it employs and we may characterize these respectively as
methods of evocation and of invocation—of command and of entreaty. Let us
consider the former first. Although it may act through many different channels,
the one great force at the back of all magic of this first type is the human will. By
this, the vitality and the nerve-ether can be directed; by this, all the varieties of el-
emental essence may be guided, selected and built into forms either simple or com-
*plex according to the work that they have to do. **By this magnetic control** (A/N*
*mesmeric) **may be gained over any of the classes of nature-spirits;** by this also*
the wills of others, whether living or dead, may be so dominated that they become
practically but tools in the hands of the magician. Indeed it is scarcely possible to
fix the limits of the power of the human will when properly directed; it is so much
farther reaching than the ordinary man ever supposes, that the results gained by
its means appear to him astounding and supernatural. The study of this subject
brings one gradually to the realization of what was meant by the remark that if
faith were only sufficient it could remove mountains and cast them into the sea,
and even this oriental description seems scarcely exaggerated when one examines
authenticated instances of what has been achieved by this marvelous power. But
in order that this mighty engine of the will may work effectively, the magician
must possess perfect confidence. [49]

This confidence brings us to what C.W. Leadbeater called the magic of command: *"We find abundant traces of this magic of command in the ceremonies con-*
nected with almost every religion in the world." [50] Ceremonies often used to contact demonic alien beings, rather than angelic ones. The purpose of Black Magic
is obviously to communicate with such demonic creatures and participate willingly or unwillingly, in their diabolical plan to establish the Antichrist.

48   C. W. Leadbeater, *Some Glimpses of Occultism*, (2nd rev. ed. Chicago: Rajput Press,
        1913.), pp 198-202.

49   *Ibid.*, pp. 202-203.

50   *Ibid.*, p. 207.

ESOTERISM AND ALIEN ENTITIES IN THE END TIMES SCENARIO

VI

The Enochian Apocalypse

llen H. Greenfield writes in his book *Secret Rituals of the Men in Black* about how the rules by so-called Alien ciphers are decoded: *"They have, in fact, not changed for at least a thousand years, possibly much longer. The rules are contained in a venerable body of knowledge loosely defined as Qubulism from the Hebrew word Qabala which* means hidden or secret. *A whole new, English-language based cipher was dictated by an Ultraterrestrial source to Queen Elizabeth's Royal Astrologer, Dr. John Dee through the trance channeling of Sir Edward Kelly several hundred years ago. It was called the language of the angels.*[1] *It's written in a script directly translatable into English, and Dee and Kelly served their government as espionage agents. They may well have used this Ultraterrestrial Cipher, termed Enochian—for espionage purposes, but, primarily, it was utilized by them to receive and use an* **Alien technology, so advanced as to be indistinguishable from magick, to learn such techniques as teleportation between planets and remote communication.** *... The Enochian cipher led directly to a more simple cipher communicated to the York Rite Royal Arch of Enoch Masons, as a series of glyphs corresponding to the 26 letters of the standard English Alphabet. Around the middle of the 19th Century, the Royal Arch of Enoch cipher was exposed to the public by a writer named Malcolm Duncan. The aliens began the slow process of communicating the new cipher to various deep agents and human allies. Madame Blavatsky of the Theosophical Society, and before her the Hermetic Brotherhood of Light, seem to have known the code, taught by their Masters, Paolos Metamon and Max Theon, probably themselves Ultraterrestrial Agents."*[2] From Greenfield we know that a supposed Alien technology, besides the Enochian cipher, was allegedly transmitted to John Dee by occult means, but what is the real mission of these Ultraterrestrial forces? What is their hidden agenda?

There is something sinister unfolding in the universe, something that prefigures an ongoing **Alien** invasion, taking place on an almost unfathomable scale.

---

1   http://www.kondor.de/enoch/sprache_e.html ‡ Archived 11th January, 2018.

2   *See* Allen Greenfield, *Secret Rituals of the Men in Black, Ibid.* [**emphasis added**].

The following research is based largely on **Donald Tyson's** short essay *Enochian Apocalypse*. If the author of this study would have been practically anyone else than Tyson, it would be nothing more than an amusing curiosity not worth mentioning in my book. Tyson however, has a certain degree of credibility in the contemporary Illuminati and magickal milieu, as he is both the published author and the editor of Llewellyn's prestigious edition of Agrippa's *Three Books of Occult Philosophy*, regarded as one of the key texts in occultism and so, it is my intent to explore thanks to his work, the possibility that Dee was indeed in communication with the same demonic hyper-dimensional aliens that thanks to the dark side of the Illuminati and corrupt Ultraterrestrial agents, like Aleister Crowley, have been working for two thousand years to invade and completely dominate our reality, to establish the Kingdom of the coming Antichrist, in time for the arrival of the long-awaited Messiah. Donald Tyson writes that:

> Between the years 1582 and 1589, the English scholar John Dee (1527-1608) conducted a series of ritual communications with a set of disincarnate entities who eventually came to be known as the Enochian angels. It was Dee's plan to use the complex system of magic communicated by the angels to advance the expansionist policies of his sovereign, Queen Elizabeth I. At the time England lay under the looming shadow of invasion from Spain. Dee hoped to control the hostile potentates of Europe by commanding the tutelary spirits of their various nations. Dee was a thoroughly remarkable man. Not only was he a skilled mathematician, astronomer, and cartographer, but he was also the private astrologer, counselor, and (some believe) confidential espionage agent of Queen Elizabeth. His father had been a gentleman sewer (a kind of steward) at the table of Henry VIII. When Elizabeth ascended to the throne in 1558, Dee was asked to set an auspicious date for her coronation. Always intensely loyal to the Protestant Elizabeth, he had earlier been falsely accused of trying to kill her predecessor, the Catholic Queen Mary, with sorcery. His intellectual brilliance and skill as a magician were famous, and infamous, throughout Europe.
>
> In his occult work, he was aided by an equally extraordinary person, Edward Kelley (also spelled Kelly; 1555-1597), the son of a Worcester apothecary, who dreamed of discovering the secret of the philosopher's stone and dabbled in the black art of necromancy. Fleeing Lancaster in 1580 on charges of forging title deeds, Kelley found it prudent to set out on a walking tour of Wales.
>
> Somewhere near Glastonbury (so the story goes) he purchased a portion of the fabled red powder that could turn base metals into gold; the source of the powder was an innkeeper who had received it from tomb robbers.[3] For the remainder of his colorful life, Kelley labored to unlock the secret of the red powder so that he could manufacture more of it himself. It was on this quest for alchemical knowledge that he sought out the library of John Dee in 1582 and it was primarily for this reason that he agreed to serve as Dee's seer. Dee was a saint, Kelley a rogue, but they were bound together by their common fascination with ceremonial magic and the wonders it promised. Dee possessed little talent for mediumship. He tried to overcome this limitation by hiring a mountebank named Barnabas Saul as his professional scryer but had poor results. When Dee learned of Kelley's consider-

---

3   See A.E. Waite, *The introduction to The Alchemical Writings of Edward Kelley*, (New York: Samuel Weiser, 1970).

able psychic abilities, he eagerly employed Kelley as his seer for the sum of 50 pounds per annum. Dee invoked the Enochian angels to visible appearance within a scrying crystal or a black mirror of obsidian by means of prayers and certain magical seals. After Kelley had alerted Dee to the presence of the spirits, Dee questioned them. Kelley reported their sayings and doings back to Dee, who recorded them in his magical diaries. The most important portion of Dee's transcription of the Enochian communications, covering the years 1582-1587, was published in London in 1659 by **Meric Casaubon** under the title **A True and Faithful Relation of What Passed for Many Years between Dr. John Dee and Some Spirits.** This fascinating work has been reprinted several times in recent decades and is readily available. The Enochian spirits got their name from the nature of the magical system they described. It was, they claimed, the very magic that the biblical patriarch Enoch had learned from the angels of heaven. The angel Ave told Dee, Now hath it pleased God to deliver this Doctrine again out of darkness: and to fulfill his promise with thee, for the books of Enoch. [4]

For Tyson, compared to Enochian:

All other forms of magic were mere playthings. Although Dee faithfully recorded all the details of Enochian magic in his diaries, he never tried to work this system in any serious way.

We cannot know the reason with certainty. In 1589 he broke with Kelley, who stayed on in Bohemia to manufacture gold for the Holy Roman Emperor Rudolph II while Dee returned to England at the request of Elizabeth, a circumstance that may have inconvenienced his plans. [5] Dee was awaiting permission from the angels to employ their magic and this permission was not given in his lifetime. It is necessary to state unequivocally for those unfamiliar with Enochian magic that neither Dee nor Kelley fabricated the spirit communications. Both believed completely in the reality of the angels, although they differed about the motives of these beings. Dee believed them to be obedient agents of God who submitted to the authority of Christ. **Kelley mistrusted them and suspected them of deliberate deception.** The dislike was mutual. The angels always treated Kelley with amused contempt. Kelley hoped the angels would communicate the secret of the red powder, which was the only reason he endured their insults for so many years. There is no space here to enter into the question of the nature and objective reality of spirits, nor is it likely that any conclusions could be reached on this difficult subject. Whatever their essential nature, the Enochian angels acted as independent, intelligent beings with their own distinct personalities and purposes. This is how Dee and Kelley regarded them and this is how I shall regard them in this essay. Using this assumption, **I will present what I believe to be the angels' secret agenda, which they concealed from Dee: to plant among mankind the ritual working that would initiate the period of violent transformation between the present aeon and the next, commonly known as the apocalypse.** [6]

4   Meric Casaubon, ed., *A True & Faithful Relation Of What Passed for many years Between Dr. John Dee (A Mathematician of Great Fame in Q. Eliz. and King James their Reignes) and Some Spirits* (Glasgow: Antonine Publishing Co., 1974), p. 174.

5   *The Enochian Apocalypse* by Donald Tyson from *Gnosis Magazine*, Summer 1996: https://www.bibliotecapleyades.net/bb/bluebook418.htm

6   *Ibid.,* [emphasis added].

Occultist Anthony Testa adds that: *"It is not surprising that the man behind the Enochian workings, John Dee was remarkable for his time, though in modern terms his credulity would seem untoward. It does, however, give us pause to consider how much the supposed rationality of the present day is merely a veneer over the primitive instincts we have inherited from our ancestors. Nevertheless, it is interesting to observe that Dee's goals were not, as it were, spiritual rapport with the angels he sought to contact, but were of a much more mundane—on a grand scale certainly—purpose.* [7]

The system of Enochian magick—if indeed it can be called such—is complex and uneven. The body of the work is developed over time and grows more complex as it develops. It also becomes more 'original' as the early work recorded by Dee is obviously influenced by a derivative of the work of occult writers before, most notably Agrippa and Trithemius." [8] Tyson describes the magick: *"As an initiatory formula designed to open the locked gates of the four great Watchtowers that stand guard against chaos at the extremities of our universe. The Watchtowers are described by the angel Ave. This clearly looks like the locked gates of the four great Watchtowers are multi-dimensional gates able to contain or facilitate the invasion of these 'alien' hyperdimensional beings. Tyson quotes some key exchanges between Dee and the alleged angels to his thesis and they are worth reproducing: The 4 houses, are the 4 Angels of the Earth, which are the 4 Overseers, and Watchtowers, that the eternal God in his providence hath placed, against the usurping blasphemy, misuse, and stealth of the wicked and great enemy, the Devil. With the intent that being put out to the Earth, his envious will might be bridled, the determinations of God fulfilled and his creatures kept and preserved, within the compass and measure of order.* [9] **These Watchtowers ... bar the chaotic legions of Coronzon from sweeping across the face of the world.** *Coronzon, the angels reveal, is the true heavenly name for Satan.* [10] *He is also known by the Enochian title of Death-Dragon or Him-That-Is-Fallen (Telocvovim)."* [11]

Choronzon 333 has been discussed previously as Crowley's ruler of the Abyss and again here with a slightly different perspective. However, it is interesting to note that the Demon Crowley popularized is equivalent to the Gnostic Demiurge Ialdaboath and the Kabbalistic Demon Samael, and as Anthony Testa writes, he is also identified in the Enochian system as the *"Death Dragon."* [12]

A description of the tablets and gates demonstrates that, regardless of the issues of unity and consistency, they were remarkably complex and interdependent. Author and Enochian expert Dean Hildebrandt describe them in this way:

The original set of calls given to Dee and Kelley were described as opening 49 gates and connected tablets. These tablets would seem to be those given in Liber Loagaeth, though the details are not clear yet. The calls open gates through which energy is transmitted and invoke the things mentioned in the calls including the I Ged

7   Anthony Testa , *The Cycles of the Aeons Book II : Angel of the Abyss,* (Anthony Testa / 2555 Working Group, freely copied and distributed on the internet, 2006), p. 82.

8   *Ibid.,* p. 85

9   *A true & faithful relation of what passed for many years between Dr. John Dee..., Ibid.,* p. 170.

10   *Ibid.,* p. 92.

11   *Ibid.,* p. 207.

12   See Anthony Testa , *Ibid.,* p. 86.

spirits. The beings invoked do not seem to be intrinsically connected with the gates, as the connected tablets are. Rather, they seem to represent one way of employing the energy. The calls have a 7-fold pattern that seems to derive from the gates. This does not fit neatly with the structures found through the calls, in particular, that of the aethers. It can be described roughly as follows: 0: These calls (0, 7, 14, etc.) seem to have a sense of reaching a sense of unity to complete the preceding calls and then returning to form to begin the next set. 1-3: These relate to some barrier to be reached through, with the first being outside projecting in, the second inside obeying the first, and the third giving a passage through connecting these two. 4: These have a quality of brightness and peace that make receptivity possible. They connect to the Worldsoul who lives at the center of the Earth. 5: These have an extraterrestrial connection admitted by means of the preceding. 6: These have a quality of earthly manifestation of higher plans. The calls involve a structure referred to in the 4th-6th calls as angles and in the 8th call as heavens, etc. [13]

According to Tyson, who cited Dee, the angel Raphael declares the expressed purpose of the Keys to Dee:

In 49 voices or callings: which are the Natural Keyes, to open those, not 49, but 48. (for One is not to be opened) Gates of understanding, whereby you shall have the knowledge to move every Gate, and to call out as many as you please, or shall be thought necessary, which can very well, righteously, and wisely, open unto you the secrets of their Cities, and make you understand perfectly the [mysteries] contained in the Tables. [14]

With this (admittedly sketchy) outline of the system, Tyson now returns to his main point: *"Dee's blindness to the true function of the Keys is curious because clues about their nature are everywhere for those with eyes to see them. The Enochian communications are filled with apocalyptic pronouncements and imagery. Again and again, the angels warn of the coming destruction of the world by the wrath of God and the advent of the Antichrist. This apocalyptic imagery is also found throughout the Keys themselves."* [15]

Tyson is on solid ground to this point, insofar as he is supported by Dee's diaries and notes. As mentioned above, the Watchtowers are described as barriers by which the *Death Dragon* himself, **Choronzon** and his host, are restricted from invading and, one would assume, destroying the Universe. Tyson questions Dee's incomprehension of the obvious, that if the Watchtowers are the fortress walls that keep out the hyperdimensional Demons, then the keys, which are explicitly for opening these very gates, are also the means by which these entities can allow the ingress of alien hyperdimensional beings, in order to herald the End of all things; something Aleister Crowley clearly facilitated with his rituals. Tyson states:

Perhaps Dee believed, as the angels deceitfully encouraged him to believe, that the gates could be opened a crack for specific human purposes and then slammed shut before anything too horrible slipped through to our dimension of awareness. Dee

13   https://hermetic.com/enochia/essay-enochiana ‡ Archived 11th January, 2017.

14   *A true & faithful relation of what passed for many years between Dr. John Dee Ibid.,* p. 77.

15   *The Enochian Apocalypse, Ibid.*

would have assumed that the harrowing of the goddess Earth and her children by the demons of Coronzon would not occur until the preordained time of the apocalypse, an event initiated by God and presumably beyond Dee's control. What he failed to understand is that the date of the initiation of the apocalypse is (in the intention of the angels) the same date as the successful completion of the full ritual working of the 48 Keys. This date is not predetermined, but will be determined by the free will and actions of a single human being. [16]

Tyson clearly identifies with the Antichrist announced in the New Testament. This is certainly plausible and more of a reality every day as we approach the 2020 turning point.

Dee, after all, was a Christian, no matter how heterodox his ideas may seem (and how much more so they would have in his day, which was a time when trials, religious wars and the burning alive of heretics was, if not an everyday occurrence, certainly a reality) and he would have been comfortable with the apocalyptic imagery that the Calls, as translated into English, were simply saturated with. [17]

So after a little more than four hundred years since Dee's death, does this mean we are finally heading for the Apocalypse? Let's remember again that for Tyson the Enochian Calls are also portions of a single giant ritual which, when completed, will usher in the destruction of the World. The Christian ideal of the End Days has always rested on the understanding that the actual events are preordained by God. This is a logical conclusion that can be drawn from the Scriptures, as in Matthew, 24 : 36—*"But of that day and hour knoweth no one, not even the angels of heaven, neither the Son, but the Father only."* This implies that God alone knows the exact day and hour of these events because God is the one who will decide when they will take place. And of course, this is the orthodox interpretation held today, as it was in Dee's time. Nevertheless, Tyson demonstrates again from Dees's own words, that the Angels have a different idea of when the Apocalypse will be initiated:

It has always been generally assumed that the apocalypse is in the hands of the angels of wrath, to be visited upon the world at the pleasure of God, at a moment preordained from the beginning of creation. In the veiled teachings of the Enochian angels, this is not true. The gates of the Watchtowers can only be unlocked from the inside. Basically, the angels of wrath cannot initiate the apocalypse even if they wish to do so. This is suggested by an exchange between Dee and the angel Ave.

This conversation with the angel Ave was presumably made through Edward Kelley as a medium, and let's not forget that Crowley himself claimed to be Kelley's reincarnation:

Dee - As for the form of our Petition or Invitation of the good Angels, what sort should it be of?

Ave - A short and brief speech.

Dee - We beseech you to give us an example: we would have a confidence, it should be of more effect.

---

16   *Ibid.*

17   Anthony Testa , *Ibid.*, p. 87.

Ave - I may not do so.

Kelley - And why?

Ave - Invocation proceedeth of the goodwill of man, and of the heat and fervency of the spirit: And therefore, is prayer of such effect with God.

Dee - We beseech you, shall we use one form to all?

Ave - Every one, after a diverse form.

Dee - If the mind do dictate or prompt a diverse form, you mean.

Ave - I know not: for I dwell not in the soul of man. [18]

The multi-dimensional gates of the Watchtowers can only be unlocked from the inside by the Angels of Wrath, who cannot initiate the apocalypse, even if they wish to do so. This is suggested by an exchange between Dee and the angel Ave. Tyson's summary in his essay, shows his allegiance to the dark side of the Illuminati, as another willing Ultraterrestrial agent:

Spiritual beings must be evoked into our reality by human beings. We must open the gates and admit the servants of Coronzon ourselves. Evocation and invocation are not a part of the business of angels, but of humans. That is why the angels needed to go through the elaborate ruse of conveying the system of Enochian magic, with the Keys and the Great Table of the Watchtowers, to Dee. If the apocalypse is to take place, and if it is necessary for human beings to open the gates of the Watchtowers before it can take place, the angels first had to instruct man in the correct method for opening the gates.

This is certainly a bold statement from Illuminati Donald Tyson, and one that is not without its issues, as we shouldn't be opening the gates of the Watchtowers to dangerous interdimensional demonic beings. Tyson also believes in Crowley's leading role in the so-called *Apocalypse Working: "Dee evidently never received the signal to conduct the Apocalypse Working in his lifetime. It was to be reserved for another century and another man. That man was Aleister Crowley."* We may also note, thanks to Tyson, that according to the angels who communicated with Dee, Choronzon himself is behind the fall of Adam:

Choronzon is mentioned only once in John Dee's diaries, during a communication from the angels concerning the expulsion of Adam from the garden of Eden: But Coronzon (for so is the name of that mighty devil), envying man's felicity, and perceiving that the substance of man's lesser part was frail and unperfect in respect to his purer essence, began to assail man and so prevailed. By offending so, man became accursed in the sight of God, and so lost both the garden of Felicity and the judgment of his understanding, but not utterly the favor of God. But he was driven forth (as your scriptures record) unto the earth which was covered with brambles. ... But in the same instant when Adam was expelled, the Lord gave unto the world her time, and placed over her Angelic Keepers, Watchmen and Princes. [19]

For Colin Low: *"In this context C(h)oronzon is identical with the Serpent of Genesis, and with the rebellious angel Samael in Jewish midrashic and kabbalistic leg-*

---

end. We can equate Choronzon with the Devil, but I must emphasise this is not the Devil of Christian myth; this is the Devil from myths that predate Christianity." Colin Low, adds later on in his brilliant essay on the subject: *"It can be seen that one slight reference to Chronozon in Dee's transcript of his conversations with angels hides a rich and somewhat muddled lore. That Choronzon is identical with Samael is evident. The lore concerning Samael is somewhat confusing, however. He tempted Adam and was cast out of heaven to earth. He was assigned to watch over the earth, but fell (with his angels) and begat monsters, culminating in the first destruction of mankind. He is chief of the evil seven (seven imprisoned stars in Enoch, seven Assyrio-Babylonian demons, seven deadly angels) that God keeps at hand for running the more unpleasant parts of the eschatological process. He will be judged at the end of time. He will be unleashed at the end of time. This apocalyptic theme is strongly pronounced in the work of both H.P. Lovecraft and the 20th century magician Aleister Crowley. Crowley had a fundamentalist Christian upbringing incorporated many elements from* The Book of Revelations *into his personal myth. He reinterpreted the symbols to suit himself, but there is no question that like Dee, he had a deep and scholarly knowledge of the book. It is often forgotten just how thorough Crowley's knowledge of the Bible: 'he could quote Biblical passages with the best.'"* [20]

Anthony Testa underlines, that it would be difficult to assert, as Tyson does, that the only way demons, including the Arch-Demon, may enter the universe is by invocation. In other words, by the willing opening of the hyper-dimensional gates by man. Are we also to believe that Choronzon was responsible for the temptation of Eve who, in turn, caused Adam to *eat of the fruit* and thus be cast forth from Eden? This thought is in no way supported in *Genesis* (or for that matter, in the esoteric doctrines of the Kabbalah. [21] As Tyson himself says:

It is evident that Dee was to be restrained from opening the gates of the Watchtowers until it pleased the angels. The angel Gabriel, who purports to be speaking with the authority of God, tells him: I have chosen you, to enter into my barns: And have commanded you to open the Corn, that the scattered may appear, and that which remaineth in the sheaf may stand. And have entered into the first, and so into the seventh. And have delivered unto you the Testimony of my spirit to come. For, my Barn hath been long without Threshers. And I have kept my flayles for a long time hidden in unknown places: Which flayle is the Doctrine that I deliver unto you: Which is the Instrument of thrashing, wherewith you shall beat the shears, that the Corn which is scattered, and the rest may be all one. (But a word in the mean season.) If I be Master of the Barn, owner of the Corn, and deliverer of my flayle: If all be mine (And unto you, there is nothing: for you are hirelings, whose reward is in heaven.) Then see, that you neither thresh, nor unbind, until I bid you, let it be sufficient unto you: that you know my house, that you know the labour I will put you to: That I favor you so much as to entertain you the labourers within my Barn: For within it thresheth none without my consent. [22]

20   Colin Low, *Dr. John Dee, the Necronomicon & the Cleansing of the World - A Gnostic Trail* at http://www.digital-brilliance.com/kab/essays/GnosticTrail.htm ‡ Archived 11th January, 2017.

21   Anthony Testa , *Ibid.*, p. 90.

22   *Cf.* Donald Tyson, *Enochian Magic for Beginners,* (Woodbury, MN: Llewellyn Publications, 2002) pp. 38-39.

Presuming the being that spoke through Kelley was the Archangel, we are left with a puzzle. Even allowing that the words here spoken are from (or by the authority) of God, it is not clear that the "harvest" here described, is in fact, the Apocalypse, though the interpretation is not without merit, and Tyson seems absolutely convinced this is the case: *"Surely nothing could be clearer. Throughout the Enochian communications, the angels euphemistically refer to the apocalypse as the Harvest. Here Enochian magic is specifically described as the Instrument of thrashing. Yet Dee did not comprehend the awesome significance of the burden that had been laid upon his shoulders."* [23]

It seems odd that the Angel would say: *"For, my Barn hath been long without Threshers. And I have kept my flayles for a long time hid in unknown places: Which flayle is the Doctrine that I deliver unto you."* Meaning that the mechanism by which the plan of salvation is to be completed is waiting on the arrival of a man, in this case, John Dee. And, once the Calls are delivered, **Gabriel finds it necessary to instruct Dee, as a parent to a child who has just received his first hunting rifle, not to use it until they (the angels) tell him it is safe to do so. In other words, the Angel gave Dee a loaded weapon—one that will destroy the entire world!** Tyson states:

Elsewhere in the record the angel Mapsama is just as explicit about the need for Dee to await permission before attempting to use the Keys:

Mapsama - These Calls are the keys to the Gates and Cities of wisdom. Which [Gates] are not able to be opened, but with a visible apparition.

Dee - And how shall that become unto?

Mapsama - Which is according to the former instructions: and to be had, by calling of every Table. You called for wisdom, God hath opened unto you, his judgement: He hath delivered unto you the keys, that you may enter; But be humble. Enter not of presumption, but of permission.

Go not in rashly; But be brought in willingly: For, many have ascended, but few have entered. By Sunday you shall have all things that are necessary to be taught, then (as occasion serveth) you may practice at all times. But you being called by God, and to a good purpose.

Dee - How shall we understand this Calling by God?

Mapsama - God stoppeth my mouth, I will answer thee no more.

At this point, Tyson makes it clear that: *"Despite these hints and many others, the angels never actually came out and told Dee that he was to be the instrument whereby the ritual formula for initiating the apocalypse would be planted in the midst of humanity. Here it would sit like a ticking occult time bomb, waiting for some clever magician, perhaps guided by the angels, to work it."* [24]

Tyson then discusses the later use of the Enochian system, primarily by Aleister Crowley and further investigates his role in the Apocalypse. It ought to be clear, however, that if Tyson's interpretation of Dee's diaries is correct—and aside from his controversial statement concerning the *Grand Ritual*—it is fully

---

23   *The Enochian Apocalypse, Ibid.*

24   *The Enochian Apocalypse, Ibid.*

supported by Dee's own work and it confirms that Dee was not in contact with angelic forces at all, but on the contrary, Dee was another Ultraterrestrial agent willing to serve demonic forces at the heart of today's New World Order. Edward Kelley warned John Dee that the "angels" they were talking to were really demons and that their goal was to destroy humanity. This ominous warning that went unheard by Dee might have been truly prophetic.

THE CONJURATION OF THE FOUR ELEMENTS BY ELIPHAS LEVI

*T*he following work by Eliphas Levi is focused on the alchemist Paracelsus, who named the four elements and their inhabitants. Many Illuminati in their sacred chambers perform this **Conjuration of the Four Elements,** so I decided to extract a couple of passages from it to include in my exposé on this subject. Eliphas Levi writes:

The four elementary forms separate and specify by a kind of rough outline, the created spirits whom the universal movement disengages from the central fire. Everywhere spirit works and fecundates matter by life; all matter is animated; thought and soul are everywhere. In seizing upon the thought that produces the diverse forms, we become the master of forms and make them serve for our use. The astral light is completely filled with souls that it disengages in the incessant generation of being; souls have imperfect wills which can be dominated and used by more powerful wills. They then form great invisible chains and can occasion or determine grand elementary commotions. Phenomena ascertained in the processes of magic and all those recently verified by M. Eudes de Merville have no other causes. Elementary spirits are like young children. They torment those more who busy themselves with them unless one has control of them by means of superior rationality and great severity. These are the spirits which we designate under the name of occult elements.

These spirits are those who often prepare disquieting or fantastic dreams. They are those who produce the movements of the divining rod, and the raps on walls and furniture. But they can never manifest any other thought than our own, and if we are not thinking, they talk to us with all the incoherence of dreams. They reproduce good and evil indifferently because they are without free will and consequently have no responsibility. They show themselves to ecstatics and somnambulists under incomplete and fugitive forms. This occasioned the nightmares of Saint Antony, and, very probably, the visions of Swedenborg. They are neither souls in hell nor spirits guilty of mortal sin; they are simply inquisitive and inoffensive. We can employ or abuse them like animals or children. Therefore, the magus who employs their help assumes a terrible responsibility, for he will expiate all the evil which he makes them do, and the greatness of his torments will be proportionate to the extent of the power which he will have exercised through their agency. In order to control elementary spirits and thus become the king of the occult elements, we must have previously undergone the four trials of the ancient initiations.

As these no longer exist, it is necessary to supply their place by analogous actions, such as exposing oneself without fear in a conflagration, of crossing a gulf upon the trunk of a tree or upon a plank, or scaling a steep mountain during a storm, or getting away from a cascade, or from a dangerous whirlpool by swimming.

FIG. 39 Illustration of John Dee and Edward Kelly and his cemetery Necromancy (ca. 1890).

The man who fears water will never reign over the undines; he who is afraid of fire cannot command the salamanders; as long as we are subject to dizziness we must leave the sylphs in peace, and not irritate the gnomes; for inferior spirits only obey a power that is proved to them by showing itself their master even in their own element. When we have acquired by boldness and practice this incontestable power, we may impose upon the elements the mandate (verb) of our will, by special consecrations of air, fire, water, and earth. This is the indispensable beginning of all magic operations.

Then Levi invites the magician to exorcise the air by blowing from the direction of the four cardinal points while saying: *"Spiritus Dei ferebatur super aquas, et inspiravit in facian hominis spiraculum vitae. Sit Michael dux meus, et Sabtabiel servus meus, in luce etper lucem. Fiat verbum halitus meus; et imperabo spiritibus aeris hujus, et refraenabo equos solis voluntate cordis nei, et cogitatione mentis meae et nutu oculi dextri. Erorciso igitur te, creatura aeris, per Pentagrammaton et in nomine Tetragrammaton, in quibus sunt voluntas firma et fides recta. Amen. Sela, fiat. Qu'il en soit ainsi."*

Next Levi invites his students to recite the prayer of the Sylphs, after tracing in the air their sign with the plume of an eagle. What I find more interesting is Levi's thoughts on the elementary spirits, and how to control them:

In order to control and subject elementary spirits we must never yield to the defects which characterize them. Thus a light and capricious mind can never govern the sylphs. An effeminate, cold, and changeable nature will never control the undines. Anger irritates the salamanders, and covetous rudeness renders those whom it enslaves the sport of the gnomes. But it is necessary to be as prompt and active as the sylphs; as flexible and attentive to images as the undines. As energetic and strong as the Salamanders; as laborious and patient as the gnomes; in a word, we must conquer them in their strength, without ever allowing ourselves to be enthralled by their weaknesses. When we shall be well fixed in this disposition, the entire world will be at the service of the wise operator. He will go out during the storm and the rain will not touch his head; the wind will not derange even a single fold of his garments; he will go through fire without being burned; he will walk on the water, and will behold the diamonds through the crust of the earth. These promises which may seem hyperbolical are only so in the minds of the vulgar; for though the sage does not do materially and precisely the things which these words express, he will do many greater and more wonderful. In the meantime, it is not to be doubted that individuals can direct the elements by the will to a certain extent, and change or really stop their effects.

Why, for example, if it is ascertained that certain individuals in a state of ecstasy lose their weight for the moment, could we not walk or glide upon the water? Saint Medard's convulsionaries felt neither fire nor sword and begged as a relief the most violent blows and the most incredible tortures. Are not the strange ascensions and wonderful equilibrium of certain somnambulists a revelation of these hidden forces of nature. But we live in an age in which men have not the courage to confess the miracles they witness, and if anyone says, I have seen or have done myself the things which I relate, he will be told, either you are making sport of us or you are sick. It is better to keep silence and act.

The metals that correspond to the four elementary forms are gold and silver for air; mercury for water; iron and copper for fire, and lead for earth. Talismans are prepared from them, having relation to the forces which they represent, and to the effects proposed to be obtained. Divination by the four elementary forms named Aeromancy, hydromancy, pyromancy, and geomancy, is made in diverse ways, which all depend upon the will and transparency or imagination of the operator. In truth, the four elements are only instruments to aid second-sight. Second-sight is the faculty of seeing in the astral light. This second-sight is as natural as the first sight, or the sensible and ordinary sight, but it can only act through the abstraction of the senses. Somnambulists and ecstatics enjoy second-sight naturally, but this sight is more lucid as the abstraction becomes more complete. The abstraction is produced by astral intoxication; that is, by a superabundance of light, which completely saturates the nervous system, and consequently renders it inactive. Sanguine temperaments are more disposed to Aeromancy; bilious to pyromancy, phlegmatic to geomancy, and melancholic to hydromancy. Aeromancy is confirmed by oneiromancy or divination by dreams; pyromancy is supplemented by magnetism; hydromancy by divination with crystals; geomancy by fortune-telling with cards. These are transposition and perfecting of methods. But divination, in whatever manner we may operate, is dangerous, or at least useless, for it disheartens the will; consequently, it restricts freedom, and fatigues the nervous system.

I hope this gave you a general idea of what the Illuminati intend with *"The Conjuration of the Four Elements."*

ALEISTER CROWLEY APOCALYPSE SUPERSTAR

*E*ven as a child, Aleister Crowley was convinced that he was the Great Beast mentioned in the biblical book of *Revelation*. He studied magic with the **Hermetic Order of the Golden Dawn**, then went on to construct his own occult system using an amalgamation of the ritual working of Abramelin the Mage, the Goetia, and the Tantric sexual techniques of the German *Ordo Templi Orientis*, among other sources. He firmly believed that he was the herald for a New Age of strife and destruction that would sweep across the world. He called this the **Aeon of Horus**, after the Egyptian God of War. As we saw earlier in Cairo in 1904, he received the bible of this apocalyptic period, *LiberAL vel Legis "The Book of the Law,"* in the form of a psychic dictation from his guardian angel, Aiwass. The book explains some of the conditions that will prevail in the **Aeon of Horus**. It also contains Crowley's famous dictum **"Do what thou wilt shall be the whole of the Law."** For Illuminati researcher Donald Tyson, it is highly significant that Crowley never considered himself to be the Antichrist. He is not the central character in the drama of the apocalypse, but the herald who ushers in the age of chaos. In a very real sense, he was the gatekeeper of the apocalypse. The text of *The Book of the Law* clearly states:

*This book shall be translated into all tongues: but always with the original in the writing of the Beast; for in the chance shape of the letters and their position to one another: in these are mysteries that no Beast shall divine. Let him not seek to try: but one cometh after him, whence I say not, who shall discover the Key to it all. Then this line drawn is a key: then this circle squared in its failure is a key also. And Abrahadabra. It shall be his child & that strangely. Let him not seek after this; for thereby alone can he fall from it. (**Liber AL III:47**)*

Crowley studied and practiced Enochian magic more often and deeply than any other magician of the Golden Dawn, indeed probably more deeply than any other human being who has ever lived. About the angelic communications of Dee and Kelley, he writes: *"Much of their work still defies explanation, though I and Frater Semper Pararus (Thomas Windram), an Adeptus Major of the A(rgenteum) A(strum) have spent much time and research upon it and cleared up many obscure points."* The record of Crowley's working of the Enochian Aethers in 1909 in the desert of North Africa is preserved in the document entitled, *The Vision and the Voice.* About it, Tyson writes: *"It possessed a profound and broad understanding of ritual magic, an understanding that was not merely theoretical but practical. No other man of the twentieth century was better suited to initiate the Apocalypse Working, even as there had been no man in the sixteenth century better suited than Dee to receive it from the Enochian angels."* [25] Tyson writes that: *"Crowley never succeeded in correctly completing the entire Enochian Apocalypse Working, which is, the primal occult Key that has never been recorded, are the eighteen manifest Keys, and the Key of the 30 Aethers in their correct correspondence with the parts of the Great Table of the Watchtowers. But he may have succeeded in partially opening the gates of the Watchtowers."* I am pretty sure he opened the gates of Hell with Victor Neuberg. It is significant that he states concerning the African working conducted with Neuberg: *"As a rule, we did one Aethyr every day."* On the method for invoking the spirits of the Watchtowers, the angel Ave Dee states:

> *Four days ... must you only call upon those names of God (on the Great Table of the Watchtowers), or on the God of Hosts, in those names:*

> *And 14 days after you shall (in this, or in some convenient place) Call the Angels by Petition and by the name of God, unto the which they are obedient.*

> *The 15 day you shall Cloath yourselves, in vestures made of linen, white: and so have the apparition, use, and practice of the Creatures. For, it is not a labor of years, nor many days.*

It seems clear to Tyson, that the complete *Apocalypse Working* must be conducted on consecutive days, one Key per day. I would guess that the unexpressed primordial Key of the Great Mother is the missing ingredient that will complete the Working, but this is a matter of practical magic. Crowley remained firmly convinced until his death in 1947, that the Aeon of Horus began in 1904, precisely at the time he received *The Book of the Law.* Fundamentalist Christians commonly believe that the end of the world will be a completely physical event, and will be sparked by some horrifying wars and plagues, and we have indeed had the worst ones in the history of humankind after Crowley's channeled work started circulating among the various Illuminati sects.

Only in the limited time span from 1945 to 1969, there were 97 wars around the globe. The total duration of these conflicts exceeded 250 years. There was not a single day in which one or several wars were not fought somewhere in the world. Imagine that the death toll already surmounted to tens of millions. At the present moment, it is difficult to remember the exact number of wars in progress or the exact number of places where war seems likely. Nor does the frequency of these wars show the slightest sign of diminishing. Even **Pope Francis**, in 2014, at a ceremony honoring WWI victims stated that: *"a World War III fought with crimes, massacres, and destruction may have started."*

As soon as one war ends, another begins. Henry Kissinger, one of the key players in the New World Order, once said: *"The Western world seems to be floating without power or rudder on a sea filled with destructive events."* This supposition is natural in view of the concrete imagery of *The book of Revelation*. The gates of the Watchtowers that stand guard at the four corners of our dimension of reality have already been opened, by occultists and dark figures in the Western Initiatic System, to admit demons like Choronzon into the physical world to corrupt our subconscious minds. Spirits are mental, not material. They dwell in the depths of the mind and communicate with us through our dreams, unconscious impulses, and more rarely in waking visions. They affect our feelings and our thoughts beneath the level of our conscious awareness. Sometimes they are able to control our actions, either partially, as in the case of irrational and obsessive behavior patterns, or completely, as in the case of full possession. Through us, and only through us, are they able to influence physical things.

The Enochian communications teach us that the Illuminati and the Invisible Masters behind them, have been wanting the Apocalypse to manifest through the magical formula delivered to Dee and Kelly, for a very long time now, but they also need humans as physical agents to manifest their plagues, wars, and famines described with such chilling eloquence in the vision of St. John. As Tyson, an Illuminati controlled occultist says: *"It is we who will let the demons of Choronzon into our minds by means of a specific ritual working. They will not find a welcome place there all at once, but will worm their way into our subconscious and make their homes there slowly over time. In the minds of individuals that resist this invasion they will find it difficult to gain a foothold, but in the more pliable minds of those who welcome their influence they will establish themselves readily."* [26] This is no joke my dear readers we need to resist! Tyson writes without shame:

> *Once the demons have taken up residence, we will be powerless to prevent them from turning our thoughts and actions toward chaotic and destructive ends. These apocalyptic spirits will set person against person and nation against nation, gradually increasing the madness and chaos in human society until at last the full horror of Revelation has been realized upon the stage of the world. The corruption of human thoughts and feelings may require generations to bring to full fruition. Only after the wasting and burning of souls are well advanced will the full horror of the apocalypse achieve its final fulfillment in the material realm. Let us suppose for the sake of argument that the signal for the initiation of this psychic invasion occurred in 1904 when Crowley received* **The Book of the Law,** *as he himself believed. Crowley's Enochian evocations of 1909 then pried the doors of the Watchtowers open a crack enough to allow a foul wind to blow through the common mind of the human race. This would explain the senseless slaughter of the First World War and the unspeakable horror of the Nazi Holocaust during the Second World War. It would explain the decline of organized religions and why the soulless cult of science has gained supremacy. It would explain the moral and ethical bankruptcy of modern times and the increase in senseless violence.* [27]

---

26   *Ibid.*

27   *Ibid.*

The Antichrist foretold in Crowley's **The Book of the Law** *to follow after the Beast, will succeed in completing the Apocalypse Working. Then the gates of the Watchtowers will truly gape wide, and the children of Coronzon will sweep into our minds as crowned conquerors. If this chilling scenario ever comes to pass, the wars of the twentieth century will seem bucolic to those who survive the slaughter.* [28]

I would like to further unveil the secret instruction prepared for the future Antichrist to be found in the work of another one of Aleister Crowley's alleged reincarnations, French occult author and ceremonial magician Eliphas Levi, born Alphonse Louis Constant (1810-1875), considered of great importance in the pseudo-religion of Thelema, and most modern mystery schools of the Illuminati network. The fact that Levi had a profound influence on Crowley, there is no doubt. Crowley translated Levi's *The Key of the Mysteries* as his own Adeptus Minor thesis, and Crowley went as far to claim in *Magick in Theory and Practice* that he was the reincarnation of Levi. Therefore, it is not unreasonable to suggest that Levi influenced Crowley in the *Apocalypse Workings*. Eliphas Levi's Baphomet was also adopted by Aleister Crowley, most famously in his Gnostic Mass and has become a key symbol of modern Satanism used in recent years by the Satanic Temple.

MESSIAH OR ANTICHRIST?

*Q*ears ago, I meditated on the following passage from The Gospel According to Matthew: *"42 Therefore, keep watch, because you do not know on what day your Lord will come. 43 But understand this: If the owner of the house had known at what time of night the thief was coming, he would have kept watch and would not have let his house be broken into. 44 So you also must be ready, because the Son of Man will come at an hour when you do not expect him."* [29]

While reflecting on these words, I discovered in the book *Dogma of High Magic,* the first Volume of the second edition of the occult classic *Dogma and Ritual of High Magic* by Eliphas Levi, originally published in French as *Dogme et Rituel de la Haute Magie* (1854-1856), and later translated into English with the title **Transcendental Magic**. A specific passage, linked to the belief and doctrine of Messianism that has always been present in the DNA of the Illuminati, but was never truly explained in such detail. I found this synchronicity interesting, even if it took me years to fully comprehend its real importance.

This passage contains in fact, the instructions for the creation of a real Messiah on Earth, or the possible preparation of a "False Messiah" by the elite of the New World Order. Basically, these could well be the instructions for the making of the Antichrist. As we know, the prevalent ideology behind the New World Order supports the idea of a God-chosen "King of the Jews" to rule over the world. This Messiah, or Antichrist, could well be selected from the ranks of the Rothschild family. Jews will administer this world empire with the help of the liberal side of Freemasonry and the Jesuits. Part of this argument is espoused in a rare, and now a suppressed book, entitled *Elijah, Rothschilds and the Ark of the Covenant* by Tom Crotser & Jeremiah Patrick (Restoration Press, 1984). This book details the Rothschild's alleged discovery of the Ark of the Covenant, a gold-covered box

28   *Ibid.*

29   NIV.

supposedly built by Moses to hold Aaron's Rod and the original Ten Command-ment tablets that, as I wrote earlier in the book, might be in a variety of places.

Apparently, the Rothschild's intend to place this object in Solomon's Temple in Jerusalem to legitimize their Messiah claim. It sounds a bit far-fetched and with no real evidence in support of such outlandish claims, but as crazy as all this may seem, there are certain words written by Eliphas Levi, a century and a half ago, that sound totally in line with this vision, and there is even a mention of the possi-ble role of the Rothschilds. Reality, or simple speculation? Here is the crucial pas-sage extracted from the chapter called *The Magical Chain*. Please study it in detail:

The great man is he who comes seasonably and knows how to innovate oppor-tunely. In the days of the apostles, Voltaire would have found no echo for his utter-ances and might have been merely an ingenious parasite at the banquets of Trimal-cyon. Now, at the epoch wherein we live, everything is ripe for a fresh outburst of evangelical zeal and Christian self devotion, precisely by reason of the prevailing general disillusion egoistic positivism, and public cynicism of the coarsest interests. The success of certain books and the mystical tendencies of minds are unequivocal symptoms of this widespread disposition. We restore and we build churches only to realize more keenly that we are void of belief, only to long the more for it; once more does the whole world await its Messiah, and he cannot tarry in his coming. Let a man, for example, come forward, who by rank or by fortune is placed in an exalted position a pope, a king, even a Jewish millionaire and let this man publicly and solemnly sacrifice all his material interests for the wealh of human-ity; let him make himself the saviour of the poor, the disseminator, and even the victim, of doctrines of renunciation and charity, and he will draw round him an immense following; he will accomplish a complete moral revolution in the world. But the high rank of such a character is more than anything necessary since, in our times of misery and charlatanism, any word issuing from the lower ranks is suspected of interested ambition and imposture. Ye, then, who are nothing, ye who possess nothing, aspire not to be apostles or messiahs. If you have faith and would act in accordance therewith, get possession, in the first place, of the means of action, which are the influence of rank and the prestige of fortune. In olden times gold was manufactured by science; nowadays science must be remade by gold. We have fixed the volatile, and we must now volatilize the fixed in other words, we have material-ized spirit, and we must now spiritualize matter. The most sublime utterance now passes unheeded if it goes forth without the guarantee of a name that is to say, of a success which represents a material value. What is The worth of a manuscript? That of the author's signature among the booksellers? That established reputation is known as Alexander Dumas who represents one of the literary guarantees of our time, but the house of Dumas is in repute only for the romances which are its exclusive productions. Let Dumas devise a magnificent Utopia, or discover a splen-did solution of the religious problem, and no one will take them seriously, despite the European celebrity of the Panurge of modern literature. We are in the age of acquired positions, where everyone is appraised according to his social and com-mercial standing. Unlimited freedom of speech has produced such a strife of words that no one inquires what is said, but who has said it. If it be Rothschild, his Holi-ness Pius the Ninth, or even Monseigneur Dupanloup, it is something; but if it be Tartempion, it is nothing, were he even which is possible, after all an unrecognised prodigy of genius, knowledge, and good sense. Hence to those who would say to me:

If you possess the secret of great successes, and of a force which can transform the world, why do you not make use of them? I would answer: This knowledge has come to me too late for myself, and I have spent over its acquisition the time and the resources which might have enabled me to apply it; I offer it to those who are in a position to avail themselves of it. Illustrious men, rich men, great ones of this world, who are dissatisfied with that which you have, who are conscious of a nobler and larger ambition, will you be fathers of a new world, kings of a rejuvenated civilisation? A poor and obscure scholar has found the lever of Archimedes, and he offers it to you for the good of humanity alone, asking nothing whatsoever in exchange. **The phenomena which have quite recently perturbed America and Europe, as regards table-turning and fluidic manifestations, are simply magnetic currents at the beginning of their formation, appeals on the part of nature inviting us, for the good of humanity, to re-establish the great sympathetic and religious chains.** *As a fact, stagnation in the astral light would mean death to the human race, and torpor in this secret agent has already been manifested by alarming symptoms of decomposition and death. For example, cholera-morbus, the potato disease, and the blight of the grape, are traceable solely to this cause, as the* **two young shepherds of la Salette** *saw darkly and symbolically in their dream.* [30]

On September 19,1846, two children, shepherds of La Salette in the French Alps, had a vision of the Virgin. Soon after on the 19th of September 1851, Pope Pius IX formally approved the public devotion and prayers to Our Lady of La Salette, referring to messages from the apparition as *secrets*. The original secrets of Our Lady of La Salette, given to Melanie Calvat and Maximin Giraud in 1846, and first transcribed in 1851, were buried in the Vatican Secret Archives for almost 150 years, before they were discovered by Fr. Michel Corteville in 1999. They were then published by Fr. Corteville along with Fr. Rene Laurentin in the 2002 book *Découverte du Secret de La Salette*.

In this version Melanie's secret differed somewhat from the later versions of her secret, published in 1858, 1873 and 1879 respectively. Prior to the publication of the 1851 originals in 2002, the vast majority of the content of Maximin's secret was unknown to the general public. As Emmett O'Regan argues in his book *Unveiling the Apocalypse*, it seems that the main reason that the secrets of La Salette were suppressed for so long, was due to their reference to a specific point in the future as to when the prophecies would begin to take place—**the year 2000.**

The secrets, revealed to the two shepherds by the Virgin Mary must have reached in some way, in their entirety, Eliphas Levi, which as you just read mentions the "two young shepherds of La Salette." This reference seems to be heavily inspired by their Apocalyptic "secrets" in the final part of a prophecy written only a few years later, in 1860, for his new friend and patron, the Tuscan Baron Nicola Spedalieri:

That is why the return of Enoch and Elijah will precede the second advent of Jesus. In his first coming, Jesus turned out to be a pontiff. In his second coming, he will be revealed as King. He is Christ. He must be the Messiah the Jews are right to wait. It was Enoch, on Mount Sinai, to give the Divine law to Moses. They were Moses and Elijah, on the Tabor, teaching Jesus the great mysteries of

30   Eliphas Levi, *Transcendental Magic: Its Doctrine and Ritual* , (London : G. Redway, 1896) pp. 102,103,104.

Christian revelation. Jesus transmitted his initiation to St. John the Evangelist and this apostle detached from the rest must remain until the Second Coming of the Master. At the moment of decomposition, inferior spirits will manifest themselves as worms on corpses. They are evoked by corruption and are being devoured by it. They are vampires of unhealthy souls. This decomposition always precedes and announces the coming on the Earth of a Spirit of regenerating in the person of the Solar Metatron. Talking boards and flying spirits announced the return of Enoch. He will return when the Papacy has lost his authority in the world and the cabalistic visions will shine.

The advent of Elijah will follow immediately after Enoch, then Jesus Saviour of the world will come back a second time. It will be preceded by the Antichrist whose mission will be to prepare the great temporal Empire of the Gospel Revelator. The astral light flushed with elemental spirits is a sign of a new creation that is being prepared. Already the keys of Solomon are found and the mysteries of High Freemasonry are explained. A school, whose beginnings are still dark and almost invisible, is being formed in the Slavic Empire, Germany, and France. In a century this school will have seven thousand adepts and its last Grand Master will be Enoch. Enoch will appear in the year two thousand of the Christian world. Then Messianism, which will be the forerunner, will flourish on Earth for a thousand years. These predictions are the summary of all prophecies and all the cabalistic calculations ... they have to be kept secret so as not to expose the most respectable labors of human genius and divining science to the profanations of ignorance. Eliphas Lévi, Paris 1860. [31]

This is a specific passage from the secrets of Our Lady of La Salette that seem to match the above in certain predictions:

Rome will lose the Faith and become the seat of the Antichrist. **The demons of the air, together with the Antichrist, will work great wonders on the earth and in the air, and men will become ever more perverted.** *God will take care of His faithful servants and men of good will; the Gospel will be preached everywhere, all peoples and all nations will have knowledge of the Truth. I address a pressing appeal to the earth: I call upon the true disciples of the God living and reigning in the heavens; I call upon the true imitators of Christ made man, the one true Savior of men; I call upon my children, my true devotees, those who have given themselves o me so that I may lead them to my Divine Son, those whom I bear as it were in my arms, those who have lived in my spirit; finally, I call upon the Apostles of the Latter Times, the faithful disciples of Jesus Christ who have lived in contempt of the world and of themselves, in poverty and humility, in contempt and silence, in prayer and mortification, in chastity and in union with God, in suffering, and unknown to the world. It is time for them to emerge and come enlighten the earth. Go, show yourselves to be my dear children; I am with you and in you, provided your faith is the light enlightening you in these evil times. May your zeal make your famished for the glory and honor of Jesus Christ. Do battle, children of light, you, the few who see thereby; for the time of times, the end of ends is at hand.*

The Church will be eclipsed, the world will be in consternation. But there are Enoch and Elias, they will preach with the power of God, and men of good-will, will believe in God, and many souls will be comforted; they will make great progress by

---

virtue of the Holy Ghost and will condemn the diabolical errors of the Antichrist. [32]

There is definitely a thin thread that unites, Marian Prophecies like this one, Allan Kardec's Spiritism, Rosicrucianism, Ufology and of course, Theosophy, all linked to the Holy Mary and Invisible Masters, like Enoch and Eliah, all messengers of a variety of Messianic revelations, that have modeled in one way or another the future beliefs of the New Age.

After Eliphas Levi's death in Paris on May 31st 1875 at the age of 65, a few months later on the 17th of November 1875 **Helena Petrovna Blavatsky, Colonel Henry Steel Olcott, William Quan Judge**, and others, founded the **Theosophical Society**, as the result of Blavatsky's relationship with these mysterious beings inspired by Eliphas Levi's work. The roots of Ufology are in some way also the same roots of Theosophy and Spiritism. In the years following the meeting with the aforementioned Spedalieri, Levi published texts which were later considered milestones in the field of contemporary theoretical magic, such as *Fables et Symboles* "Stories and Images," in 1862 and *La Science des Esprits* "The Science of Spirits," in 1865, clearly inspired by the writings of **Allan Kardec (1804-1869)**, a pseudonym of the French pedagogue Hippolyte Léon Denizard Rivail, considered the father of Spiritism, a philosophical doctrine that appeared in France in the mid-nineteenth century, whose practice was rampant in Europe in Levi's time.

Interestingly enough, before he died in 2008, the well-known demonologist and Ufologist from the Vatican, the late **Monsignor Corrado Balducci (1923-2008)**, wrote: *"In the last hundred and forty years they have appeared in succession and at a growing pace two types of manifestations."* [33] The two kinds of manifestations cited by Balducci, are Ufology, and Spiritism, described in the following way by Balducci: *"With regards to Spiritism, this is a practice which has been witnessed for millennia, but in 1847 with the Fox sisters in Hydesville (New York) it took on a very special impetus and spread rapidly in various countries. The phenomena of this nature were soon given, even by scientists, an explanation: the souls of the disembodied, that is, the dead, are the cause, and here is the spiritual hypothesis to which theologians soon opposed the demonic one. Scientists had resorted to the beyond, and one could not expect the theorists to think of a natural hypothesis. Only towards the end of the nineteenth century there were the first attempts at a natural explanation, which increased and became more and more plausible and consistent in their scientificity through the emergence of various societies: the first, the Psychic Research Society, was born in England in 1882; two years later, in 1884, the American Society for Psychical Research was founded in the United States. In 1888, Richet and Marillier gave birth to the* Société de Psycologie Physiologique *and in 1901 Marzorati founded the Society of Psychic Studies in Italy."* [34] Interestingly enough for Balducci: *"We begin to talk about UFOs exactly one hundred years after the Fox sisters, always in the United States, on June 24, 1947 when, thanks to Kenneth Arnold, the first reported related accident went into print."* [35]

---

32   http://www.traditionalcatholicpriest.com/2014/11/10/antichrist-as-foretold-by-the-virgin-mary-at-la-salette-france/ **[emphasis added]** ‡ Archived 11th January, 2017.

33   *See* Roberto Pinotti, *UFO: Il fattore contatto. Alieni intelligence ed esopolitica*, (Milan,IT: Mondadori, 2017), preface (V)

34   *Ibid.*,VI

35   *Ibid.*

UFOLOGY OFFICIALLY APPEARS IN THE VATICAN

*I*n this incredibly troubled period for humanity, fueled with speculation of a current alien invasion, something close to what St. John the Evangelist called **the Apocalypse**, seems to be gradually unfolding in front of our eyes, possibly leading to an imminent End-times scenario. For this reason, the greatest UFO experts met in the most unlikely and unusual location to date in recent years. The Vatican officially opened their doors to guest experts on Ufology at least three times in recent years, and we are told unofficially many other times, to talk about this delicate subject, which is also related to the so-called **Marian apparitions**, seen by some Ufologists as a product of alien deception, and for others as a sign of the **End-times**.

These semi official meetings in the Vatican, took place in 2002, 2010 and 2013, [36] with the support of a little-known organization called CIFAS, the **Council of International Federation of Advanced Studies**, headed by an engineer called Alfredo Magenta, member of the Scientific committee of the Italian National Ufology Center, better known with the acronym C.U.N., who is also the Western European representative of the Radio Regulations Board (RRB) of the **International Telecommunication Union (ITU) of the United Nations**, a leading communications technology agency, and a major technological resource of the New World Order. Seems like a pretty strange coincidence, don't you think?

The First Conference of C.I.F.A.S in the Vatican, dated Wednesday, February 20, 2002, was entitled **"UFOs Believe or not Believe**," and was held in the meeting room known as *La Sala del Buon Consiglio* [37] of the Church of Saint Anne in the Vatican (Italian: *Sant'Anna in Vaticano*), known as Sant'Anna de' Parafrenieri (English: Saint Anne of the Grooms), a Roman Catholic parish church dedicated to Saint Anne in Vatican City. The church is the parish church of the Vatican City State, and is placed under the jurisdiction of the Vicariate of Vatican City and is located beside the *Porta Sant'Anna* (Saint Anne's Gate), an international border crossing between Vatican City State and Italy.

Alfredo Magenta gave a brilliant report in the prestigious *Sala del Buon Consiglio* in Via del Pellegrino, in Vatican City territory, to a very restricted and selected audience. In May 2010, with the help of the new secretary of C.I.F.A.S. Vladimiro Bibolotti, the event was replicated for a much larger audience. The unusual event brought to the Vatican a very specific crowd of more than seventy people, all passionate about this topic, including top military personnel, agents of various Intelligence agencies, Freemasons, influential Jesuits, and various members of the clergy, and those that belong to the Vatican hierarchy.

"Our presence in the Vatican," explained in 2010, by engineer Alfredo Magenta *"is due to the fact that the Holy See is open to all the voices."* Magenta is at the heart of this strange movement of Italian Ufologist's tied to the Vatican and the New World Order. During the conference in 2002, Magenta made a statement that left everyone astonished. According to him: *"All these facts and logical deductions make it possible to assert, without a shadow of a doubt, that UFOs exist."* Further

---

36   http://www.cifas-italia.net/convegni.html ‡ Archived 11th January, 2017.

37   http://www.pontificiaparrocchiasantanna.it/mercoledi-culturali ‡ Archived 11th January, 2017.

declaring that: *"If what has been handed down to us in past chronicles is worthy of faith, they have been existing for at least five or six thousand years, since there has been written and painted testimonies of it."* Then some in the Conference audience asked him if extraterrestrials were real, or figments of their own imagination? *"We are not alone in the universe,"* replied Magenta, *"but we have to wait."* [38]

In April 2013, the C.I.F.A.S. returned to the Vatican, headed by Alfredo Magenta and Vladimiro Bibolotti, Secretary General of C.I.F.A.S., and now President of C.U.N., the Italian National Center for the study of UFOs, originally created in the middle of the 1960s by the late Freemason Giancarlo Barattini, and the current secretary Roberto Pinotti (also a Freemason), who has a long-standing collaboration with the superstar of Ufology, Dr. Steven Greer. Vladimiro Bibolotti told a newspaper: *"We should look for them because of a higher civilization. We can get useful answers. The fact is that the time is not yet ripe to do so."*

It seems obvious that C.I.F.A.S., and the more mainstream, C.U.N., also recognized at a Ministerial level in Italy, are both willing agents of the Jesuit clergy and Catholic Freemasonry, secretly presiding over Ufology for the New World Order. In a way, Bibbotti himself confirmed this in a brief interview given to the local Italian newspaper *Gazzetta di Parma* on July 4, 2010, when he declared: *"The subject matter is studied by the Secret and Military Services of the Great Powers of World and the greatest scientific minds have been interested. Numerous UFO sightings are well documented. From 1947 to today there have been 150,000 documented phenomena in the world that cannot be explained otherwise. UFOs are a serious thing. Who laughs about UFOs is like he laughed about microbes because he could not see them."*

Interestingly enough, at an international conference organized by C.U.N. I attended in Rome, back 2013, I met **Professor Erling P. Strand**, a former Rosicrucian Grand Master of A.M.O.R.C. in Norway, now involved in Ufology and Norwegian Freemasonry, who has recently reached the highest degree in the Swedish Rite. As Eliphas Levi wrote: *"Many important circles of Illuminati in certain northern countries have powerful chains."* Indeed, these chains are linked to the Invisible Alien Masters, as the presence of Professor Erling P. Strand in Rome, who confirms once again.

At the same conference, I met an old acquaintance of mine, **Admiral Falco Accame**, known for his in-depth research on the secret structure of the Gladio-Stay Behind operation. Accame, while chairman of the Italian Parliamentary Defense Committee, in February 1979, launched an unprecedented parliamentary investigation on unidentified objects.

Returning to the Vatican's relationship with UFOs, among the various emails concerning the UFO subject released by *Wikileaks*, one appeared three years ago that suggests the Vatican has been hiding knowledge of extraterrestrial intelligence. This revelation is based on an email dated January 18, 2015 from none other than former astronaut **Edgar Mitchell** to **John Podesta**, a Visiting Professor of Law at the Jesuit Georgetown University, who trained for a time to become a Jesuit himself, and is best known as top Democratic Party adviser, and former chairman, of the failed 2016 Hillary Clinton presidential campaign. Yes, the guy

38   http://www.cifas-italia.net/ricerche/intervento-vaticano1.html ‡ Archived 11th January, 2017.

FIG. 40 *Vladimiro Bibolotti, Giulio Perrone, Italian Airforce General Salvatore Marcelletti, Dr. Nadia DeMarinis-Giudice and Engineer Alfredo Magenta during the first historic meeting "UFOs Believe or not Believe" that took place in 2002 in the meeting room known as La Sala del Buon Consiglio of the Church of Saint Anne in the Vatican.*

who loves Aleister Crowley's inspired Spirit Cooking by Marina Abramovic, and tweeted in December 2017 "Lift the Veil" after the Pentagon UFO exposé by the *New York Times.* [39]

In the email, Mitchell requests a meeting with John Podesta along with a colleague, to discuss the Catholic Church's knowledge of alien intelligence and the perfect energy source aliens wish to give us. He stated *"It is urgent that we agree on a date and time to meet to discuss Disclosure and Zero Point Energy, at your earliest available time after your departure. My Catholic colleague Terri Mansfield will be there too, to bring us up to date on the Vatican's awareness of ETI."*

The colleague Mitchell refers to is Terri Mansfield, a lobbyist, and advocate for what she describes as non-violent alien beings in our universe. Mansfield runs the "ETI (Extraterrestrial Intelligence) Peace Task Force," a special interest group that seeks to educate lawmakers and world leaders about the promises offered to us from peaceful alien beings. Former astronaut Edgar Mitchel was the sixth man on the moon. After retiring from NASA, Mitchell became outspoken in his belief that ET's exist and have visited Earth. According to Mansfield's web-

39   *See* http://www.dailygalaxy.com/my_weblog/2017/12/disclosure-clinton-campaign-chief-john-podesta-tweets-lift-the-veil-on-secret-pentagon-ufo-program-v.html ‡ Archived 11th January, 2017.

site, there are extraterrestrial intelligences (ETIs) that are aware of humankind and wish to give us a sustainable, clean energy source capable of revolutionizing space travel: *"We educate humans about our work with our nonviolent obedient-to-God ETI, Extraterrestrial Intelligence, from the contiguous universe whose mission is to work with our scientists to bring zero point energy here for the purpose of extending life on our fragile Earth."* [40]

The internet is abuzz with speculation and theories that this email shows the Catholic Church has been colluding with world leaders to hide knowledge of extraterrestrial intelligence, and there is a lot of truth in this hypothesis.

After all, Pope Francis has been known to make unexplained remarks about the American government's knowledge of alien life, as well as several other high-ranking Vatican officials and Jesuits like the director of The Vatican Observatory (in Latin: *Specola Vaticana*), **Brother Guy Consolmagno**, an American Jesuit who grew up in Detroit, Michigan, who once said he would baptise an alien but *"only if they asked."*

At a science festival in Birmingham, he added to the controversial statement: *"Any entity – no matter how many tentacles it has—has a soul."* This reminds me of the friendly approach with the tentacle aliens present in the film *Arrival* that came out in 2016, and seems rather distant from H.P. Lovecraft's idea of the apocalyptic threat of Cthulhu, with its horrifying tentacles, that will collapse civilization into an endless dark horror. Consolmagno also said he would be *delighted* if intelligent life was found among the stars but admitted it was unlikely. Nevertheless, in February 2017, Claire Giangravè wrote in *Crux*, an independent Catholic media outlet, operated in partnership with the **Knights of Columbus**: *"So, just as a thought exercise, suppose a flying saucer landed in St. Peter's Square during the pope's weekly general audience. What would that mean for the Catholic faith?"* As it happens, Pope Francis is three years ahead of us: *"If an expedition of Martians arrives and some of them come to us and if one of them says: 'Me, I want to be baptized,' what would happen?"* the pope said during morning Mass in May of 2014.

It's simple. For the pope of the peripheries, no matter how distant they may be, the Church does not turn others away. Even if Pope Francis were able to keep his cool, anyone who has ever seen a sci-fi movie where aliens visit Earth knows that the general expectation is widespread panic, with religions being the first to crumble.

Outside Hollywood, real believers seem more composed. According to a 2011 study for the Royal Society, about 90 percent of believers felt that if intelligent life were to be discovered on other planets, they would not have a crisis of faith. The truth is that religions, being in the business of understanding the place of human beings in the world, are naturally drawn to wonder at the immensity of the sky and the vastness of space. For Catholics, enriched by Greco-Roman philosophy, the question of whether there are other worlds has had a pretty early onset. In the 13th century, Thomas Aquinas was already arguing for the existence of other worlds and beginning to wrap his mind around its theological implications in *Third Book of Sentences*. For *Crux*: *"Many Catholics have embraced the possibility of life beyond our 'pale blue dot.'"*

40   *See* http://mysteriousuniverse.org/2016/10/wikileaks-email-implies-the-vatican-has-proof-of-alien-life/ ‡ Archived 11th January, 2017.

FIG. 41 Artist depiction of Cthulhu from 2006 (image in public domain).

According to a 2015 study by Joshua Ambrosius, a professor at the University of Dayton, Catholics and "noones" are the two groups most optimistic about the possibility of discovering extraterrestrial life in the next 40 years. [41] Mr. Podesta added on Tweeter after the explosive news about the secretive Pentagon program on UFO research began circulating: "**#TheTruthIsOutThere.**"

THE KNIGHT OF UFOLOGY IN THE VATICAN

*I*n this final insight, in relation to the UFO phenomenon, we can't leave out the truly enlightened role of Consul and Knight of the Vatican **Carlo Alberto Perego (1903-1981)**, who on November 6, 1954, around the same period of George Adamski's first experiences in contactism, was witness to an extraordinary sight in the skies of Rome, near the Vatican, an event that laid the foundation of Vatican Ufology and its Exopolitical thinking. Exopolitics, as the name suggests, is, of course, the study of extraterrestrial politics. Perego who became a close friend of the late George Adamski, who he brought to Italy in 1959, found himself in an unprecedented position. In fact, thanks to his consular mandate, which led him to carry out many missions in different parts of the world, even after his activity officially ceased after the war for political reasons, Perego had the unique opportunity to be in contact with many political and military personalities of the time to discuss in detail this phenomenon.

In Italy, he befriended the influential Italian politician Giulio Andreotti (1919-2013), who is said to be the illegitimate son of a Pope, and one of the key figures in the Vatican Illuminati during his lifetime. Thanks to Andreotti, who would become one of the most powerful figures in the NATO alliance in the aftermath of World War II, Perego began extensive research on the UFO phenomenon. Even today, because of his privileged position, Perego's research in this field remains far superior to many other researchers involved in this unusual subject.

In 2010, a group of admirers published a biography entitled, *The console who revealed the mystery of the Flying Discs*, compiled by **Ivan Ceci**, and based on extensive research made by Cenci in the Italian State Archives, and also in the many memories and documents, still in the hands of the Perego family. A book that is not only defined as an essay on UFOs, but also a daring tribute to the memory of what can be considered not only a pioneer of Ufology, but a free, courageous, idealist and extraordinarily modern man, who regardless of his own privileged social status within the pyramid of power of the Vatican Illuminati, decided to not remain silent and secretive about certain topics. His life ended in isolation, betrayed by the system he served for a lifetime. The Vatican Illuminati operating in this field today seems on the contrary, more interested in manipulating this kind of information to fit their own economic interest and their own agenda, offering only half-truths to the masses.

Roberto Pinotti's website, for example, since 2013, is in the control of a company called PGB Group Srl owned by Freemason and Senior Illuminati, **Piergiorgio Bassi**, who is the vice-president of the Academy of the Illuminati and Professor Giuliano Bernardo, a figure I have written extensively about in my trilogy.

Piergiorgio Bassi, who is a staunch UFO believer, has invested a large amount of money in creating this new website for Steven Greer's collaborator Roberto

---

41   *See* https://cruxnow.com/global-church/2017/02/23/catholicism-handle-discovery-extraterrestrial-life/ ‡ Archived 11th January, 2017.

FIG. 42 *Perego dressed up in his uniform, proud of the crosses received by the various chivalric orders.*

Pinotti, positioning him as a sort of gatekeeper. Contrary to Perego, these characters who obviously live in a very different historical context, are merely blind servants of the Antichrist and the New World Order in the Kali Yuga, and certainly do not have a genuine and direct relationship with the most benevolent entities. According to Italian ufologist Maurizio Baiata, **C.U.N.**, has been infiltrated in the last decades by the **Opus Dei** (yes, that infamous organization made famous

FIG. 43 From the left, Alberto Perego, Mario Marioli, the Swiss psychologist Lou Zinsstag, and George Adamski at a dinner in a restaurant in Trastevere in 1959.

by Dan Brown in the *Da Vinci Code*), that surprise, surprise, collaborates with the Illuminati Academy of Grand Master Giuliano Di Bernardo, a Satanist.

Thanks to Cenci's research, we can explore the life of Alberto Perego in detail, who was born in Ferrara in 1903, in a bourgeoisie family belonging to a rich Italian prominent regional aristocracy. At age twenty-four, after graduating from Bologna, he entered a competition that would kickstart his diplomatic-consular career where he soon became a representative at embassies and Italian diplomatic offices abroad. The Italian Ministry of Foreign Affairs, at that time under the leadership of Galeazzo Ciano, first sent him to Brazil in Rio de Janeiro as Secretary of the Embassy, then to Africa, where he would reach the position of General Counsel at the Diplomatic seat of Susa, Tunisia. In 1937, Perego was sent by Ciano himself to the Far East, first to Bangkok and later to Singapore, with the task of treating delicate relations with Japan in view of a possible alliance against England. In those years as Galeazzo Ciano remembers in his diary, Perego would also become the protagonist of a delicate intelligence operation to recover the plans of British bases in Singapore.

Plans that Mussolini intended to donate to Japan to strengthen diplomatic relations with a view of a future alliance against the British. After the end of the war, Perego is forced to retire in post-Fascist Italy, a decision made by the tribunal instituted shortly after the end of the conflict. He settles in Rome, where he is employed by a famous Italian soda company called Chinotto-Neri, as a representative for mineral water sales. It will be in Rome, on the roof of the Neri plant, that Perego will witness his first UFO encounter, on the morning of the 6th of November 1954, with the appearance of what seemed clearly a formation in the shape of a Greek cross in the skies over the Vatican, consisting of hundreds of small luminous globes, quite similar to today's South American *flotillas*. The sighting was witnessed first hand by Perego and many other eyewitnesses.

This began his interest in the question of flying disks and unidentified objects. At first, he was convinced that this was connected to something piloted by the Russians. Perego closely investigated the phenomena, and as a result, numerous other sightings by many other witnesses were reported. Perego's research convinced him that the phenomenon could not be of human origin, but that inevitably it was extraterrestrial. In June 1957, just two and a half years after his first sighting (he later said he had about seventy sightings in total, made in various parts of the world), he published at his own expense, his first report on UFOs, titled *Unveiled the mystery of the Flying Disc*. In that first book, which he dedicated symbolically to the Deputies of the Italian Republic, Perego shows that he understood not only the size and importance of the phenomenon but also the infinite social, political, and religious implications that underlie the whole UFO phenomenon.

Despite the apathy of the political class of that time in regards to this subject, Perego received the attention of many important personalities in the political, scientific, and even in the religious world, being so well-connected to the Vatican. Among them were the Minister of Armed Forces Giulio Andreotti, Senator Angelo Cerica, Air Chief Marshal Hugh Caswall Tremenheere Dowding, 1st Baron Dowding, and NATO Supreme Allied Commander and United States General Alfred Gruenther—all with a key role in the geopolitical games of the day. Even the office of the American President John Fitzgerald Kennedy showed interest in his research. For this reason, Perego dedicated his third book entitled, *The aviation of other planets operates among us. Report to the Italians,* to JFK. Perego was a friend and an admirer of George Adamski, with whom Perego had an intense exchange of letters, and later organized in 1959, with the help of friends Mario Maioli and Eufemio Del Buono, the visit of the famous Polish contactee to Italy, where he held numerous conferences and where he had the alleged meeting with Pope John XXIII, as I mentioned earlier.

In 1958, perhaps aware of the necessity in finding support for his peculiar activities, Perego founded the **Italian Center for Electromagnetic Aviation Studies**, in Rome, where in a few years he brought together thousands of sympathizers of the UFO phenomenon, and enrolled new ones from all over the world, as testified by the newspapers at the time. Every day Perego received dozens of UFO sighting witnesses, many who turn to him in the hope of being heard and believed. In a short time, he became the reference point for Italian Ufology, and in 1958 he published his second book entitled, *They are Extraterrestrial.*

In this second book, Perego insists on the socio-political aspect of the UFO phenomenon and highlights how UFOs: *"intervened systematically to try to prevent an atomic conflict between superpowers, back then and for many years to come."* In the tense and harsh scenario of the Cold War, this seemed like good news. He also mentioned places, names, and dates of the most important UFO sightings around the world, reconstructing and analyzing each cause and effect, time and detail. He was the first to understand not only the reality of the UFO phenomenon but also his new role in Exopolitics. Perego came to such conclusions not only because of his political sensibility, but his ability to analyze. It was undoubtedly stimulated, as I said before, from some direct experience that deeply influenced his life to the point of dedicating it exclusively and almost obsessively to the study and divulgation of the truth about an extraterrestrial presence. Perego was a modern man who could grasp the extraordinary importance and, above all, the consequences of such a phenomenon. For this reason, he was a very misunderstood man, mortified by a society that perhaps was and still is, not ready to deal with such a complex and "revolutionary" reality.

But what makes Perego a figure of extraordinary importance in the history of Ufology was his ability to project the problem into a political dimension, or better yet, a socio-political one, allowing a rapid evolution in understanding. **Perego, was the precursor of exopolitics,** at a time when they had just begun to use the terms "flying disks" and "UFOs." He was, in fact, the vanguard of an entire school of thought that today is evolving, especially in the USA, towards a wider understanding of the UFO phenomenon. He was the first in Italy to use the expression "**conspiracy of silence**" in one of his books, as well as being one of the few, if not the only one, to be part of **ufology research marked by a clear ethical, moral, and civil imprint.**

It is no accident that Perego appreciated the figure of **Hermann Julius Oberth (1910-1986), Wernher von Braun,** his mysterious mentor, who was an Austro-Hungarian-born German physicist and engineer and is considered one of the founding fathers of rocketry and astronautics. He dared to slam the door on the President of the United States to reaffirm his conviction of using atomic energy for peaceful and non-military purposes only. And it is no coincidence that Perego expressed harsh words regarding **Professor Hellen Hynek** (considered by many the father of modern Ufology), defined in a chapter of his book *The Extraterrestrians came back* as the most celebrated amongst the heathens in history due to his ambiguous proximity to the U.S. military environment.

For Perego's biographer, Ivan Cenci: *"Perego wanted to continue in the footsteps of Oberth, not of Hynek, and this shows, even more, the moral burden, and his desire to maintain Ufology research independent from all forms of power, simply in the service of social and cultural life development for all of humanity."* Ivan Cenci concludes his somehow bitter statement by rightly saying:*"It is sad to remember that this very prominent figure in the cultural history of our country (N/D Italy) was forgotten, even before his death, and left in a shameful oblivion. So much so that when I started writing his biography, nobody knew anything at all about him, even when he was born or when he died, but also an intellectual oblivion, so that his works were never reprinted, Neither in Italy or abroad. Every time I read his books, I cannot help but think of what role our country would have today in the international Ufology scenario if instead of relegating him and his theories to oblivion, Italian Ufology continued on the path traced by Perego. Certainly, today's Exopolitics would speak much more Italian, and abroad they would look into the search that is done in our country and in this field surely with greater respect and admiration."*

I close with special thanks to Alberto Perego for his pioneering work for all of humankind.

THE ALCHEMY OF REINTEGRATION
AND THE PENTAGON

*A*s we approach the close of this book, I would like to speak about the role of the Rosicrucians, as well as the good side of the Illuminati and Freemasonry. Remember that the Society, or Brotherhood of the Rosicrucians, has been extensively sabotaged in the last three centuries by Witchcraft and Black Magic, just as Freemasonry has, and the Illuminati of the various mystery schools, who gradually went from Christianity to secular philosophy, ending with anti-Christian overtones, and twisted new political and economic philosophies, like Communism, and New Age religions, such as, Thelema or Scientology. For this reason, the minds of the profane, or of the uniniti ated, are filled with many prejudices on the true mission of the real Rosicrucians and initiates of today, just as they are with the real mission of Freemasonry, the most popular branch of the Western Initiatic System, that is presently living in profound crisis, mostly due to a growing Satanic infiltration.

The lack of real information on the subject, could simply be judged as surprising, if it was not clear that the malicious ignorance of a few authors and researchers was willingly repeated later without individual verifications, often pushed and manipulated by the diabolical hand of the Jesuits to keep the important subject of the alien/UFO phenomenon in a world of constant disinformation and lies. There are a few Rosicrucians who preserve a genuine relation ohip with God, and His angelic beings, as well as alien races working to protect humankind. There are others instead, who have sold their souls to the fallen angels, for materialistic power and wealth, and others who have joined the dark side, favoring an alien invasion, simply because of their weakness and stupidity, ignoring the dangers of serving the demonic side of an alien reality. In the meantime, ignorance, prejudice, envy, and presumption, have often confused the minds of critics and historians on the role of the real initiates of this troubled era, where genuine mystery schools are often confused with a variety of fake traditions, and dubious initiatic lineages.

Remember, as Frances Yates wrote: *"To the genuine Rosicrucian, the religious side of the movement was always the most important."* Strangely enough, that's not the case today, and the life of the real Rosicrucian, on the contrary of much of their modern emulators, has always been sensationally dramatic and incredibly influential. The operative branch was and still is today, when genuine, under the control of Christian Alchemists and Hermeticists working in an Invisible College, who, while proclaiming their alleged ability to transform metals into silver or gold, **are also looking for mental and moral powers,** rather than the obvious materialistic wealth.

The true philosopher will not seek fame, prestige, grandeur, or luxury, as they have been taught in a superior sphere, the truth about our existence and our real mission on Earth. Remember, the abundance of money for the real Illuminati who serve God, and not Satan's legion, is not the true purpose of life. Possessions, honor, rank, and money for the real initiate are merely superficial elements compared to knowledge, peace of mind and spiritual truth, which equals freedom. The truth seeker strengthens his soul, not giving too much importance to the materialistic realm, knowing it is volatile and impermanent. Earthly grandeur pales in the face of intellectual elevation, and completely collapses in the face of those who feel closer to the angelic militias and God, because those who we sometimes refer to as "good aliens" are always angelic in essence, and work for God.

The most fervent desire of the Rosicrucians was, and still is today, to go unnoticed and unprovable to the world, but they are always ready for action within their power and sphere of influence, working in secret and collaborating with Invisible Masters and Secret Chiefs, who are helping humanity's evolution in a constant fight against extradimensional demonic forces whose goal is to enslave us. Pope Francis once said that the one thing he is sure about in the universe and the world in which we live is that it: *"is not the result of chance or chaos,"* but rather of Divine intelligence.

The progress of our truly illuminated ones is encouraged by the continued spiritual procession of true Masters, who have enlightened humanity thanks to a pure heart, and a real understanding and connection to the Secret Chiefs and Invisible Masters at the center of everything. Do not hesitate, as the road seems long and the mind tired, to reach the highest levels of wisdom. Remember that, **Knowledge is Power,** and the *source of all wisdom* will support our weaker steps in the journey leading to Life Eternal through the **Alchemy of Reintegration** and the mysteries of penance.

Alchemy is not, as some historians of science mistakenly believe, a mythological and allusive chemistry. The most important hermetic authors warn not to be misled, not to take their affirmations to the letter, because they are expressed in an encrypted language full of symbols and allegories.

These authors have often repeated that in the end, their art is occult, that their work is not done, *with their hands*, but by *elements* that are not known. I remember Jacob Boheme, who in *Signatura Rerum* or *"The Signature of All Things"* (1622), affirmed the absolute parallelism between the achievement of the philosopher's stone desired by the alchemists, and the so-called reintegration or eternal birth pursued by Christian mystics.

The great Baron Julius Evola added that Alchemy is a science that promises to give its adherents the status that man had before his *fall*. Interestingly enough, Count Cagliostro reminds in his secret teachings, that the mysterious fruit of the great work of moral regeneration, made through the retreat of forty days, which all the truly elected of God have made, is actually called, **the Pentagon,** something Moses did, writing and engraving the names and signs of the seven archangels. Cagliostro strongly hybridized teachings fueled with magic-kabbalistic elements, occasionally reminiscent of the Sacred Magic of Abramelin, for the purpose of sharpening the subtle faculties of the body of glory, to gain the capacity to correctly contact and learn from his Invisible Master.

Reintegration, in this sense, has no moral meaning, it is concrete and ontological. Those who have achieved it possess supernatural powers, but they must purify their being, to fully be able to penetrate the abilities of their intellect and become engaged in "Contactism" on a higher level, or engage in occult practices that will invite such hyperdimensional entities. Once science fully understands and discloses the multi-dimensional reality of the UFO/alien phenomenon, the world we live in will be changed forever. At the end of 2017, the Pentagon (in this case the headquarters of the United States Department of Defense) finally admitted that it ran a secret program tasked with investigating sightings of unidentified flying objects, or UFOs. As reported by *The Independent*: *"Although the Advanced Aviation Threat Identification Programme ended five years ago, when U.S. defense officials shifted attention and funding to other priorities, it remains unclear if it has continued to investigate sightings of mysterious vehicles. The programme ran from 2007 to 2012 with $22m (£15m) in annual funding, which was hidden in U.S. Defense Department budgets worth hundreds of billions of dollars."*

The New York Times reported that: *"The shadowy program—parts of it remain classified—began in 2007, and initially, it was largely funded at the request of Harry Reid, the Nevada Democrat who was the Senate majority leader at the time and who has long had an interest in space phenomena. Most of the money went to an aerospace research company run by a billionaire entrepreneur and longtime friend of Mr. Reid's, Robert Bigelow, who is currently working with NASA to produce expandable craft for humans to use in space. On CBS's 60 Minutes in May 2017, Mr. Bigelow said he was 'absolutely convinced' that aliens exist and that U.F.O.s have visited Earth."*

As I wrote in Volume II of my *Confessions*, Bigelow works with John B. Alexander (born 1937), a retired United States Army colonel, who currently lives in Las Vegas with his two sons and his wife Victoria Lacas Alexander, and studies alien abductions. As I pointed out also in that book, what most people don't realize about Bigelow and Alexander, is that the two are members of The Temple of Set, the darkest faction of the American Illuminati, founded by Satanist and Theosophist Dr. Michael A. Aquino, a retired Lt. Colonel of the Military Intelligence who specialized in Psychological Warfare. They seem to use this research to disguise the group's more occult experiments and Satanic practices, in places like Skinwalker Ranch, also known as Sherman Ranch, a property located on approximately 480 acres (1.9 km2) southeast of Ballard, Utah, that is allegedly the site of paranormal and UFO-related activities. Colonel John B. Alexander is the author of a very interesting book on the UFO phenomenon called, *UFOs: Myths, Conspiracies, and Realities* (New York, NY: Thomas Dunne Books, 2011), a book particularly appreciated by his ex-colleague in the U.S. military, Michael Aquino, who described the whole UFO phenomena as a huge PSYOP (Psychological Operation): *"So the emerging picture on UFOs is not one of are-They/aren't-They-here, but rather of a global phenomenon of human psychology: a PSYOP campaign without anyone actually running it. Much like the traditional circus coming to town, it thrills us, scares us, and certainly alleviates boredom. John Alexander isn't about to stare it down; like everyone else, he's having way too much fun with it."*

By making such a statement publicly on an internet forum, Aquino is participating to some extent in the massive cover-up underway, of the true occult origin of the UFO phenomena. There is something sinister going on behind closed doors, with what we know now as an **Advanced Aviation Threat Identification Program.** It seems that Bigelow, Col. Alexander, and the Temple of Set are helping NASA return to its occult roots in dealing with the industry that was pioneered by Scientist and Occultist Jack Parsons of the *Ordo Templi Orientis*. Parsons and L. Ron Hubbard's rituals opened a portal that apparently never closed, and is now being used by a new generation of Satanists working with NASA to implement the last stage of a full-on alien invasion. In the meantime, apocalyptic events take place almost on a daily basis around the world, that leaves us wondering if the Invisible Masters will eventually intervene, or if we will be left alone this time, to face the terrible consequence of the many bad deals and compromises made by the dark side. This could only mean that humanity will be forced to finally face the End Times.

Ad Maiora,

Leo Lyon Zagami

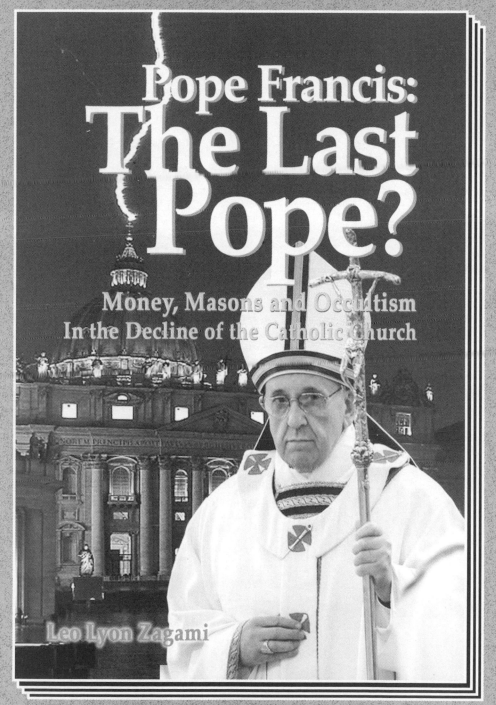

Pope Francis: The Last Pope?

Money, Masons and Occultism In the Decline of the Catholic Church

Leo Lyon Zagami

ISBN: 978-1888729542 • paperback • $16.95

TRAVEL BOOKS BY CCC PUBLISHING

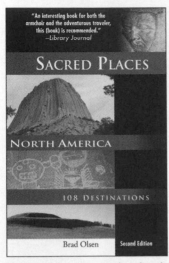

Sacred Places North America: 108 Destinations
– 2nd EDITION

by Brad Olsen

This comprehensive travel guide examines North America's most sacred sites for spiritually attuned explorers. Spirituality & Health reviewed: "The book is filled with fascinating archeological, geological, and historical material. These 108 sacred places in the United States, Canada, and Hawaii offer ample opportunity for questing by spiritual seekers."

$19.95 :: 408 pages   **paperback: 978-1888729139**

all Ebooks priced at $9.99

Kindle: 978-1888729252
PDF: 978-1888729191
ePub: 978-1888729337

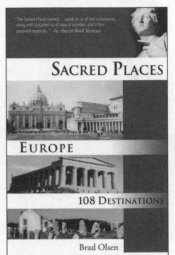

Sacred Places Europe: 108 Destinations
by Brad Olsen

This guide to European holy sites examines the most significant locations that shaped the religious consciousness of Western civilization. Travel to Europe for 108 uplifting destinations that helped define religion and spirituality in the Western Hemisphere. From Paleolithic cave art and Neolithic megaliths, to New Age temples, this is an impartial guide book many millennium in the making.

$19.95 :: 344 pages   **paperback: 978-1888729122**

all Ebooks priced at $9.99

Kindle: 978-1888729245
PDF: 978-1888729184
ePub: 978-1888729320

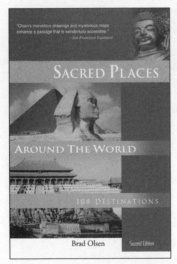

Sacred Places Around the World: 108 Destinations
– 2nd EDITION

by Brad Olsen

The mystical comes alive in this exciting compilation of 108 beloved holy destinations. World travelers and armchair tourists who want to explore the mythology and archaeology of the ruins, sanctuaries, mountains, lost cities, and temples of ancient civilizations will find this guide ideal.

$17.95 :: 288 pages   **paperback: 978-1888729108**

all Ebooks priced at $9.99

Kindle: 978-1888729238
PDF: 978-1888729160
ePub: 978-1888729313

World Stompers: A Global Travel Manifesto
– 5th EDITION

by Brad Olsen

Here is a travel guide written specifically to assist and motivate young readers to travel the world. When you are ready to leave your day job, load up your backpack and head out to distant lands for extended periods of time, Brad Olsen's "Travel Classic" will lend a helping hand.

$17.95 :: 288 pages   **paperback: 978-1888729054**

all Ebooks priced at $8.99

Kindle: 978-1888729276
PDF: 978-1888729061
ePub: 978-1888729351